UNORGANIZED TERRITORY

Fort Leavenworth

St. Louis

Missouri River

KENTUCKY

P9-DVV-427

Kearney (1846)

MISSOURI

TENNESSEE

Bent's Fort

Arkansas River

DISPUTED TERRITORY

UNITED STATES

ARKANSAS

GEORGIA

Mississippi River

ALABAMA

LLANO ESTACADO (STAKED PLAINS)

Red River

MISSISSIPPI

TEXAS

FLORIDA

Pecos River

Fort Jessup

LOUISIANA

New Orleans

Rio Grande

Austin

San Jacinto

Galveston Island

San Antonio

Victoria
Goliad

Scott (1846)

Presidio de Rio Grande

Corpus Christi

Laredo

Padre Island

Monclova

SIERRA

Mier

Fort Brown

PALO ALTO 1846

Saltillo

Taylor (1846)

MONTERREY 1846

RESACA DE LA PALMA 1846

Parras

Quitman (1846)

Ampudia (1846)

Matamoros

BUENA VISTA 1847

MADRE

Linares

Gulf

Santa Anna (1847)

Cedral

ORIENTAL

Victoria

of

San Luis Potosí

Santa Anna (1847)

Tampico

Mexico

Scott (1847)

Bay of Campeche

Guadalajara

Jalapa

Rio Lerma

MEXICO CITY 1847

Frontera

MEXICO

Puebla

CERRO GORDO 1847

VERACRUZ 1847

San Juan Batista

Rio de las Balsas

SIERRA MADRE DEL SUR

THE
TRAINING
GROUND

ALSO BY MARTIN DUGARD

Chasing Lance
The Last Voyage of Columbus
Into Africa
Farther Than Any Man
Knockdown
Surviving the Toughest Race on Earth

THE
TRAINING
GROUND

GRANT, LEE, SHERMAN, AND DAVIS IN
THE MEXICAN WAR, 1846–1848

MARTIN DUGARD

Little, Brown and Company
New York Boston London

Little, Brown and Company
Hachette Book Group USA
237 Park Avenue, New York, NY 10017
Visit our Web site at www.HachetteBookGroupUSA.com

First Edition: May 2008

Maps by George Ward

Library of Congress Cataloging-in-Publication Data
Dugard, Martin.
    The training ground : Grant, Lee, Sherman, and Davis in the Mexican
War, 1846–1848 / Martin Dugard. — 1st ed.
        p. cm.
    ISBN 978-0-316-16625-6
    1. Mexican War, 1846–1848 — Biography.   2. Mexican War,
1846–1848 — Influence.   3. United States. Army — History —
Mexican War, 1846–1848.   4. Grant, Ulysses S. (Ulysses Simpson),
1822–1885.   5. Lee, Robert E. (Robert Edward), 1807–1870.
6. Sherman, William T. (William Tecumseh), 1820–1891.   7. Davis,
Jefferson, 1808–1889.   8. Soldiers — United States — Biography.
9. Generals — United States — Biography.   10. United States Military
Academy — Alumni and alumnae — Biography.   I. Title.
    E403.D84 2008
    973.6'2 — dc22   2007041107

10   9   8   7   6   5   4   3   2   1

RRD-IN

Printed in the United States of America

FOR COLONEL GEORGE ALAN DUGARD

CONTENTS

AUTHOR'S NOTE *ix*

APPOMATTOX *xi*

PROLOGUE *3*

BOOK ONE: LINE IN THE SAND

ONE: Corpus Christi *39*

TWO: Rio Grande *47*

THREE: Rough and Ready *57*

FOUR: Fields of Fire *66*

FIVE: Call to Battle *73*

SIX: Fort Texas *77*

SEVEN: Clash *83*

EIGHT: Resaca de la Palma *94*

NINE: Brown Bess *103*

TEN: Volunteers *112*

ELEVEN: Growing Up *120*

BOOK TWO: TAYLOR'S WAR

TWELVE: Camargo *129*

THIRTEEN: *Star-Spangled Banner* *136*

FOURTEEN: Eager for Action *141*

FIFTEEN: First Mississippi *150*

SIXTEEN: The Westerner *158*

SEVENTEEN: The Rifles *165*

EIGHTEEN: Supply Train *171*

NINETEEN: Prelude *184*

TWENTY: Monterrey, Day One *197*

TWENTY-ONE: Monterrey, Day Two *214*

TWENTY-TWO: The Mortar *218*

CONTENTS

BOOK THREE: POLITICS AND WAR
Twenty-three: Change of Command   *235*
Twenty-four: The Perils of Occupation   *243*
Twenty-five: Policy and Power   *249*

BOOK FOUR: SCOTT'S WAR
Twenty-six: Transfers   *259*
Twenty-seven: The Artillery Officer   *263*
Twenty-eight: One Step Closer   *268*
Twenty-nine: California   *271*
Thirty: Taylor Stands Alone   *275*
Thirty-one: The Hacienda   *280*
Thirty-two: Lobos Island   *286*
Thirty-three: Invasion   *292*
Thirty-four: National Road   *311*
Thirty-five: Twiggs's Dilemma   *315*
Thirty-six: Reconnaissance   *319*
Thirty-seven: Pressing the Advantage   *328*

BOOK FIVE: THE AZTEC CLUB
Thirty-eight: "Nothing Can Stop This Army"   *335*
Thirty-nine: Old Glory   *352*
Forty: Conquest   *363*
Forty-one: Fourth of July   *370*
Epilogue   *375*

Acknowledgments   *381*
Appendix A   *383*
Appendix B   *389*
Appendix C   *393*
Selected Notes and Biographies   *397*
Selected Bibliography   *421*
Index   *431*

AUTHOR'S NOTE

This is not a history of the Mexican War. Rather, it is the very personal story of the young men of West Point, marching into battle for the first time, learning well the rules and tactics of engagement.

I have always been fascinated by the theme of potential, and that thematic thread weaves through my body of work. How and why individuals blossom from rather ordinary citizens into world-changing historical figures, fulfilling their innate potential even as others around them wither or let their talents lie fallow, makes for powerful narrative.

The story you are about to read is the most poignant example of potential I have yet encountered. While researching, I was struck time and again by the way a group of regular young men were transformed by their experiences under fire, and how those experiences molded them into the great generals and statesmen they would one day become. Through their letters, memoirs, and personal histories, these figures became very much alive to me. I came to understand how intimately they knew one another from their years at West Point and then on the battlefields of Mexico.

It was only when I finished writing about their Mexican War experiences that I allowed myself to read the rest of the story and look a dozen or so years down the road to the Civil War. It was thrilling to see how this brotherhood had shown the extent of their potential during the great campaigns of the Mexican War, but it was also heartbreaking to realize that these characters whom I had come to know so well would later become so devoted to killing one another. They were not dispassionate men. One can only imagine how gut wrenching it must have been to peer across a Civil War battlefield and remember the brotherhood once shared with the opposing general. The fact that many of these men resumed their friendships once that war ended is testimony to the enduring bonds forged at West Point and in Mexico.

—*Martin Dugard*
Rancho Santa Margarita, California
January 2008

APPOMATTOX

It was Palm Sunday, 1865, when General Robert E. Lee rode forth to surrender. The brilliant Confederate tactician had struggled with the decision for two days, but now the time had come. His vaunted Army of Northern Virginia, which had bewildered and frustrated its Union opponents throughout the Civil War, was camped just outside the village of Appomattox Courthouse, hemmed in on three sides by a sixty-thousand-strong Union force. Rather than try to fight his way out once more, Lee had chosen to avoid further bloodshed. It was time for the war that had divided America to come to an end.

The home of a man named Wilmer McLean was chosen, somewhat randomly, as the site where Lee would meet with the Union commander Ulysses S. Grant to lay down his sword. McLean had once lived near the battlefield of Manassas, but a shell had burst through one of his windows during the war's opening battle, and he had moved to get away from the hostilities. Now, by mere coincidence, the war had found him once again.

Lee arrived first, resplendent in polished black boots, a pressed gray uniform, an expensive ceremonial sword, and a clean yellow sash. With him were Colonel Orville Babcock and Major Charles Marshall. Lee was a stately man who had been a soldier his entire adult life. To show up for such a momentous ceremony in a uniform that was less than his very best would have been unthinkable, even on this heartbreaking occasion.

The three men sat quietly in McLean's parlor, listening for the telltale rumble of approaching hoofbeats. An orderly had been directed to stand out on the road and direct Grant toward the house.

A half hour later, at 1:30 in the afternoon, the Union general trudged up the front steps. He had ridden thirty-five miles through April mud to be there and was clad in spattered boots and a private's uniform, onto which he had pinned shoulder boards displaying the three stars of a lieutenant general. He wore no sword, sash, or sidearm, and one of his coat buttons was in the wrong hole. "Grant," noted one of his staff, Colonel Amos Webster, "covered with mud in an old faded uniform, looked like a fly on a shoulder of beef."

It was not the first time the two great generals had come face-to-face. Grant later told friends that as he walked up those steps to accept Lee's unconditional surrender, he felt a sudden embarrassment. Grant was fearful Lee would think his appearance was retribution for a long-ago rebuke during the Mexican War.

"I met you once before, General Lee," Grant began as they made their introductions, "while we were serving in Mexico, when you came over from General Scott's headquarters to visit Garland's brigade, to which I then belonged. I have always remembered your appearance, and I think I should have recognized you anywhere."

"Yes," Lee replied cordially, setting Grant at ease. "I know I met you on that occasion, and I have often thought of it and tried to recollect how you looked, but I have never recalled a single feature."

The two old soldiers sat down facing each other. Then, for the next few minutes, before getting down to the business of bringing to a close the most horrific war in U.S. history, Grant and Lee spoke of Mexico, where they had both worn blue, and where they first learned how to fight.

> *Texas was originally a state belonging to the Republic of Mexico. It extended from the Sabine River on the east to the Rio Grande on the west, and from the Gulf of Mexico on the south and east to the territory of the United States and New Mexico—another Mexican state at that time—on the north and west. An empire in territory, it had but a very sparse population, until settled by the Americans who had received authority from Mexico to colonize. These colonists paid very little attention to the supreme government, and introduced slavery into the state almost from the start, though the constitution of Mexico did not, nor does it now, sanction that institution. Soon they set up an independent government of their own, and war existed, between Texas and Mexico, in name from that time until 1836, when active hostilities very nearly ceased upon the capture of Santa Anna, the Mexican president. Before long, however, the same people—who with the permission of Mexico had colonized Texas, and afterwards set up slavery there, and then seceded as soon as they felt strong enough to do so—offered themselves and the State to the United States, and in 1845 their offer was accepted. The occupation, separation, and annexation were, from the inception of the movement to its final consummation, a conspiracy to acquire territory out of which slave states might be formed for the American Union.*
>
> *Even if the annexation itself could be justified, the manner in which the subsequent war was forced upon Mexico cannot.*
>
> —ULYSSES S. GRANT, *MEMOIRS*

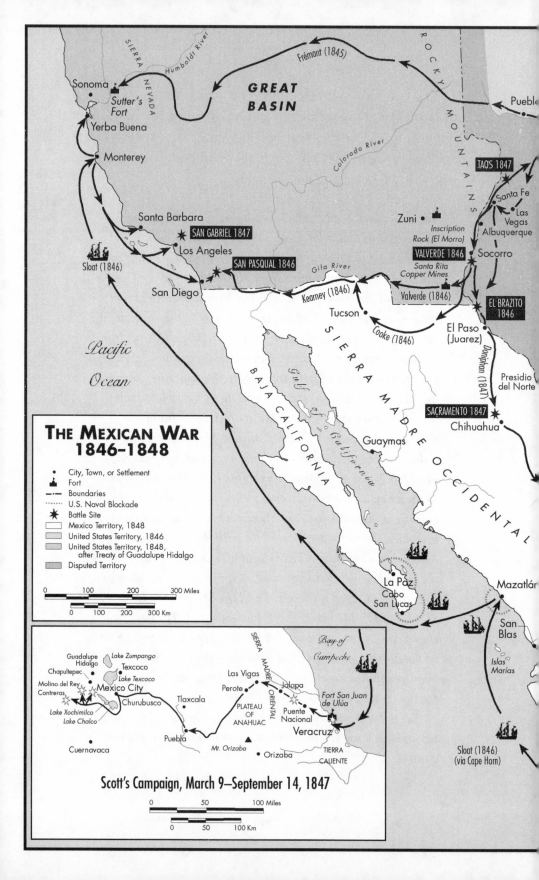

THE MEXICAN WAR 1846–1848

- • City, Town, or Settlement
- ⚓ Fort
- –··– Boundaries
- ········ U.S. Naval Blockade
- ✳ Battle Site
- ▢ Mexico Territory, 1848
- ▢ United States Territory, 1846
- ▢ United States Territory, 1848, after Treaty of Guadalupe Hidalgo
- ▢ Disputed Territory

0 100 200 300 Miles
0 100 200 300 Km

Frémont (1845)

GREAT BASIN

SIERRA NEVADA

Humboldt River

Sonoma
Sutter's Fort
Yerba Buena
Monterey

Sloat (1846)

Santa Barbara
SAN GABRIEL 1847
Los Angeles
SAN PASQUAL 1846
San Diego

Pacific Ocean

Colorado River

Gila River

Kearney (1846)

Tucson

Cooke (1846)

ROCKY MOUNTAINS

Pueblo

TAOS 1847

Zuni
Inscription Rock (El Morro)
VALVERDE 1846
Santa Rita Copper Mines

Santa Fe
Las Vegas
Albuquerque
Socorro

Valverde (1846)

EL BRAZITO 1846

El Paso (Juarez)

Doniphan (1847)

Presidio del Norte

SACRAMENTO 1847
Chihuahua

SIERRA MADRE OCCIDENTAL

BAJA CALIFORNIA

Gulf of California

Guaymas

La Paz
Cabo San Lucas

Mazatlán

San Blas

Islas Marías

Sloat (1846)
(via Cape Horn)

Scott's Campaign, March 9–September 14, 1847

Guadalupe Hidalgo
Chapultepec
Molino del Rey
Contreras
Lake Xochimilco
Lake Chalco

Lake Zumpango
Texcoco
Lake Texcoco
Mexico City
Churubusco

Tlaxcala

Puebla

Cuernavaca

SIERRA MADRE ORIENTAL

Las Vigas
Perote
PLATEAU OF ANAHUAC

Mt. Orizaba
Orizaba

Bay of Campeche

Jalapa
Fort San Juan de Ulúa
Puente Nacional
Veracruz

TIERRA CALIENTE

0 50 100 Miles
0 50 100 Km

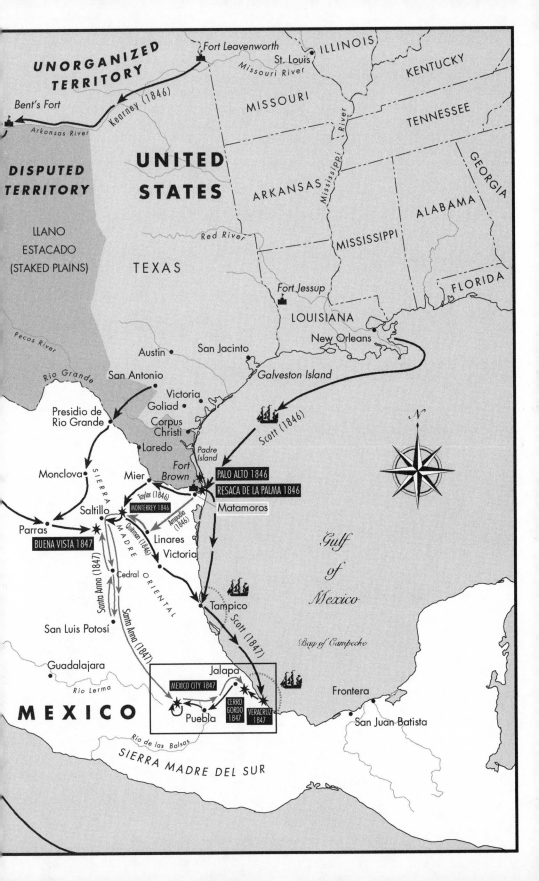

THE
TRAINING
GROUND

PROLOGUE

On March 16, 1802, President Thomas Jefferson signed into law the Military Peace Establishment Act, creating a U.S. military academy. The school would be located on a bluff at West Point, at an S-shaped bend in the Hudson River that the American general Benedict Arnold had famously offered to hand over to the British during the Revolutionary War. Major Jonathan Williams, a grandnephew of Benjamin Franklin's who dabbled in philosophy but had an even greater passion for engineering, was named the academy's first superintendent. The school opened on July 4 of that year, and three months later, Cadet Joseph Swift successfully passed a series of oral exams to become the institution's first graduate. He was just eighteen years old, and perhaps the most notable aspect of his brief tenure at the academy was that he had once threatened to kill an instructor.

Jefferson, a fifty-nine-year-old stalwart of the Democratic-Republican Party, was an avowed pacifist with a passion for global exploration. This put him in the complicated position of coveting the North American continent's unknown territories while being opposed to the military force needed to obtain and maintain them. Jefferson had once harangued George Washington about the unconstitutionality of a school that would create a warrior class. But less than three years after the great general's death, Jefferson had set aside his ideals concerning the military and expansionism, pragmatically recognizing that trained warriors would be needed to mold and protect America's future. Just twenty-three years after they had lost control of their American colonies, large numbers of British redcoats were stationed a few hundred miles north of West Point, arrayed along the Canadian border like an avenging force. Jefferson knew that the impression of a strong American military was the most effective way of averting future wars.

Just one year later, with another stroke of the pen, Jefferson purchased the Louisiana Territory from cash-poor France for fifteen million dollars. Napoleon Bonaparte needed money to fund a new series of wars and recognized that the American continent was an indefensible strategic liability for a European nation. Jefferson immediately dispatched his personal secretary, Captain Meriwether Lewis, on an epic journey to investigate this new frontier. Though Lewis led a group of men known as the Corps of Discovery, the trip was military in nature, a scouting incursion that pushed beyond the boundaries of the Louisiana Purchase all the way to the Pacific coast, reaching lands that Captain James Cook had claimed for Britain in 1778.

The logistical demands of American expansion meant that the establishment of West Point, the Louisiana Purchase, and the Corps of Discovery were very much connected. West Point's curriculum emphasized engineering and mathematics over military tactics, and it was no coincidence that Superintendent Williams was also given command of the newly formed Army Corps of Engineers: the cadets weren't being trained for battle so much as learning to build frontier garrisons and bridges and roads. The War of 1812, however, was a reminder that the army also had to be a fighting force. America won that conflict, thanks in part to the valor of West Point graduates such as that very first graduate, Joseph Swift—"Number 1" in academy lore. Swift not only distinguished himself in the field at the Battle of Crysler's Farm, but he also used his engineering skills to design New York City's defensive fortifications and then went on to help rebuild Washington, D.C., after the British burned it to the ground in August 1814.

Cadets entering West Point knew they would receive (free of cost) one of the finest engineering educations available anywhere and then graduate into a career of low pay, slow advancement in rank, and—following the War of 1812 peace treaty with Great Britain—little prospect of battlefield glory. Still, a military commission offered a level of social status and—with few exceptions—could only be attained by graduating from that academy overlooking the Hudson. As a result, and despite the trade-offs, a steady trickle of applicants eager to join the Long Gray Line petitioned their congressman for an appointment. Prospective cadets were required to be at least four feet nine inches tall, between the ages of fourteen and twenty, free of physical defect, and well educated in reading and arithmetic. Each congressman, in turn, would forward the applications on to the secretary of war, who would send them on to the president for final approval. The competition was fierce, and there were no state or regional quotas. When applying, it paid to have connections in high places.

The student body at West Point often numbered no more than 250. A typical graduating class averaged 60 cadets, all held to rigorous standards. The curriculum favored mathematics and engineering skills but also included French, drawing, chemistry, ethics, history, geography, infantry drill, and, for two hours every second afternoon, artillery practice. Alcohol, tobacco, playing cards, leaving academy grounds, and drunkenness were forbidden. Cadets were not allowed to have cooking utensils or novels in their room, and the library was open for just two hours per week, on Saturday afternoons, as reading excessively for pleasure was considered detrimental to a budding soldier's focus on his studies. These rules were broken on a regular basis, the resulting punishment sometimes as grand as expulsion or, more commonly, demerits, often resulting in diminished cadet rank and status. As intended, however, the tight strictures and modest enrollment brought about a deep and positive sense of community. The cadets learned well the strengths and weaknesses of their peers and were such a close-knit bunch that one graduate referred to the corps of cadets as "the very Siamese twins of society." Long before Shakespeare wrote his famous St. Crispin's Day speech in 1599, in which Henry V proclaims his soldiers to be a "band of brothers," military men everywhere understood what that phrase meant; so, in time, did the men of West Point.

Some of those brothers would make indelible marks on American history. In its first five decades alone, West Point graduated men whose names would become synonymous with the nation: Jefferson Davis, Robert E. Lee, William Tecumseh Sherman, Thomas "Stonewall" Jackson, George Gordon Meade, and many more.

The least of those brothers, academically speaking, were those who graduated last in their class each year — the goats. Among these was George Pickett, a Virginian who became something of a cult figure for graduating fifty-ninth in a class of fifty-nine and then later led one of the most famous cavalry charges in the history of modern warfare.

Lee was, perhaps, the best of them. A methodical perfectionist and son of a Revolutionary War hero who later fell on hard times, the Virginian finished second in the class of 1829. He did not receive a single demerit during his four years at West Point, a record that could never be broken. In 1852 he would return to act as superintendent.

Two of Lee's forebears had signed the Declaration of Independence, but a third — Lee's father — had a far more profound place in American history. Henry Lee was better known as Light-Horse Harry for the dashing manner in which he charged Lee's Legions, his combined infantry-cavalry unit of partisan soldiers, into battle during the Revolutionary War. Lee, who graduated from the College of New Jersey in 1773 (the institution changed its name to Princeton University in 1896) at the age of eighteen, was not only one of George Washington's favorite officers but also one of the youngest. At the age of twenty, he was a captain in the First Continental Light Dragoons; two years later he was a major; and at the Battle of Paulus Hook in 1779, for which Congress voted that a special medal be cast to commemorate his midnight attack on a British fort in New Jersey (which netted 158 prisoners and saw fifty British soldiers killed), Lee was all of twenty-three.

Washington soon promoted Lee to lieutenant colonel and transferred his unit to the Carolinas, where they joined forces with southern units led by Francis "the Swamp Fox" Marion and Thomas "the Gamecock" Sumter to harass the British. Lee's Legions fought with distinction at the battles of Camden and Guilford Courthouse before returning north again, where they served at the Battle of Yorktown, which all but ended the Revolutionary War.

Once the conflict ended, the five-foot-nine bundle of energy and ambition found himself at loose ends. Lee was instrumental in helping to ratify the U.S. Constitution and went on to serve as governor of Virginia. But he spent his money poorly, speculating on properties and soon finding himself so deeply in debt that his wife, Matilda, put all of her own assets in a trust to protect them from his creditors.

Matilda, who was also Lee's second cousin, died in 1790, and three years later Henry remarried, a woman almost half his age. Ann Hill Carter Lee gave birth to six children. The fourth, a boy who came into the world on January 19, 1807, was given the name Robert Edward, for two of her brothers.

By then, Light-Horse Harry Lee's financial misadventures had long derailed his promise. He had served in Congress for a term, had been briefly considered for a presidential nomination, and had written the words that Chief Justice John Marshall used to eulogize George Washington—"first in war, first in peace, first in the hearts of his countrymen." But soon after young Robert Edward was born, confiscation of family assets became a regular part of the family equation. For a year, beginning in the spring of 1809, Light-Horse Harry was cast into a debtor's prison, where he wrote his memoirs of the Revolutionary War. The family was destitute by the time he was released, with every property and dwelling sold to pay bills.

As devastating as that surely was, Harry Lee's worst problems were before him. In July 1812, while defending a friend who shared his opposition to America's new conflict with Britain, he was beaten for nearly three hours by a pro-war mob. They poured hot candle wax into his eyes, slashed at him with knives, and even tried to cut off his nose. Harry suffered serious internal injuries, his face was permanently disfigured, and his speech was slurred for the few remaining years that he lived. In 1813 he abandoned his family and traveled to Barbados at the behest of President James Monroe, hoping to regain his health. That summer day, five-year-old Robert Edward said good-bye to his father for the last time. On March 25, 1818, while finally making his way home to Virginia, Light-Horse Harry Lee died on Cumberland Island, off the coast of Georgia.

Robert Edward Lee was eleven at the time. His mother was raising the family in Alexandria, in a small house on Washington Street. Ann Carter Lee was only in her midforties, but she was already dying from the stress of too many years spent struggling to keep the family together in the face of Harry Lee's many setbacks. She had loved her husband dearly and was proud of his many accomplishments, but she was just as adamant that her five children not be like him. Ann was a gentle woman who instilled in her children a disdain for all things impulsive and reckless, and daily preached a gospel of personal discipline and self-restraint. Those lessons would define Robert E. Lee for the rest of his life. He would never drink, swear, or gamble, just as his mother had hoped.

The seeds of Ann's teachings first bore fruit in the years following Henry's death. After Robert's older siblings, Carter, Ann, and Smith, moved away, he became the head of the household, left to care for his now-invalid mother and younger sister Mildred. He was growing—eventually reaching five feet ten and a half inches—and becoming a handsome young man, with a strong chin, wavy brown hair, and dark brown eyes. He was intellectual yet rugged, fond of study and just as fond of swimming in the nearby Potomac River or trekking through the forests and hills outside town.

In 1823, Robert finished his studies at a small academy in Alexandria and applied to West Point. The family attorney, William H. Fitzhugh, wrote a letter of introduction, and Robert boldly bypassed the congressional selection process by presenting the letter directly to Secretary of War John C. Calhoun. On March 11, 1824, Lee was formally notified of his appointment. His enrollment was pushed back an entire year, however, because of an unexpected surplus of qualified applicants. Lee passed the year in productive fashion, preparing himself mentally for West Point by studying at a new boys' school that had, coincidentally, just opened next door to the Lee home, and meeting the Marquis de Lafayette, the famed Frenchman and Revolutionary War hero who had once been a peer of Harry Lee's and had called upon the late general's widow during a triumphal return to America.

On July 1, 1825, Robert Edward Lee reported to West Point. "His personal appearance surpassed in manly beauty that of any cadet in the corps," said a fellow cadet effusively. "Though firm in his position and perfectly erect, he had none of the stiffness so often assumed by men who affect to be very strict in their ideas of what is military." Here, along the Hudson, he had found himself.

Lee blossomed at West Point. Not only did he excel in his academic subjects and display exemplary conduct, but he also grew fond of reading on concepts beyond the academy's purview, devouring topics such as travel and philosophy in his spare time. His grasp of mathematics was so advanced that he was asked to serve as an assistant professor in that subject.

Lee shared his time at West Point with other future generals and national leaders like Joseph E. Johnston, Jefferson Davis, and W. N. Pendleton, but none of them possessed Lee's self-discipline and desire to compete for the top spot in his class. His own curiosity cost him that prize: though he dedicated his final year to studying and abandoned all pleasure reading, he fell short of his goal and finished second. Still, by all measures, his time at West Point had been magnificent.

On July 10, 1829, less than two months after her son's graduation, Ann Carter Lee passed away. A devastated Lee was at her side. Soon, though, another woman became prominent in his life, as Lee rekindled his relationship with an old friend from a distinguished family. Mary Anne Randolph Custis was a descendant of George Washington. Her family estate, Arlington, overlooked Alexandria. Lee had visited it often since childhood, for the Lees and the Custises were distant relations. Mary was twenty-one and frail, with a sharp nose, a quick smile, a habit of being late, and mousy blond hair that she parted in the middle and wore in ringlets down to the base of her neck. Their relationship steadily became more formal during the summer of 1829—Lee, the dashing and earnest young lieutenant, and Mary, the socialite known for her kindness and good graces. They were married the following summer. Over the next fourteen years, they would have seven children.

In the meantime, Lee's career beckoned. He was often away from home, sent to build forts, embankments, wharves, locks, and other vital infrastructure in faraway outposts on the Georgia coast and the upper Mississippi and in closer locales such as New York Harbor. He wore the uniform of a soldier, but his daily duties were those of a highly trained engineer. This pattern would solidly define the next fifteen years of his life — a series of summer construction projects followed by winter journeys home to be with Mary and the children, who usually did not travel with their father.

Lee was thorough in his work, careful in his dealings with his fellow officers, and in every way the opposite of his father, never associated in the least with scandal. But the peacetime army was no place for advancement, even for a man of his caliber. By the spring of 1844, almost a decade and a half after graduating, he was still just a captain.

As luck would have it, Lee received orders to return to West Point at that time, assigned, along with several of his fellow officers, to spend two weeks helping to administer the cadets' final exams. Among these officers was Major General Winfield Scott, commanding general of the army. The two got to know each other on a somewhat formal basis, and Scott came away with a favorable impression of Lee. This likely would have meant nothing at all, had hostilities between the United States and Mexico not increased over the next two years. When they did, however, Scott would remember Lee and call upon him to prove himself on the field of battle.

SOMEWHERE IN THE middle of the West Point alumni hierarchy, between the capricious nature of the class goats and the perfection of Lee, was a small young man from Ohio. His given name was Hiram Ulysses, but his fellow cadets called him simply Sam—or if a last name was required, Sam Grant. The Ohioan wanted little to do with the army and had only come to West Point to please his father. Grant was clean shaven and square jawed, stood five eight, and weighed just 120 pounds; he had steel blue eyes, auburn hair that he would part on the left until the day he died, and, concurrent with his arrival along the Hudson, a nagging cough—compliments of West Point's drafty dormitories—that made him wonder if he had tuberculosis. Friends considered him noble and powerfully loyal and thought it obvious that the introverted young man had little if any experience when it came to the opposite sex. Yet they marveled at the way he sat a horse and at his almost spiritual connection with those animals. Still basically a boy, he was already complicated.

Grants had lived in America for eight generations, dating back to the arrival of the Englishman Matthew Grant, who sailed to Massachusetts on the *Mary and John* in 1630. Sam's great-grandfather had been a commissioned officer in the British army who died in 1756 during the French and Indian War. His grandfather Noah fought for the colonists at the Battle of Bunker Hill and then served clear on through the Revolutionary War, mustering out after the grand finale at the Battle of Yorktown. Afterward, Noah joined the large number of settlers marching westward in search of opportunity. He ended up in Ohio, where he fathered nine children. Unable to support them all, Noah sent the more capable off to make their way in the world. Noah's fourth child, Jesse, was kicked out at the age of eleven. Never having forgotten the years of poverty that ensued, he grew into a tightfisted and controlling man with an ironic fondness for personal luxury. A tanner by trade, he married the warm and devout Hanna Simpson in 1821. Their first child, a son, was born on April 27, 1822, in Point Pleasant, Ohio. Selecting the boy's name was no easy matter. Relatives gathered from far and wide to offer their opinions before the family finally settled on Hiram Ulysses—his father being partial to the former and his grandmother having a fondness for the Greek hero. His father's preference would go to waste when Grant applied to West Point seventeen years later. The congressman making the appointment knew that the child went by Lyss, so he assumed Ulysses to be a first name. He also made the mistake of believing that the Grants had followed the common practice of using the mother's maiden name in the middle. Thus Hiram Ulysses Grant became Ulysses S. Grant. Lyss didn't learn that his name had been changed until he signed in at West Point, and officials there, showing the stubborn military logic that Grant would come to despise, refused to reverse the blunder. His fellow cadets soon took the mistake a step further. "I remember seeing his name on the bulletin board, where the names of all the newcomers were posted," noted William Tecumseh Sherman, a cadet three years ahead of Grant. "I ran my eye down the columns, and there saw 'U.S. Grant.' A lot of us began making up names to fit the initials. One said, 'United States Grant.' Another 'Uncle Sam Grant.' A third said, 'Sam Grant.' That name stuck to him."

Jesse Grant had submitted Sam's application without telling his son; Grant got his revenge by being an indifferent cadet. "A military life had no charms for me. And I had not the faintest idea of staying in the army even if I should be graduated, which I did not expect," he once explained. "I did not take hold of my studies with avidity. In fact, I rarely ever read over a lesson a second time during my cadetship."

Engineering, that backbone of the West Point curriculum, was a dry topic for the detached and somewhat romantic Grant. Making matters worse, he had a limited background in math, a topic vital to engineering success. Rather than tackle the problem through study and self-discipline, Grant preferred to read novels and other books unrelated to military life whenever possible. His disdain for West Point was so great that when Congress introduced a resolution in December 1839 that would abolish the military academy, Grant pored over newspaper accounts of the ensuing debate, praying the measure would succeed so he could return to Ohio without being considered a failure. "I saw in it an honorable way to obtain a discharge," he stated plainly. The bill, much to Grant's chagrin, failed.

Year by year, his apathy grew. Grant was promoted from cadet private to the rank of corporal as a sophomore, and then to sergeant during his junior year. But he received so many demerits that he was stripped of rank and was made a private once more; he was in the bottom half of his class academically—ranking 25th in his class of 39 in artillery tactics, 28th in infantry tactics, and, when it came to conduct, 156th out of 253 in the entire school. Surprisingly, the only class at West Point in which he performed well was mathematics, for which he had such a natural aptitude that his earlier lack of education was soon forgotten.

Yet there was more to this quiet cadet than even he realized. "He was proficient in mathematics but did not try to excel at anything except horsemanship," remembered a fellow cadet. "He was very daring. When his turn came to leap the bar, he would make the dragoons lift it from the trestles and raise it as high as their heads, when he would drive his horse over it, clearing at least six feet." Grant had a steadfast quality that drew others to him, and a powerful gift for observation and analysis. He was elected president of the Dialectic, the cadet literary society, and was chosen to join a secret society called the T.I.O.—twelve in one—whose members wore rings engraved with those initials, promising to wear them until their wedding day, at which time they would give the rings to their wives. "We all liked him. He had no bad habits," remembered his classmate D. M. Frost, who would go on to become a general. "He had no facility in conversation with the ladies, a total absence of elegance, and naturally showed off badly in contrast with the young Southern men, who prided themselves on being finished in the ways of the world."

One of those much more refined southerners was James Longstreet, a strapping young man born in South Carolina and raised in the Georgia hills, who went by the nickname Pete. Longstreet was a year ahead of Grant and had the careless grace of a man thoroughly comfortable in his own skin. He was loud and larger than life, fond of whiskey, practical jokes, cards, and breaking academy rules. The tall, broad-shouldered Longstreet and the diminutive Grant were physical opposites, but they were also kindred spirits who formed a lasting bond. "We became fast friends the first time we met," Longstreet said of Grant, whom he described as possessing "a noble heart, a loveable character, and a sense of honor which was so perfect." The unlikely friends would later see battle in two wars. The first time they would fight on the same side; the second time they would not.

As ADMISSION TO West Point required a recommendation from the applicant's congressman, the student body revealed a geographical diversity uncommon at most American educational institutions. Here a boy from Vermont could meet another from Georgia; a Maryland native would room with someone from Massachusetts.

There was, however, not a single Texan to be found during Grant's time along the Hudson. The reason was simple: West Point students had to be Americans. Texas was an independent nation, a democratic republic with its own president and congress, almost constantly at war with the Comanche and Mexican nations, and so vast that the combined square mileage of America's original thirteen colonies could almost fit within its borders.

Some saw Texas as a buffer between the United States and Mexico. Others saw Texas as an impediment to America's growth. Therein lay the roots of war.

The seeds themselves had been planted centuries before, when the first intrepid English (and later, American) men and women struck inland from the Atlantic, seeking better places to live. This individual penetration was the hallmark of America's expansion—not growth by governmental decree, but colonist after colonist, striking out to find a better life in the wilderness. For generations they pushed inexorably west, until they were no longer called colonists but settlers and pioneers, in a nod to their courage, sense of exploration, and proprietary interest in land that was frequently not theirs to take.

Not many of those adventurers favored Texas—not at first. The landscape didn't extend an easy welcome, the climate was contrary, and the dearth of natural resources meant there were few obvious opportunities to accrue wealth. Texas was a land of low mountains, few lakes, sediment-filled rivers, thunderstorms, tornadoes, hurricanes, withering heat, bracing cold, and an abundance of freshwater streams—the lone natural feature that could possibly be considered an asset, were it not for their tendency to become utterly dry in the summer and unrepentantly torrential during the long, rainy winter. Texas was the nesting ground of alligators, catfish, snapping turtles, bloodsucking insects, fifteen varieties of poisonous snakes, and a small, undeniably odd mammal whose body was cloaked not in fur but in a bony shell that looked like battle armor—the armadillo.

It took a sturdy individual to make a life among those biblical hardships, and Texas's settlers possessed a desperate, hardscrabble quality, partly because many of them had failed elsewhere. Texas was their last stand, and those who came and stayed bonded fiercely with the land, realizing, quite rightly, that its challenges molded their characters and toughened their hides each and every time they stepped outside.

These American pioneers were not the first people to experience Texas's challenges. Its first inhabitants had crossed a land bridge from Asia ten thousand years earlier. Some of those migrants settled on the flat coastal plain fronting what would become known as the Gulf of Mexico. Others preferred the arid land far to the west, and others still the forested hills and rolling plains in the center of the region. A tribe known as the Caddo, who lived in the pine forests of east and northeast Texas, first used the word *taysha* to describe a friend or an ally. The Spanish, who arrived in the sixteenth century with their horses and dreams of building roads and Catholic missions, gave the word a Castilian spelling and applied it to the region at large. Thus the land became known as Tejas and then Texas, the benevolence of the original term diminishing with each spelling change and the flow of blood and history. In 1716, Texas became part of a larger colony known as New Spain, overseen by a Spanish viceroy in Mexico City. New Spain's southern border was the Central American isthmus; its northern border was unspecified but was thought to be somewhere around North America's forty-second parallel, where the lands later known as California and Oregon met. A stubborn brown river neatly bisected New Spain, marking the distinct border at which Texas began. Born as a snow-fed mountain stream at the Continental Divide, some twelve thousand feet up in the San Juan Mountains of the New Mexico region, the river was known as the Posoge (big river) by the Pueblo Indians. Others would name it Río de Nuestra Señora, River of May, and Río Turbio (Turbulent River). It was the explorer Juan de Oñate, in 1598, who reverted back to the Pueblo name, only now in Spanish: Río Grande (or Rio Grande in English).

Over the next years, famed explorers such as Francisco Coronado and Hernando de Soto made forays across the Rio Grande and throughout Texas. The Spanish were not usually welcomed by the local tribes — as evidenced by the 1554 massacre of shipwrecked sailors on what would later become known as Padre Island. Such hostility, combined with a lack of the gold and other mineral resources that had been discovered farther south, meant that Texas was among the last regions of New Spain to be settled. The New Mexico region to the west, for example, contained twenty missions built between 1598 and 1680, but the first mission built on Texas soil was not erected until 1682.

With or without churches, the settlers systematically subjugated the indigenous cultures. Scores of Indians were slaughtered. Many of the women were taken as brides or used as concubines, and children born out of these relations between the Indians and the Spanish invaders were known derogatorily as *mestizo*.

For decades, the Spaniards mapped the land, naming rivers, towns, and geographic features and claiming every inch of the territory as their own, even though it was so vast that when the French tried their hand in Texas in 1685, it took the Spanish four long years to find them (though by then the French, too, had been massacred). In 1820, a failed lead industry kingpin named Moses Austin traveled from Saint Louis down to the regional capital in San Antonio to ask the Spanish government for a land grant and permission to settle the first American colonists in the region. Spain agreed. Austin died soon after, so it was left to his son, Stephen, to finish the job.

In February of that year, the northern half of New Spain had become an independent republic known as Mexico, the name coming from the Aztecs, who referred to themselves as the Mexica. The new Mexican government rescinded Austin's land grant, but Stephen Austin quickly traveled to Mexico City and successfully lobbied for its return. In December 1821, the first American colonists entered Texas. In exchange for a thirty-dollar payment, each of the three hundred incoming families received 4,428 acres. The Texians, as the American residents called themselves, were required to become Mexican citizens and pay Mexican taxes, forbidden to own slaves, and forced to convert to Roman Catholicism, Mexico's national religion. Nevertheless, so many Americans took advantage of this generous offer that within a decade the Mexican inhabitants of Texas were outnumbered almost six to one.

MEANWHILE, EXPANSION WAS changing the character of the United States.

Before the War of 1812, the United States had considered itself a nonaggressor nation, isolationist by default. There was no need, went the popular logic, to interfere with the sovereignty of other countries; the United States needed only to fill in its natural borders to continue growing. (Of course, this conceit ignored the fact that such expansion meant dispossessing and warring with the many native nations that blanketed the continent.) More pressing issues, such as the ongoing experiment in democracy and the challenge of maintaining independence from Britain, made the notion of instigating a foreign invasion seem ludicrous.

But then America won that second pivotal war with Britain. The following year saw the conclusion of the Napoleonic Wars, which had ravaged the European continent for more than a decade. Spain came out on the losing end, bringing about the demise of its empire in the Americas, leaving Puerto Rico and Cuba as its lone remaining holdings.

Most of those former Spanish colonies — among them Mexico, Argentina, Venezuela, Bolivia, and Paraguay — reinvented themselves as democratic republics. Not surprisingly, none of this sat well with traditional European powers. France, Austria, Russia, and Britain all made plans to topple the young democracies and claim the new nations as their own in order to gain colonies and resources.

The United States, on the other hand, took pride in the fact that other nations had copied their innovative form of government. Realizing, quite rightly, that the armies of Argentina, Venezuela, and other new democracies were too weak to beat back a large-scale European invasion, the United States shrugged off its isolationist mind-set and thrust itself into the role of protector. In November 1823, then secretary of state John Quincy Adams conceived a doctrine spelling out America's enhanced role in world affairs. Drawing on America's ascendance after the War of 1812, and on the lessons learned in 1818 while standing up to Spain during seminal disputes over Florida and over the fate of an American citizen held hostage in a Spanish prison, Adams proposed a foreign policy founded on the twin pillars of defensive strength and nonaggression, buttressed by the threat of war whenever and wherever American interests came under attack in the Western Hemisphere.

Adams shared his proposal with James Monroe and then stood aside as it became known as the Monroe Doctrine, named for the man who announced the new direction in an address to Congress on December 2, 1823. Monroe, the fifth president of the United States, made it clear that American forces would not wage war in Europe. By the same token, European nations were unwelcome within America's sphere of influence. Such an intrusion, Monroe warned, would be considered "dangerous to our peace and safety." The United States' army and navy were pitifully small, a threat to no one, but Monroe promised that appropriate military response would follow.

Europe's monarchies were furious about the upbraiding from what they still considered an infant nation. They knew that

Monroe's words were not altruistic but a thinly veiled attempt to protect U.S. interests, targeted foremost at Russia, which had designs on the Pacific Northwest. American pioneers were flocking into the territories of Oregon, California, and Texas, none of which belonged to the United States (Oregon belonging to England, and the other two being the property of Mexico). British foreign secretary George Canning (who had previously urged an Anglo-American partnership to keep the Holy Alliance of Russia, Austria, Prussia, and France out of the Americas because they were known to believe that democracy was a threat to absolute monarchy) was particularly offended. He felt that Monroe's comments were directed at Great Britain.

In 1827, John Quincy Adams—by then America's sixth president—offered to buy Texas from Mexico for one million dollars. The offer was refused. Adams's successor, Andrew Jackson, upped the purchase price to five million dollars. He was also refused. With rejection, tensions increased, and as more settlers flocked to the region, whispers of a secessionist rebellion grew to a full-throated roar. On October 1, 1835, a 140-strong Texian contingent attacked a squad of 100 Mexican cavalry on the rain-swollen banks of the Guadalupe River. The Mexicans retreated, and a revolution was born. A provisional Texas government was formed as the Texian army, which grew to 2,000 men, swept across the region, rolling up victories over their unprepared foes.

Come the new year, the Mexican dictator Antonio López de Santa Anna—a ruthless and self-absorbed general with a fondness for public executions—personally led an army of 6,000 men from Mexico City to Texas. On February 23, 1836, he cornered some 200 Texians at a small adobe structure known as Mission San Antonio de Valero—nicknamed the Alamo—and lay siege for thirteen long days. He suffered some 400 casualties, but Santa Anna had men to spare and the Texians did not.

On March 2, 1836, Texas boldly declared its formal independence from Mexico. Four days later, the Alamo fell. Santa Anna ordered that those defenders not already dead be massacred. In case there was any doubt about his intentions, he commanded the Mexican band to play the *Degüello,* a dirge synonymous with throat slashing, as his troops moved forward to invest the Alamo.

Santa Anna was far more ruthless three weeks later, when a Mexican force accepted the surrender of 300 Texians at Goliad. Once the Texians—expecting to be taken prisoner—had given up their weapons, Santa Anna ordered them shot.

But it was the Alamo that festered most in the Texians' craw. Until then, their rallying cry had been "Come and take it." Soon the far more rousing "Remember the Alamo" took its place. Inspired, the Texians fought back with devastating results. On April 21, Santa Anna was defeated and taken prisoner at the Battle of San Jacinto. On May 14, he signed the Treaty of Velasco, granting Texas's wish for independence. Texian general Sam Houston ordered that Santa Anna be sent to Washington, D.C., under armed guard to confirm this arrangement with President Jackson. Houston's plan went awry when the bitterly disappointed people of Mexico deposed Santa Anna before the meeting could took place. As a result, when Santa Anna and Jackson officially met, the general no longer had official power to broker treaties. Britain, France, and the United States all recognized Texas as an independent territory, but the new Mexican government refused to accept this arrangement. With that, another fuse was lit.

Now known simply as Texans, the citizens of Texas lived under constant threat of a punitive invasion. In September 1842, Mexican forces crossed the border at the Rio Grande, took possession of San Antonio, and slaughtered a band of Texans seeking to reliberate the city. Unable to hold the position, Mexico settled for a symbolic victory and retreated back across the river after just a week. They had not reconquered, but the Mexican army was making it clear to Washington that it was capable of crossing the border and inflicting terror at will.

As sam grant was graduating from West Point the following June, U.S. president John Tyler was busy lobbying the Senate to annex Texas into the Union—a gambit that had the tacit approval of the nearly one hundred thousand Texans. The Mexican government vigorously opposed such a move, of course, and talk of war between the United States and Mexico increased.

By the spring of 1844, Grant was posted to the Jefferson Barracks in Saint Louis. Soon, for the first time in his life, he was deeply in love. Julia Boggs Dent was the nineteen-year-old daughter of a plantation owner; her brother had been Grant's roommate at West Point, and she was also Pete Longstreet's cousin. Until Julia, Sam Grant's lifetime list of passions could be summed up in a single word: horses. But something in the outspoken young woman had changed all that. She was not conventionally attractive. Short and athletically built, with dark brown hair and eyes, Julia had a slightly bulbous nose and a cast in one pupil that gave her a walleyed gaze. Yet she was a spirited and sharp-witted young woman and, like Grant, was fond of reading novels and riding horses. He was not the first man drawn to the dynamic force of her personality, willing to overlook her plainness. Julia was a popular guest at the military balls and various galas marking the Saint Louis social season—such a popular guest, in fact, that there were whispers about previous romantic entanglements with the various young men of Jefferson Barracks. Grant was the West Point graduate, trained to be an officer and a gentleman, but it was Julia who was wiser to the ways of the world.

He called her Julia, while she referred to him, somewhat chastely, as "Lieutenant" or "Mr. Grant" in the presence of others, and "Ulysses" when it was just the two of them. "He was always by my side," she wrote, "walking and riding." Their behavior was platonic in all respects, in the manner of two good friends who simply enjoyed spending time together, confiding thoughts and observations. He never stole a kiss or publicly held her hand, and she would have been thoroughly shocked if he had.

As the young pair went about their walks and rides, Grant could hardly have known that the Texas controversy and Julia Dent would become the two most powerful and influential forces in his life, shaping his worldview, guiding him through the transition from cadet to warrior, and molding him into the man he would one day be.

It was not clear that war was inevitable, and many soldiers likely had mixed feelings about fighting, but when the Third Infantry received orders in late April 1844 to ship out from the Jefferson Barracks for Fort Jesup, Louisiana, the handwriting was on the wall. Grant's Fourth Infantry was sure to follow. The reluctant soldier responded by finding a way to delay his departure. He asked for, and received, leave from duty to visit his parents in Ohio. Before embarking, he stopped at the Dent household and spent the day with Julia. He didn't think of himself as being in love, but given his imminent departure and Julia's habit of flirting with the socially connected young bachelors of Saint Louis, he wanted to make their relationship more permanent. As they sat alone on the great porch in front of her house, Grant summoned his courage and then proposed—though not in so many words. "He took his class ring from his finger and asked me if I would not wear it," she remembered.

West Point had been issuing the gold bands to its graduates since 1835. One day the tradition of class rings would be commonplace at colleges everywhere, but it was at the U.S. Military

Academy that the practice originated. The band symbolized the years of struggle each cadet had endured, as well as a powerful common bond that could be invoked long after they left the military. Two strangers might be passing each other on a busy city sidewalk but know worlds about each other just by glancing down and spying that gold ring on the other's finger.

So for Sam Grant to offer that special band to Julia Dent was more than just a casual proposition. It was his way of inducting her into his world, with all the hardships and adventures that came with the army life. And Julia knew what the ring symbolized. Grant had once told her that when the day came that he offered his class ring to a woman, the request would signify their engagement.

She declined.

Grant rose to his feet. Wounded, he asked Julia if she would think of him while he was away. Julia didn't have an answer. "I, child that I was, never for a moment thought of him as a lover. I was very happy when he was near, but that was all," she later wrote.

It was only after Grant galloped out the iron front gates of White Haven (as the Dent estate was known) and boarded a steamship for Ohio that Julia realized her true feelings. She was miserable throughout his absence. The emotion was made stronger when the Fourth Infantry finally received orders to ship out for Louisiana on May 7. Lieutenant Robert Hazlitt, a close friend of Grant's, warned Julia about the possibility that she might never see him again. "If Mr. Grant were not out to see us within a week," she wrote, summing up the conversation, "we must understand that he had gone on down the Mississippi and would not be at the Barracks again.

"Saturday came and no Lieutenant. I felt very restless and, ordering my horse, rode alone toward the Barracks," she went on. "I halted my horse and waited and listened, but he did not come."

At the same time, Grant had come to realize that his powerful attraction to Julia had only intensified. "I now discovered that I was exceedingly anxious to get back to Jefferson Barracks, and I understood the reason without explanation from anyone," he later recalled.

Hazlitt, who had packed all of Grant's belongings and carried them ahead to Fort Jesup, sent a kindly letter to Ohio telling Grant not to open any mail postmarked from the Jefferson Barracks until his leave expired. This allowed Grant to feign ignorance about his unit's shipping out and also gave him one last chance to slip away and make his case with Julia when he returned from leave.

That day came on May 20. Lieutenant Richard "Dick" Ewell, an eccentric friend from West Point, was the duty officer. Ewell was energetic and profane, spoke with a lisp, swore constantly, and had chronic dyspepsia, a habit of tilting his head to one side while speaking, and eyes that bulged from his skull. Ewell was not a shining example of regimental decorum. So when Grant applied for one more week of leave to spend time at White Haven, the unconventional Virginian was just the sort of man who would readily agree—and he did.

Grant galloped his horse Fashion to Julia's house. The road was muddy from heavy rains. The Gravois Creek, normally nothing more than a trickle, was a raging torrent that had overflowed its banks. Yet Grant needed to cross, for the Gravois Creek lay between him and White Haven. "I looked at it a moment to consider what to do. One of my superstitions had always been when I started to go anywhere, or to do anything, not to turn back, or stop until the thing intended was accomplished," he wrote. "So I struck into the stream, and in an instant the horse was swimming and I was being carried down by the current."

Grant didn't panic. Putting steady and even pressure on the reins, he guided the horse through the roiling waters. By the time Grant reached the far bank, his entire uniform was a soggy mess. Though careless and even sloppy in many ways, Grant was determined to look his absolute best for Julia. Instead of racing toward White Haven, he trotted Fashion to the home of Julia's older brother John, two miles down the road. There Grant borrowed fresh, dry clothes and then resumed his mission.

Julia was lying down for an afternoon nap when her maid rushed in, saying that Sam Grant was riding up to the house—and in civilian attire. Julia leaped from her bed and rushed to the window.

"Sure enough, there he was," Julia wrote. But rather than hurry from the bedroom to greet him, she did as Grant had done, taking a few extra minutes to look in the mirror and primp so she could look her finest. "As soon as I could arrange my toilet, I repaired to the sitting room, and to my surprise, found Lieutenant Grant in the dining room, not far from my door."

Grant spent the next week riding back and forth between the Jefferson Barracks and White Haven. He and Julia attended a wedding together in Saint Louis, where she was surprised to discover that she was far more interested in her escort than in the society bachelors trying to win her attention.

Finally it was time for Grant to ship out, perhaps never to return. Once again, he sat down alone with Julia to discuss their future. This time, both understood the depth of their feelings. Said Grant, "I mustered up the courage to make known, in the most awkward manner imaginable, the discovery I had made on learning that the Fourth Infantry had been ordered away from Jefferson Barracks. The young lady afterwards admitted that she too, although until then she had never looked upon me as other than a visitor whose company was agreeable to her, had experienced a depression of spirits she could not account for when the regiment left."

Once again, Sam Grant slipped his gold West Point ring from

his finger and asked his beloved Julia to wear it, definitely proposing marriage. She said yes — under one condition: "I begged
him not to say anything to Papa about our engagement, and he
consented to this simply on account of shyness. When he asked
me to wear his class ring I took it and wore it." She, in turn, gave
Grant a lock of her hair.

ON JUNE 8, 1844, the matter of annexing Texas was put to a
vote.

American distrust for Great Britain had diminished little since
the Revolutionary War and had only been reinforced by the War
of 1812. It was a time when the sun truly never set on the British
Empire, and there was widespread fear that Britain would seek
to establish a new toehold on the North American continent by
bringing Texas into the fold. Slavery in Texas would then be
banned, as it had recently been in Britain's other possessions.
Many southerners feared that escaped slaves would then flood
into Texas, seeking sanctuary. They also hoped to increase their
power by adding Texas to the Union as a slave state.

Tyler had been extremely vocal in defending slavery, and
his secretary of state, John C. Calhoun, had even written to
the British government about the virtues of this practice. As a
result, many senators who had no love for Britain but even less
for slavery now lined up against Tyler's resolution. When it came
time to vote, the U.S. Senate overwhelmingly decided against the
measure, thirty-five to sixteen. Texas would remain an independent nation.

But the battle was far from over. A cornerstone of the decade-old
Whig Party was their staunch opposition to a strong executive
branch. Yet rather than let the Texas matter die, Tyler decided to
force it through Congress as a joint resolution (needing approval
in the House and Senate, but by a simple majority rather than

two-thirds). This last-ditch effort to push his agenda sealed his fate within his party. The Whigs turned their back on the unrepentant Tyler when it came to selecting their 1844 candidate, making him the first incumbent president in U.S. history not to win his party's nomination. With just a few short months left in his term, Tyler rededicated himself to American expansion via the joint congressional resolution.

For years, American political writers had argued that the United States had a God-given right to expansion, because it was more virtuous than other nations. John L. O'Sullivan, a zealous Democrat, had argued that America was "the Great Nation of Futurity" in a November 1839 issue of the *United States Democratic Review*. "Our annals describe no scenes of horrid carnage, where men were led on by hundreds of thousands to slay one another," wrote O'Sullivan. He repeated two words over and over in that essay: *manifest* and *destiny*, both in reference to America's inherent moral authority to expand its boundaries. He would later combine the words into a single sweeping pronouncement. The United States, O'Sullivan would write, had a "manifest destiny to overspread and to possess the whole of the continent which Providence has given us for the development of the great experiment of liberty and federated self-government entrusted to us."

That vainglorious notion was a subcurrent to American life during the 1840s, as evidenced by the ever-growing number of pioneers flooding to settle lands west of the Mississippi. To Tyler and an increasing number of politicians, the next logical step was to wrestle Oregon away from Britain, snatch California and New Mexico away from Mexico, and add Texas to the Union. That last item on the list, thanks to Texas's pro-American leanings, was the most logical place to start.

Annexation became a vital part of each candidate's campaign platform in the 1844 presidential election. When Martin

Van Buren, a northern Democrat who had been leading in the polls and was the favorite to win his party's nomination, went on record as opposing annexation, the southern voting bloc threw their weight behind Tennessee firebrand James K. Polk, who sought a "reannexation" of Texas, as if the territory had once been American. The dark horse Polk prevailed for the Democratic nomination and would face Whig Henry Clay, who wanted Texas to join the Union, but only if it could be accomplished without war.

Polk was a lawyer and a slave owner whose gift for oratory had earned him the nickname Napoleon of the Stump. He was dogmatic in his Jacksonian belief in American expansion—so much so that he had earned a second sobriquet: Young Hickory. A small, thin man with pursed lips, steel gray eyes, and graying black hair that he combed straight back from his high forehead, Polk had a peevish and self-important air and the habit of affecting a folksy twang when speaking before constituents. His childhood had been marred by a surgery that left him impotent (a hole was drilled through his prostate—without the use of anesthetic—to alleviate painful urinary stones). As an adult, Polk was known for his zealous pursuit of personal ambition and ideals, as well as for an enormous personal dislike for the Whigs. Polk would be forty-nine on November 2, which would make him the youngest president in history if elected.

By cleverly twining the possible annexation of Oregon with the Texas issue, Polk succeeded in winning not only the southern states, but also portions of the industrial North. Still, it was clear that Polk, with his eagerness to wage war, did not enjoy the backing of the entire nation. He won by the narrowest of margins: Polk and Clay each received 48.1 percent of the popular vote. The difference was Polk's 170 electoral votes to Clay's 105.

On February 28, 1845, just days before leaving office (until the passage of the Twentieth Amendment in 1933, the inaugural date was fixed by the Constitution as March 4), Tyler finally pushed his joint resolution for Texas annexation through Congress. On March 1, he signed it. In one of his last acts as president, Tyler then instructed the U.S. chargé d'affaires to Texas, Andrew Jackson Donelson—an 1820 graduate of West Point and a nephew of the former president—to relay the terms of statehood to Texas president Anson Jones. If Texas voted to join the Union, it would become a single slave state, which could then divide itself into as many as four additional states if it chose. In addition, Texas would enjoy all the benefits that came with being a state, among them political stability, a sound currency, military protection from Mexican and Indian forces, a postal service, and congressional representation. The deadline for acceptance was set at January 1, 1846. After that, the deal was off the table.

Polk made Texas the centerpiece of his inaugural address. As he spoke, thunderstorms raged. Gazing out from the Capitol's east portico onto a sea of umbrellas, Polk could see spectators standing ankle deep in freezing mud. "Foreign powers should therefore look on the annexation of Texas to the United States not as the conquest of a nation, but as the peaceful acquisition of a territory once her own," he gravely intoned.

Mexican officials read between the lines of Polk's speech and immediately broke off diplomatic relations with the United States. Using the only bit of political leverage they possessed, they belatedly offered to formally recognize Texas as an independent nation. They were acting at the behest of Britain and France, which favored a buffer nation between Mexico and the United States. The two European nations feared that if American expansion was left unchecked, the United States might someday take on dimensions even larger than New Spain, covering the entire North American continent—including Canada. As long as Texas held fast, remaining a nation unto itself, Britain and France were confident that they could control the size and shape of the budding American empire.

Of the two countries, Britain fretted most about America's growth. Years before, the two nations had signed the Anglo-American Convention of 1818, establishing peaceful cohabitation of Oregon. But rampant American settlement of that territory was putting a strain on the joint ownership agreement. And with Polk's election, there was a growing national clamor in the United States to annex Oregon and remove the British altogether — by force, if necessary.

Britain and France formally requested that Texas take at least ninety days to study all sides of the annexation issue. Texas president Jones, who reveled in being at the center of all the international wheeling and dealing, agreed. He saw the two European powers as allies — Britain in particular — to the point that he became blinded to the reality that their interests were entirely self-motivated. "Texas was then a rich jewel lying derelict by the way. She was without a friend who thought her of sufficient consequence to take her by her hand and assist her in her accumulated misfortunes," Jones later wrote. "Guided by her interests and a far-reaching policy, England had become such a friend."

For his part, Mexican president General José Joaquín de Herrera feared war with America. Land speculators had flooded into Texas during 1844, bringing the non-Mexican population up to one hundred thousand — a formidable number of people allied against his nation. But for the sake of appearance, Herrera could not bend to American pressure. Polk didn't help matters any by opening diplomatic talks with a proclamation that the only issue not open to discussion was Texas.

As tensions mounted between the United States and Mexico, international opinion came down solidly on Mexico's side. The *Times* of London wrote of "the enormous wrong done to Mexico

by this aggression of the United States, and the probable consequences of that wrong to British interests." On May 17, in Mexico City, the Mexican government initialed a British-brokered
treaty recognizing Texas as an independent republic. President
Jones began playing both sides against the middle, using the
diplomats of Britain and France as power brokers, seeking to
gain the best deal for his nation as he decided whether independence or annexation was the wiser move. But on June 4, Herrera
reneged. He once again stated that Texas rightfully belonged to
Mexico. He ordered his army to assemble for war.

Polk did the same. He commanded Brevet Brigadier General
Zachary Taylor to march the American army on Texas.

TAYLOR, A SHORT and fiery second cousin to former president
James Madison, went by the nickname Old Rough and Ready.
"In his manners and in his appearance, he is one of the com-
monest people in the country," marveled one of Taylor's fellow
generals. "Perfectly temperate in his habits, perfectly plain in
his dress, entirely unassuming in his manners, he appears to be
an old gentleman in fine health, whose thoughts are not turned
upon his personal appearance, and who has no point about him
to attract particular attention. In his intercourse with men, he is
free, frank, and manly; he plays off none of the airs of great men
I have met, and the more closely his character is examined the
greater beauties it discloses."

Taylor had been raised on the Kentucky frontier and had little
formal education, and he possessed such disdain for military decorum that he almost never dressed in uniform. Yet he was an officer
through and through. The sixty-year-old Taylor had been thoroughly schooled in the art of warfare during a military career span-
ning almost four decades and a vast assortment of armed conflicts
that ran the gamut from the somewhat conventional battles of the

War of 1812 to the guerrilla engagements of the Seminole Wars. War with Mexico, with its European-trained generals and vast spaces, would likely mean a little of both. Old Rough and Ready was the ideal man for the job.

DESPITE ITS TICKS and mosquitoes, Camp Salubrity (as the bivouac near Fort Jesup was known) turned out to be a relatively pleasant posting. Grant even gave the Louisiana woods credit for improving his health. "I kept a horse and rode, and stayed out of doors most of the time by day, and entirely recovered from the cough which I had carried from West Point, and from all indications of consumption," he wrote.

The commander was Colonel Josiah H. Vose, an older man unconcerned with military rituals such as daily drill, which meant that the junior officers had a great deal of free time on their hands—perhaps too much. Pete Longstreet and Sam Grant made regular trips into Natchitoches, where they played a rugged new game called football, drank, and wagered on horse races. After the discipline of West Point, and with the ongoing uncertainty of impending war, the officers of Camp Salubrity were more than happy to live it up.

"There were five days of races at Natchitoches. I was there every day and bet low, generally lost," Grant wrote his friend Robert Hazlitt on December 1.

The Army of Observation had little to do but await further orders. As the blazing summer turned to a most bearable fall and winter, those orders were slow in coming, so the great pines were felled and cabins were built, giving the camp a more permanent air.

UPON RECEIVING POLK'S directive, Taylor promptly ordered an elite mounted outfit known as the Second Dragoons to ride overland from Fort Jesup to Corpus Christi, a flyblown smuggler's haven on the Gulf of Mexico. It took them thirty-two days to travel the 501 miles, but they arrived in the coastal fishing outpost in good shape, ready to take on the Mexican army, which was arrayed 200 miles south, along the Rio Grande. In a best-case scenario, the Mexicans would march north and attack first, instigating war and invading America in one fell swoop, making the United States a victim rather than a belligerent. If that were the case, antiwar protesters would be silenced and international opinion would likely favor America. Taylor would have no choice but to fight back, and Polk's ambitious national expansion would begin.

As the dragoons made camp, Grant and the rest of Taylor's force traveled to the war by steamship. Departing Natchitoches, Louisiana, on July 2, 1845, they journeyed down the Red River, and then the Mississippi, to New Orleans, which was in the throes of a yellow fever epidemic. While they were there, Texas accepted the United States' statehood offer. On December 29, 1845, as Grant shivered through a wet Texas winter on the beach in Corpus Christi, Texas became the twenty-ninth state, now within—and protected by—a much more powerful republic. Anson Jones, by necessity, was turned out of office. Thirteen years later, the man who would go down in history as the last president of Texas would die a lonely suicide in a Houston hotel room.

Mexico responded to Texas's statehood by ousting President Herrera. On January 4, 1846, General Mariano Paredes y Arrillaga took office in his place and immediately announced that Mexico considered its borders essentially the same as had existed before Texas won its independence. From a diplomatic standpoint, war now seemed inevitable.

Meanwhile, Taylor's army drilled in the rain on the beach in Corpus Christi. Their presence had not thus far incited a Mexican attack. "We were sent to provoke a fight," Grant noted with an ironic shrug, as if he were an impartial observer instead of a would-be combatant, "but it was essential that Mexico commence it."

Mexico wasn't taking the bait. Their army had more horses, more men, and more guns and was entrenched in well-fortified defensive positions on the southern side of the Rio Grande. There was no need to invade America and invite international judgment by waging war on Polk's terms.

Early in 1846, Polk ordered Taylor to give the Mexicans something to shoot at.

In the second week of March, the young officers of West Point gathered to lead a march on Mexico. Some had fought in battles against the Seminoles, violent and bloody affairs involving great loss of life on both sides; yet in their minds, this conflict marked the first time they were actually marching off to wage war on another nation. Never did it enter the officers' minds that the battlefields of Mexico might teach them the tactics and lessons they would later use to wage war on one another.

I

LINE IN THE SAND

The men engaged in the Mexican War were brave, and the officers of the regular army, from highest to lowest, were educated in their profession. A more efficient army for its number and armament I do not believe ever fought a battle.
— Ulysses S. Grant, *Memoirs*

ONE

Corpus Christi

MARCH 11, 1846

It was just after dawn when the soldiers of the U.S. Army's Fourth Infantry assembled, rank and file, for the long march to war. Amid a great shuffling of black leather brogans and last-minute adjustments of pistols, muskets, sabers, cartridge belts, bedrolls, india-rubber canteens, and the M1839 forage caps that would keep the South Texas sun off their heads, the nearly five hundred men organized themselves by their separate companies.

A soft wind blew in off the Gulf of Mexico as the men awaited the order to move out. It was a subtle reminder that spring had arrived after a winter they would long remember for torrential rain, flimsy white tents, and rampant dysentery. Given a choice between spending one more day in Corpus Christi and charging straight into a Mexican artillery battery, most of the Fourth would have chosen the cannon every time.

With the exception of the regimental band, which wore bright red, every man's uniform was blue, America's official national color. The enlisted were mostly immigrants, German, Scottish, and Irish boys who joined the army for the seven dollars a month and the promise of regular employment. The officers were almost all West Point trained and the sons or grandsons of men who fought in the wars of 1776 and 1812. Some were old enough to have fought the British themselves. Among the West Point graduates was Sam Grant, who just wanted out of Corpus Christi. He had camped on the beach for seven long months, and what had begun as a military idyll had become a bivouac hell.

"I do not believe there is a healthier spot in the world," he had blithely written to Julia shortly after he'd first arrived. Grant loved the outdoor lifestyle. He had filled his off-duty hours hunting, riding horseback, and losing at cards and had even been cast as the female lead in a production of *The Moor of Venice,* which was being staged at the new eight-hundred-seat theater the officers had built. (His theatrical career ended before it began: Lieutenant Theodoric Porter, the male lead, objected to performing opposite a man in drag, and an actress was imported from New Orleans for the actual performance.) Those diversions, combined with General Zachary Taylor's penchant for casual leadership, meant that Corpus Christi was good duty when the weather was nice.

Grant also liked the fact that most of his friends from West Point were in Corpus Christi. In fact, nearly two hundred academy graduates rounded out the officer corps. Even as the army prepared for war (indeed, a surprise Mexican attack on their camp could have come at any time), there was a burgeoning sense of sadness among the officers because they feared the conflict would be diplomatically resolved before they tested themselves on the field of battle. Grant was dismayed to note that this zeal for war had less to do with right and wrong than with personal advancement and glory. "The officers are all collected in little parties discussing affairs of the nation," he wrote Julia on May 6. "Annexation of Texas, war with Mexico, occupation of Oregon, and difficulties with England are the general topics. Some of them expect and seem to contemplate with a great deal of pleasure some difficulty where they may be able to gain laurels and advance a little in rank." With war came promotion and perhaps glory and riches. Death and dismemberment, for many American troops, were secondary concerns.

Yet even in the best of times, conditions were treacherous, and it became difficult for Grant to maintain his high spirits. The camp was infested with snakes, and more than one man woke in the night to find a deadly rattler coiled in his bedroll. Thick black clouds of flies covered the tents and food, swarming into men's mouths as they tried to sleep or eat. And a predatory militia of camp followers had wandered down from Louisiana to take advantage of the soldiers. This band of pimps, whores, gamblers, and desperadoes was described by one soldier as "all the cutthroats, thieves and murderers of the United States and Texas." Corpus Christi had been a quiet and desolate smugglers' outpost before Taylor's Army of Occupation arrived. In less than a year it had become a haven for gambling, prostitution, and loan-sharking—the last a result of the U.S. Army's inability to pay the soldiers for months at a time.

Grant wasn't a complainer, but if he were, his letters to Julia during the winter months could have gone on and on about the harsh northerly winds, the punishing rain and thunderstorms, and the unprotected coastal plain where there wasn't so much as a tree to block gales ripping in off the Gulf. The army's Quartermaster Corps, unaccustomed to providing for the needs of a wartime force, had disbursed flimsy, floorless tents; as a result, Grant and the rest of the four-thousand-man force slept in the cold mud, protected from the elements by thin woolen blankets. Fevers and diarrhea became so common that one-sixth of the American contingent was on sick call at any given time.

Instead of griping, Grant wrote love letter after love letter to Julia, rambling on and on about wanting to resign his commission just so he could be with her—and during the long, miserable winter he came very close to doing just that. But by March, when the rains had ended and conditions were finally right for the Army of Occupation to mobilize, he knew that such an act would have been perceived as cowardice and an abandonment of his West Point brethren. The cold, hard facts were this: in order to see Julia again, he might need to fight the Mexicans. There was no way of escaping back into her arms until the conflict was ended. "Fight or no fight, everyone rejoices at the idea of leaving Corpus Christi," he wrote to Julia. Others may have been heading south dreaming of glory; Grant headed south to get back to Saint Louis.

In all, nearly thirty-five hundred U.S. troops were marching to face a Mexican army that would soon number more than twice that size. They had come to Corpus Christi from posts great and small all around America (frontier outposts were often manned by a single company numbering just fifty-five men). Not only was their winter drilling under Taylor a crash course in how to function as a large armed force, but it also marked the first time in three decades that the bulk of the U.S. Army was in the same place at the same time.

To avoid ambush during the march to Mexico, General Taylor divided his army into four columns, each leaving a day apart. The first column had left on March 8. The cavalry, in the form of Colonel David Twiggs's Second Dragoons, led the way alongside a company of horse-drawn light artillery. Two more brigades of infantry and artillery trailed in their dusty wake. Grant and the Fourth Infantry were the final elements of Taylor's enormous caravan. On March 11, they struck their tents and gathered in formation on the sands of Corpus Christi, preparing to cross the

Nueces River and venture into the no-man's-land buffering the American and Mexican armies.

The Fourth was commanded by Colonel William Whistler, an aging alcoholic who had alternately served with distinction and gotten so thoroughly inebriated that he'd been threatened with dismissal from the service. His time in uniform had begun during the presidency of John Adams and continued through America's expansion. Whistler, who had first been commissioned in 1801, was taken prisoner by the British during the War of 1812, for many years withstood hardship and prolonged separation from loved ones as a fort commander on the turbulent American frontier, and performed admirably as leader of the Fourth Infantry in Corpus Christi. The son of a Revolutionary War soldier, he was a besotted living bridge between America's past and its future.

Taylor and his staff began the march with Whistler's column. When the last man was safely away, the general galloped ahead to catch up with the forward elements. Taylor trusted Whistler to bring up the rear.

The enlisted were on foot, while the officers would travel the two weeks from Corpus Christi to the Rio Grande by horse. It would be a dry, dusty trip across a barren salt plain, sure to blister the heels and crack the tongues of the foot soldiers. Many officers, foreseeing those hardships, had compassionately purchased a cheap six-dollar mustang for their personal servants. But Sam Grant—ironically enough, the Fourth's undisputed top horseman—was prepared to walk.

There were two reasons for this. The first had to do with fairness: if his men were going to slog twenty miles a day across the Texas wasteland, so would he. The second was more practical: Grant no longer possessed a horse. A week earlier he had owned three mustangs, but a careless groom let them run off. Grant was a proud man. He was bad at managing money but was not in the habit of begging or borrowing when funds ran short. "I determined not to get another, but to make the journey on foot," the young lieutenant promised himself.

Yet news of Grant's missing horses had gotten around. It was only natural that a group of officers who already knew one another through their common educational background and various army postings, and who had endured a hard winter in Corpus Christi together, would gossip like a sewing circle. These officers knew that Grant was so gifted on horseback that he had been commanded to give a special equestrian jumping demonstration at his West Point graduation and that he'd broken a supposedly unrideable wild mustang while in Corpus Christi, saddling the horse and galloping across the plains for hours until it stopped trying to buck him off and calmly consented to his commands. If Grant were less likable, his fellow officers might have reveled at seeing him walk all the way down to Mexico, looking as blistered and sunburned as some Irish immigrant private. But Grant was the sort of undersized, hardworking, self-effacing individual that other men felt compelled to take care of. And so they did.

A few days earlier, Grant's company commander had pulled Grant aside to discuss the march. Captain George Archibald McCall was a forty-four-year-old Philadelphian. Rangy, with a handsome face and neatly trimmed beard, McCall was widely respected as a great soldier and a gentleman—and like Grant, a consummate horseman. (He sold one of his favorite buggy horses to Zachary Taylor, who then rechristened the animal Old Whitey and made it synonymous with his oversize personality.) McCall preferred traveling by horse over any other mode of transportation, including trains or steamboats. Not surprisingly, the idea of Grant's traveling on foot made McCall anxious. The march would be daunting, to say the least. Grant's ability to lead

men into battle might be impaired if he were exhausted and foot-
sore. Casually, in the manner of an inquiry rather than an order,
McCall asked if Grant planned on buying a new steed. "No,"
Grant replied, adding that he belonged to a foot regiment and it
was natural for him to walk.

"I did not understand the object of his solicitude," a puzzled
Grant later wrote of the encounter. McCall pretended to let the
matter drop. It was not as if he had an extra horse. Of the captain's two expensive steeds, it was clear to Grant that McCall
would ride one and his servant the other.

So when Brevet Second Lieutenant Sam Grant lined up alongside his men on the morning of March 11, he was sure that he
was about to march two hundred miles to the Rio Grande on
foot, without fanfare or sympathy.

Captain McCall had other plans. "There, Grant," he yelled,
pointing to an unbroken mustang, "is a horse for you."

Grant studied the animal. It was a spirited three-year-old
colt, one of the thousands that roamed the Texas prairie in
herds so great that Grant thought it would take a land the size of
Delaware to contain them. Though wild, they were exceptional
horses, with a bloodline running back to the Arabians brought
to North America by Spanish soldiers centuries earlier. Traders
frequently rode out to capture the animals and sell them to the
army — or in this case, to McCall, who had used his own money
to purchase the mustang for the unhorsed lieutenant.

Grant was deeply touched. He thanked the captain and
quickly threw a saddle on his new mount. "I saw the captain's
earnestness in the matter, and accepted the horse for the trip.
The day we started was the first time the horse had been under
saddle. I had, however, but little difficulty in breaking him,
though for the first day there were frequent disagreements with
us over which way we should go, or whether we should go at
all," wrote Grant. "At no time during the day could I choose

exactly the part of the column I wanted to ride with; but, after that, I had as tractable a horse as any with the army, and none that stood the trip better."

And so it came to pass that when Sam Grant rode off to war for the very first time, he sat astride a headstrong, unpredictable, slightly aimless young horse—an animal, in fact, with a spirit much like his own.

TWO

Rio Grande

MARCH 20, 1847

Thanks to McCall's act of kindness, Grant's journey south was actually somewhat pleasant. A carpet of wildflowers covered the land, their vivid yellows and purples framed by budding shoots of green prairie grass, all set against the backdrop of a vast blue sky. "I observed in great abundance the spiderwort, phlox, lupin, fireplant, lobelia inflata, primrose, etc," one officer wrote in great detail. Grant was amazed by a horizon so vast and empty that he thought he could see the curve of the earth. A few days out of Corpus Christi, Grant and a band of officers left the boredom of the march during a rest break, spurring their mounts out toward a series of low hills to gaze in awe at a great herd of wild horses. "As far as the eye could reach to our right, the herd extended," Grant wrote. "To the left it extended equally. There was no estimating the number of animals in it."

For soldiers on foot, the journey was far less idyllic. Their boots, those army-issue leather brogans, were designed to fit interchangeably on the right or left foot, making for great discomfort over such a long distance. Game was hard to come by, so they lived on rations of bacon, salted pork, and crumbling, barely edible, maggot-infested biscuits. Water was even scarcer than predicted. The troops' thirst was made worse when Mexican scouts, seeking to harass the American advance, set fire to the prairie on March 14. The flames quickly raced inland and away from the army, driven by winds blowing in off the Gulf, but the damage was done. All that remained of the grass and wildflowers was a thick layer of soot. The Fourth Infantry's footsteps sent the black gray dust flying up into their mouths and nostrils, forcing many of them to march with handkerchiefs tied over their faces. Their blue uniforms were coated in ash, with no cool stream nor even a muddy lake in which to wash it off. "The men," Grant noted with understatement, "suffered."

Nine days after setting out, filthy and exhausted, Grant and the Fourth caught up with the rest of Taylor's army on the banks of a tidal river known as the Arroyo Colorado. Mexican soldiers had been spotted on the far shore. Taylor had no way of knowing how many enemy troops were hiding there, but from the scores of Mexican bugles blowing up and down the river, it certainly sounded as if the enemy had him outnumbered.

The Arroyo Colorado seemed just deep and wide enough to give the Mexicans a powerful tactical advantage. They merely had to wait for the Americans to begin crossing, and then let forth a hail of artillery and musket fire. Taylor's men would be stranded midriver, battling the current, incapable of fighting back, and soon weakened if not decimated altogether.

Yet Taylor was a wily general, capable of seeing a battlefield with the same analytical calm with which other men viewed a chessboard. One way or another, he needed to cross that river. Conventional tactics stipulated that infantry and cavalry should be sent across to wage war on the ground as Taylor's artillery batteries bombarded enemy positions from his side of the river. His army was vulnerable if they tried to ford piecemeal. Crossing en masse was still somewhat suicidal, but at least then the

Americans had the benefit of numbers: many men might die, but many more might make it across to do battle.

Instead, Taylor halted the entire army. By the time Grant arrived, days later, the northern bank of the Colorado was a scene of organized chaos: thousands of soldiers; hundreds of mules, horses, and bellowing oxen; and, from the other shore, the annoying blare of unseen Mexican bugles, blowing nonstop from the thick scrub.

A work party of American soldiers swung their axes under the glaring Texas sun, chopping away trees and shrubs to clear a trail down to the water, even as a second group stripped to the waist and wielded shovels to level off the steep drop from the banks down into the sluggish current. The soldiers might have looked like a very determined band of settlers, were it not for the artillery crews calmly aiming their cannons toward the Mexican positions, eager, after year upon year of practice, to fire upon a live enemy for the first time.

Grant was a compulsive observer, constantly watching and appraising so that he might understand a person or an activity better. He normally revered Taylor, a man whose disdain for affectation and military pomp mirrored his own. Yet as he studied Taylor's inability to cross the river, and the logjam of American troops now exposed to Mexican fire, anger flashed through the young lieutenant. The Arroyo Colorado should have been easy to cross. It was only a hundred yards wide and not much more than waist deep. From Grant's point of view, Taylor had made a mess of things by neglecting to bring along materials for a temporary bridge.

The lack seemed a glaring omission, for it had been known all along that the predominant geographical obstacles Taylor's army would face on its path into Mexico were Texas's broad, sluggish rivers, among them the Nueces, the Arroyo Colorado, and the Rio Grande. Yet neither Taylor nor his staff had had the forethought to bring along pontoons, an engineering novelty that had been developed during the Seminole Wars. Such an oversight seemed to Grant not only ludicrous but humiliating. If the American army was trying to intimidate the Mexicans with their professionalism, they were doing a very poor job of it.

THERE WERE MORE than just buglers on the opposite bank of the Colorado. "Mexican lancers were on the southern side," noted Second Lieutenant Pete Longstreet, "and gave notice that they had orders to resist our further advance." He had no doubt that there would be a battle if Taylor's army crossed the Arroyo Colorado.

Longstreet could hardly wait.

Since childhood, he had dreamed of being a soldier. And unlike those men whose dreams and physical attributes didn't mesh, the strapping southerner was born to be a great warrior. He was tough, having spent his childhood roaming the rugged Appalachian forests. He was shrewd, a serious cardplayer who won far more than he lost. His personal charisma was so great that some considered him a giant, even though he wasn't much more than six feet tall. But most of all, Longstreet was calm under pressure and deeply persevering. If the Mexicans contested the crossing, Longstreet would happily be in the thick of the fight. And then, he was sure, he would methodically dispose of anyone who tried to stop him.

Longstreet was Dutch on his father's side, descended from Puritans who had fled to America in 1630 and settled in New Jersey. It was Longstreet's grandfather William who moved his family south, settling near Augusta, Georgia, where he invented a steamboat prototype that successfully traveled eight miles on the Savannah River. But William was unable to procure a patent, despite years of trying, and never received proper credit for his revolutionary invention. Ten years later he moved again, this time to South Carolina.

It was on his grandfather's plantation in Edgefield, 20 miles north of Augusta and 150 miles northwest of the bustling port at Charleston, that James Longstreet the future soldier was born on January 8, 1821. The third of seven children, he was named after his father. His mother was the former Mary Ann Dent, who claimed she could trace her lineage to both Chief Justice John Marshall and William the Conqueror. Longstreet had no middle name but was given the nickname Peter at an early age — "rock" in Greek — for his strength and sturdy character.

Longstreet spent his childhood roaming the fields and forests around his father's large farm, learning to shoot and ride, feeling at home in the out-of-doors. Daily chores developed muscle to go with instinct, and Longstreet grew into a strapping, independent young boy, seemingly destined for a life in the country.

But he dreamed of being a general. Longstreet loved reading books about great warriors like Napoleon and Washington, and believed wholeheartedly that his ancestral link with William the Conqueror made him a natural soldier.

His father not only respected those dreams but also put forth a plan to help make them come true. When the boy was nine years old, his father packed him off to Augusta, where he would live with his uncle and get the sort of proper education that would allow him to enter West Point. The move from countryside to city was a dramatic lifestyle change, yet Longstreet adapted and even flourished. His uncle, a portly and influential local figure, sent the youngster off to the Richmond County Academy, a rigid private school where classes were conducted from dawn until dusk, ten months a year. By the time Longstreet matriculated at West Point at the age of sixteen, he had been educated in math, Latin, and Greek.

Sadly, his father didn't live to see Longstreet become a soldier. A cholera epidemic killed him in 1833, and Longstreet's mother moved away from the farm and relocated to the Alabama coast. Longstreet never saw much of her after that.

At West Point, Pete Longstreet was an even greater rebel and poorer cadet than Sam Grant. He graduated fifty-fourth out of fifty-six in the class of 1842, an esteemed bunch that would see seventeen of its members become generals. Longstreet was their equal in many ways, but his standing was pulled down by demerits, a fondness for sports above study, and a disdain for military discipline. (For instance, the food at West Point was a daily variation on overcooked beef, with boiled potatoes thrown in for variety, so Longstreet was fond of sneaking off the grounds to eat and drink at a local inn that was expressly off-limits to cadets.) Comfortable in his own skin, he was equally at home displaying proper etiquette at a formal military ball and swearing crudely in the field. "As I was of a large and robust physique," Longstreet admitted years later, "I was at the head of most larks and games." His classmates, noting that physique, named him Most Handsome Cadet. That description would stick for years to come, though he would eventually grow a long beard to hide his mouth, which a classmate once described as coarse.

Longstreet's poor grades meant that he, like his good friend Grant, couldn't select his postgraduate posting. As a result, all that West Point engineering training went by the wayside, and he was assigned to the infantry, which almost guaranteed that promotions would be few and far between.

Also like Grant, Longstreet fell in love after reporting for duty at the Jefferson Barracks, just outside Saint Louis. The woman in question was Louise Garland, and her father was Lieutenant Colonel John Garland, the regimental commander. Longstreet's eccentric classmate and fellow infantry officer Lieutenant Richard Ewell (the man who allowed Grant his predeployment leave to see Julia at White Haven) considered Louise to be one of just two attractive women in Missouri—the other being her sister Bessie. "This is the worst country for single ladies I ever saw," Ewell wrote to his brother. "They are hardly allowed to come of age before they are engaged to be married, however ugly they may be. Except the Miss Garlands, I have not seen a pretty girl or interesting one since I have been here."

Louise was seventeen when she first met Longstreet in the spring of 1844, a petite beauty who owed her dark black locks to her Chippewa Indian mother. The attraction between Louise and Pete Longstreet was obvious to both of them early on, and before shipping out for Camp Salubrity, Louisiana, he asked her father for permission to marry her. The request was approved, with the stipulation that the wedding not take place until Louise was a few years older.

Thus Brevet Second Lieutenants Pete Longstreet and Sam Grant were both engaged men as they settled in at Camp Salubrity. But whereas Grant was heartsick for Julia, writing letters that pleaded for her to reaffirm her love (which she did, though not as often as Grant would have liked), Longstreet had taken the separation from Louise in stride. He had passed the time near Fort Jesup among the rogues and rascals, playing poker, particularly a game called brag. (Longstreet was renowned for his ability to bluff. Grant, on the other hand, was miserable at cards.) A brevet second lieutenant earned less than thirty dollars a month—not quite a dollar a day. "The man who lost seventy-five cents in one day was esteemed a peculiarly unfortunate person," Longstreet said of Grant, who frequently lost that much before excusing himself from the table.

Longstreet had been transferred to the Eighth Infantry in March 1845 and reassigned to Fort Marion, Florida. More than two hundred years old, the fortress had a decidedly medieval feel, with moats, a dungeon, and twelve-foot-thick walls facing out at the Atlantic. The Eighth was a battle-hardened outfit, having spent the previous few years waging war against Florida's Seminole tribe. A far cry from the horse races and poker games of Camp Salubrity, Fort Marion was an appropriately disciplined military garrison for a self-confident young soldier to make the mental transition to his first taste of combat.

By September 1845, Longstreet and Grant were reunited in Corpus Christi, where they spent that awful winter awaiting the order to march on the Rio Grande. By the time Taylor's army proceeded south the following March, they had spent two full years living under the shadow of war. It had been a stretch of boredom and inertia, card games and hunting trips and living in tents, their personal lives on hold until politicians in Washington and Mexico City could decide their fate.

But now all that was past. As Pete Longstreet and Sam Grant faced south on a fine spring morning, looking across the muddy, inconsequential tidal flow of the Rio Colorado, battle was no longer some abstract image but was being vividly brought to life by the horns and lancers they could hear and see on the far bank.

Longstreet had laid eyes on few, if any, foreign soldiers in his life. The same was true of almost every officer and enlisted man along the river. It was titillating to stare over at the nameless, faceless army on the opposite shore, with their brightly colored uniforms and their exotic language, which very few Americans spoke and even fewer saw the need to learn. Most of the Americans didn't know, for instance, that the Mexican army was much like their own in many ways, structured in the European manner, with infantry, cavalry, engineers, and artillery, or that the total size of the Mexican army — 18,882 regular soldiers, 10,495 militiamen, and 1,174 irregulars — outnumbered theirs almost five to one, which was perhaps a case of ignorance being bliss.

Nor did most Americans know that the Mexicans were

divided into five separate armies, each focused around a region of the country. Nor that the cavalry, which they could so clearly hear across the river, were the Mexicans' most elite corps, composed of nine regiments (each broken into four squadrons that were made up of two companies of roughly thirty-five to fifty-five men), or that the horsemen were extremely well armed, often carrying an arsenal of pistols, sabers (with long blades designed for slashing, making them ideal weapons for soldiers on horseback), lassos (ideal for capturing a man and dragging him to death), a blunderbuss-style shotgun known as an *escopeta,* and a nine-foot-long lance—a weapon that had first been used prominently by William the Conqueror's troops at the Battle of Hastings in 1066 and had seen little design change since the Middle Ages. "The Mexican soldiery," reported the *Times* of London, are of "middle stature, or below it, small-boned, slightly built, graceful, with a smooth, soft, glossy skin, scarcely any muscle, no visible sinews, and of extremely light weight. He can be agile for a short time, but is constitutionally indolent. This is the Mexican Indian from the interior. The soldiers of mixed blood, partaking of the more northern races, and of old Spain, are stronger, rather sinewy, and capable of more continued exertion."

Longstreet visualized the battle in his head and liked what he saw. "We looked with confidence for a fight and the flow of blood down the salt water," he wrote enthusiastically.

On the morning of March 20, a Mexican officer splashed across the river on horseback. Captain José Barragan carried with him a proclamation that had been circulated to Mexican citizens, ordering them to take up arms against the American soldiers. The proclamation was glorious and poetic, issued by Mexican general Francisco Mejía in Matamoros. It went on to say of the Americans that "posterity will regard with horror their perfidious conduct" and that "the flames of patriotism which burn in our hearts will receive new fuel from the odious presence of the conquerors." In closing, it referenced Mexico's national War of Independence and promised the Mexican people that "the cry of Dolores and Iguala shall be re-echoed with harmony to our ears, when we take up our march to oppose our naked breasts to the rifles of the hunters of the Mississippi."

Captain Barragan promised Taylor that if his army tried to cross the river, the Mexicans would have no choice but to use force. And then, before mounting his horse for the ride back to his own lines, Barragan warned the Americans to turn around.

Taylor's response was not at all what the Mexicans had hoped for.

THREE

Rough and Ready

MARCH 21, 1846

Barragan might as well have insisted that the Americans attack immediately, for his defiant words had that very effect on Old Rough and Ready. The American commander brusquely ordered that the Rio Colorado be crossed. At 10:30 on the morning of March 21, one day after Barragan's visit, Taylor commanded four companies of infantry to wade the salty river (thanks to the Colorado's close proximity to the Gulf of Mexico) and assault the Mexican positions. It would be the first time since the War of 1812 that American troops had battled another regular army. The honor of leading the two-hundred-man force was given to Captain Charles Ferguson Smith. Grant knew Smith well: the dignified and fearless Philadelphian had been commandant of cadets when Grant was at West Point.

Smith's men wore a red stripe down the side of their uniform trousers as they splashed into the river, the stripes signifying that they were artillery soldiers trained to do double duty as infantry. These "redlegs" were supported by their gunnery brethren as they waded farther and farther into the brackish water, until it grew so deep that their stripes and sky blue tunics were underwater and only their heads and forage caps were visible. The men held their muskets high over their heads, keeping the barrels and cartridges dry but rendering Smith's troops defenseless against Mexican sharpshooters, which was the brutal, awful point of Taylor's sending such a small force across: to draw enemy fire. The moment such an attack commenced, American artillery would respond with their cannons, but not until then. Smith and his men were as exposed and vulnerable as a group of soldiers could ever be.

Grant, Longstreet, and the rest of Taylor's army were arrayed up and down the bank, mesmerized by the sight. No one dared speak; the silence on the American side was complete. "This was perhaps one of the most exciting hours of my life," wrote Captain Kirby Smith, West Point class of 1826. "All, from the General-in-Chief to the smallest drummer boy, felt morally certain that we were on the verge of a fierce and bloody conflict, yet I saw no one who was not cheerful and apparently eager for the game to begin."

It was a false alarm. "I do not remember that a single shot was fired," Grant wrote, remembering the disappointment.

"When they were halfway over and not a shot fired, the disappointment of the men was shown from right to left in muttered curses," noted an obviously disgusted Smith.

The Mexicans were bluffing. In a ruse designed to thwart the American advance, a very small corps of musicians had been moving from position to position, blowing trumpets night and day. "They gave the impression that there was a large number of them," Grant realized later, "and that if the troops were in proportion to the noise, they were sufficient to devour General Taylor and his army." The Mexican lancers were long gone by the time the Americans waded across, having taken their creative band of buglers with them. "The Mexicans had no artillery," rationalized Longstreet, "and could not expose their cavalry to the fire of our batteries; they made their formal protest, however, that the crossing would be regarded as a declaration of war."

As the band struck up "Yankee Doodle" and the rest of Taylor's force began to wade the Rio Colorado, Grant spent hours keenly observing the nuances of military logistics. "The troops waded the stream, which was up to their necks in the deepest part," he noted. "The bank down to the water was steep on both sides. A rope long enough to cross the river, therefore, was attached to the back axle of the wagons, and men behind would hold the rope to prevent the wagon from beating the mules into the water. This latter rope also served the purpose of bringing the end of the forward one back, to be used over again." Concluded Grant: "In this manner the artillery and transportation of the 'army of occupation' crossed the Little Colorado River."

For a junior officer, this was vital knowledge. To learn about war at West Point was valuable. But to actually be out on the Texas plains, watching as men stood in the cold river hour after hour, straining to successfully maneuver a vast caravan of supplies and animals, was another thing entirely. This was the sort of immediately practical information Grant might be called upon to impart if it ever came his turn to lead an army into battle. Grant studied the crossing so thoroughly that he could clearly recall its details almost forty years later.

BY MARCH 28, Taylor's army had reached the Rio Grande. Mexico, the land that had haunted their dreams and conversations for two years, lay on the opposite shore. The river was muddy and thin. The current veered between sluggish and deceptively fast. Cotton grew wild on the banks, its puffy white buds nestled in among the mesquite and palmetto. The thriving city of Matamoros fronted the river on the Mexican side. The houses were made of wood and bricks. Its entire population of a few thousand citizens stood on their rooftops to peer across at Taylor's arriving army. American soldiers could hear the peal of church bells and even watch with longing as the young local girls came to the river and undressed to bathe.

Taylor's camp was on a dusty patch of freshly tilled farmland, just inland from a bend in the river that thrust itself like a sharply pointed finger into the Mexican landmass. The Americans bivouacked in full sight of the Mexican army, daring them to provoke an attack. A pole was stuck upright in the fertile soil, and the Stars and Stripes was raised with great ceremony and blowing of horns. "For the first time this banner waved proudly before our forces, as if taking possession of what by every title properly belonged to us," wrote a Mexican officer, watching from Matamoros. "The soldiers of the army of the North were incensed in observing this insult of the enemy. Their cry was for the contest, and they beseeched their General to permit them to avenge the outrage."

But while his troops were inside the city's fortifications and armed for battle, Mexican general Mejía forbade any attack unless the Americans tried to cross the river. Taylor, who had no intention of doing any such thing, ordered his men to pitch those familiar white tents in a square formation, with their supply wagons positioned in the center for protection.

In this way, the two armies faced off, waiting to see who would make the first move.

"MY DEAR JULIA," Grant began his letter the next day. He missed her terribly and longed for a reunion. When he was with Julia, Grant was at his best. But with this great distance between them, he now found himself at loose ends. "A long and laborious march and one that was threatened with opposition from the enemy, too, has just been completed, and the Army now in this country are laying in camp just opposite the town of Matamoros. The city from this side bears an imposing appearance and no doubt contains four to five thousand inhabitants."

Grant didn't know the true size of the Mexican army, nor that the Americans' foes enjoyed a formidable advantage. But it didn't take a military genius to realize that Taylor's forces were relatively small and that the nearest source of fresh ammunition and food was thirty miles away on the Gulf of Mexico, where ships were being offloaded at a place called Port Isabel, which the Mexicans had evacuated. With little trouble, the Americans in both places could easily be surrounded and cut off. In many ways, Taylor's army was in a position very much like that of the Alamo defenders, which had fallen ten years earlier that month.

Taylor immediately ordered the construction of a proper defensive structure. Designed by Captain Joseph K. F. Mansfield, a Connecticut-born engineer who had specialized in fort building for two dozen years, it would be laid out in a roughly rectangular shape, with six diamond-shaped bastions on which to mount cannons thrusting out from the edges and corners. The structure would be capable of housing eight hundred men, with walls nine feet high and fifteen feet wide, made of thickly packed dirt and timber. A moat measuring twenty feet wide and eight feet deep would ring the perimeter. Fortified subterranean chambers would provide safe storage for ammunition. The men would live in tents pitched on the small parade ground, out of range of rifle fire but not of the long, parabolic lob of an artillery shell.

The days soon took on a predictable schedule. Each morning began with reveille, assembly, and roll call. Morning mess was from 6:30 to 7:30, after which construction began. Known as "fatigue" work, daily manual labor with a shovel or pickax was a constant part of a soldier's routine (officers did not share in fatigue work), even in times of peace.

Under more normal circumstances, the morning would also include sick call, general assembly, and drill, before an hour break for lunch at noon. This would then be followed by a second fatigue call. At 6:00 P.M. would come dress parade and an evening roll call, followed by dinner. The drummer's tattoo at 9:00 would be the invitation to one final roll call, then taps and lights out. But the urgency to build Fort Brown meant that almost all drill and assembly was dispensed with. Days and nights were a continuum of reveille, mess, fatigue call, taps, and sentry duty.

Construction proceeded at a feverish pace. A thousand men at a time dug into the earth and heaved their shovels of dirt into the great piles that slowly took on the shape of Mansfield's design. There were days when thunderstorms turned the soil into a muddy quagmire, and others when heat and ungodly Texas humidity made the dawn-to-dusk work schedule seem punitive. Yet construction never stopped, not for any reason.

Taylor delayed all travel to Port Isabel for supplies until the fortress was complete, fearing that he lacked the manpower to split his forces in order to simultaneously defend a supply train and his tenuous position on the Rio Grande. In the meantime, cavalry patrols rode out in search of Mexican scouts or some other such sign that the enemy was planning to cross the Rio Grande upriver and mount a surprise attack. American scouts heard rumors from local residents that six hundred Mexican dragoons had crossed on March 29. Whether they were in Texas, had returned to Mexico, or had actually crossed at all was anyone's guess. That dangerously large body of horsemen was never found.

Tensions escalated after Mexican patrols captured, and then returned, two American scouts. On April 10, Quartermaster Trueman Cross ventured out of the camp for an ill-advised solitary horseback ride through the countryside and never came back. The aging veteran of the War of 1812 had been sick, and many thought he might have fallen off his horse. But rumors of a less accidental demise gained credence when one of the patrols sent to find his body was ambushed and an American officer, Lieutenant Theodoric H. Porter, was killed. Porter was a popular man, the son of a naval commodore and seemingly destined for a greatness all his own. (Back in Corpus Christi, he had been the actor who objected to performing opposite Grant in *The Moor of Venice*.) No one knew for certain whether bandits or a Mexican army patrol had killed him, but the young lieutenant's murder was a cause for shock and quiet fury. Many soldiers were incensed that an infantry officer had volunteered to do a chore more suited to cavalry and snobbily acted as if he had it coming. Others saw Porter's death as an omen of things to come. Convinced that there was no way Taylor's puny force could defeat the Mexicans, these overnight cowards swam the Rio Grande in the dead of night to desert. Many were Irish Catholic immigrants who sympathized with the Mexicans because of their shared faith and felt themselves religiously persecuted in the predominantly Protestant U.S. Army. American sentries had standing orders to shoot all deserters on sight—but only while the deserters were still in the river. If the deserters reached the other side, they were safe; shooting them once they'd reached Mexican lines would be an act of war.

On April 11, Major General Pedro de Ampudia paraded into Matamoros with a two-hundred-man escort of light cavalry. Ampudia was a Cuban-born Spaniard with a pronounced paunch, deep circles under his eyes, and a long, white goatee that contrasted sharply with the black hair atop his head. He was respected if not beloved. Ampudia had crushed a citizens' rebellion in the Yucatán in 1841 and an uprising in Tabasco in 1844, where he shot all of its leaders—though not before ordering their throats slashed. The Americans could hear the echoing bong of church bells and the celebratory firing of muskets that accompanied Ampudia's arrival, giving the moment a raucous feel. Three days later, an infantry force of twenty-two hundred under Major General Anastasio Torrejón joined Ampudia's men. The newly arrived Mexicans confidently aimed cannons across the river, directly at Taylor's new fort. At the same time, as if to accentuate American weakness, Colonel William Whistler, the commander of the Fourth, was arrested for repeatedly stumbling through the ranks shit-faced drunk — no minor accomplishment in an army where alcohol was the universal salve.

And still — despite the manic pace of the new fort's construction, the Mexican troop buildup, the desertions, the disappearances, and the deaths — Grant kept trying to convince himself there wouldn't be a war. Even when a fresh batch of reinforcements and supplies arrived from Port Isabel during the second week of April, he thought it was just saber rattling. The American camp was within easy reach of Mexican cannons in Matamoros, yet not a single shot had been fired. As Grant saw it, the two armies were at the epicenter of an overblown international crisis, with the world watching and waiting to see which side blinked first. Someone would have to back down.

"My Dearest Julia," Grant wrote on April 20, craving a reunion with his fiancée. "Everything is quiet here. We are only separated by a narrow stream from one of the largest cities in Mexico, yet not a soul dare cross. Everything looks belligerent to a spectator but I believe there will be no fight. Occasionally they make a threat, but as yet their threats have all ended in bombast. It is now the opinion of many that our difficulty with Mex will be settled by negotiation and if so I hope my dear Julia to hear the Fourth Infantry ordered to the upper Mississippi before the end of warm weather."

Privately, Grant wondered what would happen if he was wrong. There was talk that captured Americans would be marched to prisoner-of-war camps hundreds of miles south.

There were also rumors that opposition general Ampudia was fond of boiling prisoners' heads in oil.

Grant found solace — and denial — in the reality that Mexico and the United States were not actually at war. So while the Mexicans "hovered about in such great numbers that it was not safe to send a wagon train after supplies," it was easy to blame the deaths of Porter and (presumably) Cross on bandits or accidents and not soldiers and to believe that there had been no real hostilities. With an optimism born of lovesick naïveté, Grant continued to hope that the dispute could be settled diplomatically.

That was not to be.

On April 23, Mexico secretly declared war on the United States. On April 24, Major General Mariano Arista arrived in Matamoros to relieve Ampudia as commander of Mexico's Army of the North. The red-haired Arista, who spoke fluent English and had once lived along the Ohio River very close to Grant's hometown, wasted no time showing why he had been entrusted with such a conspicuous command. By three o'clock that afternoon, Taylor's scouts were reporting that Mexican forces were mobilizing to cross the Rio Grande upriver and downriver of the new fort. Dragoon patrols soon trotted out of the American camp to see if the rumors were true. Grant, like the rest of the infantry, stayed behind. It had been a somber afternoon. There had been a funeral procession for Colonel Cross, whose body had been found, stripped and battered almost beyond recognition. The scene was made all the more wrenching by the sight of Cross's distraught son, who was also a soldier, marching alongside the flag-draped casket, and Cross's horse being led to the grave site. The animal was draped in black, with Cross's empty boots placed backward in the stirrups, according to military custom, signifying a horse whose rider has died.

The time for mere saber rattling was past. War between the United States and Mexico was about to begin.

FOUR

Fields of Fire

April 25, 1846

Captain William Joseph Hardee, a southern Georgian by birth, was tall and lean, with pale blue eyes and a courtly manner—as well as a modish French cut to his upturned mustache and thick billow of narrow beard that made the ladies swoon. The epitome of the dashing cavalry officer, Hardee was certainly no pencil-pushing engineer. He was a warrior through and through, fiery and opinionated, educated in the military arts at West Point, infatuated and engrossed by the smartest ways to trap and kill men. Hardee was one of those select souls who would be utterly lost when there was no war to fight, predestined to spend his life as a mercenary or a tactician for hire, anything to apply his considerable mental and physical prowess to making the world a better—or, depending upon which side you were on, more violent—place in which to live.

Since having graduated from West Point in 1838, he had already put this knowledge to use during two years of fighting the Seminoles in Florida with the Second Dragoons. His daring and intellect had come to the attention of no less than American secretary of war Joel Roberts Poinsett, who ordered

Hardee to the elite French military school at Saint-Maur for courses in advanced cavalry tactics. Of the 637 officers currently serving in the U.S. Army in April 1846, few had greater tactical awareness.

So Hardee's first instinct, as the men of the Second Dragoons approached the large rancho on the Rio Grande to investigate rumors of Mexican troop movements in Carricitos, was to be cautious. There was just one gate leading in and out of the property, which meant that once he and the rest of the cavalry entered, they could easily be trapped. In fact, the opening wasn't a gate at all but a narrow passage through an impenetrable tangle of scrub grass and mesquite that surrounded the ranch house on three sides. The fourth side, of course, was the Rio Grande itself. The river here was wide and swift and an unsound avenue of escape. To Hardee's trained eye, the ranch was a place where an army could easily be penned in and slaughtered.

The smart move would have been to send a small scouting party inside to search for the Mexican troops, while holding the bulk of the mounted force outside the ranch to keep a sharp eye out for a surprise attack. But Captain Seth Thornton, Hardee's commanding officer, was unworried, convinced that there were no enemy soldiers in the area. He ordered his entire outfit, sixty-three men in all, to follow him into the ranch so that he might question the owners.

Hardee was bone-tired. The dragoons had ridden through the night, traveling almost forty miles in the darkness. They had stopped only to grab a few hours' sleep and breakfast, then mounted up once again at dawn. Now they were drowsy and impatient, eager to make a cursory pass through the bottom-lands along the river before trotting back to tell Taylor that the rumors were false.

Hardee was the son of a son of a soldier, with a grandfather who had fought in the Revolutionary War and a father who had served in the War of 1812. He knew that fatigue made men lower their guard, even in war, when the need to be vigilant was greatest. So despite his lack of sleep, he grew nervous as the train of dragoons rode through the narrow gap in the mesquite. "The whole guard entered in single file, without any guard being placed in front," he noted, "or any other precautions taken to prevent surprise. Captain Thornton was prepossessed with the idea that the Mexicans had not crossed, and if they had, they would not fight."

Hardee rode in the rear of the column and was the last man to enter the rancho, or "plantation," as he thought of it, having grown up on an estate known as Rural Felicity, deep in cotton country. Here, the main house was two hundred yards inside the "fence," which was made of thick natural vegetation covered in thorns. Hardee trotted his horse up to the porch. He knocked. No one was home.

The dragoons spread out to search for someone who might answer questions about troop movements in the area. "At last," Hardee wrote, "an old man was found." Thornton rode over to question the elderly gentleman. The morning was calm. Nothing seemed out of the ordinary—for a moment or two. But then one of the dragoons turned to the east and saw a most terrifying sight: Mexican soldiers, too many for him to count, and all marching smartly toward the Americans. "The cry of alarm was given, and the enemy were seen in numbers," Hardee later wrote, with a great deal of understatement. The Georgian whirled his horse. A sixteen-hundred-man contingent of Mexican cavalry, light infantry, and sappers had surrounded the rancho and were pouring in through the lone entrance. The Second Dragoons weren't just trapped; they were moments away from being annihilated.

Thornton, acting quickly, led a frantic charge toward the gate. It was their only hope of escaping alive. The attack failed as soon as it began, with the Mexicans firing several rapid volleys at the approaching horsemen. Thus the men of the Second Dragoons, one of the army's most elite fighting forces, panicked. All sense of organization was lost. They galloped their horses up and down the fence, desperate to save themselves. Unit brotherhood was a thing of the past. Thornton led the retreat, such as it was, racing along the perimeter, frantically searching for a second opening. The Mexican firing never ceased.

Hardee galloped his horse to Thornton, thinking he had a solution — the only solution — to their life-and-death dilemma. Both were young men, on the cusp of thirty. They had been together at West Point and had fought alongside each other in the Seminole Wars. They had learned a great deal about warfare in their short lives, but nothing had prepared them for being surrounded by a fighting force that outnumbered them thirty to one, trapped inside a preposterous natural barrier, with absolutely no way out.

Hardee caught up to his classmate. Their horses were at full gallop as he screamed that their only hope was to dismount and hack through the chaparral barrier with their cavalry sabers. Thornton seemed to agree, but with the resignation of a commanding officer who had lost all control: the terrified dragoons had refused when Thornton ordered them to stand and fight. There seemed little chance they'd listen now.

Nostalgia was a thing of the past. Hardee took control. "The direction which Captain Thornton was pursuing would lead to the certain destruction of himself and his men, without possibility of resistance, [so] I turned to the right and told the men to follow me. I made for the river, intending to either swim it or place myself in position of defense." Twenty-five men followed Hardee down to the Rio Grande. They had no other choice: if they wanted to live, the river was their only way out.

Yet swimming was out of the question. The river was shallow near the bank, with a muddy bottom so soft that the horses began sinking down into the muck. Venturing farther out—whether in the saddle or on foot in an attempt to swim—might mean getting hopelessly stuck, making horses and riders easy targets for even the most pitiful enemy marksman.

Hardee spun away from the Rio Grande. The time had come to stand and fight. He could hear the battle raging near the farmhouse. Thornton and his men were being cut down, but the Mexican infantry hadn't yet advanced to the river, giving the Georgian time to plan. He assembled the dragoons, lining them abreast along the riverbank, then checking each man's armament, one by one, to make sure that they were prepared for battle. Each had started the day with the standard weaponry issued to all American cavalry: an 1840-model cavalry saber, a single-shot pistol, and an 1843-model breech-loading carbine (loaded from the rear of the barrel, as opposed to tamping a charge down from the forward opening).

Hardee was shocked to discover that many soldiers had dropped their weapons during the retreat. Theirs would be, unfortunately, a suicide charge. "Almost everyone had lost a saber, a pistol, or carbine. Nevertheless, the men were firm and disposed, if necessary to fight to the last extremity," he noted.

It hadn't been more than fifteen minutes since the American soldiers had marched onto the ranch. The battle itself was just five minutes old. Riderless American horses galloped in circles, their empty saddles attesting to the dragoons' decimation. Thornton, miraculously, had escaped into the chaparral unseen. He now hid there, dust-covered and dripping sweat, peering through the thorns and bramble as Hardee and his men prepared to mount the final cavalry charge of their lives. Mexican horsemen ringed the chaparral to prevent Hardee's escape. The infantry of Brigadier General Anastasio Torrejón walked haughtily to the river, guns leveled, ready to finish the Americans off.

Hardee reverted to his training.

It didn't take a tactical genius to see that a charge would be futile. He and his men were surrounded and barely armed. The dragoons would be cut down in a hail of musket fire the instant they spurred their horses. He'd heard the rumors about Mexicans treating prisoners atrociously during their battles with the Texans, but Hardee knew what he had to do. "I went forward and arranged, with an officer, that I should deliver myself and my men as prisoners of war, to be treated with all the consideration to which such unfortunates are entitled by the rules of civilized warfare."

With that, Hardee surrendered.

Bodies of American soldiers littered the ranchland as Hardee was marched to General Torrejón. One second lieutenant, a classmate of Longstreet's named George T. Mason, lay dead in the green spring grass, a sword clutched in his right fist, killed as he tried to fight his way off the battlefield rather than surrender.

Hardee saw no sign of Thornton.

NOT ALL OF the dragoons had been slain, much to Hardee's relief. In addition to his small force, twenty more men were in Mexican custody. When Hardee finally met face-to-face with Torrejón, he was prepared for the worst.

Torrejón was a mestizo. He had a hard and unattractive face and possessed a reputation for cunning and for setting traps. Hardee now knew that all too well. But Torrejón was also compassionate. The battle was through. He saw no need to butcher the Americans. Torrejón sent the prisoners back to Matamoros, where they were treated with cordial respect. Thornton was captured several days later and joined Hardee as a prisoner of war. They were lodged in a large hotel, where life was amazingly luxurious. Not only did they dine regularly with General Ampudia—the man reputed to boil heads in oil—but the Mexican army paid them a daily allowance equal to half their regular pay. General Arista "intended to supply all our wants himself," wrote Hardee in a letter that was sent across the river to Taylor. "These promises have already been fulfilled in part."

In fact, Hardee was living better than he would have on the American side of the Rio Grande, eating fresh food instead of salt pork out of a barrel, sleeping in a real bed instead of on a muddy bedroll, and having a roof over his head to keep him dry when thunderstorms came. This peaceful reverie would soon come to an end. Thanks to Thornton's inept tactical blunder, Taylor dashed off an urgent message to Washington, asking for immediate reinforcements. The missive confirmed the news that President Polk had awaited so eagerly: "Hostilities may now be considered as to have commenced."

FIVE

Call to Battle

May 3, 1846

To the brothers in arms along the Rio Grande, no triumphal call to battle marked the Mexican War's official beginning. Nor did they have the benefit of an elaborately worded decree. The precise moment when each man realized that Mexico and the United States were shooting at each other in earnest was, in fact, unique. For Captain William Hardee, it came as Torrejón sprung his trap. General Zachary Taylor's war began when he sent the courier galloping away from camp with that vindicating message for President Polk. And for Lieutenant Sam Grant, the first war of his young life began at dawn on a Sunday, as he lay sleeping.

It was just moments before the regimental bugler would blow reveille. Once again Grant huddled in a grimy white tent on a fly-choked Texas beach, but instead of Corpus Christi, it was the coastal supply depot of Port Isabel. The fort was finally finished. Taylor had marched the bulk of his army twenty-seven miles east to the Gulf of Mexico. His stated intent was to pick up provisions and armament — which he would indeed do. But the maneuver was also Taylor's cagey attempt to draw the Mexicans away from the fort. He wanted to fight them out in the open on a proper battlefield, rather than in what it was increasingly apparent was an Alamo-like setting that robbed the Americans of mobility and cavalry.

As Grant opened his eyes to greet the day, the sound he heard most powerfully was not the soft crash of Texas breakers or the early morning warble of seagulls but the distant rumble of a prolonged and hostile artillery bombardment. "As we lay in our tents along the sea shore, the artillery at the fort on the Rio Grande could be distinctly heard," he wrote of that moment. "The war had begun."

A skeleton force had stayed behind to defend the newly finished earthworks along the Rio Grande (referred to sometimes as Fort Taylor but more often as Fort Texas). It comprised the Seventh Infantry and a detachment of artillery specialists, all under the command of Major Jacob Brown. The Seventh had earned the nickname the Cotton Balers for allegedly taking cover behind cotton bales during the Battle of New Orleans. This group of roughly five hundred men now crouched behind walls fifteen feet thick, armed with four behemoth eighteen-pound cannons and a much less lethal battery of six-pound guns under the command of Lieutenant Braxton Bragg.

Grant knew the two men by reputation only. Brown was that rare officer who hadn't graduated from West Point, having enlisted during the War of 1812 and worked his way up through the ranks. He was in his midfifties, old for a major, and his career had been undistinguished and unsullied, spent in backwater postings like Council Bluffs, Iowa, and Little Rock, Arkansas. Yet Brown was beloved by his men, and the sort of quietly confident leader who was sure to remain calm as the enemy lay siege to the army's newest fortress.

Bragg was different. The North Carolinian was a tyrant, despised by his troops for his fanaticism about discipline and protocol. He had finished fifth in the West Point class of 1837, which had graduated more than a dozen future generals—a startling figure, given that it comprised just fifty men. Bragg was lean like a knife's blade, tall, with iron gray eyes, great bushy eyebrows, and a sharp, unshaven chin whose point was accentuated by whiskers extending clear down both sides of his face to the jawbone. He was prone to depression, hypochondria, boils, and chronic diarrhea. Strangely, despite all this, women found him to be extremely charming. Bragg could display a sly sense of humor to those he pursued. Among his men, however, such attributes might be spoken of but were never witnessed.

Bragg's character was potentially assailable, but his ability and intellect were not. Actually, he was something of a military genius. Bragg's specialty was artillery, which seemed like nothing more than a fancy word for cannons to nonmilitary observers. Such naïveté denied the complexity of nineteenth-century weaponry. There were large cannons for heavy bombardment and fort defense, small cannons for mobile battlefield use, and mortars for lobbing shells great distances. There were cast-iron cannons and the more lightweight bronze cannons. There were guns and howitzers; solid cannonballs, artillery shells, hollowed cannonballs filled with explosives, canister rounds, and those deadly bundles of shot known as grape.

Bragg was adept at mobilizing and firing all of these weapons. Yet his favorite was the six-pounder (guns took their name from the heft of the solid cannonball that fit most snugly in their muzzle), the smallest cannon in the modern American military arsenal. Those small guns were perfect for battlefield use—light, horse-drawn, joyously mobile—and were quite effective against an army marching shoulder to shoulder into battle. But a six-pounder could inflict only minimal damage against heavy fortifications; if and when soldiers of the Mexican army swarmed the walls of Fort Texas, those guns would be ideal for close combat, spraying them with lethal rounds of canister and grapeshot.

Until then, it would be up to the behemoth eighteen-pounders to lob down hellfire on the Mexican positions across the river. Eighteens were capable of demolishing almost anything. It was hoped those big guns could destroy just enough of Mexico's defensive positions for the fort to hold out until Taylor's return.

Scouts galloping into Port Isabel soon reported that Mexican troops had taken up a blocking position on the only road leading back to Fort Texas. That was good news to Taylor, for the Mexicans were now out in the open, right where he wanted them.

Not so for Grant. He was terrified and repulsed by the distant belch of cannons. He had no desire to fight; not in the open or huddled behind a bunker. He felt certain he wasn't cut out for war. "For myself, a young second lieutenant who had never heard a hostile gun before, I felt sorry that I had enlisted," he finally confessed. Yet Grant's conviction that once he started something, he must continue forward until the thing was through, was stronger than any impulse to flee. The only way of relieving Brown, Bragg, and the Seventh Infantry — and returning home to Julia — was by pushing the Mexican forces back across the Rio Grande. Like it or not, war was Grant's destiny.

He wrote to Julia. More than anything, he wanted to be sitting with her on the front porch at White Haven. "As soon as this is over, I will write to you again. That is, if I am one of the fortunate individuals who escape," he said, trying to reassure her but failing miserably. "You don't know how anxious I am to see you again, Julia."

It crossed his mind that the letter might be his last.

SIX

Fort Texas

May 3, 1846

The stranded soldiers defending Fort Texas left their tents to shave as the regimental drummers beat morning reveille. "We had just commenced washing, etc., before going to work, when the batteries of the enemy opened, and their shots and shells began to whistle over our heads in rapid succession," a young lieutenant named Napoleon Jackson Tecumseh Dana wrote to his wife, Sue. "They had commenced in real earnest, and they fired away powder and copper balls as if they cost nothing and they had a plenty of ammunition."

Infantry soldiers sprinted to man the parapets while artillerymen raced to their cannons. Lieutenant Bragg and his complement of field artillery took aim at the Mexican positions as the four eighteen-pounders under the command of Captain Allen Lowd fired onto the enemy batteries. Each big gun weighed more than two tons. Standing on the breastworks, looking across the Rio Grande, the American troops could clearly witness the destruction their superior artillery rounds were inflicting. One enemy cannon exploded into the air in pieces, leaving the brains and torn limbs of dead and wounded men littering the ground.

A half hour after the two sides began trading fire, a brown-haired sergeant named Weigart became the first official American casualty of the war. He was peering out at the enemy when a piece of grapeshot blasted through his chin and exited the back of his head. Weigart dropped facedown. Hair and blood matted the gaping hole in his skull. A sergeant standing nearby mistook Weigart's body for that of an Irish soldier named Shea, who had a profound reputation for cowardice. "Shea is killed, sir," the orderly sergeant informed his commanding officer in a shaking voice. "No, I ain't, sir," cried out Shea, standing up from the spot where he'd been hiding.

The captain ordered that Weigart's body be dragged to a hospital tent. An hour later, a second Mexican shell scored a direct hit on the hapless sergeant's corpse, entirely severing head from body. A party was sent out to bury the remains in the dark quietly that night, exiting the fort to dig a grave alongside a wall that could easily be seen by Mexican troops. The work was perilous—they could have been captured and taken prisoner at any time—but the men got the job done and returned to the relative safety of their beleaguered earthworks, which in reality weren't much safer.

The nighttime silence along the Rio Grande came after a pummeling day of fighting. The din along the river had been tremendous. American gunners fired more than 350 cannon rounds, so many that they had to stop shooting after six hours for fear of running out. The Mexicans, meanwhile, lobbed more than 1,200 rounds on the earthworks. Wrote Dana, "We could not answer their guns anymore but keep our means for an emergency, and as they did not do us the least injury in that six hours firing, we concluded that it was unnecessary to throw away any more of our powder and shot unless they materially improved their firing.... We treated all their noise with silent contempt, and our men screened themselves from the shot and slept on their arms."

Key to the fate of the American soldiers was their army's return. Fort Texas was sturdy enough, holding up spectacularly to the bombardment, with little damage to show for the hours of punishment. Yet the fact remained that the trapped Seventh would run out of food and ammunition if Taylor didn't arrive soon. No matter how effective the cannons inside the fort might be, or how inefficient the Mexican gunners, the U.S. soldiers could not endure indefinitely. The siege would break them. Sooner or later the Seventh would either starve to death or be forced to surrender.

The situation took a heartbreaking turn for the worse at mid-morning on the fourth day. Major Brown was making his daily rounds of the defenses. It was a normal walk-through: shells burst all around; his men dodged incoming artillery, staying low and pressing their bodies against a wall whenever they heard the telltale whine that signaled a new attack.

Brown paused to direct a squad building a bombproof shelter, ignoring cannonballs whistling all around him. In a brilliant example of war's sudden surprise, a Mexican howitzer shell blasted into his right leg, tearing away everything below the midthigh. Shredded muscle and jagged lengths of bone marked where the limb had been severed. Two soldiers, stunned by what they'd just witnessed, hoisted Brown off the ground and carried him quickly into the hospital tent. The military surgeon had seen few injuries in his career, let alone a shattered leg. Moving quickly, knowing that immediate treatment was the key to saving Brown's life, the surgeon reached for the box containing his amputation scalpels and bone saw. A crowd gathered in the sweltering tent to console their commander. They believed the fort would surely fall if Brown's fortunes took a turn for the worse. "Men, go to your duties," Brown reassured the dumbstruck soldiers. "Stand your posts. I am but one among you."

The surgery was brutal yet delicate. The amputation utensils were removed from their case. They were clean but not sterilized, the concept of infection being then unknown. Likewise, there was no pain relief to offer Brown, just a jolt of medicinal whiskey and either a stick or a chunk of leather on which to bite down. Amputation victims were known to thrash wildly during the operation, so two strong men restrained Brown's arms after he was lowered onto the surgical table. His left leg, the good one, was lashed to the table so that he would be unable to twist his body or kick as the surgeon sliced into him.

A tourniquet was cinched around the femoral artery. The surgeon then snipped away loose muscles and tendons from the end of the destroyed leg. He wielded a very long and slender scalpel, taking care to leave a flap of skin big enough to cover the stump. Next the surgeon cut into the meaty end of Major Brown's thigh, slicing clear down and around the bone.

He reached for his saw. Rather than cut off the femur's shattered tip, the surgeon pushed the muscle away from the femur until three inches of thigh bone were revealed. That way, after he had sawed it off, two to three inches of muscle would lie between the end of the bone and the flap of skin, ensuring that the femur wouldn't poke through the end of the stump once Brown was sutured. Later, when he was fully healed, a wooden prosthetic leg would be fitted over the major's amputated limb, allowing him to walk again.

The surgeon, according to procedure, used his right hand to hold the saw, placing his left index finger directly on the bone to serve as a cutting guide. The work proceeded relatively quickly: Brown's femur was sawed off, arteries and veins were sutured, water (also unsterilized and perhaps bearing a touch of Rio Grande mud) was splashed on the wound, and then the flap of flesh was sewn over the stump.

Once the surgeon finished, he ordered that Brown be carried down into the safety of the underground ammunition magazines. Brown would recover in the sweltering, airless room until the siege ended. This postoperative recovery setting was hardly ideal, and Brown's chances of survival, like that of his fort, depended upon Taylor's hasty return.

A few hours later, Mexican general Arista sent four officers to broker a surrender. They informed the lonely men of Fort Texas that a large enemy force had blocked the road between Fort Texas and Port Isabel. The Seventh was unlikely to be rescued or resupplied, stated Arista's emissaries, and should surrender now before they began the long, slow death from starvation and dehydration that often accompanied a siege. Brown's replacement as fort commander was Captain Edgar S. Hawkins. Arista gave him one hour to make his choice.

Hawkins was a forty-five-year-old New Yorker who had the dubious distinction of having required six years to graduate from West Point (which he had entered at the tender age of thirteen). He had spent most of his career in garrisons along the American frontier. So he possessed ample experience in hostile border environments such as the one in which he now found himself. Hawkins listened closely as an interpreter who spoke very poor Spanish read the Mexican demand; then he called a council of his officers before issuing a response. Among them were the artillerymen Bragg and Lowd, Captain Joseph Mansfield, the fort's designer, and Dana. The council quickly made its decision.

"My interpreter is not skilled in your language," Hawkins sent word to Arista, in a tone both defiant and courteous. "But if I understand you correctly, I must respectfully decline to surrender."

Arista's furious reply was to launch the most withering artillery barrage the Americans had seen so far. Shrapnel and shells dropped on Fort Texas like summer rain. The U.S. tents, pitched carefully along the inside walls of the fort, were shredded by the flying metal. One piece of shot flew just over Captain Hawkins's head while he ate breakfast. A single artillery shell pierced three horses that were standing side by side, killing them all. One soldier had a shell explode beneath his feet and escaped unharmed. Another experienced the odd sensation of having a shell roll over his back. He, too, was unharmed.

In fact, despite the intensity of the barrage, the only casualties were fifteen horses and the military band's drums and brass instruments, which were smashed by a direct hit on the chest in which they were stored.

By the fourth day of the Fort Texas siege, morale was finally dropping low. Troops were becoming more and more disheartened. Ammunition and food were running out. All eyes scanned the horizon for Taylor's return. Yet they saw nothing.

Then they rejoiced at a most wondrous sound.

Amazingly, after what seemed like an endless week of waiting, the men "heard cannonading about eight miles away, and immediately knew that the general was on the move and had met the enemy." It was Friday. Their siege was six days old. At long last, the reinforcements were close.

Yet their hopes were premature — and they knew it. Between Fort Texas and Taylor lay a massive Mexican force. Taylor had wanted his wide-open fight. He was about to get it. The lonely men of Fort Texas could only pray that he would win.

SEVEN

Clash

MAY 8, 1847

G rant could not see Fort Texas, but he could clearly see the Mexican army. They were three-quarters of a mile away, porched across the horizon like condors, half-hidden by a dense copse of chaparral on a plain known as Palo Alto. Their sharpened bayonets and polished brass cannons reflected the afternoon sunlight. The Mexican uniforms were a wild palette of colors and designs, plumes and epaulets, from the green and red of the lancers to the infantry's dark blue and yellow. There was, in fact, nothing uniform about them, for every unit adorned itself with a different design and color scheme. They would have been ridiculous if they weren't so deadly: Grant estimated that they numbered six thousand or more, with the cavalry on the right and left sides of their lines and seven units of infantry in between.

Grant chose to focus his analytical powers not on fashion, but on the Mexican weaponry, his spectacular numeric disadvantage, and basic tactics: to Grant's right was the road leading back to Fort Texas. On the far side of the road was thick chaparral. In front of Grant and the Americans was a rolling, grass-covered prairie, pocked here and there by small ravines. On the opposite side of the prairie was more chaparral, a line of trees—and a vast array of shiny Mexican bayonets. Presumably, the Mexicans had several cannons camouflaged in all those trees and mesquite, but Grant could only make out shapes that may or may not have been artillery.

Grant and the other American troops stood in shoulder-high Indian grass, the fierce yellow sun burning their faces. They were exhausted, having slept poorly the night before. "The mosquitoes seemed as thick as the blades of grass on the prairie, and swarmed and buzzed in clouds, and packs of half-famished wolves prowled and howled about us. There was no need for the sound of reveille. The wolves and mosquitoes, and perhaps some solemn thoughts, kept us on the *qui vive*," Longstreet vouched for their long night out in the open. Then, no excuses, it was up at dawn to resume

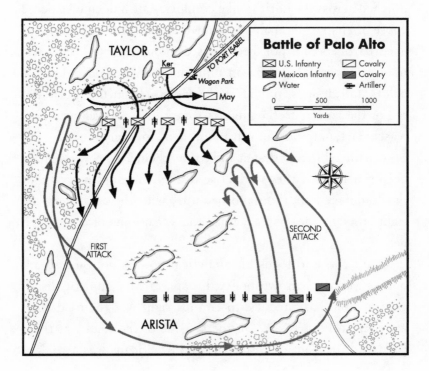

the march to Fort Texas. They drowsily marched the one-lane road in a dusty column of men, mules, oxen, horses, wagons, and cannons that stretched for three miles.

At two in the afternoon, when reports confirmed that Mexican troops had blocked the road, General Taylor ordered his army to assemble for battle. The six infantry regiments spread abreast across the prairie in close order, with artillery units positioned between them. He placed the eighteen-pounders at the very center. Instead of traditional solid cannonballs, the big guns were being loaded with rounds of canister and grape.

A canister round was essentially a long tin cylinder packed with lead or iron balls, each the size and shape of an eyeball. When the cylinder was slid into the cannon's muzzle, the fit was snug, with just one-tenth of an inch difference between the diameter of the gun tube and the width of the cylinder, a measurement known to artillery specialists as windage. The instant the cannon was fired, the force shoved the balls forward against the tip of the cylinder, which was destroyed as the spheres burst through the tin and sprayed from the cannon like large shotgun pellets. Maximum effective canister range was four hundred yards, but as with a shotgun, canister rounds were most deadly when the target was very close. Sometimes two rounds were fired from the same barrel at the same time. Known, most literally, as double canister, this especially lethal method of killing was often saved for times when the enemy loomed too close for comfort, like those terrifying moments when a position was on the verge of being overrun.

Grape was a larger and equally lethal antipersonnel round that had greater range. When first designed for the siege of Constantinople in 1453, the balls had been packed in a small burlap sack that was tied with string, making the armament resemble an oversize bundle of grapes, hence the name. By the nineteenth century, a metallic container divided into three sections had replaced the sacks. Each section was packed with sawdust and three cast-iron balls roughly the size of a man's fist. Because of its size, grape was used in the larger-diameter barrels of siege and fortress cannons. In the case of Taylor's army, that meant the eighteen- and twelve-pounders. Grape rounds worked on the spray-and-maim premise—and with devastating effect. They could easily disable a man from nine hundred yards away.

Taylor's plan was to open the battle by peppering the Mexican ranks with canister and grape. If all went well, the scatter-shot armament would not only kill and disfigure a large number of his opponents but also cause the Mexican soldiers to panic and break ranks. In the confusion that followed, his infantry units could rush into the breach and do their business.

The Mexican forces maintained their position as the Americans slowly marched forward through the tall grass. Taylor's all-important cannons were pulled by pack animals, with the guns themselves mounted on spoke-wheeled carriages. The lethal eighteen-pounders were not normally used in the field—they were cumbersome and hard to move, ill suited to the speed of battle; Taylor only had them along because they had just arrived on a boat from New Orleans, and he was transporting them from Port Isabel to Fort Texas. They were a liability, so heavy that six yoke of oxen were required to pull each gun forward, and the animals' deliberate plod had set the pace at which Taylor's army moved during the march to Palo Alto.

Grant, somewhat absurdly, was still in denial. "Even then, I did not believe they were going to give battle," he later admitted. He was shortly disabused of his ignorance. Once the Americans closed to within two-thirds of a mile, the Mexicans fired, "first with artillery and then with infantry." As expected, the Mexicans had hidden their British-made nine-pound cannons in the chaparral, disguising their precise location to achieve maximum surprise. The combination of cannon and musket fire sent a fabulous din through the air and was meant to rattle the Americans. It didn't work. Taylor's men held their fire and moved forward.

The open prairie favored a cavalry battle, but that was a fight Taylor knew he would lose. His dragoons were outnumbered two to one. Combine that superiority with the entrenched Mexican artillery and infantry, and the American horses and troops could be slaughtered by the bushel. So while it wasn't glamorous, and it wouldn't make for great copy in all the Washington newspapers, Taylor intended to fight a defensive battle, using his artillery to even the odds. His instincts were in opposition to the most bedrock of American tactical philosophies (borrowed, like most other U.S. military beliefs, from the French) — that aggressive tactical offensives would always win out over an entrenched enemy. "A general who waits for the enemy like an automaton, without taking any other part than that of fighting valiantly, will always succumb when he shall be well attacked," the French military theorist Baron Antoine-Henri Jomini had written in his widely read 1838 treatise *Summary of the Art of War,* the bible of American military thinking. But Taylor had learned his trade well in four decades of soldiering. His battle plans were dictated not by a manual but by his own gut instincts.

Unfortunately for the Mexicans, their leaders weren't as adroit as Taylor. There were three hard-and-fast rules about the use of solid cannonballs, known well by every artillery officer in the field: never fire solid shot until the infantry is within a thousand yards; make sure the battleground is covered with trees and rocks, to increase the odds that balls will ricochet unpredictably; and use solid cannonballs when the enemy is marching in close formation for the most lethal effect.

The Mexican artillery violated two out of the three.

They started by firing too soon. If Arista had waited until the Americans were closer, the Mexican cannons could have done horrendous damage to Taylor's formations, which were marching into battle upright and close together, in the manner of Europe's great armies. But Arista was overconfident and eager. He misjudged the Americans, believing they would panic and break ranks, and as a result he commenced the artillery barrage when they were more than twelve hundred yards off. The cannonballs dropped harmlessly to earth, far short of their targets. He had also chosen his armament poorly, firing puny bronze four-pounders that—even if they somehow reached enemy lines—lacked lethal firepower. As for any ricochet danger, there was none: the tall prairie grass was so pliable that the cannonballs passed straight through, like a hot knife through butter, or bounced along in such linear paths that they were easy for even the most slow-witted soldier to dodge.

Most infuriating to the Mexican gunners, though, was that they had the third rule on their side but it didn't matter. The Americans didn't panic, nor did they break ranks. They marched forward, maintaining close formation in order to concentrate their musket-firing power, and offering the Mexicans a prime target all the while. Yet even when the clumped Americans came within range, the weak and avoidable cannonballs had no effect.

Taylor, riding Old Whitey, called a halt when the two armies were separated by just five hundred yards. He wore a floppy palmetto hat to keep the sun off his face, and a plug of tobacco bulged in his cheek. As always on the battlefield, Taylor's bearing was nonchalant, as if all the shooting and dying were some sort of casual affair he had mistakenly stumbled upon.

Yet Taylor was far more intense than he liked to let on. Scrutinizing his army, he quickly decided he didn't like the positioning of his artillery. He ordered the gunners to wheel their cannons just a little farther forward, and so they rolled closer to the Mexican lines: the twelve-pound howitzers, which fired a dangerous high-trajectory shot, the lighter six-pound flying artillery, and even the mammoth eighteen-pounders.

Then each of the seven-man gun crews began its dark ballet: the tampion, or lid, was removed from the muzzle; the gun leveled and aimed; the powder wad and round shoved down into the muzzle with a rammer; the primer placed into the gun vent; a lanyard uncoiled and stretched to its full length, the gunner always holding this firing mechanism in his right hand. The men didn't have to think about what they were doing, for they had practiced this again and again, more times than they could remember. They worked as one, with fluid precision, their every movement preceded by a barked command, from "Take implements" to "Ram" to "Heave," then "Ready."

The final instruction, that fatal barked command they all awaited, was "Fire." The gun crews sweated in the heat, their hearts racing as they prepared to blast men into pink mist for the first time.

Taylor ordered his gunners to do their job.

Grant could only admire the brutal demonstration. "The infantry stood at order arms as spectators, watching the effect of our shots upon the enemy, and watching his shots so as to step out of their way. It could be seen that the 18-pounders and howitzers did a great deal of execution."

Indeed. "Every moment we could see the charges from our pieces cut a way through their ranks, making a perfect road," Grant added, describing the gruesome effects of canister and grape. "Their officers made an attempt to charge us, but the havoc had been so great that their soldiers could not be made to advance."

Up and down the rows, Grant and his fellow West Point alumni got their first taste of war. Longstreet, over on the far left, dropped back with the Eighth Infantry to protect that flank from a charge by Mexican cavalry. "Prince" John Magruder, the flamboyant lieutenant who had designed the theater back in Corpus Christi, was right up front with the First Artillery, lobbing cannon rounds. Lieutenant George Gordon Meade, serving as a messenger for Taylor, galloped his horse across the battle-field from one command to another.

Grant was surprised to discover that he felt no fear. In his usual detached manner, he became so absorbed in watching the war that he behaved as if he were not part of it. He was bemused by the sight of overly eager American soldiers firing their Model 1822 flintlock muskets at targets several hundred yards away — a distance well beyond their range and design. Indeed, the musket was so inaccurate that it worked best when fired in volleys, into tight bunches of enemy at close quarters, then followed up by a bayonet charge. Firing from more than fifty yards away was a waste of powder and ball — or as Grant put it, "a man might fire at you all day without your finding out."

Once the Americans were close enough that the Mexican artillery could do real damage Grant's personal detachment evaporated as men around him began to fall. "Although the balls were whizzing fast and thick around me, I did not feel a sensation of fear, until nearly the close of firing a ball struck close to me, killing one man instantly. It knocked Captain [John] Page's under jaw entirely off and broke in the roof of his mouth," Grant wrote. "The under jaw is gone to the wind pipe and the tongue hangs down to the throat. He will never be able to speak or eat."

The Mexican forces knew that movement was the key to victory — in particular, movement toward the all-important American supply column. The wagons were parked to the rear of the battlefield, guarded by an American cavalry outfit under the command of Captain Charles A. May. If nothing else, the Mexican forces were determined to capture those wagons or at the very least set them aflame and render them worthless.

General Torrejón sent his cavalry off into the chaparral to the right of the American forces as the battle raged, hoping to use the cover of the thick vegetation and the low hills to hide his men.

But the land was swampy, as Taylor well knew. The Mexican cavalry bogged down. Not only that, but the American Fifth Infantry had anticipated the move and taken up positions on the edge of the chaparral. As Torrejón's men charged the Fifth in force, eight hundred lance-carrying Mexican cavalry, looking like medieval throwbacks, galloped into the American rifles. The Americans, their bayonets affixed, formed themselves into a hollow square, four lines facing outward toward the points of the compass. The men of each line stood shoulder to shoulder, with another rank lined up behind them to fire a quick second volley while the first line reloaded.

Cavalry charges had been a staple of battle for centuries, and as far back as ancient Greece, infantry had formed into a square to defend against an onslaught. The hollow square required a great deal of nerve on the part of the foot soldier, for it was imperative for the lines to stand firm at all costs. Its weakest strategic points were the corners, but fainthearted soldiers who turned and fled were an even more deadly liability.

It had been three decades since an American force had formed such a square, whether they could pull it off was anyone's guess.

The Americans held their fire until the lancers were just fifty yards away. "The front of the square attacked, poured in its volley of buckshot and balls," wrote one lieutenant. "Horses, officers, and men of the lancers were brought to the ground. Many more of them reeled in their saddles, wounded. Some were thrown, and the rest, in confusion, galloped back to their own side of the field." The Mexicans fell back to regroup. When they attempted to range even farther out in a last-ditch attempt to attack the wagon train, they were shocked to discover the Third Infantry waiting with a pair of cannons to block them.

Meanwhile, farther to the left, Grant and the Fourth were taking the brunt of the battle. Their artillery was systematically mowing down the Mexican forces, but time and again they regrouped, their lines bloodied but unbroken, their numerical superiority making itself known. Arista's men returned fire with such ferocity that the Fourth began taking fantastic casualties and had to pull back. The Mexican troops were not their only danger: a prairie fire started by a powder wad that had fallen onto the grass threatened to engulf the Fourth. But though fire scorched the dry battlefield grass and raised so much smoke that fighting actually halted on both sides for an hour, no one was burned.

Like a curtain raised before a spectacular second act, the dissipating smoke gave way to more ferocious shooting. Fighting raged throughout the afternoon. Both sides were mentally and physically exhausted by the time the sun began to set. Fighting finally ceased for the night when the sky grew too black for either side to see what they were shooting at. The Americans promptly dropped to the ground and slept, resting upon the exact spots where they had stood when the sun dropped, unwilling to concede so much as an inch to the enemy. Somewhere out in the darkness and chaparral, the Mexicans did the same. The cries and moans of the wounded carried through the night, sometimes Spanish, sometimes English, always lonesome and heart-wrenching.

Grant, exhausted after the long day of marching and fighting, had no trouble resting. "I believe all slept as soundly on the ground at Palo Alto as if they had been in a palace. For my own part I don't think I even dreamed of battles."

In the predawn darkness, as Grant lay dreaming, Taylor called a council of war. He was worried and asked his key officers whether he should press the attack. Seven of the ten said no. But artillery specialist Captain James Duncan boldly declared, "We whipped 'em today, and we can whip them tomorrow."

Taylor was fortified. "That is my opinion," he declared. "Gentlemen, you will prepare your commands to move forward."

Yet when the sun rose, the Mexican army was gone. It had

retreated so quickly that surviving soldiers abandoned their personal baggage. The garbage of war littered the chaparral. Corpses dotted the grassy plain, and the air reeked of rotting flesh. Numerous Mexicans had been cut in two by the canister and grape. Bodies without heads, legs, and arms lay in the Texas dust. The Americans found one dead Mexican cavalry officer with a daguerreotype image of his sister tucked in one pocket, and another soldier with letters waiting to be mailed home tucked into the bill of his cap. When translated, the letters told of a poor army where the men were always hungry, surviving on a small daily ration of salted meat.

Wounded Mexican and American soldiers were taken to a field hospital. They were treated side by side. Taylor chose to bury the dead before chasing the enemy, and Grant spent the morning supervising a burial party. "It was a terrible sight to go over the ground the next day and see the amount of life that had been destroyed. The ground was literally strewed with the bodies of dead men and horses. The loss of the enemy is variously estimated from 300 to 500. Our loss was comparatively small," he wrote. "About twelve or fifteen of our men were killed and probably fifty wounded." The difference in the battle had been Taylor's deliberate use of artillery. Having wasted much of their firepower on their initial, premature assaults, the Mexicans fired just 750 rounds during the long afternoon, while the Americans launched almost 3,000 projectiles into the enemy ranks.

Yet there was little time for self-congratulation. Fort Texas was still under siege, and the Mexican army, wherever they were, still held the road. Just before noon, Taylor ordered his men to march forward once again. This time he intended not only to relieve the fort but to push the Mexican army back across the Rio Grande—and perhaps to follow them if conditions were right.

EIGHT

Resaca de la Palma

MAY 9, 1846

War," Sam Grant wrote of his first taste of combat, "seems much less horrible to the persons engaged in it than to those who read of the battles."

Lieutenant George Gordon Meade understood that sentiment very well. Palo Alto was his first taste of battle, too. Meade had found it nothing short of exhilarating. "I was in the action during the whole time, at the side of General Taylor, and communicating his orders, and I assure you that I have had my '*baptême de feu.*'"

At thirty-one, Meade was the oldest second lieutenant in Taylor's army. Other officers might have been discouraged lagging so far behind their peers, but not Meade, a man who had already lived an extraordinary life. He had an open face, kind blue eyes hidden behind spectacles, and a long, brown beard. Meade was married to the former Margaretta Sergeant, the daughter of John Sergeant, who had been Henry Clay's running mate in the 1832 presidential election. They had wed on Meade's twenty-fifth birthday and now had two young sons and a six-month-old daughter, all of whom he pined for during the long Texas days and nights. Saying good-bye on the day he departed for the war had been a "terrible agony" for the reserved cartographer. "No one can tell how my heart was rent at parting with you," he wrote Margaretta three days later.

Meade was, despite his slow progress up the career ladder, an elite individual in myriad ways. For starters, he was a member of that select band of officers known as the Corps of Topographical Engineers. In all of the U.S. Army, just forty-four men were so designated. They were a unit without a past, so to speak, for the "topogs" had never been employed in an actual war; Mexico would be the first.

Members of the Topographical Corps possessed a singular form of expertise. On the one hand, they were primarily engineers. But unlike members of the more traditional and much larger Corps of Engineers, who specialized in bridge and fort

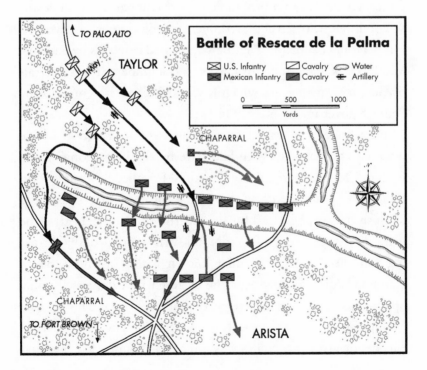

Battle of Resaca de la Palma

construction, the topographer's job was to map the land, surveying natural and man-made features for military purposes and building roads, lighthouses, and canals when needed (the Mexican army's lone engineering corps, the Zapadore, performed both engineering specialties). Very often, topographical engineers worked alone, riding out into the countryside to gaze upon the land. In this way, they behaved very much like explorers, appraising the unknown and returning with not just a perfect new map but also detailed information about local plants and animals, the current and depth of rivers, and the sort of rock formations that studded and scarred the landscape. A good topographical engineer was equally at home holding forth with generals, scientists, and civil engineers, for the information he discovered in the course of his duties was precious to them all.

Meade was born on New Year's Eve, 1815, in Cádiz, the booming Spanish port from which Columbus once sailed. His father, Richard, ran a profitable export company. Business was so good that he often accepted fine paintings in lieu of payment. His personal collection eventually included canvases by Rubens, Van Dyck, Titian, and Goya, as well as a Gilbert Stuart portrait of George Washington, which Richard Meade presented to the Spanish government as a gift in 1818.

Debt collection was constantly an issue in a nation whose national treasury had been laid bare by the Napoleonic Wars. Richard Meade had allowed Spain's Loyalist government to use his ships and wealth in their cause, but when he pressed the Spanish treasurer general for the return of those assets after the war, the government of Ferdinand VII responded by throwing him into a waterfront gulag known as the Castillo de Santa Catalina. For two long years he suffered in a dank cell while Spain ignored diplomatic overtures that might secure his release. Young George's mother—Dona Margarita Coates Butler de Meade, or just Margaret—was forced to abandon her husband in order for the family to stay afloat financially. She took the children to America to be with relatives who lived there, leaving behind their handsome whitewashed home, with its floors of Italian marble and its walls lined with old masters.

Richard Meade might have spent the rest of his life in the Castillo de Santa Catalina, but fate intervened on March 15, 1818, when Andrew Jackson celebrated his fifty-first birthday by marching his volunteer army into Spanish-held Florida to make war on the local Indians. The rationale—that the United States had to invade in order to ensure its own security—was a feeble excuse for the American government to flex its muscles against a down-on-its-luck world power. Growing American furor over Richard Meade's imprisonment counterbalanced the Spanish outrage over Florida. On April 4, 1818, the U.S. Senate, in the strongest terms possible, demanded that Meade be released unharmed or "whatever personal injury may be done him should be retaliated against by the employment, if necessary, of the whole force of this nation." No less than Henry Clay and John Quincy Adams took up the cause. "The imprisonment of Richard W. Meade is an act of cruel and unjustifiable oppression," Clay declared. He added that it was the duty of the American government "to afford Mr. Meade its aid and protection, and that this House will support and maintain such as the President may hereafter adopt."

In the end, the Spaniards sold Florida to the United States for five million dollars and released Richard Meade in June 1818. (Spain refused to ratify the Florida treaty until language erasing Meade's financial claims against the Spanish government were included in the deal.) The conflict over, Meade's sympathizers vanished. He sailed home to America, his business in ruins, the U.S. government having also rejected his claims.

Seven years later, Richard Meade died at the age of just fifty. The family, while not destitute, was now far from wealthy. In a cost-cutting move, fifteen-year-old George, the ninth of eleven Meade children, was sent off to West Point to gain a free education. Appropriately, it was President Andrew Jackson who signed the boy's appointment.

Margaret Meade was anguished about sending her boy away, a feeling she would not share with him until fifteen years later, when it looked as if he would soon see battle. "Although in my ignorance I was cruel enough to send you to West Point," she wrote George on the eve of the Mexican War, "it was the moral standing of the institution, and the education you could not escape if you remained there, also the intention of your lamented father, who said your mathematical head fitted you for it, that led me to commit the act."

Like Grant and Longstreet, Meade hadn't been a model cadet, placing halfway down his class in chemistry, artillery, conduct, infantry tactics, and final standing. He was assigned to the artillery after graduating in 1835, but—never having learned to enjoy military life—Meade resigned his commission one year later. He took a surveying job with a southern railroad, but after meeting Margaretta in 1840, Meade rethought his earlier decision. He had been raised to prize a high social standing. A military commission, despite the army's abysmal pay scale, afforded him a status that he lacked as a railroad survey engineer. In 1842 he reapplied to the army and was assigned to the Topographical Corps—which was why, eleven years after graduating from West Point, Meade was such an aged second lieutenant.

Meade had suffered greatly after arriving at Corpus Christi in September 1845, taking to bed with fever and jaundice brought on while making maps in the torrential winter rain. Yet he had refused an opportunity to return home, because the war was his chance to finally receive promotion, and going home would mean that others would advance instead of him. But as the weeks and months progressed, Meade's reasons for wanting to be at the front changed. He found himself swept up in the emotions of war and began to care deeply for the men around him. He mourned the death of Colonel Trueman Cross, the quartermaster ambushed by Mexican militia, and grew uncharacteristically furious at reports that Mexican general Ampudia had been seen wearing Cross's gold watch. "This dastardly act," he wrote, seething, in a letter home, "has inspired us all with a burning desire to avenge the Colonel's murder." Personal advancement became a secondary concern.

Thus, when he heard the first cannonballs dropping on Fort Texas, Meade was thrilled that the war had begun. During the battle at Palo Alto, he and his fellow topographical engineers set aside their usual duties and found themselves in the thick of the action. Lieutenant Thomas Woods worked with an artillery battery, using his knowledge of the terrain to help sight the eighteen-pounders; Lieutenant Jacob Blake acted as a forward scout, boldly riding his horse to within fifty yards of the Mexican lines before the battle began, making careful mental notes about the size and location of infantry units, and the caliber and position of their artillery, in effect giving Taylor a visual map of the enemy's strength and tactics; and as a battlefield messenger for Taylor, Meade had been a crucial communications link between Taylor and his subordinates.

The following morning, that glory was diminished when Blake was wounded in a freak accident. As he dismounted from his horse and unbuckled his gun belt to sit down to rest, one of his pistols dropped to the ground and discharged a round. The ball struck Blake in the abdomen. "That poor Blake," Meade wrote to Margaretta, "after having gallantly borne himself through the conflict yesterday, unfortunately shot himself accidentally today, just as we marched, and it is feared the wound is mortal." It was. Blake passed away in the afternoon, wishing to the end that he had died from a bullet on the dusty plains of Palo Alto instead.

By the time Blake died, Taylor was already chasing the Mexican army back toward Matamoros, advancing down the slender thoroughfare that sliced across the landscape like a dusty scar. Meade described the terrain to Margaretta in a letter the next day. "From the Palo Alto to the river there is a thicket in this country called chaparral, which is almost impassable when you are off the road, and which consists of thick thorny bushes that will tear your clothes to pieces in trying to get through," he wrote. To make better time, Taylor had ordered the supply train to stay behind with a small complement of infantry and artillery. While strategically savvy, this bold gambit reduced the size of the attacking American force to just seventeen hundred men. The Mexican army had ample reinforcements waiting in Matamoros. Once again they would outnumber the Americans three to one.

Taylor was convinced that the Mexicans had hidden in the chaparral yet again, waiting to spring another trap. In response, on May 9 he sent an advance party out to search for the enemy. These scouts were a handpicked corps of 150, under the command of Captain George McCall and artillery officer Charles Ferguson Smith, who had led the crossing of the Rio Colorado. The two were ideal for the job. The dashing McCall was an expert in close-combat skirmishes, having battled the Seminoles in the swamps of Florida. Smith, whose big, drooping mustache and narrow eyes gave him a ferocious, predatory look, had taught infantry tactics at West Point for four years. If any men could divine the strengths and weaknesses in Arista's lines, it was McCall and Smith.

Patiently and methodically, they worked their way along the road on horseback, searching for the enemy. The land was riven by dry streambeds and small pools of water, delineating long-ago paths of an even greater Rio Grande. The main road from Port Isabel to Matamoros—the Camino de Matamoros—dipped down into these ravines, or *resacas,* on its linear journey inland. The Mexican army—if it was still out there—was hidden in one of those chasms.

By 3:00 P.M., McCall and Smith had found it. The Mexicans had taken up positions inside the Resaca de la Palma, named for the palm trees lining its banks. The ravine was a dozen feet deep and an eighth of a mile wide, and the Mexicans were spread along a mile-wide front. Trees had been chopped down and piled across the road like stacks of cordwood to make the position more impregnable. Arista had selected the site well, the ravine being lined on both sides with thick forest. Unbeknownst to McCall and Smith, Arista had temporarily paused the siege of Fort Texas and ordered the soldiers there to reinforce his ranks. The chaparral prevented Arista from using his cavalry, but it provided his troops with excellent fighting positions. He was depending upon superior numbers and that superb defensive location to win the battle.

McCall ordered his scouts to show themselves just long enough to draw enemy fire, hoping to learn the location of enemy gun positions. They did more than offer the Mexicans a glimpse: Arista's men were so well hidden in the chaparral that the American scouts almost walked directly into their fortifications, resulting in a quick burst of artillery fire that killed five men.

The deadly encounter had revealed a battery of eight cannons positioned alongside the road, their barrels aimed directly toward the approaching Americans. McCall retreated, sending a handful of his men back to inform Taylor of the findings and forming the rest of them into a fighting square. There, in that no-man's-land between the Mexican and American lines, the squad waited for Taylor to bring his army forward.

Taylor's army marched toward the Mexican line. Once again,

it was the Mexicans who would fire first—and this time they were using the proper lethal armament. "A heavy discharge of grape was fired into our advance, showing that the enemy still disputed our march," Meade noted wryly.

As he did the day before, Taylor moved his artillery to the front of the column. The oxen dragged two eighteen-pounders and a pair of twelve-pounders forward. And while the chaparral that hid the Mexicans also provided perfect cover for the Americans, allowing the guns to be drawn perilously close to the Mexican lines, it was also so tall and thick that the artillerymen couldn't accurately aim. It would be up to the infantry to find gaps in the chaparral and overrun the Mexican positions.

This suited Meade just fine. His sadness about being separated from his wife and children had been set aside. He was enjoying the war very much. Meade was proud that Taylor was using him as a messenger, and he took an almost glib satisfaction in noting that "an officer of the General's staff had his horse shot under him, not two yards from me, and some five horses and men were killed at various times right close to me."

It was as if Meade had committed an act of bravery just by being in the vicinity of someone else's death.

NINE

Brown Bess

MAY 9, 1846

The Mexican soldiers hadn't eaten in more than twenty-four hours and were losing faith in their officer corps. Despite the decline in morale, they prepared to stand fast against the American onslaught.

But the officer corps wasn't the only test of their faith. A Mexican soldier crouched in the folds of Resaca de la Palma needed to look only to the weapon in his hands to cast further doubt on the Mexicans' ability to defeat the Americans. The gun was a British-made "Brown Bess" musket, a smoothbore flintlock that had a range of less than a hundred yards. Part of the British army's Land Pattern musket series, first introduced in 1722, the .75-caliber gun weighed ten pounds, had a walnut stock, and could be fitted with a seventeen-inch bayonet—which was important because the gun's accuracy was so minimal that the manufacturers had never bothered to install a gun sight. The Brown Bess (a nickname believed to stem either from slang for England's Elizabeth I or from *braun buss,* German for "brown gun") had long been used throughout the British Empire, and both redcoats and rebels had fired it during America's Revolutionary War. But in 1838 the British began moving toward a percussion-cap rifle and sold thousands of their Brown Besses to Mexico. As Arista's men stood fast and awaited the American onslaught, the majority of them were armed with a century-old relic that possessed such a fearful recoil that most Mexicans fired from the hip so that the gun didn't break their facial bones (which would prove to be a problem inside the *resaca*, where shooting from a prone or kneeling position with the stock nestled against the cheeks was ideal).

They had the advantage when it came to sheer numbers, but their best hope lay in allowing the Americans to draw close. The Mexicans could then let loose a volley and swarm toward the enemy en masse in a bayonet charge—a case of their tactics being restricted by their weapons.

IN MCCALL'S ABSENCE, Grant was thrust into the role of temporary company commanding officer. He reveled in the "honor and responsibility," but found himself simultaneously eager to lead men into battle and fearful of getting them slaughtered. When Taylor gave the order to advance, Grant and his men were on the army's far right flank. What followed was an ungainly, uncertain march into the Mexican position. Though the Mexicans knew that the Americans were on their way, and were poised to open fire the instant they saw a blue uniform, all the Americans could see was a thorny wall of chaparral. Grant led his company "through the thicket wherever a penetrable place could be found, taking advantage of any clear spot that could carry me towards the enemy." "At last I got up pretty close without knowing it," he recalled. "The balls commenced to whistle thick overhead, cutting the limbs of the chaparral right and left. We could not see the enemy, so I ordered my men to lie down—an order which did not have to be forced."

Pinned down, Grant ordered a retreat. He and his men fell

back into the dense brush so that Grant could study the landscape and find a better place to attack. Up and down the American line, other officers were doing the same. Individual military
units were unable to see one another, so junior officers and company commanders improvised a new strategy, advancing bit by
bit, searching for an elusive hole in the chaparral that would
allow them to attack without being mowed down.

As they did so, they realized that they had waded not onto
a battlefield but into a well-laid trap. The Mexican forces were
spread in front of and inside the rugged ravine, a strategic conceit
brought on by their numerical superiority. General Arista knew
that the Americans would be unable to outflank his men, thanks
to the chaparral, and that any breakthrough on his right was
impossible because the ravine wound to the north on that side;
if Taylor attempted an attack there, his army could be trapped
within the gulch, an easy target for artillery and infantry sharpshooters. As Arista had planned it, the Americans had no choice
but to attack head-on, into the maw of a fortified, well-manned
defensive position. All through the night and morning, his artillery had dug in. The fresh replacements who had forded the Rio
Grande from Matamoros were rested and fed, with plenty of
ammunition at the ready and the luxury of spending hours concealing themselves among the trees and earthen crags, digging
in while they awaited the Americans. The Mexican army was
fighting on Texas soil, but they planned to defend it as if it were
still their own. Arista's army was buoyed by the prospect, and
deeply confident of victory.

But Taylor had the rare gift of being able to conceive instant
battlefield stratagems that never occurred to other leaders. He
knew that if he spread his men across the entire length of the
canyon, as Arista had done, his troops would be easily overwhelmed. And though Palo Alto had been a victory, he couldn't
afford to be foolish. The few thousand American men inching

forward through the chaparral were the only soldiers he had. In fact, those troops represented almost the entire U.S. Army. America's prewar force numbered just 6,562 officers and enlisted men. With two-thirds of those men stationed with Taylor in Texas, that left just a few thousand soldiers to guard the entire Canadian border and western frontier. Arista didn't just have more soldiers at his disposal than General Zachary Taylor; the Army of the North outnumbered that of James K. Polk, commander in chief and president of the United States.

But Taylor had a plan: to follow Napoleon's axiom that "fire must be concentrated on one point, and as soon as the breach is made, the equilibrium is broken and the rest is nothing." It was a premise borrowed from Alexander the Great, Hannibal, and Caesar. Taylor would concentrate his forces on a single point at the center of the Mexican line. They would burst through like a fist shattering a thin pane of glass, using their speed and guile to make up for inferior numbers. McCall would lead the way.

The attack would have to be brisk. If the Mexican line held, Arista could reposition his forces, encircling the Americans and using the chaparral as a natural barricade to prevent them from escaping. "The determination today was to go the whole hog and charge at once, without standing off at a shooting distance," an officer noted.

Bayonets were fixed. Brogans were tied. Prayers were murmured. Then the Americans charged, screaming as they ran forward, a bansheelike wail piercing the thick Texas air.

The Mexican artillery fired point-blank into the wall of onrushing American troops. Their cannons were Napoleonic War surplus nine-pounders that had been purchased secondhand from Britain in the 1830s. Arista's gun crews included as many as seven men, each wearing the dark blue coats and trousers and black stovepipe shako hats of Mexican foot artillery. Working at top speed, they could fire a round every three minutes—but more often it was one round every five. When the enemy was a quarter mile away, that was more than enough. But the enemy wasn't a quarter mile away; Taylor's army was running right at the cannons, without regard to their safety. Mexican canister rounds were still hot out of the barrel as they claimed their first victims. Survivors reported that their clothes caught fire when the fabric was nicked by passing shot. But although some Americans went down, more remained upright and closed in on Arista's increasingly concentrated troops.

Not to be outdone, American cavalry charged ahead of the infantry, their horses dodging their comrades on foot as well as chaparral and cannonballs on the path to the Mexican defenses. This, too, was a Napoleonic tactic: first the cavalry and infantry, then the light artillery, always moving forward.

It worked. Mexico's frontline artillery crews, stunned by the American onslaught and lacking time to reload, were quickly overrun. For the rest of the Mexican army, it was vital that they stand their ground. If they fell back now, there was little to stop Taylor from sweeping in and charging down the road into Matamoros.

The Americans overran the cannons and collided with a wall of Mexican infantry and cavalry. The combat now was mostly hand-to-hand. Both sides were armed with bayonets and sabers, but they just as often swung the wooden butt of a musket as a weapon.

The next two hours saw an explosion of mayhem and carnage, yet Taylor's plan was unfolding just as he'd scripted it. And with the cavalry and infantry holding the center, American light artillery now moved forward to fire canister and grape rounds into the heart of the Mexican ranks. This prevented Arista from sending reinforcements into the thick of the battle.

Another obstacle facing the Mexican troops was Arista himself. He was confident that the American charge was a diversion, so he remained in his tent, writing at his desk, and entrusted the battle to Brigadier General Rómulo Díaz de la Vega. Even when reports filtered back to his campsite, making it clear that the attack was not a ruse, Arista failed to believe them.

Once the center of their line had been obliterated, the Mexican troops panicked. It was now obvious that their right and left flanks were incapable of collapsing onto the Americans, which had been their only chance to overwhelm Taylor's army. Men began to sprint toward the Rio Grande. The distance to the river was three miles. Many didn't make it that far, hacked to death by the blade of an American cavalry saber as they ran for their lives. Numerous Mexicans hid in the chaparral to await the end of the battle, when they would give themselves up as prisoners of war. In all, more than four hundred Mexicans were captured, including General Díaz de la Vega, a gracious man who was dumbfounded by the defeat. "If I had had with me," he marveled, "$100,000 in silver, I would have bet the whole of it that no 10,000 men on earth could drive us from our position."

Arista had eluded capture by fleeing his tent just in time. American troops ransacked its belongings, coming away with a silver dining set and another, far more valuable bit of plunder: a topographical map of the Texas frontier, showing roads, villages, and mule trails. The Americans had been feeling their way through the countryside without any such guide. As a means of anticipating Mexican strategy and deploying troops, the map was priceless to Taylor.

GRANT AND HIS men missed out on the bayonet charge. Rather than join the action, he had held his company back, waiting for conditions to improve. "I at last found a clear space separating two ponds. There seemed to be a few men in front and I charged upon them with my company. There was no resistance, and we captured a Mexican colonel, who had been wounded, and a few men."

Just as Grant was congratulating himself, a group of American soldiers marched toward him from the direction of the Mexican position, and it dawned on Grant that he had not "captured" the wounded colonel and those few men. The line of battle had already moved far forward, and Grant was merely taking custody of men who had been overlooked during the charge.

Grant remained infuriated at his cowardice in holding back his company during the infantry charge. "The ground had been charged over before," he wrote. "This left no doubt in my mind that the battle of Resaca de la Palma would have been won, just as it was, if I had not been there."

Nonetheless, he had fought. His letter to Julia that day was written from the captured Mexican camp on the south side of the Resaca de la Palma. Lacking a writing desk, he set his paper atop the head of a captured Mexican drum.

Longstreet, too, was thinking of home and his beloved Louise—and had been during the battle itself. "A pause was made to dip our cups for water," Longstreet later recalled, "which gave a moment for other thoughts; mine went back to her whom I had left behind. I drew her daguerreotype from my breast-pocket, had a glint of her charming smile, and with quickened spirit mounted the bank."

Meade had done little but observe, yet he was euphoric about the action-packed spectacle he had witnessed. "They gave away in all directions, and there was a total rout of the Grand Mexican Army that was going to eat us up. We captured seven pieces of artillery, all their pack mules, several hundred in number, all their ammunition, several hundred stands of arms, and all their baggage. Took one general, two colonels, several captains and subalterns, and some hundred and fifty men, prisoners." Then he added, as if aware that his gloating was inappropriate: "It is supposed to take all day today and tomorrow to bring in their dead and wounded off the field, as the ground is said to be literally strewn."

Indeed, the Mexicans had suffered 256 killed and 182 missing—losses that dwarfed the Americans' 127 casualties. Corpses—horses, mules, and men—carpeted the road. Flies coated the bodies in thick black swarms, and the hot afternoon air reeked of death. The bulk of the Mexican fatalities was not due to American bullets but to the tricky currents of the Rio Grande. Unable to swim, yet so overcome with fear that they leaped into the river anyway, scores of soldiers drowned; their bodies would litter the muddy banks for miles and miles in the days to come, many of them naked, their uniforms having been swept away by the river as submerged rocks and branches held them underwater. Rotting in the sun, bloated beyond recognition, these men became carrion for coyotes, crows, and the turtles that made their home in the red river clay.

WITH THE BATTLE won, the American soldiers turned their thoughts back to Fort Texas. The first order of business was to make sure it was still in American hands. Without it, they were without a home, naked against a surprise Mexican attack.

Closer and closer they marched, until finally, looking into the distance, they could see the U.S. flag flying over the embattled structure—shot full of holes by Mexican snipers, barely fluttering in the languid heat after six days of bombardment, but atop the flagpole nonetheless. The fort had held.

The men inside that fort were more than just soldiers of the Seventh Infantry; they were friends and comrades who had shared the beach at Corpus Christi, the Rio Colorado crossing, and all those long hours plunging shovels into the ground and reshaping the earth into an ingeniously designed defensive fortress. The tattered flag that marked their survival was a deeply welcome sight.

Weary from battle, Taylor's army marched into Fort Texas.

TEN

Volunteers

MAY 11, 1846

Jefferson Davis was chronically restless. As the freshman congressman from Mississippi, he had such great legislatorial potential that former U.S. president John Quincy Adams had predicted "he will make his mark, mind me," after Davis gave an eloquent floor speech on the annexation of Oregon early in his term. Adams's praise was the sort of career-making benediction that would inspire most young politicians to pursue their calling with greater diligence. But by May 1846, after Davis had spent just six months in office, Congress was beginning to bore the thirty-seven-year-old. For inspiration, he was setting his sights on a new ambition: war.

Not only was Davis prepared to vote in favor of a resolution that would send American troops into Mexico (and perhaps into Oregon to fight the British after the Mexicans had been dealt with), but Davis personally lusted to lead them into battle. Given his status and West Point education, the job was almost his for the taking. There was, however, a formidable obstacle between Davis and his first taste of combat: a rather determined woman by the name of Varina Davis—his young and sharp-tongued wife.

Long before entering Congress, and even before becoming a successful plantation owner, Davis had been an officer in the U.S. Army. The work had been challenging and the hardships many, but he had done well during his six years in uniform. He had resigned his commission in haste, in order to marry and settle down with the love of his life. In the eleven years of struggle and mourning since, he had come to regret that decision. Now, as a formal request from President James K. Polk for fifty thousand troops, ten million dollars in military appropriations, and a formal declaration of war with Mexico reached Congress, Davis saw his chance. He had long backed Polk's pro-southern, pro-expansion, pro-slavery policies. When the issue was put to a vote, Davis was one of the 174 congressmen voting in favor. Only 14 voted against it (most notably the Monroe Doctrine author John Quincy Adams), while 20 members of Congress abstained.

Those numbers were misleading. The nation and the Congress were bitterly divided on the war. Leading members of Polk's Democratic Party, such as John C. Calhoun, Thomas Hart Benton, and even Secretary of War William L. Marcy, counseled the president against the conflict. They argued that America was overextended militarily. Should Britain choose to commence hostilities in Oregon, the United States would be forced to wage war on two fronts—a disastrous policy, given the puny size of its army and the logistical impossibility of supplying forces separated by thousands of miles and a rugged, roadless continent.

But Polk—whom Varina Davis dismissed as "an insignificant looking little man"—saw the war as a means of unifying the country behind his policies. Polk cleverly bundled his war declaration with an appropriation request to provide funds for Taylor's troops, already engaging the Mexican forces in Texas. At a time when Americans were cheering the victories of Taylor's army, even as many of those same citizens were opposed to further hostilities, Polk's careful wording transformed the measure into a referendum on patriotism. Thus, even antiwar northern Whigs ended up voting in favor of a conflict they did not want.

No matter where they stood, the Washington politicians risked little but their careers with a yes or no vote. Davis was the rare legislator willing to back up his stance by marching off to the front lines. His years at West Point had been the making of him, not just as a man but also as an American. "Those who have received their education at West Point, taken as a body, are more free from purely sectional prejudices, and more national in their feelings than the same number of persons to be found elsewhere in the country," he later wrote. The irony in this statement would become apparent only years later.

Davis's straight-backed posture was that of a man who had once been an officer of some distinction, but the truth was that his military service was bereft of glory. He was a lively man whose ego sometimes got the best of him, a character trait that resulted in his (unsuccessful) court-martial for insubordination in 1835 and hastened the end of his army career. For a man accustomed to success in all aspects of life, his lack of military commendation rankled. He ached to march into battle and make a name for himself. If nothing else, he would also advance his political fortunes, for the people of Mississippi were even more gung ho about the war than he was.

Varina adamantly opposed the idea of her husband's running off to play soldier. After all, he was finally getting established in Congress after the middling success of his army days and the equally mediocre years he had spent as a plantation owner, which were lived largely in the shadow of his older and more successful brother Joseph. Politics, not war, seemed to be Davis's calling. Indeed, with his strong jaw, piercing eyes, and powerful oratorical style, he seemed to have been born for the profession. Making the matter even more complicated was the fact that Varina, a sensuous beauty who had just celebrated her twentieth birthday, adored Washington, D.C. Though the nation's capital was still a city in name only, with few monuments or majestic buildings to mark it as much more than a series of connected villages (the Capitol still lacked its rotunda, the Mall was partially swampland, and fund-raising efforts for a towering obelisk monument that would honor George Washington had churned sluggishly along for decades, with no end in sight), she was much taken with its social scene. To see her husband at the center of it all, meeting occasionally with the president and helping to plan a grand new museum with money bequeathed by the Englishman James Smithson, was to watch history being made. To leave it all and return to their bottomland plantation as Davis galloped off to war, perhaps never to return, made little sense to Varina.

Yet if ever there was a war that Jefferson Davis had been born to fight, the conflict in Mexico was it. After all, Davis was the namesake of America's third president, the man who had pushed to expand the country. As an adolescent, Davis had spent a week at the home of Andrew Jackson, another strong advocate of American expansion. And after graduating from West Point in 1828, Davis had served nearly his entire six-year military career on the frontier, extending America's borders westward. He had built forts in the Wisconsin wilderness, had fought briefly in the Black Hawk War of 1832, and had been selected to become one of America's first cavalry officers when the First Dragoons were formed the following year, with the intention that they would protect settlers from Indian attack.

Davis was not insensitive to his wife's concerns — at least to those more profound than the mere loss of a social life. Varina, after all, was not the first woman who had disrupted Davis's military ambition.

Davis met Sarah Knox Taylor, the daughter of none other than General Zachary Taylor, shortly after completing his checkered career at West Point, where he was almost expelled three times for alcohol-related incidents and ultimately graduated with a poor class standing. After learning basic infantry skills at the Jefferson Barracks, he was posted to the wilds of what would later be known as Wisconsin, Illinois, Minnesota, and Iowa. Taylor was Davis's commanding officer at Fort Crawford, in the heart of the Wisconsin Territory, for a year, beginning in the spring of 1832. It was there that Davis met the then colonel's eighteen-year-old daughter. Slender and witty, Knox, as she was known, was a pretty, petite woman with hazel eyes and long brown hair. She was known to be a splendid dancer. Davis fell for her gradually, but soon they were in love. When he asked Taylor for his daughter's hand, however, the gruff senior officer refused. Taylor had often lamented the vagaries of military life, with its hard travel, dangerous duty, and months and years of enforced separation. Appalled by the fact that he barely knew his children, Taylor was firmly opposed to Knox's marrying an officer. A schism developed between the two men. Taylor and Davis maintained their professional relationship, but the smitten young lieutenant was forbidden to court the colonel's daughter.

The young lovers saw each other on the sly for the next three years. The charade might have gone on much longer had Davis not been brought before the court-martial for "conduct subversive of a good order and military discipline" on February 12, 1835. The trial was held at Fort Gibson, an outpost on the Arkansas River. Davis's crime was that he had refused to rise for reveille on a cold and rainy Christmas Eve, 1834, even though he was wide awake and already dressed in full uniform. His commanding officer then placed him under arrest because he found Davis to be contemptuous and disrespectful when confronted about his actions.

Davis acted as his own defense attorney and won. Shortly afterward he requested leave, not intending to return. On June

17, 1835, Davis married Knox at her aunt's home in Louisville. He wore a waistcoat and a stovepipe hat; she wore a dark dress and bonnet. Neither of her parents attended. That evening, the newlyweds boarded a paddle wheeler bound for Vicksburg.

On June 30, 1835, Davis formally resigned his commission. He and his new bride returned to the Mississippi Delta, the region in which he had grown up. His older brother Joseph, a prominent local landowner, lent Davis the money and the land to plant crops on property right next to his own plantation, Hurricane. The acreage was fertile bottomland, located on a curve in the Mississippi known, appropriately, as Davis Bend. The land still needed to be cleared of briars and trees, and Jefferson and Knox would have to build a home, but it was a fine start to a marriage delayed too long by the exigencies of the service. Their future seemed limitless.

Three months later, Knox was dead.

The summer heat and humidity of the Mississippi Delta was a haven for mosquitoes and tropical diseases. Davis and Knox were both struck down by malaria shortly after their arrival and took straight to bed. One day, in a state of delirium, Davis awoke to hear Knox in her room, singing a popular song known as "Fairy Bells." He rose from bed and staggered to her. She died that day, with her heartbroken young husband at her bedside. Sarah Knox Taylor Davis was just twenty-one.

Davis was soon drowning in grief. He threw himself into clearing land for planting and read great works of philosophy. As a young man he had been anything but sober, a fun-loving partygoer with a rounded face and warm, bright eyes, a passion for life, and a habit of scoffing at authority. But after Knox's death he slowly took on a severe look. He never totally gave up drinking or smoking—indeed, Davis almost died on a trip to Washington, D.C., in 1838, after falling face-first into a creek and striking his head on a rock during a drunken late night stroll—but in time his face assumed a gaunt, haunted appearance that would make him look malarial even when he was quite well.

In the midst of his loss, Davis thought he might find solace in the rigors of military life. The purpose of that 1838 visit to Washington was to apply for a new commission. There was talk that Congress might fund three new regiments, and he hoped to reenter the military as a member of one of them. However, just one new regiment was added to the army, and Davis did not receive an appointment. He returned home to Brierfield, his plantation, to continue life as a farmer. Soon after, Davis focused his attention on politics. His political inspiration was Thomas Jefferson, as his father's had been. He strongly believed in states' rights and in reducing the size of the federal government, just as Jefferson had. As a slave owner and as a man who had openly disdained his Yankee counterparts during his time at West Point ("you cannot know how pitiful they generally are," he had written to Joseph), Davis was troubled by the growing antislavery movement in the northern states. He became active in Mississippi politics, learning firsthand the exhaustion of campaigning and the elation of a powerfully delivered stump speech. He ran for Congress in 1843 and lost handily. Two years later, having become deeply entrenched within the state Democratic Party's hierarchy, he was elected easily. In between the initial loss and the subsequent victory, he met and married Varina Howell, younger than Davis by two decades. His tone in their letters was occasionally paternal, but on the whole, theirs was a loving and equitable marriage. Varina was jealous of the great demands that politics put on her "Jeffy" but was nevertheless thrilled with the rewards. Having a husband in the U.S. Congress was something she had never anticipated but grew to enjoy a great deal.

War with Mexico had the potential to change all that.

Davis had learned the importance of paying attention to his

constituents. So when the Mississippi newspapers ran headlines screaming "To Arms To Arms" and some seventeen thousand men raced to Vicksburg to volunteer for military duty in Taylor's army, Davis paid attention. Even before that, his desire to see battle had been getting the best of him. In a letter written on May 12, a day before Congress took a formal vote on the war, Davis confided to a friend that if the people of Mississippi asked him to go to war, he would do so. "If they wish it, I will join them as soon as possible, wherever they may be."

If there were any doubts in Davis's mind about the positive effects it might have on his career, a May 21 rally in New York City confirmed the war's phenomenal popularity: fifty thousand people gathered in front of city hall to show their support for the conflict in Mexico. In Philadelphia, the *North American* wrote, "Upon the duties which the present crisis invoked, our country has but one heart."

Davis and Varina fought bitterly when she learned of his intentions. She pleaded with him not to go, and Davis ultimately bent to her will. Concerned for his wife's "weaknesses which spring from a sensitive and generous temper," Davis promised Varina that he would not accept a commission. But back home in Mississippi, volunteer regiments were being formed. Two of those came from Warren County, in which Vicksburg and Davis Bend were both nestled. There was a growing public outcry that Davis command a Mississippi regiment. Davis kept it a secret from Varina, but in his heart he had already broken his promise: he had every intention of accepting a command, if offered, to lead the men of Mississippi into battle. He would go to Mexico.

ELEVEN

Growing Up

May 24, 1846

S am Grant was growing a beard. It had taken a while to fill in, but by late May his facial hair was finally beginning to flourish. He was surprised at its flaming red color but nevertheless quite sure that the beard had a manly effect on his appearance. "My Dear Julia," he wrote, "do you ever see me anymore in your dreams? How much I wish you could see me in reality! I am certain that you would not know me. I am as badly sunburnt as it is possible to be, and I have allowed my beard to grow three inches long." Grant was no longer the naive young lieutenant who had sailed from Saint Louis two years earlier. He had changed. He was becoming a battle-hardened soldier.

The engagements at Palo Alto and Resaca de la Palma were career and emotional turning points for Grant and the others who had fought in them. But that would only be clear years later; now they were just battles that had needed to be won so that the young men could return home. It was the same for those who had been part of the triumph at Fort Texas.

Remarkably, only two Americans had died there. The first was the hapless Sergeant Weigart. The second was Major Jacob

Brown, who had succumbed to his horrific wound mere hours before the siege came to an end. The major had suffered terribly in his final days. "It was so hot he could scarcely breathe. Of course, his fevers raged," wrote Dana. "He is a very serious loss to our regiment, one which we will not be able to replace. He was a perfect bulldog for the fight."

Soon after, the earthworks along the Rio Grande were finally given an official name: Fort Brown.

An exclamation point had been added on May 18: Taylor's army crossed the Rio Grande by flatboat and occupied Matamoros without a shot being fired. It was Lieutenant George Gordon Meade who canvassed the riverbanks for the perfect crossing site.

Matamoros was flea-bitten and dusty, occupied by whores, farmers, peasants, and those Mexican officers and soldiers who had chosen to quit the war rather than accompany their army inland to the city of Monterrey,* where General Arista was planning to make another stand. Soldiers who had been wounded at Palo Alto and Resaca de la Palma had risen from hospital beds to join the retreat, terrified that the Americans would torture or simply kill them. That march had turned into an ordeal all its own, with many of Arista's men committing suicide rather than die from the thirst and starvation that eventually defined the desperate journey.

They would have been far better off remaining in Matamoros. Taylor wanted no cruel behavior directed at the Mexicans, be they prisoners of war or private citizens. His aim was to build trust and cooperation. "It was the policy of the commanding general to allow no pillaging, no taking of private property for public or individual use without satisfactory compensation, so that a better market was afforded than the people had ever known."

The Americans searched the town's small adobe homes and

---

*The American spelling of Monterrey used one *r* at the time of the Mexican invasion. This was subsequently changed to the modern spelling.

community buildings for any supply depots the Mexican army might have left behind. They were shocked by the vast quantities of abandoned munitions: grenades, gunpowder, twenty-five hundred pounds of cannon powder, and more than thirty thousand musket cartridges. The Mexicans had spiked most of their cannons (destroying the weapon's tube by firing the gun while it was packed with sand or rocks or driving a spike or file into the gun's vent) and pushed them into the river, but a few pieces of heavy artillery were discovered intact, including one cannon hidden in a church belfry.

There was more: barrels of clothing, desks, muskets, bayonets, and vast quantities of playing cards. Tobacco was an illegal commodity in Mexico and was carefully packed in barrels to be sold on the black market. More than two hundred thousand cigars were discovered, and Taylor ordered them distributed to his army.

The locals eagerly sold the Americans fresh vegetables, eggs, sugar, and milk from their personal stores. After months of army rations, it was a welcome change of fare for Taylor's men. Such niceties gave Matamoros a pleasant air, but Grant knew that the situation was about to take a drastic turn. "Up to this time," he later explained, "Taylor had none but regular troops in his command." But now that Mexico had been invaded, volunteer regiments were forming all over America, eager to join in the fight. These citizen soldiers had little, if any, military training. Nobody knew how they would fit in with the officers and soldiers of the regular army. Yet Taylor needed these reinforcements if he was going to pursue Arista deep into Mexico.

The plan approved by Congress on May 13 gave each state a recruiting quota. The new soldiers would be transported by river or sea to New Orleans and then either overland or by sea to the mouth of the Rio Grande. The volunteers had the option of enlisting for the entire war or for twelve months. They would provide their own uniforms and horses and would receive the same pay as regular soldiers. The officers would be chosen by an election among the men and would be equal in authority and pay to their regular army counterparts. Only Polk could appoint generals and staff officers, and those were subject to Senate approval.

Needless to say, the officers and soldiers of the regular army were not happy about this turn of events. Many had spent their entire adult lives in the army, seeing little promotion while enduring great hardship and familial separation. It galled them that they would be forced to salute a group of well-connected, undisciplined civilians who didn't know rank and file from a fighting square and who had never heard a shot fired in anger.

Those first volunteer units began arriving on May 24. A regiment from New Orleans marched inland from Port Isabel, some six hundred men in all. They were a sorry lot, ill disciplined and "used up" in the estimation of one American officer.

Grant took the newcomers' presence in stride. As always, his thoughts were on ending the war as soon as possible. If that meant bringing in volunteer regiments, no matter how ragged they might be, he was willing to endure their presence. He hadn't been in the army long enough to be passed over for rank, and he had few plans to remain in the service after the war was over. "My dearest Julia," he wrote, "I feel as if I shall never be contented until I can see you again, my Dear Julia, and I hope to never leave you again for a long time."

Bearded, sunburned, and now battle-hardened as he might be, one thing had not changed about Sam Grant: he was hopelessly under Julia's spell. "P.S. The two flowers you sent me come safe, but when I opened your letter the wind blew them away and I could not find them. Before I seal this I will pick a wildflower off the bank of the Rio Grande and send you."

FOUR DAYS LATER, it was Meade who wrote home. "I really consider spending a day in my tent, uninjured, equivalent to passing through a well-contested action," he told Margaretta. Meade was not trying to be glib. The volunteer regiments had only been in camp a few days, and already their sense of entitlement and lack of discipline were causing major problems. Many came from slave states. These "soldiers" refused to do chores such as chopping firewood or hauling water, which they considered slave labor. After the euphoria of arriving at the war, most of the volunteers had settled into a routine of daily drunkenness. A standing order against firing guns in camp was totally ignored. Most of the volunteers were still back across the river at Fort Brown, but they gathered regularly on the north bank of the Rio Grande to fire their muskets at Matamoros. Not only were the lives of innocent civilians at risk, but the tents of regular army officers were pitched in the town.

The thought of remaining in his shelter and risking having a volunteer's bullet strike him annoyed Meade no end. He spent his days riding his horse through the Mexican countryside, inspecting roads and abandoned fortifications. With Blake dead, he was the lone topographical officer in camp. Even with the captured map, the Americans knew little about the Mexican landscape, so it was Meade's duty to ride out alone to make charts and observations about what Taylor could expect to find when he marched toward Monterrey. The stark landscape appealed to Meade, and he was surprised to find himself taken with the local culture. He thought the women were demure and graceful and began teaching himself a few words of Spanish so that he might talk with them.

Meade was a quietly courageous sort who gave little thought to the bandits that were said to roam the area or to any vestiges of Arista's army that might be hiding out. The long rides along the Rio Grande were a tonic, just as the excitement of battle was. He was no longer consumed by thoughts of going home.

As soon as he returned to Matamoros, Meade's mood darkened. Other officers enjoyed the place, but to Meade it was a depressing town where most of the houses were made of logs and the grand cathedral near the central plaza was an unfinished eyesore. He turned up his nose at the women, whom he considered "old hags, worse looking than Indians."

But Meade saved his most pointed criticisms for the volunteers. General Taylor had absolutely no control over their behavior, and their own officers seemed uninterested in imposing discipline. The citizen soldiers traveled back and forth across the Rio Grande at will to frequent the saloons and gambling halls that were springing up to service the American army. They stole and butchered local cattle and sometimes even shot Mexican citizens just for sport. The majority of volunteers were Protestants with a strong bias against people of other religions and cultures (more than one resident of Matamoros was murdered just for being a brown-skinned papist), which made for a natural clash with the Irish Catholic immigrants that composed a large chunk of the regular army's enlisted ranks.

Most infuriating of all to soldiers like Meade, the American people viewed the volunteers as being better, more patriotic soldiers than the regular army. The men of West Point, the public thought, were a second-class bunch who served for money — mercenaries. The volunteers, on the other hand, were brave men willing to risk their lives out of love for their country.

"They expect the regulars to play waiters for them," wrote a disgusted Meade. The very presence of the volunteers was an affront to the sacrifices he'd endured for his country since the very day he entered West Point. "No, soldiering is not play, and those who undertake it must make up their minds to hard times and hard knocks."

But there was little he could do about them other than complain. Taylor would need much of the summer to mount his assault on Monterrey. The occupying force — regular and volunteer alike — were destined to spend a long, hot season in Matamoros, waiting for the order to move out. And when they did so, much to Meade's disgust, they would do it together.

II

TAYLOR'S WAR

The Mexican war was a political war, and the administration conducting it desired to make party capital out of it. General Scott was at the head of the army, and, being a soldier of acknowledged professional capacity, his claim to the command of the forces in the field was almost indisputable, and that does not seem to have been denied by President Polk, or Marcy, his Secretary of War. Scott was a Whig and the administration was democratic. General Scott was also known to have political aspirations, and nothing so popularizes a candidate for high civil positions as military victories. It would not do, therefore, to give him command of the "army of conquest." The plans submitted by Scott for a campaign in Mexico were disapproved by the administration, and he replied, in a tone possibly a little disrespectful, to the effect that, if a soldier's plans were not to be supported by the administration, success could not be expected. This was the 27th of May, 1846. Four days later, General Scott was notified that he need not go to Mexico. General [Edmund P.] Gaines was next in rank, but he was too old and feeble to take the field. Colonel Zachary Taylor—a brigadier-general by brevet—was therefore left in command.

—ULYSSES S. GRANT, *Memoirs*

TWELVE

Camargo

JUNE 14, 1846

The spring rains were replaced by a summer heat so fierce that one officer described the beating sun as having "force enough to bake one's brains, however thick the skull may be." Matamoros and Fort Brown were transformed into full-fledged frontier depots. Taylor prepared to move his headquarters upriver to the town of Camargo, which would be used as a base for the assault on Monterrey — or wherever the Mexicans would make their next stand. Arista had moved inland, and so would the Americans.

Camargo was an ideal jumping-off point. It was closer to the action. Men and supplies could quickly be ferried there from Port Isabel and Matamoros by steamboat.

From Camargo, Taylor's army would travel overland, on foot and horseback, deep into Mexico. His chief quartermaster was in the process of buying two thousand pack animals to supplement the mules, horses, and oxen already ferrying supplies. Steamships had begun arriving in Matamoros on a regular basis, much to the delight of the local residents. The boats were brought from New Orleans and were specially selected for their shallow draft (which made their six-hundred-mile journey through rough ocean to the Rio Grande a nautical marvel). Their presence made transportation of supplies much easier. The normal wagon caravan making the regular journey to Port Isabel for supplies numbered 240 wagons and stretched across the Texas prairie in a single-file line three miles long. A steamboat carried almost as much and did so at much greater speed.

Both were in short supply. The wagons were more problematic. Wagons were not mass-produced in a central factory or production plant; they were built one by one, by craftsmen specializing in wagon construction. Every village and town throughout America had such individuals. The trick was finding them, getting new wagons assembled, and shipping them to Matamoros. Even with steamships hauling many of the supplies, Dana estimated it would require some fifteen hundred wagons to transport Taylor's munitions and stores from Matamoros to Camargo. However, just seven hundred were on order. Until Taylor had these wagons—or found some other means of hauling his army's provisions deep into Mexico for the next stage of the war—the Americans were forced to spend day after infernal day waiting.

And waiting. And waiting. With every passing hour the Mexican army disappeared farther into the interior, digging themselves in and fortifying their position for the war's next great battle.

An adage of war states that time always favors a defensive force. This all but ensured that the next clash would not be so haphazard as Palo Alto or as lopsided as Resaca de la Palma. The Mexicans would reinforce and resupply.

Taylor had no choice but to wait.

Most days were filled with trivia and tedium. For Napoleon Dana, the hours were spent fretting over the money he owed a fellow soldier, the large sum he owed Weigart's family (before his demise, the dead sergeant had requested that Dana hold his wages for safekeeping and act as his executor if he died, but

Dana had foolishly spent the money), trying to buy a gold cross from a local senorita in the hopes of sending it home to Sue as a gift (the young woman demurred, saying that she had to ask her mother first), watching the occasional fistfights between the regular army soldiers and the volunteers, and witnessing some of the seedier by-products of occupation. There were "fandangos" going on over in Matamoros each week, American officers and the local women meeting for a night of dancing and strong punch. "I heard there was to be a 'high-flung' fandango last Tuesday night," Dana wrote to his beloved, "something extra above the ordinary things of the kind at which all the beauty and fine dresses and so forth and so forth were to appear. Well, I thought to go over with the rest to take a look. So I went with Captain Ross, Porter and Clitz. I went in, and one look around was enough for me. I remained about two minutes and declared my determination to come home, to which all the party assented, and off we came. There were about forty of our officers in there and about twenty Spanish girls. I inquired particularly if there was not a mistake in the place, but I was told no, that was the high-flung fandango. If this was it, I would like to see a common one for curiosity sake. I believe I have felt fleas on me ever since."

DAY BY DAY, the U.S. Army grew. Volunteers poured off steamships at the mouth of the Rio Grande. They came from all over the country (except antiwar New England), their daily additions to the ranks dashing the regulars' hopes of fighting the war on their own. Torrential rains fell an average of four hours each day, thanks to the onset of hurricane season. Not only was Taylor's expanding army constantly either wet or smelling of mildew, but the rain overwhelmed the camps' meager sanitary systems, allowing human waste to flood into the river.

The volunteers, in particular, lacked a fundamental knowledge of hygiene. They saw nothing wrong with drinking water straight from the Rio Grande. Most were soon enduring the early stages of cholera: watery diarrhea, profuse vomiting, and leg cramps. The scorching Texas sun helped to create a vicious circle of dehydration—thirsty men craved water to sate their thirst, unaware that the very same water was making them sick. In extreme cases, soldiers went into shock. Many died.

For Sam Grant, clinging like a delusional optimist to the ever more irrational hope that the war would end any day, being away from Julia was much more of a problem than the threat of cholera. Regular soldiers didn't know much more about disease prevention than the volunteers—indeed, the practice of boiling drinking water was as unknown as the concept that disease was spread through minute germs and bacteria. Yet certain lifesaving traditions were a part of army life, passed down from soldier to soldier over the generations. Simple and born of intuition, they were a part of every professional warrior's way of doing business. Brackish or muddy water was to be avoided at all costs. Regular soldiers made it a habit to drink a great deal of coffee, which provided their bodies with boiled fluid, even if such protection was usually accompanied by a gritty taste reminiscent of a freshly dug well.

So as the ignorant newcomers clutched their abdomens and squatted over slit trenches in the shrubs along the Rio Grande, a robust Sam Grant fantasized about making love to Julia—a fantasy he was not afraid to share. "I recollect you did volunteer some time ago, or what showed your willingness to do so, you said that you wished we had been united when I was last in Mo and how willing you were to share a tent with me," he said in a roundabout fashion. "Indeed Julia, that letter made me feel very happy."

Grant mailed the letter and eagerly awaited a response. The mail service that soldiers relied on was painfully slow (telegraphs were still in their infancy and were limited mostly to connecting the eastern seaboard's major cities). It took seven days for the letter to reach Port Isabel, and another week after that to travel up the Mississippi to Saint Louis. Grant kept one nervous eye on the calendar as he waited for Julia's reply, and the other on Taylor's army as the great movement inland finally began.

July progressed, with Grant waiting for mail and the inevitable word to move out, praying his long-awaited missive would arrive first. It didn't. On July 25, Grant wrote to Julia once again. Taylor's army was already on the move and he would soon join them. "You must not neglect to write often Dearest, so that whenever a mail does reach this far-out-of-the-way country I can hear from the one single person who occupies my thoughts. This is my last letter from Matamoros, Julia," he wrote. "At present we are bound for Camargo and thence to Monterey, where it is reported that there is several thousand Mexican troops engaged in throwing up fortifications."

THE UNITED STATES had been sharply divided about the potential for this war in the years leading up to the formal declaration. The split had taken place mainly along the North-South—pro-slavery versus abolitionist—line. Even as a wave of jingoistic patriotism swept through the nation and volunteer regiments were quickly being filled with soldiers eager to join the fight, it was no surprise that pockets of antiwar fervor began developing in the North. An editorial in the June 12 edition of the *New York Tribune* was typical of such sentiment: "They may shout and hurrah, and dance around the bonfires that will be lighted, the cannon that will roar in honor of some field of human butchery; but to what end? Is not life miserable enough, comes not death soon enough, without resort to the hideous energy of war? People of the United States! Your rulers are precipitating you into a fathomless abyss of crime and calamity! Why sleep you thoughtless on its verge, as though this was not your business, or murder could be hid from the sight of God by a few flimsy rags called banners? Awake and arrest the work of butchery ere it shall be too late to preserve your souls from the guilt of wholesale slaughter! Hold meetings! Speak out! Act!"

But the antiwar crowd was in the minority. Walt Whitman, the twenty-seven-year-old editor of the *Brooklyn Daily Eagle*, mirrored the national mood as he equated support of the war with being a true American. "There is hardly a more admirable impulse in the human soul than patriotism," wrote Whitman. Displays of national pride had been minimal during the Thirty Years' Peace. Taylor's victories had changed all that. The conflict marked the first time in American history that all its soldiers fought under the Stars and Stripes rather than merely under their own regimental colors. (Army regulations in 1834 had stipulated it as the official flag of the U.S. forces. An 1818 act of Congress had decreed that the flag would have thirteen stripes and one star for each state, with new stars to be added on the Fourth of July following a new state's admission. As the Mexican War got under way, the flag had twenty-seven stars, with a twenty-eighth soon to be added to symbolize Texas's admission.)

So patriotism was not just a mood or an impulse to citizens and soldiers; it could be physically embodied in a symbolic banner around which pro-war factions could rally just as easily as soldiers on the front lines. And it was: cities fluttered with red, white, and blue.

Another unique aspect of the American patriotic response involved God. Mexico was a deeply Catholic nation, with cathedrals and ritual church attendance a staple of life for the majority of the population. The same could be said of predominantly Protestant America, which was, theologically speaking, still very much influenced by the founding Puritans.

However, the link between the war and Manifest Destiny, with its emphatic belief that God favored the United States over Mexico, made for a strikingly evangelical form of patriotism. As American citizens cheered the volunteers rushing into their town squares to enlist, the assemblages often felt like a combination between a Sunday morning service and a Fourth of July celebration, complete with bands playing "Yankee Doodle" and fevered speeches comparing the Mexican War with the Crusades.

And even when those soldiers marched off to war, that cocktail of patriotism and faith traveled right alongside. On June 1, 1846, Captain R. A. Stewart, a Methodist minister and sugar farmer from Louisiana, celebrated the first American church service on Mexican soil since the war's beginning. Standing on a dusty patch of farmland outside Matamoros, Stewart reminded his all-combatant flock that God intended Anglo-Saxons to rule North America as an "order of Providence." All devout Americans would stand by the troops as a display of their faith and patriotism.

Such talk was heady—and premature. As spring turned to summer, the American army had not been seriously tested. Casualties had been light. The war was having little impact on most of the nation. Patriotism, thus far, had come cheap.

But as Taylor prepared to escalate hostilities by leaving Texas and pressing the fight onto Mexican soil—lands that had nothing to do with Manifest Destiny and that only a meager handful of U.S. citizens coveted—it remained to be seen if the American people would continue to support a cause that was about to lose its moral certainty.

"We," Grant wrote of the change in the war's focus, as evidenced by the new name given Taylor's force, "became the Army of Invasion."

THIRTEEN

Star-Spangled Banner

JULY 4, 1846

"If the American army is yet to undertake a campaign south of the Rio Grande, its greatest perils are yet to come," the *Times* of London predicted somewhat ominously on June 15.

That same day the United States and Great Britain signed the Treaty of Oregon, ending all threat of hostility between the two countries. The specter of a two-front war no longer hung over the United States. President Polk was free to concentrate all his military might on Mexico.

Working off plans drafted by Major General Winfield Scott, the vainglorious yet brilliant commanding general of the U.S. Army, Polk quickly focused America's ambitions and plans. The war's goal was to make the Rio Grande the nation's southern border and to bring California into the Union.

A four-pronged attack would make this possible.

Part one was Taylor's ongoing advance into Mexico; part two would be a second column of American troops marching south from San Antonio under the command of Brigadier General John E. Wool, in order to protect Taylor's right flank; part three was an improbable two-thousand-mile overland march by U.S.

dragoons from Fort Leavenworth, Kansas, to San Diego, California; and part four was a naval blockade of all Mexican ports on the Atlantic and Pacific to prevent the importation of arms from Europe.

The Treaty of Oregon made it all possible. Britain had agreed to cede Oregon to the United States, in exchange for keeping sole possession of all lands north of the forty-ninth parallel, an act formally defining the northern border of the United States for the first time since the Louisiana Purchase. The British press, which had been watching the conflict with Mexico closely, seemed to take a certain glee in predicting American calamity. "The hot weather has set in; the yellow fever is raging on the coast; and to advance into the interior of Mexico at this time will be an operation of extreme difficulty," chuckled the *Times*.

None of that dissuaded Jefferson Davis. Though still officially a congressman, his new title was Colonel Davis, commander of the First Mississippi Regiment (the unit's title was deceptive: they were the *only* Mississippi regiment). His pay rate was seventy-five dollars a month. On July 3, the War Department had ordered him to leave at once for Mexico, where he would report directly to General Taylor. Now, as America celebrated its seventieth birthday, he and Varina boarded the caravan of stagecoaches that took them over the Appalachians via the National Road. For safety from robbers and other predators, stagecoaches seldom traveled alone, with as many as six journeying together at one time. A typical stage was pulled by four horses, with nine passengers inside the cab and up to four more sitting outside in the open air.

The Davises would be taken to the Ohio River, where they would then board a steamboat that would ferry them down to the Mississippi.

Mississippi meant "Big River" to the Native Americans who first settled on her banks. The grand title failed to convey the

majesty of a waterway stretching from Canada down into the
Gulf of Mexico and had no equal north of the equator—not
even the similarly named Rio Grande. The river flowed through
America like a promise that would always be kept, expanding
the nation's boundaries by doubling as the nation's travel hub:
settlers headed toward the Santa Fe and Oregon trails gathered
on its banks to stock up on provisions to load aboard their covered wagons; traders bound for a summer in the Nebraska and
Dakota territories bundled their wares and crowded the stone
riverfront wharves of cities like Saint Louis, awaiting passage on
steamboats headed north to the Missouri River; travelers from
the East journeyed down the Ohio River until it merged with the
Mississippi, then changed boats at Cairo, from there continuing
downriver to New Orleans or upriver toward Saint Louis and
points beyond.

The riverboat segment of Jeff and Varina Davis's journey
would last nine days. Appropriately, given the patriotic fervor
attending their trip and the date Davis chose for his departure,
they cruised the Mississippi River aboard the paddle wheeler
Star-Spangled Banner.

Davis had not resigned his House seat when he accepted his
new commission, and he was nakedly honest when discussing
his motivations in a letter to his sister Lucinda. "It may be that
I will return with a reputation over which you will rejoice," he
stated plainly.

The time for fighting his decision was long past. Varina had
been devastated, but her husband had refused to change his
mind. "I have cried until I am stupid," she wrote to her mother.
"If Jeff was a cross bad husband, old, ugly, or stupid, I could better bear for him to go on a year's campaign, but he is so tender,
and good that I feel like he ought never to leave me."

Davis was risking Varina's life as well as his own—though

that was her own doing. As if she'd learned nothing from Knox's death, she would be returning to the Deep South at the exact same time of year that mosquitoes and malaria had killed his first wife.

Davis had implored Varina to agree to remain in Virginia, for her own safety and his peace of mind. But since her social standing would wither notably without her husband in Washington, she was adamant about returning to the South. Varina planned to travel to her parents' home in Louisiana once Davis went off to war. She thought it a better place to spend the time than alone at Brierfield or even at nearby Hurricane. Her exposure to Davis Bend would be minimal — but even that made Davis nervous.

He was bursting with pride that his constituents had chosen him to lead the First Mississippi into Mexico, and he longed to do more than just perform gracefully under fire. Indeed, Davis yearned to bring glory upon himself and his men by making sure they were the best-trained, best-equipped, and bravest volunteer fighting force that it was possible to assemble on such short notice. He immersed himself in a pocket field manual while aboard the *Star-Spangled Banner,* lifting his head from the pages just long enough to explain the meanings of "enfilading, breaking columns, hollow squares, and what not" to his wife from time to time.

Davis and Varina arrived home on July 13. He soon entrusted his brother with a letter of resignation from Congress but gave him explicit instructions not to submit it unless the war became a political liability.

Davis hastily made arrangements for Varina's safety and well-being and placed his longtime favorite slave James Pemberton in charge of the plantation in his absence.

Jefferson kissed Varina good-bye the very next morning and boarded yet another steamboat, this one bound for New

Orleans. He was accompanied by a slave named Jim Green and an Arabian horse called Tartar, named for the Turkish warriors who once rampaged across Europe with Genghis Khan.

The Tartars were infamous for pillaging and looting, and otherwise changing the course of Western civilization.

FOURTEEN

Eager for Action

JULY 14, 1846

With Manhattan's skyline to his right, the residential borough of Brooklyn to his left, and the green black waters of the Atlantic Ocean straight ahead, First Lieutenant William Tecumseh Sherman could finally rest easily: he was on his way to the war. For six crazed weeks, starting in early June, Sherman had finagled and schemed his way from an unchallenging post with the recruiting department into an assignment with an artillery company bound for combat.

Wiry and intense, a red-haired dervish whose unkempt and often casual appearance belied deep wells of inner passion and, sometimes, depression, Sherman now stood on the decks of the store ship *Lexington* along with the 113 enlisted men, five officers, and assistant surgeon of Company F of the U.S. Army's Third Artillery.

They were all bound for California, in anticipation of the war's second front opening there soon. The passage would be arduous and long—perhaps six months. The route would take them down along the coast of South America and around Tierra del Fuego before turning north to the California coastal port at Monterey.

If F Company had been an infantry outfit instead of artillery, they could have marched to California more quickly. But they were not, and dragging cannons from one side of the North American continent to the other was deeply impractical.

Sherman was extremely ill suited to such a passive mode of transportation. The young officer from Ohio, sixth in the West Point class of 1840, could only pace the decks in frustration, praying all the while for smooth seas and a following wind.

This depressed him no end, but the alternative was not traveling to the front lines at all. A Seminole War veteran who had never seen action, Sherman had been on duty as a recruiter when he heard about shots being fired on the Rio Grande. He was overwhelmed by an eagerness to finally take part in some battle — *any* battle — if only to hold his head high among fellow West Point alumni. "In the latter part of May when at Wheeling, Virginia, on my way back from Zanesville to Pittsburg, I heard the news of the first battle of Palo Alto and Resaca de la Palma," he wrote of his zeal, "and, in common with everybody else, felt intensely excited. That I should be on the recruiting service when my comrades were actually fighting was intolerable."

The railroad tracks heading west stopped abruptly at the Allegheny Mountains. Sherman had to race for his post at Pittsburgh aboard a stagecoach. A letter was waiting from an old classmate informing him that the Third Artillery had just received orders for California and that Sherman should apply for permission to join them. A whirlwind odyssey of rule bending immediately followed, during which Sherman had fled the recruiting office (he left a corporal in charge) in a desperate quest to secure a transfer to Company F. The clock was ticking. Once that ship sailed for California, Sherman's hopes of seeing combat sailed with it. Relegated to the recruiting office once again, he would be destined to spend the war traveling up and down the Ohio River, pleading for able-bodied men to join the U.S. Army.

But he had been in luck. "I got my orders about 8 P.M. one night," Sherman wrote. "The next morning traveled by stage from Brownsville to Cumberland, Maryland, and thence by cars to Baltimore, Philadelphia, and New York, in a great hurry lest the ship might sail without me."

It hadn't. The *Lexington* was a former sloop of war commissioned exactly twenty years and three days before Company F's departure for California. It had been refitted in 1840 as a store ship and had its twenty-four cannons reduced to just six. It had been a proud vessel before the castration, seeing action in the Mediterranean, Caribbean, and South Atlantic. In particular, the *Lexington* had played a decisive role in the Falkland Islands crisis of 1831, its mighty twenty-four-pounders raking the village of Puerto Soledad in response to the seizure of U.S. fishing boats by the Falklands' Argentine governor. The *Lexington* was 127 feet from stem to stern and 33½ feet at the beam. In its glory days its crew had numbered 190. Now it required just 50 sailors to set a course and trim the sails. Those men, however, combined with Company F, meant that the *Lexington*'s slim hull was near full capacity once again. The ship's crew slept in hammocks between decks, while the enlisted soldiers were crammed into bunks built along the hull and amidships. Over the course of the voyage, it was understood that soldiers would be pressed into service performing nautical and maintenance duties alongside the sailors.

Sherman and the other army officers (who would also serve in nominal fashion alongside their naval counterparts) slept two to a room. He shared a berth with First Lieutenant Edward Ord, who had also been his roommate at West Point.

They were alike in many ways, particularly in their keen intelligence and disdain for pressed uniforms and combed hair. Ord, a mathematical genius who was reputed to be a descendant of Britain's King George IV, was "unselfish, manly, and patriotic" in Sherman's eyes. Small wonder that the two got along: Sherman could have used those words to describe himself. Theirs was a friendship that would endure for almost five decades.

Ord was the friend who had alerted Sherman that Company F was short a junior officer, thus making it possible for Sherman to apply for the vacancy and be onboard the *Lexington* in the first place. Their cabin was small and cramped, with barely enough room for their bunks and chests of personal belongings. Sherman, who possessed a great flair for the theatrical, liked to call it a stateroom.

Sherman was twenty-six, born into a family whose history was intertwined with that of a young United States. The first Shermans had sailed from Essex County, England, in 1634, just fourteen years after the *Mayflower* voyage. Roger Sherman, a distant relative, signed the Declaration of Independence. The family was situated in New England for the first century and a half after their arrival, then moved west after the Revolutionary War to take advantage of a land grant. In this way, Charles R. Sherman, a twenty-one-year-old attorney, brought his young bride, Mary, to Ohio in 1811. He left a year later, enlisting to fight the British during the War of 1812.

As was their custom when waging war in North America, the British army enlisted the help of Native American tribes. One such tribe was the Shawnee, led by a charismatic orator named Tecumseh. "Live your life," Tecumseh had said in 1809, rallying other tribes to fight encroachment by American settlers, "that the fear of death can never enter your heart."

Ironically, Tecumseh's maverick style struck a nerve with those same settlers. They identified with his independence, courage, and refusal to quit in the face of long odds. He even won the respect of men who took up arms against Tecumseh's cause—men like Charles Sherman. He admired Tecumseh and his tactics very much, so much so that when Mary bore their second son, in 1816, Charles was determined to name the boy after that Shawnee chief. Mary would have none of it. She insisted upon James, after her brother (Charles and Mary's first son, born in 1810, was named Charles—but for her brother by that name). When the Shermans finally had a third son in 1820, Mary bent.

"When I came along, on the 8th of February, 1820, mother having no more brothers, my father succeeded in his original purpose," Tecumseh Sherman later wrote of his mother's lack of enthusiasm for the offbeat moniker.

Tecumseh Sherman, or just "Cump," was only nine when work called his father away from home in June 1829. Charles Sherman had risen to become a member of the Ohio Supreme Court. His duties that summer were to ride horseback from town to town, presiding over the circuit court. He was thirty-nine and healthy.

Sherman later wrote about his father's last day in court: "He took his seat on the bench, opened court in the forenoon, but in the afternoon, after recess, was seized by a severe chill and had to adjourn the court. The best medical aid was called in, and for three days with apparent success, but the fever then assumed a more dangerous type, and he gradually yielded to it."

Tecumseh Sherman's words, lacking in emotion and abounding in simplification, sounded like those of a grown-up describing the awful turn of events as diplomatically as possible to a nine-year-old boy.

Mary now had no source of income. Rather than subject her children to a life of poverty and want, she sent some off to live with neighbors. Tecumseh would be raised by a prominent local judge named Thomas Ewing. Though the boy, like generations of his relatives, had been raised Episcopalian, Ewing's Catholic wife insisted that he be baptized into her faith. Not only that, but Maria Ewing found the child's true name deeply inappropriate for a Christian youth. She chose to call him William. Forever after he was officially William Tecumseh Sherman.

Thomas Ewing was an important Whig politician who would one day hold a cabinet-level position as the first secretary of the interior. In 1836, the year that Sherman made up his mind to attend West Point, Ewing was a U.S. senator. Arranging an academy appointment was hardly an issue.

On his way toward the Hudson, Sherman stopped in Washington to visit Ewing. He happened to be walking past the White House when his eyes befell Andrew Jackson on the lawn, fretting over policy with his advisers.

Sherman stopped dead in his tracks to watch. "I recall looking at him a full hour, one morning, through a wood railing on Pennsylvania Avenue, as he paced up and down the gravel walk on the north front of the White House," Sherman later recalled. "He wore a cap and an overcoat so full that his form seemed smaller than I had expected."

Standing near Jackson were Washington's other major power brokers: Vice President Martin Van Buren, John Calhoun, Henry Clay, and Daniel Webster.

West Point, with its focus on fraternity and discipline, was the ideal university for Sherman. Not that he showed any great potential as a soldier or a leader—just the opposite. Sherman's grades were exemplary, but his tendencies toward independence and impulse were his undoing. He racked up demerit after demerit, never rising above the rank of cadet private during his entire four years. "Then, as now, neatness in dress and uniform, with a strict conformity to the rules, were the qualifications required for office, and I suppose I was found not to excel in any of these," he later wrote with a shrug.

Sherman was posted to the Third Artillery after graduation. In due time he was sent to Florida, where the Seminole Wars had taken on the feel of a mop-up action. Sherman would remember his time in Florida for its shark-filled ocean waters, its mangrove swamps, and the delicious dinners of sea turtle steak. His chief duty was rounding up rogue bands of Seminoles for deportation to their new homes in Oklahoma. "We at Fort Pierce made several excursions...into the Everglades, picking up here and there a family, so that it was absurd any longer to call it a 'war.'"

Sherman, however, was constantly one remove from the action. Fellow officers like Brevet Brigadier General Zachary Taylor, Colonel William Worth, and Lieutenant Braxton Bragg made their reputations during the Seminole Wars, but Sherman never got the chance to prove himself in battle. He was transferred from Florida to an outpost in Alabama. From there he spent time in New Orleans and Charleston.

Sherman traveled through chunks of the South on horseback, studying the lay of the land, memorizing the topography, and making a mental map of its roads and of the paths of its streams and rivers. In time he could travel just as knowledgeably through the swales and mountains of Georgia as through his native Ohio. Sherman never forgot those lessons.

"The knowledge thus acquired was of great use to me, and consequently to the government," he would later note with some understatement.

As 1845 TURNED into 1846 American soldiers massed in Corpus Christi, anticipating the start of yet another war. Sherman was posted to Charleston's Fort Moultrie, light-years from combat. That thriving port, with its wharves and shops and ships laden with cotton, was good duty. An artificial island made up of rocks that had formerly been used as ballast in cotton ships was sprouting in the middle of the bay. Military engineers had dumped the rocks there on purpose and then leveled them once the mound rose high enough to poke out of the sea. A fort was being built on top of this artificial foundation.

Despite the close proximity to Fort Moultrie and another installation named Fort Johnson, the new fortress was considered vital to America's coastal defenses.

In 1817, President Monroe had advocated a network of new defenses to prevent invasion by sea. Over the protests of the U.S. Army's Corps of Engineers, Monroe appealed to France for help in their construction. The Napoleonic War veteran General Simon Bernard was commissioned to design some two hundred fortresses on the Atlantic and the Gulf of Mexico. Sumter, the pentagonal fort Sherman could see being built atop the pile of rocks in Charleston Harbor, was named for South Carolina's Revolutionary War hero, the legendary General Thomas "the Gamecock" Sumter, who had fought with Light-Horse Harry Lee. It would have brick walls five feet thick and room enough to house 135 guns and garrison 650 men. The first rocks had been dumped into the harbor in 1829.

In 1846, as the first shots were fired on the Rio Grande, Fort Sumter, in Sherman's words, "was barely above the water."

On May 1, Sherman was transferred to the recruiting service. Polk's call for volunteers had not yet gone out. There was a sense that the army would need more men to fight Mexico (the Northeast was a hotbed for recruiters, thanks to the surplus of able-bodied farm laborers and immigrants; one 1842 study had shown that half of all regular army enlistments were from either New York or Pennsylvania). For an officer during a time of war, the assignment was a career death sentence.

But that was someone else's problem now. Sherman stood aboard the swaying, creaking decks of the *Lexington*.

"Live your life that the fear of death can never enter your heart," said Tecumseh.

That's exactly what First Lieutenant William Tecumseh Sherman was trying to do—if only he could be a part of the action. His military career had been lackluster so far, and he had always arrived at war too late.

It was his deepest desire that California would change all that.

FIFTEEN

First Mississippi

July 17, 1846

O n a sweltering midsummer day, Colonel Jefferson Davis
disembarked in New Orleans to meet his troops for the
first time. Three miles south of the city, the 936 officers and
men of the First Mississippi were camped on the very site where
Andrew Jackson had fought the Battle of New Orleans—yet
another coincidence in which Davis's past and present collided.

The men of the First Mississippi were as flamboyant as their
commander was ambitious. Each state's volunteer regiment was
allowed to design its own uniform. One group of Kentucky volunteers dressed in tricornered hats and hip boots made of red
goatskin. Still other volunteer regiments wore various shades of
green, pink, and gray. For their part, the men of the First Mississippi had chosen to adorn themselves quite smartly in broad
black straw hats, white trousers made of a heavy-duty "duck"
cotton fabric that was more often used for making tents, and garish red shirts. In addition, almost every man—including lowly
privates—traveled with a personal slave or servant to attend to
his needs, for the members of the First Mississippi came from
some of the state's finest families. Davis, who hadn't made time

to have a uniform tailored before leaving Washington, was the sole member of the unit who arrived in Saint Louis clad in civilian clothing.

Despite its historical impact, the campsite selected by interim commanders Lieutenant Colonel Alexander K. McLung and Major Alexander Bradford was abysmal. The regimental tents were pitched in a plantation field made swampy by frequent rains. Thick black clouds of mosquitoes tortured the men by day and by night. Vast puddles of water and mud pocked the area, and those impressive white trousers worn by each man were soon a filthy brown. Even worse, the regimental drinking water was also used for bathing and for washing clothes. Dozens of men staggered to the sick list.

When the call for volunteers had gone out in early May, some seventeen thousand enthusiastic Mississippians had swelled the streets of Vicksburg. Now, the initial burst of patriotism had been replaced by the rigors and realities of life during wartime. The mud and dysentery—not to mention alligators and mosquitoes—of a Louisiana swamp were not what those once-eager men had had in mind when they raced to volunteer. With every day spent in camp, awaiting the long-delayed order to ship out for the Rio Grande, morale plunged further and further.

Davis had arrived at a catastrophe in the making.

The scene of failure and mismanagement cried out for bold and immediate leadership—something Davis recognized immediately. He was appalled by all he saw: the morass at Chalmette Plantation (the legal name of the fields housing the troops' tents), the growing number of incapacitated troops, the absence of the special .54-caliber percussion-cap rifles he had ordered specially for his men, and the emotional gloom that had left his fellow Mississippians regretting their decision. Davis's first order of business was relocating his troops to indoor quarters closer to New Orleans. He then busied himself with finding the missing shipments of rifles and securing berths on ships bound for Port Isabel.

Davis had learned a thing or two about political muscle during his short time in Congress. He quickly got his way.

By July 22, the men of the First Mississippi, who had (thanks to Davis) spent the previous five days living in the relative comfort of dry cotton sheds, were saying good-bye to New Orleans and clambering up the gangplank of a tall ship. Each man's gear locker included a dress cap, a forage cap, two flannel shirts, two pairs of full-body underwear, a uniform coat, four pairs of socks, a woolen jacket, four pairs of overalls (three woolen and one cotton), a cotton jacket, a frock, a wool blanket that served as a bedroll, and canteens made from hollowed gourds or molded india rubber. The men were mostly farmers in real life and got paid very little for the privilege of risking their lives for their country. A private earned just eight dollars a month. Yet they were thrilled to be sailing, at long last, to war.

Finding ships for the entire regiment and its supplies was an arduous process, so even though Davis longed to be astride Tartar in Mexico as soon as possible, he waited until the last man decamped on July 26 before setting sail himself. Six days later he disembarked near the mouth of the Rio Grande, onto a sandy, treeless offshore landmass known as Brazos Island, bringing to an end a turbulent month of cross-country travel and career change. His arrival went unmarked by marching bands, fanfare, or even the presence of General Taylor and his army. In any case, a celebration would have seemed cruel. Texas made the Chalmette Plantation look like paradise.

Bugs were everywhere. The Mississippians had never seen such swarms of flies and mosquitoes. This was particularly remarkable because they came from a state *known* for its swarms of flies and mosquitoes. There were no trees in their temporary new home, just a bustling new army camp and a standing order to remain on Brazos Island until there was room on a steamboat heading upriver to Camargo. The summer heat had reached its peak, beating down with the sort of ferocity that made even the most rugged individual seek out the merest sliver of shade. The only respite came from the hurricane season's fierce northerly winds. But those also swirled the sand every which way, adding a fine layer of grit to the hard bread, fatty bacon, and bean soup that the men lived on, day after day.

Davis took the conditions for granted. Wars were seldom fought in comfortable surroundings. His focus was on getting his men ready for battle. If Davis had anything to say about it, the First Mississippi would not be like the other volunteer regiments, with their drunkenness, sloppy appearance, and disdain for regulation. They would be men of honor and valor, soldiers whose behavior would not bring shame of any kind to the great state of Mississippi. He drilled them constantly to instill discipline and order. Davis also posted an around-the-clock guard at the camp, even though the Mexican army was hundreds of miles away.

THE LONG-AWAITED RIFLES would be another way of setting Davis's men apart. In his mind, the fighting man's musket was an antique, ill suited for the modern battlefield. The evidence was too powerful to ignore. The standard-issue gun used throughout the regular army was the Model 1822 flintlock, a smoothbore musket fifty-seven inches long, with a forty-two-inch barrel. The term *smoothbore* meant that there were no internal spiral grooves, or "rifling," in the barrel.

The two main forces affecting a projectile in flight are air resistance and gravity. The musket ball was particularly susceptible to both because it was shot from the barrel without any significant spin or rotation. As Isaac Newton noted as far back as the seventeenth century (the German physicist Heinrich Magnus would confirm his finding in 1853), all spheres effect a tumbling, spinning motion in flight. However, if the axis of that rotation is not parallel to the direction of travel, that object will begin to curve. Sometimes the curve is to the right or to the left, and sometimes it is simply straight down. As applied to the musket, the random tumbling affected accuracy and range by causing bullets to veer off course or plummet into the ground. This made the musket a liability when firing at great range, as Sam Grant had noted at Palo Alto.

A rifle's internal spiral grooves gave the bullet (not a ball) a deliberate spin as it exited the barrel. Forcing the bullet to spin on an axis parallel to its direction of travel negated the tumbling effect and minimized the effects of wind resistance and gravity. This greatly increased accuracy and range. On a good day, in a gentle breeze, a Model 1841 percussion-cap rifle with its .54-caliber bullet was capable of killing a man from one thousand yards away. And its thirty-three-inch barrel was also two feet shorter than a musket's, making for a lighter and more mobile weapon.

Just as notable was the use of percussion caps, which allowed the rifle to be fired in all weather conditions. There was never any worry about gunpowder charges getting wet, as with muskets. The explosive mixture that propelled the bullet from the gun was encased in a metal cartridge. And not only were percussion caps waterproof, but they were also easier to load and fire than musket balls and paper gunpowder charges.

Back on March 23, Davis had taken the floor in Congress to argue in favor of a bill that would fund two new army rifle regiments. Noting that the British and French had already begun using rifles, he argued that America was "now falling behind" in terms of military weaponry.

But that bill had been reworded by the time it passed, so that it merely funded new musket regiments. Soon after, Davis had argued in favor of a second bill that would fund a regiment of rifle dragoons. It had passed on May 19 and was signed into law that same day.

As soon as it became clear that Davis would be leaving Congress to join the fighting, he had insisted that each and every man in his regiment be outfitted with a rifle.

It wasn't that simple. The U.S. Army had slowly begun to insinuate the rifle into combat ranks, but it was standard army procedure to outfit only two companies of each infantry regiment with the Model 1841 rifle (there were ten companies to a regiment, meaning that the other eight still carried muskets). In the eyes of the army's top commanders, the lack of a bayonet mount made the rifle a liability, and they feared being overrun in close-quarters fighting. That, plus the musket's many years of proven service, made it a familiar favorite. Indeed, battle tactics had been planned around its shortcomings. To change weapons and strategies on the eve of combat struck many officers as a needless gamble.

Davis didn't care. He ordered a thousand 1841s directly from the manufacturer, the Eli Whitney Company of New Haven, Connecticut. To compensate for the lack of a bayonet mount, Davis had commanded the First Mississippi's soldiers to arm themselves with a secondary weapon for close-quarters fighting, whether it be a knife, a saber, an artillery sword, or even one of the brand-new Colt revolving pistols.

General Winfield Scott, the army's top general, had tried to thwart Davis. "He expressed a doubt as to the propriety of supplying a whole regiment with percussion arms and positively insisted that at least six of the companies should bear muskets, instead of rifles," Davis wrote. "I knew the confidence the men I was expecting to lead had in rifles, and their distrust of the musket then in use and therefore notwithstanding my reluctance to oppose the General insisted upon the thousand rifles."

Just to make sure he got those precious new guns, Davis had

made the savvy move of enlisting President Polk's assistance. Polk, of course, wanted a favor in return. A bit of political horse trading ensued.

Polk promised Davis his thousand rifles in exchange for his vote on a crucial tariff bill then making its way through Congress. Proposed by Treasury Secretary Robert J. Walker, the bill would lower tariffs in the hopes of increasing Treasury revenue through increased trade. Walker was a Davis confidant who also made his home in Mississippi. Forty-five years old and eager to impose his antiprotectionist views on the national economy, the former U.S. senator wielded immense political clout. By voting in favor of the Walker Tariff, Davis was courting favor with the president and treasury secretary—the two most powerful men in Washington.

There was just one problem: the tariff bill was extremely divisive, literally pitting North against South. Northern manufacturing states opposed it, saying they needed protection from foreign competition; the agricultural southern states argued that the lower tariffs would allow greater international sales of cotton and other such goods. The crucial swing vote would come from the western states, which at the time consisted of the Great Lakes and Mississippi River valley regions. In exchange for southern backing of a pro-West measure known as the Harbors and Rivers Bill, sponsored by South Carolina senator John C. Calhoun, the western voting bloc would cast its ballots in favor of the Walker Tariff.

The measure would go before Congress on July 3. Davis, at Polk's personal request, had delayed his departure for Mexico accordingly so that he could first cast his vote on that very close bill.

The Walker Tariff passed. The next morning, Jefferson Davis had left Washington with Varina, secure in the knowledge that his rifles would be delivered to the Mississippi First.

But by August 3, as Davis and his men adjusted to life at the mouth of the Rio Grande, those rifles still hadn't arrived.

On the very same day, in far-off Washington, having successfully attained the pro-southern Walker Tariff and no longer needing the support of the western voting bloc, President Polk blithely vetoed the Harbors and Rivers Bill.

Western states were outraged by Polk's unabashed act of partisanship toward the South and soon formed a congressional voting alliance with the North. Among the new bloc's demands was that slavery be permanently excluded from all western territories. Fifteen years hence, the split that commenced with this issue would drive a wedge between North and South. When that time came, Jefferson Davis would find himself at the head of a great and terrible rebellion. But first—now—there was Mexico.

SIXTEEN

The Westerner

AUGUST 3, 1846

The president's veto of the Harbors and Rivers Bill was just one beef Abraham Lincoln, a westerner, had with James K. Polk. Like Polk, Lincoln was a deeply partisan politician, loyal to his party and its ideals. In his case, the party in question was Whig. And now, on the same day that Jefferson Davis was arriving to fight the Mexican War, Lincoln had been elected to Congress. For the first time in his political career, the lanky veteran of the Illinois legislature would stride onto the national political stage.

The honor was a long time coming. The thirty-seven-year-old Lincoln had coveted Springfield's congressional seat for years, but in the name of party unity he had held off.

Back in 1842, he had plotted a congressional candidacy but had realized that the field was overcrowded with Whigs. At the party's convention in Pekin that year, Lincoln had introduced a resolution designed to fix that problem. Rather than force pro-Whig voters to divide their votes between him and two other candidates, Lincoln suggested that the three men rotate the job. Each would agree to serve just one term in the House and then let another run for the office. The resolution passed. Lincoln, knowing that his day was imminent, stepped aside. Thirty-two-year-old John Hardin received the Whig Party nod and was duly elected. In 1844, Hardin left office in favor of Lincoln's good friend Edward Dickenson Baker, after whom Lincoln's six-month-old son was named. The British-born Baker was duly elected and traveled to Washington to serve out his two-year term.

Lincoln was next. Early in 1846, he began making campaign plans.

But Hardin had enjoyed his time in Washington, with the power and prestige that attended national office. He reneged on the deal and began planning a campaign of his own. Lincoln was an imposing six feet four and had a thoughtful disposition and calm demeanor that led some to overlook his deeply competitive nature. Hardin certainly did. Lincoln began writing letters to Whigs throughout the district, seeking their support; he questioned those who were opposed to his candidacy, and he lobbied Whig newspapers to support him. Stung, Hardin pulled out of the race.

Now Hardin and Baker were off to war with Illinois's volunteer regiments. The Irishman James Shields, a close political acquaintance and a man with whom Lincoln had nearly fought a duel several years earlier, was soon to join them. There was political capital to be gained from soldiering, and all three were eager to display their heroism against Mexico.

Lincoln had no interest in that sort of fight; he had already earned his military stripes, serving as a captain of the volunteers during the Black Hawk War. This short conflict between the Illinois militia, the U.S. Army, and a disgruntled sixty-five-year-old Sauk warrior named Ma-Ka-Tai-Me-She-Kia-Kiak—Black Hawk—was grounded in America's westward expansion and the practice of displacing Indians from their tribal lands in favor of incoming farmers and other settlers. An avenging Black Hawk's rampage in the spring of 1832 had proved disastrous for his tribe, and by September of that year he was being escorted to a prison cell at the Jefferson Barracks by Lieutenant Jefferson Davis, who had missed all but the last battle of the war because of a sixty-day furlough.

Lincoln's contribution to that war was also slight but was notable for his determination to serve. His captaincy in the Fourth Regiment of Mounted Volunteers was short lived — the Illinois regiments enrolled men for just thirty days at a time. Lincoln was a captain from April 21, 1832, until mustering out on May 27. He immediately reenlisted, but as a private, the rank he would hold until his unit was deactivated on July 10. Lincoln never saw combat, but he traveled widely through Illinois and Wisconsin during the course of the conflict. Years later he would look back fondly on his election to captain and subsequent service as "a success which gave me more pleasure than any I have had since."

Lincoln was that sort of man, offbeat and adventurous, with a quietly competitive spirit. It was the pioneer's attitude, one that came naturally through his lineage. He was born in Kentucky and lived there until moving to Illinois at the age of twenty-two. "My paternal grandfather, Abraham Lincoln, emigrated from Rockingham County, Virginia, to Kentucky, about 1781 or 2, where, a year or two later, he was killed by Indians, not in battle, but by stealth, when he was laboring to open a farm in the forest. His ancestors, who were Quakers, went to Virginia from Berks County, Pennsylvania," he noted. His own mother died when Lincoln was ten, and he was raised by his father on the Kentucky frontier at a time when bears roamed the forests and there was no doubt the land was pure wilderness. Schools were in such short supply that the basics of reading, writing, and arithmetic were the extent of most education. "If a straggler supposed to understand Latin happened to sojourn in the neighborhood, he was looked upon as a wizard," Lincoln wrote.

Classroom studies were sandwiched between working in the fields. Lincoln received just one year of formal education and, as he noted later, had "not been to school since." "The little advance I now have upon this store of education, I have picked up from time to time under the pressure of necessity," he wrote. Lincoln was being modest. He had an intelligence bordering on genius and was deeply ambitious. Though his formal education may have ended in early childhood, he was profoundly intellectual.

He entered politics after moving to Illinois. It was a rather abrupt career change—with the exception of one year spent working in a small store, he had been a farmworker his entire life and had even navigated a flatboat down the Mississippi to bring produce to market. Lincoln's first campaign was for the Illinois legislature. He lost, though that was not surprising, considering that he had just moved to the state and had interrupted his campaign to enlist for the Black Hawk War.

It was the last election he would lose for many years to come. Lincoln served three terms in the legislature, always studying on the side. In 1842 he wed Mary Todd, whose blue eyes and dimples had caught Lincoln's eye at a party. She was attractive, though not pretty, just as the clean-shaven and gray-eyed Lincoln was distinctive without being handsome. Their courtship did not go smoothly, and at one point she broke up with him, but their marriage was fruitful. Their first child, Robert, was born almost nine months to the day after their wedding; Edward came along three years later.

The time span between Lincoln's election to Congress and the day he first set foot on the floor of the House of Representatives was remarkable for its length. The Thirtieth Congress would not hold its first session until December 6, 1847, some sixteen months after the election. (Although the Thirtieth Congress technically ran from March 4, 1847, to March 3, 1849, their first meeting was delayed until December by Article I, Section 4, of the Constitution, which stipulated that "the Congress shall assemble at least once in every year, and such meeting shall be on the first Monday in December, unless they shall by law appoint a different day.")

It was an auspicious time in America's history to hold a national elected office, a time when a congressman's vote could influence the shape and direction of the country for decades to come. Already, Whig politicians were attacking the war. Many of them saw it as unconstitutional. A group known as the Conscience Whigs argued that the spread of slavery was an underlying cause. With the Whigs controlling the House, 115–108, Lincoln's vote would most often be in the majority.

The war, however, was extremely popular in Illinois. Of the state's seven seats in the House of Representatives, six were controlled by pro-war Democrats. His opponent for Congress, a fiercely evangelical old circuit judge named Peter Cartwright, had taken pains to cast Lincoln as a secular deist who belonged to no specific Christian denomination. Being antiwar as well as anti-God could very well end Lincoln's career.

Illinois was a frontier state and populated with residents who believed powerfully in Manifest Destiny. The Black Hawk War was their own, much smaller battle to rid their lands of an unwanted native populace that loomed as an impediment to growth. Some 8,370 Illinois men volunteered for just 3,720 spots in the state's Mexican War regiments. The conflict offered them something Illinois could not: a job. The state was in the midst of a financial crisis. Farmers were unable to sell their crops, there were too many men for too few jobs, and there was such a chronic cash shortage that barter was the most popular form of mercantile exchange. Lincoln and his law partner, William H. Herndon, often accepted produce in exchange for legal services.

For a politician, the war was a guaranteed way to make a name for oneself. Small wonder that Lincoln's fellow Whigs had raced off to it. Baker had personally raised one of the four Illinois regiments. Hardin had led an emotional call to arms at a pro-war rally in Springfield: "Let us not say Taylor and his brave men can whip Mexico without our aid," he cried. "This is not the language of brave men. Let us have a hand in whipping her. Let our people answer 'Aye' in one universal and glorious response."

In fact, most antiwar Whigs were from places like New England, which represented the staid, industrial America many residents of Illinois had abandoned for the wilds of frontier living. And though Illinois had been a state since 1818, the twenty-first admitted to the Union, it was only a few decades removed from being part of a region known as the Northwest Territory, so called because it signified the farthest edge of the American wilderness, divided from the rest of the continent, pre–Louisiana Purchase, by the Mississippi River. Illinois was still wild enough that major blizzards in the winters of 1830 and 1836 killed scores of travelers caught in the vast spaces between settlements. Its populace viewed the war in purely emotional terms, for in the Texans' plight it was easy to see themselves.

Lincoln could be just as emotional. His upbringing and those adventures on the Mississippi guaranteed that no one could doubt his credentials as a frontier "westerner." But he was also a deeply political animal. Lincoln was notably quiet on the Mexican War during his campaign. He urged Illinoisans to support the flag and the troops (he conspicuously made no mention of supporting the president). Privately, Lincoln was beginning to view the war as Polk's underhanded attempt to push a personal agenda and deflect the public's criticism of his shortcomings. The president, Lincoln would later note, hoped "to escape scrutiny, by fixing the public gaze upon the exceeding brightness of military glory...that serpent's eye, that charms to destroy."

This deep Whig-Democrat divide, felt so acutely by the army, was even more pronounced in the halls of Congress. Those halls and that schism loomed prominently in Lincoln's immediate future.

SEVENTEEN

The Rifles

AUGUST 19, 1846

Finally, Davis's rifles arrived. A Treasury Department cutter delivered crates full of the brand-new weapons to the sands of Brazos Island. On August 24, armed and ready, the First Mississippi boarded steamships for the long journey up the Rio Grande to Camargo.

They were lucky to get the ride. Taylor's ambitious plans to move his army upriver by steamboat were solidly at odds with reality. Like so many other aspects of the Mexican War, in which outdated War of 1812 mind-sets had to be replaced with a more up-to-date approach, the U.S. Army's approach to logistics remained antiquated. This had already become apparent through Taylor's inability to get his hands on enough wagons to haul supplies. It was even more obvious on the subject of water craft. The army had very few steamboats, and the U.S. Navy, which had begun blockading Mexican ports, lacked the sort of shallow-draft vessels necessary to navigate inland waters. The few that existed were often barely afloat, thanks to shipworms boring into their wooden hulls. The impact was immediate. "My operations are completely paralyzed," Taylor groused.

The solution was to rent steamboats from private contractors. There was no set fee structure, so each ship's captain set his own price. Inevitably, deals were made and then broken by captains seeking top dollar for their services. Troop movements were delayed for days as soldiers awaited their boat. "She is expected down every hour," Napoleon Dana had written about their promised vessel, the *Aid,* a side-wheel shallow-draft steamboat weighing 137 tons. "And I think it highly probable that we will move day after tomorrow, possibly tomorrow, and maybe not for several days. We are in readiness at any moment."

Dana was overly optimistic. The *Aid*'s owner wanted $250 to deliver soldiers to Camargo, but the quartermaster would go no higher than $100. Negotiations broke down and then ended altogether. A second vessel, the *Neva,* arrived in a pouring rain on June 27 to pick up Dana and elements of the First and Seventh infantries. "This will save us sixty miles' march over bad roads," he exulted in a two-paragraph letter just an hour before shipping out.

The *Neva* was an accident waiting to happen. Its three boilers were weak, overheating, and liable to explode without warning. The strain of carrying five hundred barrels of provisions, plus men and personal belongings, would be far too much and the risks far too high. A disgusted Taylor decided the *Neva* would return to Port Isabel for new boilers. The good news for Dana and his men was that they spent the night aboard the steamboat as they awaited the decision about whether to proceed. Rain was drenching Fort Brown and Matamoros. A roof over their heads was far preferable to yet another miserable, muddy night in a tent. The bad news was that, like many of his fellow soldiers, including Grant, Dana ended up walking to Camargo.

The journey was predictably horrendous. "During the day the sun is very powerful, making it hot and sultry with scarcely a breath of air stirring," he wrote one day. Because of the heat, there was an evening march and a morning march; the long, ragged column slept in the middle of the day and night. Discipline was lax, and the natural obstacles, such as the heat and the waist-deep mud the men encountered while wading the recently flooded river bottoms, prevented speedy progress.

Camargo was on the San Juan River, at a point three miles upriver from its confluence with the Rio Grande. The trek from Matamoros, though just a little more than a hundred miles, averaged nine days for most outfits. "After a fatiguing march," Grant wrote to Julia, "my company has arrived at this place. When we left Matamoros on the 5th of August, it had been raining a great deal, so that the roads were very bad, and, as you well may guess, in this low latitude, the weather was none the coolest. The troops suffered considerably from heat and thirst. Matamoros is a perfect paradise compared to this place."

Camargo had recently been flooded, and the high-water mark could be seen six feet up doorframes in some parts of town. The plaza itself had been scrubbed of grass and was now just a barren patch of white sand. Those floods, and the influx of American soldiers, were all the motivation most local residents needed to evacuate to high ground inland. There they planned to rebuild their city.

Dana's letter to Sue describing Camargo was typically elaborate. "It has some fine houses but none over one story, and like all Mexican houses, flat and tiled on top such as you hear of at Jerusalem in olden times. But like all the Mexican towns we have seen, all the houses on the suburbs are made of cane and thatched with straw. None have wood floors or glass windows, and in fact most of them have no windows at all."

"We are now encamped, my dearest wife, in the plaza, or public square, of Camargo, K and I companies on one side, C and F on another, and D and E on another, whilst the guardhouse, hospital adjutant's office, and so forth occupy the hills. The church is on my side of the square and is by far the prettiest one we have yet seen, though its style of architecture is ancient and odd. It is also the only one we have seen with a finished steeple. It is quite a picturesque building and like all Mexican churches has three bells of different sounds in its steeple." As Dana and the other Americans would soon learn, the bells rang four times a day, providing a natural source of reveille each morning and a nine o'clock reminder to go to bed each night.

THE FIRST MISSISSIPPI'S steamboat journey to Camargo may have been less physically demanding than that of the soldiers who marched, but it was no pleasure cruise. In fact, they might have been better off on foot. "Everybody dissatisfied, unhappy, the boat fetid and stinking, and many, very many, sick. I was suffering dreadfully with the universal complaint, diarrhea, so hot, such a dreadful stench from the necessities, biscuits half cooked, no place to poke one's head in where a moment's comfort could be found, night or day. The sick strewed about, some delirious and crying out for their friends. I became so weak I could scarcely walk," wrote one member of Davis's regiment in his journal.

The ordeal lasted just six days. As they traveled inland, the oceanfront humidity of Brazos Island was replaced by the still and dry desert heat. The swirling sand was replaced by the fine grit of desert dust. As the Mississippians' boat veered from the Rio Grande and up the San Juan for the final three miles of their journey, the landscape remained brown and covered with scrub. That is, until Camargo hove into view. White tents now carpeted the riverbanks. A thin haze of fine caliche dust, stirred up by men and horses, hung over the town like a pall. Taylor's army had overflowed the town square and was now camped along the San Juan, some fifteen thousand strong.

Camargo lacked Brazos Island's infuriating swarms of flies and mosquitoes but more than made up for those pests with deadly scorpions and biting ants. And those thousands of American soldiers camped along the riverbank were once again breeding cholera and dysentery by urinating in the river and using the water for cooking, drinking, and bathing ("The water here," one insightful volunteer wrote of life on the Rio Grande, "opens the bowels like a melting tar")—or in many cases, by *not* bathing at all. A report issued months later by Senior Surgeon R. S. Satterlee noted that "many patients received into our hospitals who probably have not washed their persons for months, and who for weeks have not changed their underclothes, and who are not only filthy but covered with vermin. This remark does not apply, of course, to our brave and faithful soldiers who are an ornament to any service, but particularly to the recruits, a great part of whom are indolent and of course filthy."

The result was an appalling number of deaths. Unmarked graves soon lined the San Juan. Regimental bands so often played a death march for funerals that Camargo's mockingbirds learned to mimic the refrain.

The First Mississippi had already sent 108 men home because of illness. Another 70 were so sick that it appeared they would soon join them, and a handful of Davis's men had died. This had reduced their strength by just over 20 percent. Davis, however, was in robust health. This was fortunate, since he had marched off to war seeking glamour and glory; a sickness-related discharge would have had just the opposite effect.

All Davis could do was make the best of the situation and await further orders. He didn't have to wait long. On September 7, the Rifles marched out of Camargo as part of a three-division American invasion force that was pushing hundreds of miles south into the heart of Mexico. The road led first to Monterrey, where it was rumored that the Mexicans were fortifying to make a stand. Should the war go on, that same road would continue all the way south to Mexico City. The First Mississippi, who would soon be rechristened the Mississippi Rifles, in honor of their being the first rifle regiment in U.S. Army history, would be playing catch-up with the other American squads. General Worth and the Second Division had crossed the river into Mexico on August 19.

Owing to his lack of wagons, Taylor had chosen to leave the bulk of his volunteer force in Camargo, destined to wait for their short enlistments to expire so they could turn right around and head home. Taylor had handpicked those outfits that would accompany him into the field. By sending them forward, Taylor was acknowledging the Mississippi Rifles, though reduced in strength, as an elite volunteer element. This was due to the discipline and military air Davis had instilled — and also to Davis's past relationship with Taylor.

It was just as Davis had wanted it.

EIGHTEEN

Supply Train

SEPTEMBER 13, 1846

Promotion to the leadership of Company C back in July marked the first time in his career that Grant officially had men serving under him. The company was the smallest grouping of soldiers to receive an alphanumeric designation. A battalion was a group of companies that assembled to execute a specific task but then separated when the task was finished. A regiment was a permanent collection of ten companies, a brigade was a collection of regiments, and a division was a collection of brigades.

But the company was the basis of all those groupings. Army regulations stipulated that each be composed of fifty-five soldiers, including a lieutenant and a noncommissioned officer. Before the war, the company had been considered the perfect outfit to man frontier forts, making it feasible to imagine that, had Grant been similarly promoted in peacetime, his command would have been far more prestigious. But there was no frontier outpost for Sam Grant. In fact, he didn't even have a full complement of soldiers. Wartime attrition had affected unit size throughout the army, and the strength of Company C hovered right around three dozen men.

Nonetheless, it was a command, and Grant was rightfully pleased to be given the job. The highlight of his brief tenure was the long march from Matamoros to Camargo. Company C was part of a brigade that accompanied the cavalry and artillery to Camargo via an overland route along the Rio Grande's south shore. Grant got to know his men, copying Taylor's practice of memorizing each soldier's name. These were the soldiers he would soon lead into battle. Grant prepared for that moment as he marched, analyzing their character strengths and weaknesses, just as he analyzed his own, so that when it came time to fight, he would know the strong and the weak, assigning them missions accordingly.

THE GLORY OF command was fleeting. The exigencies of the service being what they were, and with the bulk of Taylor's armies being transported by mules (the army's Quartermaster Department had sent buyers through the Mississippi River valley, purchasing as many of the animals as possible), it was decided in August that someone with a talent for handling equine creatures should be appointed as the regiment's new supply clerk. That new quartermaster was Sam Grant.

He was not the least bit happy about it. Just as there were vast differences between horses and mules, so there was a gap between leading an infantry company into battle and dispensing its supplies. Disparaging the Quartermaster Corps was something of a sport among troops on the Mexican border ("the jackass of a quartermaster," Dana had written, expressing a typical sentiment), and the last thing Grant desired was to be so downgraded. He fought back. "I respectfully protest against being assigned to a duty which removes me from sharing in the dangers and honors of a service with my company at the front, and respectfully ask to be permitted to resume my place in line," he immediately wrote to Brevet Colonel John Garland, his commander.

Garland's response was swift and succinct. "Lt. Grant is respectfully informed that his protest can not be considered. Lt. Grant was assigned to duty as Quartermaster and Commissary because of his observed ability, skill, and persistency in the line of duty. The commanding officer is confident that Lt. Grant can best serve his country in present emergencies under this assignment." If there was any doubt, Garland added in closing: "Lt. Grant will continue to perform his assigned duties."

Grant was unaware of the oblique honor, but his reassignment had come directly from General Taylor, who had noticed Grant's diligent work ethic as far back as Corpus Christi. Taylor had been riding Old Whitey along the beach one day when he observed Grant overseeing a work party clearing underwater obstacles. The men weren't doing the job to Grant's satisfaction, so he had waded in up to his waist to direct them, much to the amusement of onlooking officers. They mocked him from the shore for his drenched uniform. Taylor quickly shut them up. "I wish I had more officers like Grant who would stand ready to set a personal example when needed," Taylor had said.

Taylor was actually paying the young lieutenant an enormous compliment with the assignment. The steady movement of supplies to frontline troops was vital. The flow began back in Philadelphia, at the Schuylkill Arsenal, the Quartermaster Department's main depot. The U.S. Army had divided its logistical support into three units: Ordnance, Subsistence, and Quartermaster. The first group was in charge of bullets and guns, and the second oversaw bulk foods (in particular the barrels of salt pork, flour, and cured beef that formed the bulk of the army diet). Everything else that a soldier might need fell under the quartermaster's purview: uniforms, tents, saddles, manuals, and so on. However, the quartermaster was also in charge of transportation, establishing and maintaining supply depots, and ensuring a steady flow of provisions and material to the troops. Since among these provisions and materials were bullets, guns, and food, quartermasters were actually responsible for every aspect of supply, even those aspects they weren't officially responsible for. But whereas Ordnance and Subsistence operated in the rear, quartermasters were constantly shuttling to and from the front lines, delivering supplies.

Before the war, the Quartermaster Department had been restricted from accumulating more than six months of provisions and gear, basing their figures on the small size of America's standing army. Now, as volunteers flooded the ranks and there was an instant demand for ammunition, uniforms, shoes, and transportation, quartermasters scrambled to purchase equipment. The plea for tents was so great that a national shortage of the "duck" cotton used most commonly in their construction forced the use of flimsy muslin instead. A lack of shoes had the army parceling out contracts to cobblers. Fabric was purchased in bulk and then delivered to private seamstresses, who sewed uniforms from the comfort of their homes.

From Schuylkill, the goods were shipped to a second depot in New Orleans, then loaded on sailing ships for the journey to Port Isabel. Steamboats ferried them upriver to Camargo. There the all-important supplies were distributed to individual units, then loaded onto mules and wagons for the march into Mexico. Here the problem turned from one of production into one of transportation—and of mules in particular. If these notoriously stubborn animals could not be made to perform their job, all that production begun in far-off Philadelphia would be for naught. Taylor needed diligent officers who were good with pack animals. Grant failed to notice the compliment. Happy or not, on August 14 he officially became regimental quartermaster.

On September 5, the Fourth Infantry marched away from

Camargo, bound for Monterrey. When General Worth had passed through two weeks earlier, he had had the foresight to put his men to work widening those trails into a passable road. It was soon a most busy thoroughfare.

Over the course of four weeks, some 6,640 American soldiers, 1,500 pack mules, and 180 wagons carrying 160,000 rations plied that hot, dusty path—the largest movement of American troops in history. Taylor's quartermasters hadn't been able to meet the general's urgent demand for a mass production of supply wagons, so the few he possessed were forced to make an endless round-trip journey. To make the wagoneer's job easier, Taylor insisted that all soldiers and officers travel without personal luxuries—no camp tables, chairs, or other superfluous items. "We will live like real soldiers on nothing but hard fare to eat, hard ground to walk on, only blankets to sleep on, and lots of watchfulness," one young officer wrote to his family back home. "It will be a fine life to make us hearty and strong."

Grant set to managing the regimental supplies with all the professionalism and enthusiasm he could muster. His day began before sunrise, just after the troops had eaten breakfast and begun their march. The enlisted men carried all their personal belongings, including clothing, ammunition, bedding, and a haversack containing the midday meal. Many had begun carrying their water in gourd canteens, preferring them to the army-issue metal or india-rubber variety, which gave the water a foul aftertaste. Officers, however, marched with just a canteen and their weapon. They were entirely dependent on Grant for their food, tents, personal items, and bedding.

Because of the lack of wagons, Grant, the teamsters, and the soldiers under his command then spent several hours loading their mules for the day's march. This was a frustrating undertaking in and of itself. "The tents and cooking utensils had to be made into packages, so that they could be lashed to the back of mules. Sheet iron kettles, tent poles, and mess chests were inconvenient articles to transport in that way. It took several hours to get ready to start each morning, and by the time we were loaded some of the mules first loaded would be tired of standing so long with their loads on their backs. Sometimes one would start to run, bowing his back and kicking up until he scattered his load; others would lie down and try to disarrange their loads by attempting to get on top of them by rolling on them; others with tent poles for part of their loads would manage to run a tent pole on one side of a sapling while they would take the other," he wrote.

Grant added a grace note to his frustrations: "I am not aware of ever having used a profane expletive in my life, but I would have the charity to excuse those who may have done so, if they were in charge of a train of Mexican pack mules."

Lieutenant Samuel French, an artillery lieutenant who graduated from West Point in Grant's class, wrote of a typical morning loading the mules: "One was lassoed and throwed and the pack saddle put on. Then, for his load, two barrels of crackers were securely put on," French remembered. "He surveyed the load from right to left with rolling eyes, squatted low, humped himself, sprang forward, stood on his forefeet and commenced high kicking, exploded the barrels of hardtack with his heels, threw the biscuits in the air with the force of a dynamite bomb, and ran away with the empty barrels dangling behind, as badly scared as a dog with tin buckets tied to his tail."

The mules were the most obvious symbol of a very frustrating time for Grant. He felt powerless. He hated his new job, was angry that he hadn't seen Julia in a year and upset that her father had prohibited them from getting married during his last leave. Most of all, he deeply resented having to wage war in Mexico.

To Grant, Palo Alto and Resaca de la Palma were proof that the Mexicans had lost. Their insistence on retreating farther and farther into their country rather than surrendering enraged him.

"If these Mexicans were any kind of people they would have given us a chance to whip them enough some time ago and now the difficulty would be over; but I do believe they think they will outdo us by keeping us running over the country after them," he wrote to Julia.

His letter of September 6 was one rant after another. "Julia, ain't you getting tired of hearing war, war, war? I am truly tired of it. Here it is now five months that we have been at war and as yet but two battles. I do wish this one would close. If we have to fight I wish we could do it all at once and then make friends," Grant wrote bitterly.

Despite his misery, Grant was a professional. He deftly guided his complement of wagons and mules through the ranks of men marching the dusty road into Mexico. They may have started every morning far behind the troops, but by the time the soldiers made camp each night, Grant had already arrived and unloaded his tents, poles, cooking gear, and provisions. "There was no road so obstructed," wrote Second Lieutenant Alexander Hays, "but that Grant, in some mysterious way, would work his train through and have it in the camp of his brigade before the campfires were lighted."

Not all quartermasters were as ambitious as Grant. There were several instances of baggage trains never catching up with the columns of soldiers, forcing the officers to sleep out in the open, without even a thin wool blanket between them and the hard ground. The desert temperatures, which rose to such withering heights during the day, plummeted each night. Cold and lack of food had a crippling effect on morale, so Grant's nascent talents as a quartermaster were greatly appreciated by the men of the Fourth. He was so busy that he didn't write a single letter to Julia during the entire march.

Despite the fact that the United States had officially invaded Mexico, the truth was that the extent of the American incursion was minimal until August 1846. From Port Isabel to Matamoros to Camargo, Taylor had simply followed the course of the Rio Grande inland. He hugged the border between the two nations, positioning all his troops within miles—and often within eyesight—of the river. As invasions went, it was rather modest, from close-up seemingly just another chapter in the decade-long border war between Mexico and Texas.

At first the penetration from Camargo to Monterrey was more of the same. The American army traveled in a west-by-northwest fashion, parallel to the Rio Grande, until they got to Mier, 120 miles from Matamoros. There they wheeled ninety degrees to the left and marched seventy-five miles due southwest into the heart of Mexico. Mier was atop a hill, with two churches, streets naturally paved by the rocky ground, and two streams running through the middle that came together to form a large creek, known, unforgettably, as the Alamo. Mier had recently been savaged by Comanches. After the locals pleaded for protection, it was agreed that a force of a hundred American soldiers would remain behind in town.

On a map, it was almost possible to draw a straight line that began in Washington, D.C., passed through Mier, and ended in Monterrey. This line represented both the genesis and the hopeful conclusion of the Mexican War. Taylor, for one, didn't think that General Ampudia and the Mexican army would defend Monterrey. The Mexican retreat, he believed, had just been a way of testing the United States' will. The Mexican army would cede those towns along the Rio Grande, knowing that the U.S. Army would one day leave, after which they could be recaptured. Only by penetrating deep into Mexico and once again defeating the Mexican army could the Americans show a willingness to elevate the conflict beyond a mere border squabble—even if it meant marching all the way to Mexico City.

It was deeply symbolic that Mier was the fulcrum of Taylor's advance. The last great border war between Texas and Mexico had been fought in 1842. A band of three hundred starving Texans had crossed the Rio Grande two days before Christmas, searching for food for themselves, their horses, and their families. They thought they found it in Mier. The Texans had spent the past year fighting the Mexicans rather than tending to their farms and families. Two months earlier, thirty-six of their brethren had been blown to bits by Mexican cannons in a conflict just east of San Antonio known as the Dawson Massacre. So when they galloped into Mier, they came as bullies, impotent when facing the Mexican army but all-powerful against the peaceful citizens of Mier. The Texans presented the residents with a staggering list of essential items to be handed over immediately. Included were forty sacks of flour, twelve hundred pounds of sugar, six hundred pounds of coffee, and "200 pairs of strong, coarse shoes, 100 pairs of pantaloons, and a hundred blankets." The mayor of Mier, who knew that more than three thousand Mexican troops were within a day's march of the town. He argued for time to gather so many disparate items.

The Texans galloped back to their side of the Rio Grande in exchange for a promise from the mayor that food and supplies would soon be delivered to their camp. If that promise was broken, the Texans vowed to return.

The Mexican army marched into Mier the next day. It was Christmas Eve, but General Pedro Ampudia was not in a giving mood. He positioned his men on the town's flat rooftops and then waited to spring his trap. He didn't have to wait long.

The Texans galloped back at twilight on Christmas Day, armed to the teeth and eager to extract vengeance. Ampudia's men eagerly opened fire. The Texans were outnumbered ten to one, but more than held their own. Husbanding ammunition and choosing targets carefully, they patiently picked off the Mexican sharpshooters, evening the odds.

The fighting descended into a musket battle that raged for nineteen hours in the city's streets. Some six hundred Mexicans were killed; in contrast, just thirty-one Texans died. But by noon on December 26, the Texans had run low on musket balls. Ampudia sent a messenger to inform them that Mexican reinforcements were galloping to Mier. This was a hoax, a painful battle ruse that the Texans would not find out until after they threw down their arms and surrendered.

The surviving Texans would bitterly regret their decision not to fight until the last man. The Mexicans considered them vigilantes, not prisoners of war, and treated them as criminals. The Texans were marched to Matamoros, where they were held before continuing their march once again, this time toward a prison hundreds of miles south in Mexico City. At the town of Salado, roughly a third of the way from Mier to their waiting cells, they rebelled and escaped on foot into the nearby mountains.

But as the Texans had shown when they first arrived in Mier, they had little talent for living off the land. Starving and dehydrated, all but three were soon rounded up and returned to Salado. When word of their escape reached the Mexican dictator Antonio López de Santa Anna—the same Santa Anna who had defeated the Texans at the Alamo—he was furious. Santa Anna ordered that each of the prisoners be shot. When the regional governor refused to carry out the command, Santa Anna schemed a far more twisted manner of dealing with the Texans. Each was to partake in a life-and-death lottery. The prisoners would be blindfolded and forced to withdraw a single bean from an earthen jar filled with dry white beans, among which were seventeen black beans. When that day, March 25, 1843, came, every man drawing a black bean was shot at dusk. One Texan fell to the ground, pretending to be dead; he escaped that night, only to be captured and shot soon afterward.

The remaining Texans continued their march south to Mexico City at gunpoint, where they were imprisoned at the maximum-security Perote Prison in the heart of Mexico's capital. Their case soon attracted international attention. Diplomats from the United States and Great Britain lobbied to set them free. This effort was ultimately successful, although many of the Texans died before their release was secured in 1844.

These memories were fresh in the minds of American soldiers marching through Mier toward Monterrey. The Black Bean Episode, as it had come to be known, was by no means ancient history. That deadly lottery had taken place during Grant's final months at West Point, and the final Perote prisoners were released while he was stationed with Longstreet at Camp Salubrity. There was even a Mier veteran among the troops. Lieutenant Colonel Samuel Walker of the First Texas Division had been a private during the Battle of Mier, but he had gone on to become one of the leaders of the Salado escape and was one of the three Texans who had avoided recapture. Walker had gotten his revenge by fighting at the battles of Palo Alto and Resaca de la Palma, yet he was by no means through.

As he had in Matamoros, General Taylor insisted that his army not follow a scorched-earth policy, which invading armies had used for thousands of years. There was no raping and pillaging. Instead of just helping themselves to cattle and crops and whatever else they required or wanted, the American soldiers were required to purchase what they needed. The most important of the commodities was corn. Without corn it was impossible to feed the horses and mules or to make corn bread to supplement the men's meals. Though initially scarce, as the landscape grew more lush and tropical with Monterrey's approach, corn could soon be had for just a dollar a bushel. And while the daily search for corn was still a burden to Grant and the other quartermasters, they were at least appeased by the news that Taylor planned to modify his policy toward the locals when they reached Monterrey. Instead of paying for everything, Taylor planned to force civil authorities to provide all his army required, including corn and flour.

Until then, they continued to march. The American army tramped into the foothills of the great Sierra Alva, a spur of the Sierra Madre range that runs down the spine of Mexico. Here the streams ran clear, and large boulders had recently tumbled into the road, dislodged by heavy rains.

The road led them through gorgeous Cerralvo, an old Spanish town of some eighteen hundred people, with a distinctly European appearance: a crumbling castle made of gray stone; a cathedral with a high steeple from which emanated the sound of chimes; a network of canals; the aroma of fresh flowers from the many formal gardens; and a clear stream running through the center of the main street, spanned by ornate bridges arching gracefully from one side to the other. The temperatures were pleasant, a calming departure from the heat of Camargo. Brief daily downpours had the effect of cleansing the air, and many soldiers quickly proclaimed it to be the most welcoming spot they had yet seen in Mexico.

Taylor's army camped outside town, arranging their tents in the familiar company rows, but muddled on the next day, pausing only in the village of Marín—though not to sightsee. The time had come to prepare for battle. Taylor waited for the soldiers and wagons and mules and cannons that had set out from Camargo in his wake, gathering his entire force for the final push into Monterrey.

Like spectators in a great drama, the local citizens watched the invasion with some fascination, but they also sang out words of warning. "The forward division halted again at Marín, twenty-four miles from Monterrey," Grant would remember later. "But this place and Cerralvo were nearly deserted, and men, women, and children were seen running and scattered over the hills as we approached. But when the people returned they found all their abandoned property safe, which must have given them a favorable opinion of *Los Grengos* — 'the Yankees.'" "We saw Mexicans sitting in their doorways along the route to see us pass. They had lost all fear of us, now that they saw we had no intention of injuring peaceful citizens," wrote Lieutenant Abner Doubleday of New York, an 1842 West Point graduate. "They said to us 'Mucho fandango a Monterrey,' which is equivalent to 'they are getting up a dance for you in Monterrey.'"

The Mexican army had spent the entire summer preparing Monterrey for Taylor's fandango. On the nineteenth, the American troops moved within three miles of that vital stronghold. It was, at long last, time to dance.

NINETEEN

Prelude

J efferson Davis, his lack of uniform giving him a decidedly unmilitary appearance, inspected the Mississippi Rifles as they stood, rank and file, in the American encampment outside Monterrey. The formation was tight, the rows neat and bodies erect. All around the Rifles, row after row, acre after acre, mile upon mile, white tents were being pitched as Taylor's army made itself at home.

After dismissing his troops, Davis surveyed Monterrey, three miles to the south. Heavy fog had hung over the city that morning, hiding it entirely from the Americans. But as the sun climbed higher in the sky, the fog burned off, dramatically revealing the object of their long march. Monterrey was a large Mexican city of ten thousand residents, with a cathedral and rows of flat-roofed stone houses. Founded in 1596 by the Spanish, it had been a small settlement until the Mexican War of Independence but had since flourished, becoming the commercial hub of northern Mexico and capital of the Nuevo León state. The city rested on a plateau, built along the banks of the Río Santa Catarina (already very familiar to the Americans as the Río San

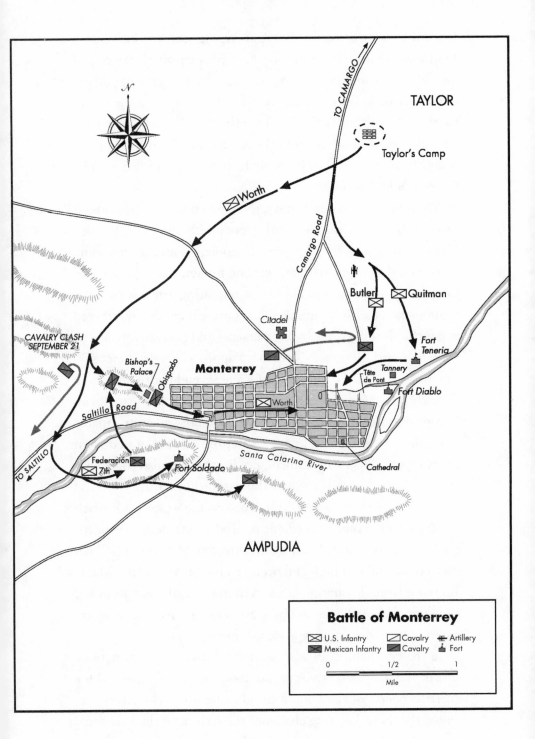

TAYLOR

TO CAMARGO

N

Taylor's Camp

Worth

Camargo Road

Butler

Quitman

Citadel

Fort Teneria

CAVALRY CLASH
SEPTEMBER 21

Bishop's
Palace

Monterrey

Obispado

Tannery

Tête
de Pont

Fort Diablo

Saltillo Road

Worth

TO SALTILLO

Federación
7th

Fort Soldado

Santa Catarina River

Cathedral

AMPUDIA

Battle of Monterrey

U.S. Infantry   Cavalry   Artillery
Mexican Infantry   Cavalry   Fort

0   1/2   1
Mile

Juan, the name it assumed at Camargo), with the lush Sierra Madre rising sharply to the south. A pass cut by the river was the only way through those jagged peaks, leading farther inland to the city of Saltillo. Compared with the harsh desert environment and shabby adobe cities along the Rio Grande, Monterrey was an oasis of civilization to the Americans. "This is the most beautiful spot that it has been my fortune to see in this world," Grant would describe it.

Yet at this moment in history, there was nothing idyllic about Monterrey. It was studded with forts and batteries. A tricolor Mexican flag hung limply from a flagpole, pointedly reminding Davis and the others that they were on foreign soil. The city was the ideal defensive stronghold for a retreating army, with fortifications made of solid granite. A prominent citadel, weathered to a forbidding dark hue by the elements and time, rose from the plain to guard Monterrey's northern approach. A dry moat surrounded the citadel's walls, which were seven hundred feet long on each side. Mexican cannons—aged castoffs imported from Europe that were heavy and hard to reload but still quite capable of decimating any army that came within range—jutted from the parapets. American soldiers, predictably but also somewhat ominously, had already begun calling it the black fort.

There were even more fortifications on the western approach to Monterrey. Loma de Federación and Loma de Independencia were a pair of hills looming over the city like sentinels. Each was a thousand feet high and occupied by the Mexican soldiers. The view from the summits was stunning and all-encompassing, allowing the Mexicans a bird's-eye view of American troop movements as the army approached the city.

In the center of it all was Monterrey itself, with its narrow streets and alleys and thick wood doors, seemingly tailored for guerrilla operations and house-to-house fighting. Monterrey presented the most daunting challenge the Americans had yet seen.

There were no sweeping vistas as there had been at Palo Alto or Resaca de la Palma, where the terrain had been suited to cavalry charges and an artillery battle. Taylor, perhaps making his first blunder of the war, had even left most of his large cannons back at the Rio Grande, thinking they would slow down his army during the rugged overland journey.

Monterrey would be a more intimate battle. The fighting would be hand-to-hand and the enemy so close that a man might smell the other's breath as they fought. "The city has to be carried," one American officer noted. He then added with prescience, "The bayonet will probably have to do the work."

The Mexican army had made great changes in leadership in the three months since both sides had last met. Gone was Major General Mariano Arista, whose overconfidence had cost him Palo Alto and Resaca de la Palma. Replacing him as commander of Mexico's Army of the North had been General Francisco Mejía, who in turn was replaced by Ampudia. As the Americans knew all too well, Ampudia was also the man who had orchestrated the massacre at Mier two years earlier.

Ampudia owed his new command to none other than General Antonio López de Santa Anna, the infamous butcher of the Alamo, Goliad, and the Black Bean Episode. Santa Anna's postwar exile had come to an end during August, as Taylor's army prepared to move from Camargo toward Monterrey. President Polk had foolishly arranged for Santa Anna to be smuggled back into Mexico from his exile in Cuba on August 14, with the understanding that the Mexican general would find a way to rise to power and then align himself with the American side. Santa Anna wasted no time in taking control of the Mexican army, but rather than befriend the Americans, he now ached to defeat them. Though based hundreds of miles south in Mexico City, Santa Anna had been in constant contact with Ampudia via messengers on horseback.

Santa Anna had originally ordered Ampudia to march his army all the way back through the narrow notch in the mountains to Saltillo, there to make a stand. The rotund major general, however, feared his men would mutiny if he retreated too far into the Mexican interior. He also recognized something Santa Anna could not have known from so far away: Monterrey's tremendous military advantages. With the broad plain sprawled before the city, and the mountains providing natural protection to the rear, an attacking army could approach from only one direction. By fortifying Monterrey's approaches, Ampudia could draw Taylor's army in and then decimate it.

Santa Anna had poured in reinforcements, and Ampudia had pressed local men into service, giving him an army numbering seventy-three hundred regulars and three thousand raw newcomers. Recognizing that mere manpower was not enough, Ampudia had also ordered Mexico's two top military engineers to transform the city's tangled streets into a deadly labyrinth. Mariano Reyes, a lieutenant colonel, and Luis Robles, a captain, designed a complex network of revetments, breastworks, gun platforms, and impromptu fortresses that offered maximum defensive protection. Cavalry and infantry alike had worked together all through the summer, filling sandbags and building walls across thoroughfares. The men had drilled holes into the sides of many homes and city buildings to serve as gun ports, placed sandbags atop flat-roofed houses to protect Mexican soldiers as they fired down on the Americans, and barricaded city streets to prevent easy troop movement. Some streets even had cannons strategically situated to fire into an oncoming force.

There was more. Sensing that the citadel and two fortified hilltops might not be enough to stop the Americans, Ampudia had turned a former tannery into a heavily armed and manned redoubt. La Tenería, as it was known, now garrisoned 350 soldiers, and earthen berms concealed four specially built cannons atop the roof.

Ampudia had also ordered the hasty construction of breast-works at the northwest and northeast approaches to Monterrey—the directions from which the Americans would travel. Even the La Purísima Bridge, with its prominent statue of the Virgin Mary, was defended by an earthworks and three cannons. Monterrey, one American officer noted as he surveyed the seemingly impregnable defenses for the first time, "is a perfect Gibraltar." Remembering those great cliffs rising from the Hudson, he added that Monterrey was "a second West Point in strength."

With the road north from the Rio Grande now blocked by Taylor's army, Ampudia was left with just two military choices: flee through that cut in the mountains to Saltillo or defend Monterrey until the last man.

Quite obviously, the Mexican general wasn't going anywhere.

DAVIS KNEW LITTLE of the city's amazing defensive details as he gazed across the plain. He and the other Americans were camped in an area three miles long and three-quarters of a mile wide that the people of Monterrey called the Bosque de San Domingo (American troops had misidentified the local oaks and bald cypresses and renamed the campground Walnut Springs).

No matter what the camp was called, the First Mississippi and the other volunteer regiments were not entirely welcome. The ongoing animosity between regular army and volunteer soldiers drove a divisive wedge through the campsite, particularly now that the regulars had seen combat and were skittish about depending on the untried volunteers for support in the battle that was soon to come.

That wariness was well founded. Even without combat experience, the regulars had endured years of training and discipline specifically designed to harden them for engagements such as Monterrey. While the volunteers had been farming or sitting in some plush office back in their hometown, sleeping with their wives, and generally coming and going as they pleased, the regulars had lived in barracks and tents and had put up with military rigors: morning reveille; brutal punishments such as flogging with a lash and "bucking and gagging," which saw a soldier hogtied for hours with a stick in his mouth; a meager diet of bread, salted pork, and weak coffee; and even sleeping two to a bed when posted to a barracks. Discipline was strict: an officer was allowed to strike an enlisted man at any time, without provocation and without fear of punishment. Those that chose to flee army life by deserting were whipped fifty times with a cowhide lash if caught. Then, his back still dripping blood, the deserter's head would be shaved and he would be dismissed from the service to the beat of a drum ("drummed out of the army" was the official phrase). There was little adventure to being a soldier, and little chance for advancement. The only time of day when a man could relax and find peace was at dusk. "Later in the evening, after having answered our names at retreat, which was beat precisely at sunset, groups assembled round the tent doors, to smoke, chat, tell tales, or sing songs. . . . At nine o'clock we fell in, to answer our names at tattoo roll call, when the drums and fifes played a few merry tunes, after which the roll was called and we were then dismissed to bed. About fifteen minutes were then suffered to elapse, when the drummer beat three distinct taps on the drum, at which signal every light in tents or quarters had to be extinguished, and the most strict silence preserved, on pain of the offender being sent to the guard-house — the immediate punishment for all willful infractions of the rules of the service," wrote one enlisted soldier.

The volunteer regiments hadn't gone through any such hardship. For them, becoming a soldier had been as simple as answering a patriotic rallying cry. They'd sailed off to war as bands played and women cried. Places like New Orleans and

Brazos Island and even Camargo were their first introduction to military living. Their lack of discipline and disrespect for the protocol had caused immediate friction between them and the regulars. As the volunteers began drinking too much, brawling too much, arguing constantly about whether slavery was acceptable, getting sick, and deserting back to their farms and families with little threat of punishment, the divide grew.

The Mississippi Rifles' dandy red and white uniforms, their cutting-edge armament, and the fact that they'd taken a steamer all the way upriver to Camargo rather than walked was yet another reason for the regulars to loathe them. Military discipline was designed to immunize men against lapsing into chaotic behavior during the heat of battle. The regulars had already proved themselves in Palo Alto and Resaca de la Palma; nobody knew how the volunteers would behave under fire. Thus Taylor's decision to separate his army into three divisions—two composed solely of regular army soldiers and a third made up of volunteer recruits. The Mississippi Rifles were grouped with the First Tennessee (which had been joined by the First Kentucky and the First Ohio, under the command of Thomas L. Hamer, the congressman who had submitted Grant's application to West Point and changed the young man's name in the process). Taylor had marched his troops toward Monterrey in order of battle, with the volunteers taking up the rear. It was unstated but understood that the Third Division of Taylor's army wouldn't see action unless absolutely necessary. This subtle point was reinforced when Taylor ordered an armed reconnaissance of the city on the afternoon of September 19 but didn't allow a single member of the volunteers' division to join the task.

Davis's presence only made things worse. The majority of regular army officers were Whigs. This group included both Taylor and his boss back in Washington, Major General Winfield Scott. President Polk's Democratic Party had a long-standing distrust of the armed forces, believing that the nation had little need for a standing army. Volunteers like Davis were his ideal soldiers. "It has never been our policy to maintain large standing armies in time of peace," Polk had declared before the war began. "They are contrary to the genius of our free institutions, would impose heavy burdens on the people and be dangerous to public liberty. Our reliance for protection and defense on the land must be mainly on our citizen soldiers, who will be ever ready, as they have been ever ready in times past, to rush with alacrity, at the call of their country, to her defense."

The president's disdain for the Whigs was public knowledge. While he was Speaker of the House during the mid-1830s, debate between the Democrats and Whigs had been particularly heated and all too often took on personal overtones. Democrats held the slimmest of majorities — 108–107, with 24 independents — so throughout Polk's reign as Speaker he constantly battled to keep his party allied, recruiting independent votes (one Democratic measure, adopted from a long-held belief of Andrew Jackson's, argued for the abolition of West Point, but as Sam Grant was all too aware during his plebe year, the measure failed) and jousting verbally with Whigs. Polk's smug behavior and insults offended many Whig members of Congress, who heckled him from the floor of the House and challenged him to at least two duels (which Polk refused to accept).

Polk was getting his revenge as president. To the disgust of the regular army corps, he had begun appointing Democrats from the volunteer ranks to fill openings for new senior officers. Though Colonel Jefferson Davis had not been appointed by Polk, they were members of the same political party and shared a close bond. This combination of high rank, volunteer status, and Democratic allegiance, as well as Davis's unequivocal support of Polk, threatened to make him a pariah at Walnut Springs.

The saving grace was Taylor. His army had arrived in

Monterrey eleven years, almost to the day, after the death of
Sarah Knox. This sad anniversary marked a pivotal moment in
the reconciliation between Davis and the general, an unlikely
chance for redemption and healing that neither one could have
anticipated. The regular army's officer corps may have distrusted
Davis, but Taylor did not—and that was enough. The Mississippi Rifles would not be in the first wave of attackers, yet they
were a definite part of Taylor's strategy for seizing Monterrey.

Taylor's battle plans were born on the evening and night of
September 19. That day's armed reconnaissance under Brevet Major Joseph K. F. Mansfield, the brilliant career engineer
who had earned a battlefield promotion for his design of Fort
Brown, had detailed Monterrey's stunning new defenses. A frontal assault or an extended siege was out of the question because
the American army lacked large cannons and mortars. Instead,
the bulk of Taylor's forces would take up positions on the plain
north of the city walls. Jefferson Davis and the Mississippi Rifles
would stand among that broad phalanx. The army's rank and
file would remain in formation, just as at Palo Alto. And just as
on that prairie battlefield, the Americans would be a long-range
target for Mexican cannons as they stood out in the open.

That was the point: they were a decoy. As they drew fire and
attention, Brigadier General William Worth would march west
and then south in a grand loop that would circumvent the hilltop
fortresses at La Federación and La Independencia. The plan was
to mount a surprise attack that would block the road to Saltillo,
serving the twofold purpose of sealing the Mexican army inside
Monterrey and cutting the city off from the rest of Mexico. It
would, in effect, become a military island. Worth would then
continue his broad sweep and enter the city from the west,
bypassing La Independencia and La Federación, if possible, since
storming the heights by force might mean huge casualties.

Worth's flanking movement would also set in motion a

pincer action. His Second Division would hammer the city from the high ground to the west; Taylor's First and Third divisions—Mississippi Rifles included—would simultaneously launch a two-pronged frontal assault on Monterrey, charging in from the north and the east. The only remaining compass point would be blocked by the Río Santa Catarina, its shallow but swift current providing a neat southern boundary to the battle, hemming in the Mexicans inside the city.

The plan was bold. Military thinking held that an attacking force should outnumber an entrenched defender by three to one in order to ensure success. The overmatched Taylor was putting that theory to the test—and then some. He was also flirting with disaster by splitting his small army, just as he had done at Palo Alto, where his had been the army on the defensive.

The key to Taylor's plan was stealth and speed.

Neither one materialized.

ON THE AFTERNOON of the twentieth, Worth and his Second Division augured northwest out of Walnut Springs, setting Taylor's plan in motion. He led a force of 1,651 regular army soldiers, along with the First Texas Mounted Rifles. The Texans were an unusual force: trained and armed like infantry, but with every single man mounted on horseback. This made them an agile, deadly fighting machine. Another band of Texans, the Second Mounted Rifles, were being held in reserve, prepared to gallop to the rescue should Worth get in a jam. Topping it all off, Worth's force included two companies of "flying" artillery, so called because their lightweight, horse-drawn bronze six-pounders (and on occasion twelve-pound howitzers) could easily be galloped to any strategic position on the battlefield. The British army had pioneered the concept with their "horse artillery," but the Americans were taking it to a new level. Ten companies composed each

U.S. artillery regiment, and one company per regiment was designated as "flying." The six-pounder had a range of fifteen hundred yards and weighed less than half a ton. By attaching the wheeled gun carriage to a limber, which was then fastened to a horse, it was possible to quickly repel a surprise cavalry assault or a sudden infantry flanking movement. From the cavalry to the infantry to the lightweight horse-drawn cannons, Worth's was a division designed for nonstop movement.

The lot of them would march to the Saltillo road, staying hidden from the Mexicans if at all possible. They would seize the road, keeping their distance from the guns atop La Independencia and La Federación, and then invade the city from the west.

Taylor planned to launch the second half of the offensive on his side of the city, so cutting off the Saltillo road before sunrise the next morning was paramount. If there was any general upon whom Taylor could depend to complete that task, no matter what the obstacles, it was Worth. He was fifty-two, a handsome and sometimes petulant man with wavy hair and a barrel chest. A Quaker by birth and a soldier by choice, he began his career as a private during the War of 1812 and rose through the ranks to become an officer. A round of grape had pierced his thigh at the Battle of Lundy's Lane during that conflict, leaving him lame in one leg. Worth, who had later served as commandant of cadets at West Point, had the distinction of being Taylor's favorite general — and easily the most capable.

Sadly for Worth, the Mexicans had not spent the summer fortifying their city only to have him sneak around the back and invade through its weakest point. Their lookouts caught sight of Worth's force and quickly figured that he meant to block the Saltillo road. They would give him that, for the Mexicans had no use for the winding dirt thoroughfare until the battle was won. However, the heights of La Independencia and La Federación were of vital strategic importance. Rather than bother with an attempt to hold the Saltillo road, Ampudia rushed reinforcements to La Independencia, which featured two sturdy stone forts.

As storm clouds gathered, Worth's army marched through the afternoon across recently harvested fields of sugarcane and corn. The rich soil caked to their feet, and the uneven stalks jutting from the ground slowed their march to an anguished plod. The horse-drawn six-pounders bogged down in the mud. By sunset, Worth's division had managed to travel only six miles in four hours. He was reluctant to push on in the darkness, fearful of his army's getting split or of a sudden Mexican attack. Just as much as he needed to sever the Saltillo road by daylight, Worth needed to keep his men out of danger. As the rain began, he pressed on—but carefully.

"We were soon all wet through to the skin," Dana wrote. "It soon turned so dark you could not see your hand before you, and the cold was keenly felt through wet clothes. We marched forward two miles farther, and there on the wet ground of a hillside with no cover, wet clothes, on a cold and cheerless night, and as dark as pitch, we lay on our arms with nothing but our coats and not even able to take exercise to keep warm."

The troops were exhausted, but the order to sleep in the field was hardly welcomed. The Second Division had left their tents at Walnut Springs in order to travel light. They would doze fitfully in the cool mountain air, their bodies trapped in the harsh cocoon of a strafing wind, muddy soil, and freezing rain. A warming flame would have been nirvana and would have made the night pass more quickly, but the downpour and the wartime need for concealment made campfires impossible. The result, Dana wrote to Sue, "was the most cheerless, comfortless, unhappy night I ever spent."

TWENTY

Monterrey, Day One

SEPTEMBER 21, 1846

K nowing that his troops were paying close attention to his behavior, General Zachary Taylor oozed a calculated confidence as the time for battle drew near. His optimism wasn't altogether feigned.

The Fourth Infantry, minus Grant, had spent a long and laborious night out on the open plain in front of Monterrey. The quartermaster was watching the battle plan unfold from the safe distance of Walnut Springs. The view was unique, and one he might not have enjoyed on the front lines. He was, in effect, seeing the feints and parries of battle from the same perspective as General Taylor. Five hundred unobstructed yards of flat earth separated their forward position from the city walls. Taylor had sent two companies of artillery along with Worth, which left few cannons at his disposal. The remaining guns consisted almost entirely of Lieutenant Braxton Bragg's and Brevet Captain Randolph Ridgely's horse cannons. Traditional military doctrine held that artillery was static, anchored to one position on the battlefield at all times because of its ponderous weight. The two primary battlefield weapons were the traditional field gun, which utilized a low, flat trajectory when fired, making it ideal for anti-personnel rounds, and the howitzer, which featured a shorter barrel but elevated the muzzle upward, for a blast that rained down razor-sharp shrapnel from above (the third form of cannon, the mortar, launched projectiles at a severe upward angle and was better utilized as a siege gun than as a field piece).

Bragg and Ridgely were just two of the young American officers at the forefront of the revolutionary new "flying artillery" concept. Captain Samuel Ringgold, the fifty-year-old son of a congressman, was considered by many the "father of modern artillery" and the man who had done more than any other American to promote the new concept. Ironically, he had been mortally wounded on the plains of Palo Alto while applying those tactics in actual combat for the first time. Now it was left to Bragg and Ridgely to carry on his legacy.

For now, Taylor resorted to the traditional. Though he had ordered the heavy artillery left behind in Camargo, he had hedged his bets by dragging three very large guns up from the Rio Grande. There was nothing "flying" about the pair of twenty-four-pound howitzers and the cumbersome ten-pound mortar now being moved into siege range. Once in position, these guns—courtesy of Company C, First U.S. Heavy Artillery—would be capable of dropping monstrous shells on Monterrey. Taylor's scouts had discovered a natural hedgerow out on the plain, big enough to conceal those cannons and hundreds of men. During the night the artillery and soldiers had dug into the depression behind that berm. "The point for establishing the siege battery was reached, and the work performed without attracting the attention of the enemy," Grant noted.

Grant's Fourth Infantry, which had also supported Ridgely's artillery at Palo Alto, spent the night of September 20 as part of a forward egress from Walnut Springs. The men huddled together in the brisk air. Their bodies had been warmed at first from the labor of placing the guns, but now they were chilled and their clothes were still damp with sweat. Back at Walnut Springs, watch fires kept soldiers warm when breaks in the weather made it possible, but fire was out of the question for the forward troops. Side by side, some standing watch, some curled up on the ground, they waited out the darkness, praying for morning to come, even though they knew all too well that daylight would not deliver them from their misery. Come dawn they would be warmed by the sun and would then race, on command, toward the unknown of Monterrey's defenses. As cold as the night might have been, nothing made them tremble inside the way thoughts of the impending attack did.

Their safety blanket was those three big guns. Combined with Bragg and Ridgely's flying artillery, the howitzers and mortar formed an unusual aspect of Taylor's strategy. Normally, heavy artillery might be used to besiege the city, as the Mexicans had attempted at Fort Brown. Or the guns could be used against columns of infantry, as at Palo Alto. But during his reconnaissance on the nineteenth, Major Mansfield realized quite astutely that the Mexican army would never leave the city. Their battle plan was to draw the Americans in to create an optimal field of fire. Taylor's men, if all went according to plan, would march straight into the fortified kill zones. But relying so heavily on these strongpoints meant the Mexicans were effectively stuck: they couldn't travel from strongpoint to strongpoint without risking annihilation, and they couldn't march out onto the prairie without throwing their entire battle plan into disarray.

Taylor's artillery had just enough firepower to prove Mansfield's analysis was correct. The big guns were trained on the Black Fort and La Tenería. These would keep the Mexicans pinned down inside their fortifications. Should Ampudia's army venture out, most likely with a cavalry force, the artillery would cut them down. And when the time came for an American assault, those cannons would lay down suppressing fire to protect the American charge.

That protection had its limits. Any frontal assault on Monterrey was going to be bloody.

At dawn, Worth's forces rose from the ground several miles to Taylor's right. Once again they slogged toward the Saltillo road. As they did, the big guns of Company C, First U.S. Heavy Artillery, opened fire. The diversionary tactic was designed to keep the Mexicans focused on the First and Third divisions, distracting them from sending further reinforcements to block Worth's advance.

The Mexican batteries answered loud and clear. "At daylight," Grant wrote with understatement, "fire was opened on both sides and continued with, what seemed to me at that day, great fury."

The advantage was clearly with the defenders. Hidden within La Tenería and the Black Fort were thirty cannons—all of them trained on the spot five hundred yards across the open plain where American bodies were pressed as flat as humanly possible against the wet soil. Only a lip of earth stood between them and those Mexican cannons.

Grant could take it no longer. "My curiosity got the better of my judgment, and I mounted a horse and rode to the front to see what was going on."

A GREAT DEAL was going on, all over the battlefield. Worth's division, for instance, was finally reaching its objective. "We started to place ourselves in the position of the Saltillo road," Second Lieutenant George Gordon Meade wrote to his wife, "by which we should cut off the retreat of the enemy and have an eye to the advance of his reinforcements, said to be daily expected." Among his troops were three infantry divisions: the Fifth, the Eighth, and the Seventh. Pete Longstreet was in the Eighth, his men marching in a narrow picket line. Dana was in the Seventh. Meade rode close to Worth as part of the Topographical Corps, the general's indispensable guide to the landscape and defenses that lay just ahead. Meade was famished. He had been caught out with the rest of the two-thousand-plus force during the rainy night. He had slept as best he could, wrapped in his trusty cloak, which was made waterproof by its india-rubber lining. The lack of campfires had prevented the troops from cooking even a simple evening meal. Now his stomach rumbled and a deep chill lingered in his bones.

Up at the very front of the taut column, the Texas cavalry served as the advance guard. They were followed closely by the three units of infantry and two more of flying artillery.

The twin summits loomed above Meade's left shoulder— Independencia closest and Federación on the far side of the river. The fortress on that peak belonged to the local archbishop. Like the Black Fort on the opposite side of Monterrey, it had been given a nickname by the American forces—in this case, quite logically, the Bishop's Palace. At 6:30 hellfire rained down from the fortified sanctuary; a horse was killed, a wagon was struck, and a soldier in the Fifth Infantry lost his leg. Yet the American flanking movement had taken Worth's men farther and farther west of the city, pointedly ensuring that the Americans were just beyond truly effective artillery range. The Mexicans helped out by using solid rounds that lacked explosive charges. The balls of iron were more a nuisance to the Americans than anything else—a reminder to look lively and pay attention. When Meade had ridden out with Major Mansfield as part of the initial Monterrey reconnaissance, the Mexicans had been so accurate that a passing cannonball whooshed within two feet of Meade's pant leg—and almost crushed the nearby Zachary Taylor. The Mexican gunners may have had inferior munitions, but they were no amateurs.

The Texans, hungry after the miserable night, had ridden ahead and then dismounted to eat from a cornfield. Just north of the Saltillo road, they chose a poor time and place to stop. "As we were turning the corner of the road entering the valley, the enemy showed himself with a large cavalry force, some two thousand, with some five hundred infantry, evidently intending to dispute our passage," wrote Meade.

Those two regiments of Mexican cavalry—the Jalisco Lancers and Guanajuato Lancers—launched a sudden attack.

As the Texans hurried back to their mounts, Longstreet took the initiative and led his men forward to counterattack. His quick action gave the Texans time to take cover near a wooden fence and begin firing straight into the Mexican horsemen. "The Mexican cavalry charged on our people most gallantly, but were received with so warm a fire as to throw them into confusion," Meade exulted.

The Mexican lancers pulled back to regroup. Meanwhile, Worth's two batteries of flying artillery charged toward the front of the American column and unlimbered their cannons. Within minutes the six-pounders were hurling canister rounds into the massed Mexican horsemen. The carnage was instant, maiming and killing men and horses. Blood, lances, and plumed stovepipe shako hats littered the ground; the morning air was rent by the screams of dying men and animals. Among the fallen was Lieutenant Colonel Juan Nájera, the commander of the Jalisco Regiment.

The attack had been nothing less than a suicide charge. "The infantry and a portion of the cavalry retired towards the town, but twelve hundred of the cavalry went in the direction of Saltillo, and have not been heard from since," wrote Meade. As Mansfield had predicted, the Mexican army was in full defensive mode, ill prepared to venture outside Monterrey's city walls. That a single horse regiment had lost one hundred men, with another three hundred wounded, before fleeing to fight another day was an indication that the battle for Monterrey was no place for their cavalry.

Soon, Meade and the other Americans were not just taking and holding but crossing beyond the Saltillo road. This sealed the Mexican army inside the city. Worth ordered a messenger to gallop back toward Taylor with the news that "the town is ours."

The time was early, shortly after 8:00 A.M., and the message as premature as the day was young. Controlling the Saltillo road was a fine accomplishment, but it was no guarantee that the Americans would enter Monterrey, let alone take the city.

Meade rode alongside General Worth as the commander devised a strategy. Worth had a reputation for behaving impulsively, but now he remained collected. "We were on the Saltillo road beyond the gorge through which it passes into town, and…this gorge was heavily defended by artillery on the tops of those hills, and by a strong work around the Bishop's Palace, on one hill, and a redoubt opposite, on the other." The dilemma was whether it was smarter to send an assault force up the slopes of La Independencia and La Federación, or simply to continue sweeping around to the southernmost side of the city, probing for a more vulnerable place to enter.

Worth appraised the battlefield with his veteran eye, focusing on the enemy's control of the high ground. "The examination," the general later wrote, revealed "the impracticability of any effective operations against the city, until possessed of the exterior forts and batteries."

Worth had to alter his plans if they were to stand any chance. "It now became necessary to take those heights before we could advance upon the town," Meade later remembered, breaking the situation down to its simplest terms in a letter home. The hills would be assaulted, one at a time, regardless of the human cost.

Shortly after noon, Captain Charles Ferguson Smith and his red-legged infantry—the same men who had so bravely waded the Rio Colorado five months earlier—forded the Santa Catarina and then began clawing their way up Federación's rocky slope. This time they were joined by two hundred Texas Rangers.

The gritty force took fire from the moment they stepped into the river and then became pinned down as they climbed. Worth ordered the Seventh Infantry to move forward and reinforce them. "Up the hill we went with a rush, and the Texans ahead like devils," Dana wrote Sue, trying to sound fearless. "On we came like an irresistible wave. Nothing could stop us."

AT THE SAME time, on the opposite side of Monterrey, the Fourth Infantry was still being held in reserve, back by the three siege guns. An affable Georgian and the son of a Revolutionary War major general, General David E. Twiggs ("a grand looking old man, six feet two in stature, with long flowing white hair and a beard which hung over his broad breast like Aaron's" was how one officer described him) would normally have been in command of the First Division, but he had inadvertently taken an overdose of laxative before the battle, believing that a bullet would pass through his body without harm if his bowels were properly loosened.

Lieutenant Colonel John Garland had assumed command of Twiggs's division. Garland was a capable man and had served in the military for more than three decades. But he had never led a charge, and now his brave leadership was undermined by bad tactical decisions. As he cautiously led eight hundred soldiers of the First Division forward under withering fire from the Black Fort and La Tenería, the open plain left his men unprotected, with nowhere to take cover. The units fragmented into smaller groups as they ran forward. The Maryland and District of Columbia volunteers veered too far to the left, toward La Tenería, and were soon subjected to an even greater profusion of artillery and musket fire. Almost all of them lost their nerve. They turned and fled back to Walnut Springs, leaving just one commander and a band of seventy men to press onward into the city.

On the right side of Garland's advance, the regulars pressed on, advancing slowly toward the city walls. La Tenería rose to their left and the Black Fort to the right. The plan was for Garland to make his way into the city and then meet up with Major Mansfield, Taylor's superscout, who would have sneaked into Monterrey to conduct yet another reconnaissance. Mansfield would help lead the way through the maze of streets so that they might attack La Tenería from the rear.

Grant arrived in the small depression behind Taylor's big guns. He was on horseback, still studying the battle as a passive observer. He could hear gunfire from inside the city as Garland's men began a series of street battles on their way to La Tenería. Reinforcements were clearly needed. Taylor decided on a two-pronged response: the Third Division, which included Jefferson Davis and the Mississippi Rifles, would charge directly at La Tenería, and Grant's Fourth Infantry would simultaneously rush forward to reinforce Garland. "I had been there but a short time when an order to charge was given," Grant noted. "Lacking the moral courage to return to camp—where I had been ordered to stay—I charged with the regiment."

So it was that Sam Grant and Jeff Davis rode into battle together.

"As soon as the troops were out of the depression they came under fire from the Black Fort," Grant wrote. The Fourth was totally exposed, with no place to take cover on the flat plain. The Mississippi Rifles and the First Tennessee were farther to the left, temporarily screened from the Black Fort's guns. "As they advanced they got under fire from batteries guarding the east, or lower, end of the city, and musketry. About one-third of the men engaged in the charge were killed or wounded in the space of a few minutes."

The losses were horrendous, with hundreds of American bodies maimed and pierced by a relentless stream of flying metal—rounds of grape and canister musket balls and pulverizing barrages from the Black Fort's eighteen-pounders. "We were being *enfiladed*," one astonished Maryland volunteer would later write, choosing a chilling military term that described troops' being exposed to gunfire along the entire length of their formation. It was slaughter—and for the first time in the war, Americans were on the receiving end.

Grant and the Fourth retreated to get out of range, moving parallel to the city walls instead of fleeing backward. "When we got to the place of safety the regiment halted and drew itself together—what was left of it." In the midst of it all, he thought of his dearest Julia and his love for her.

Grant was one of the few saddled members of the Fourth; even the regimental adjutant, First Lieutenant Charles Hoskins, was on foot. The thirty-two-year-old Hoskins was an 1836 graduate of West Point who had spent much of his career in frontier outposts such as Kansas and Oklahoma. Grant had known him since their time at the Jefferson Barracks. Not only did Hoskins outrank Grant and carry the regimental colors, but he was also in poor health. Grant offered up his horse. Hoskins graciously accepted, not bothering to command Grant to return to Walnut Springs or even register surprise that his regimental quartermaster was in the thick of the charge instead of tending to the company mules. It was understood that Grant would remain at the front.

Desperate to be mounted when the next charge came, Grant scrambled to find a horse. He "saw a soldier, a quartermaster's man, mounted not far away. I ran to him, took his horse and was back with the regiment in a few minutes. In a short time we were off again; and the next place of safety I can remember being in was a field of cane or corn to the northeast of the lower batteries." Hoskins—and Grant's original horse—were nowhere to be seen, and the lieutenant soon learned why. "The adjutant to whom I had loaned my horse was killed, and I was designated to act in his place."

Temporarily at least, Grant was no longer a quartermaster. With the Fourth now having lost a third of its officers and men, he was responsible for carrying the regimental colors into Monterrey.

It was shortly before eleven in the morning as the Fourth rested up for the next charge, finding relative comfort and cover in the shelter of some low houses on the edge of town. They could hear the musket fire as the First Mississippi, off to the far left, stormed the bastion at La Tenería. Mexican general Mejía had just reinforced the former tannery with 140 more light infantry and an additional cannon.

Davis was on foot. The high-strung Tartar was safely back at Walnut Springs with Davis's longtime slave Jim Green. Three hundred yards out, the First Mississippi came under attack and took cover to return fire. Davis's men were flustered by the brand-new experience of having men shoot at them, and it showed most of all in their marksmanship. Despite the Whitney rifles' superior range, the First Mississippi's bullets weren't killing any Mexicans. "Damn it," Davis griped to one of his officers, pacing back and forth behind his lines, "why do not the men get nearer to the fort? Why waste ammunition from such a great distance?" But it was not the gap between the Mississippi volunteers and their enemy that was the problem: Davis's regiment was "seeing the elephant," as American soldiers described that first overwhelming whoosh of combat. They were not turning in panic, as most of the Maryland and District of Columbia volunteers had during Garland's attack, but they were also too timid to press the battle.

Davis was so sentimental that he sealed letters to Varina with a kiss, but on the battlefield he swore a blue streak, despite having repeatedly promised his wife that he would quit using profanity. Now he screamed at the Rifles to move forward, each well-chosen word designed to terrify and motivate even the most timid planter or banker-cum-soldier. The First Mississippi heeded his command until, 180 yards from the fort, they threw their bodies to the ground once again, pinned down by Mexican fire. "Now is the time," Davis fumed. "Great God, if I had thirty men with knives I could take that fort."

The First Tennessee was to their right. Together they made an imposing force, but they had to act immediately.

The guns of La Tenería went inexplicably quiet at that very moment. When the Third Division commander General Quitman was slow to issue fresh orders, redheaded Lieutenant Colonel Alexander McClung of Mississippi's Company K took matters into his own hands. With a cry of "Charge!" McClung impulsively rushed to the fort, waving his saber. Davis and the First Mississippi rose as one and sprinted behind him, heedless of the fact that their rifles lacked the bayonets necessary for the close-quarters fighting that surely awaited those lucky enough to make it over the walls.

Quitman hastily ordered the First Tennessee—whose muskets *did* possess bayonets—to do the same. Letting loose with a piercing battle cry of their own, they sprinted straight at La Tenería. The fort's guns opened fire, barking musket balls and grape at the frenzied Americans. In seconds the landscape was splattered with blood, bones, and brains, and so many of the First Tennessee died that forever after they were known as the Bloody First. McClung clambered up the fort's rampart and waved his sword to encourage the troops. Davis was close behind. Spying a

General Zachary
Taylor

An aging General
Winfield Scott,
pictured at the start
of the Civil War
*(Photograph by
Mathew B. Brady.
Courtesy of NARA)*

General Antonio
López de Santa
Anna

A young Sam
Grant (left), shown
with good friend
Alexander Hays
*(From the collection
of Keya Morgan,
New York City)*

Stonewall Jackson, pictured during the Civil War

A young Robert E. Lee
(Courtesy NPS)

Robert E. Lee, the
aging officer whose
career appeared to
be going nowhere,
shown in 1841

General William Tecumseh Sherman *(Photograph by Mathew B. Brady. Courtesy of NARA)*

General James Longstreet,
pictured during the Civil War

Jefferson Davis
and his young
bride, Varina

Jefferson Davis, shown while president of the Confederacy *(Photograph by Mathew B. Brady. Courtesy of NARA)*

James Walker's *Storming of Chapultepec*

nearby sally port (a small opening through which the defenders could enter and exit unobtrusively), Davis burst into La Tenería. He was the second man into the fort—but far from the last. American volunteers surged over walls and squeezed through openings, anything to find a way into La Tenería. McClung was felled by a musket ball that tore through his left hand, entered his torso at the hip, and exited at his spine. He would live, though only after being wrapped in a blanket and hidden in a culvert until the battle for La Tenería was through.

Which it soon was. Thanks, in part, to Davis's bravery and gallant leadership, the Americans soon controlled the fortress.

It was noon. The commander of the Mississippi Rifles had officially made a name for himself—but his wartime heroics were far from over.

FARTHER TO THE right, Colonel Garland and an injured Major Mansfield were leading a frantic retreat from the outskirts of Monterrey. Those city streets had initially been a sanctuary after the nonstop hail of bullets during their long charge across the plain. The soldiers' chests had heaved from the dash, sweat flecking their foreheads and darkening the blue armpits of their tunics—yet they had felt deeply elated to still be alive. The euphoria soon wore off. The Americans were new to street fighting and quickly made the fatal mistake of maintaining column formation—that is, marching rank and file in straight, orderly lines—as they crept through the unfamiliar lanes. But the wide-open dirt streets offered no cover. The Mexicans fired down on Garland's troops from rooftops and secret gun emplacements, popped up suddenly from behind low stone walls, blasted point-blank rounds of grape from perfectly camouflaged cannons, and blocked many of the streets with heaps of wood and dry brush to better contain the Americans.

Once it became clear that Garland and Mansfield would be unable to navigate the streets without additional firepower, Lieutenant Braxton Bragg and his mobile artillery were summoned to break the bottleneck. Yet Bragg's usually nimble six-pounders presented problems all their own. Their small shells proved laughably ineffective, literally bouncing off the four-foot-thick stone walls protecting the Mexican gunners. Making matters worse, Mexican cannons quickly cut down ten of Bragg's artillerymen and a dozen horses.

In tragically comic fashion, when the order to retreat — "retire in good order" — was called, the city streets proved too narrow for Bragg's cannons to be turned around while harnessed to a horse. Garland's embattled infantry had to save the day by manually lifting and pivoting each gun — no small feat, considering that a single cannon weighed 880 pounds.

Mansfield had been shot through the calf, but with a white handkerchief wrapped around the bloody bullet entry, he led the way out of town. Infantry soldiers ran close behind, and Bragg's horse-drawn cannons trailed in their wake, taking "the streets by which we had entered — there was no difficulty in finding our route, for it was painfully marked," said one officer, since almost half of Garland's men lay dead or dying along Monterrey's suddenly terrifying streets.

THE AMERICAN ARMY was having far more success atop La Federación. The hill featured two prominent fortified heights, and these had to be taken one at a time. The first one was captured early in the afternoon, just as Garland's men were blundering through Monterrey. "When we were at the top of the hill, we saw right before us and a little lower than we their second height. There was a stone fort on it, and the top of the hill was covered with large tents," Dana wrote, remembering the triumph.

"We were flushed with victory. A tremendous shouting and yelling was raised and all cried out, 'Forward!' The sight was too tempting and we must have the second hill before sunset."

The Americans took fire from a Mexican nine-pounder as they swarmed the small redoubt. "We routed them from their fort. They fled like good fellows, scarcely stopping to look behind once," wrote Dana. "We placed our colors on the hills and cheered like real Americans."

Cannon fire from the Bishop's Palace atop La Independencia ended the celebration. Shells landed uncomfortably close to the American troops, kicking up dirt and spraying splinters of rock. As if Worth's men needed another reminder, it was clear that capturing La Federación was tactically meaningless if the Americans did not also claim its sister hilltop of La Independencia. As long as the Mexicans held that bit of high ground, the American advance would be in jeopardy.

As C. F. SMITH'S MEN were capturing La Federación, Grant and the Fourth crept into Monterrey, hoping to capture Fort Diablo, a small fortification five hundred yards southwest of La Tenería, defended by more than a hundred Mexican soldiers under the command of Colonel Ignacio Joaquín del Arenal. El Fortín del Rincón del Diablo rested on a long ridge above the Río Santa Catarina, anchoring the left side of the Mexican lines. Capturing El Diablo would give American forces tentative control of Monterrey's perimeter.

Once inside the city, the Americans were again driven back by point-blank canister rounds. Comrades were blasted into red and left sprawled, dead and maimed, on the streets. The brigade was horrified. "The slaughter here was terrific; ten of our gallant officers fell to rise no more, and some ten others were wounded, some beyond the hope of recovery. The two regiments constituting the brigade were literally cut to pieces," one officer wrote. Taylor ordered that all American forces retreat from the city. The dead and wounded were left behind.

The only American toehold inside Monterrey was La Tenería. Davis's Mississippi Rifles remained there with Bloody First Tennessee, awaiting further orders. Captain Randolph Ridgely, Taylor's top artillery specialist, had made his way to them and was repositioning the captured Mexican cannons. They would be aimed no longer toward the American lines but into the city itself, at the Mexican army.

When the First Mississippi and First Tennessee were finally relieved and allowed to march back across the plain to the siege guns, a weary but elated Davis was content to travel at the rear of the column, with the wounded and the feeble. As they trudged through a cornfield lined with chaparral, Mexican lancers leaped their horses over the thorny berm and "commenced slaughtering stragglers and wounded men," in the words of one witness. A voice soon cried out above the chaos—it was Davis, forming his men into a line and shouting for them to take careful aim. His quick action drove away the lancers and saved countless American lives.

Later that night, Grant ventured alone back out onto the battlefield to search for his friends among the dead. Taylor's army had suffered 394 wounded and killed that day, a figure that equaled more than one-tenth of the men who saw battle—and almost twice as many casualties as Ampudia. Grant's dear pal Robert Hazlitt had been among the killed. As he searched for the body, a wounded soldier cried out to him. Grant tended to the man with water from his canteen, gently washing grime from the soldier's face with his handkerchief. Wooden ambulance wagons would be along in the morning to collect the soldiers of both sides. Should he make it through the night, that wounded man would be carefully lifted inside and carted back over painfully bumpy ground to a primitive field hospital. Grant offered what comfort and hope he could, knowing that the man faced a long, cold night out in the open.

Taylor's army had been just half the size of the Mexican force at the start of the day. To lose so many men, in such a short time, was appalling. Even Grant, who idolized Taylor in so many ways, labeled the battle plan of September 21 "ill-conceived." As he walked back to Walnut Springs, he was overcome by an unexpected sense of loss. And he knew, like the rest of his fellow soldiers, that more death was to come.

TWENTY-ONE

Monterrey, Day Two

SEPTEMBER 22, 1846

A few short hours after Grant returned to his tent, American prospects took a sudden turn for the better. At three in the morning, Worth ordered the five hundred regular soldiers and Texans camped at the base of La Independencia to quietly begin making their way up the eight-hundred-foot-high hill. Worth's men faced the demanding chore of capturing two separate fortresses. First they would attack a small redoubt known as Fort Libertad; the second target would be the Bishop's Palace, also known as the Obispado.

Longstreet was among them. The night was cold and wet, with a howling wind making conditions nearly unbearable. For three long hours the clandestine force climbed in pitch-blackness and pelting rain. They uttered not a sound, lest the Mexican sentries hear them. The steep hill was covered with thick bushes and rocks. Just before sunrise, a heavy fog slipped in, further concealing the Americans. By the time the rising sun burned off the mist and gave them away, they were just a short sprint from the summit.

Worth's men were crouched fifty yards from Fort Libertad

when the sentries first spied them. The Mexicans fired immediately. The Americans pressed carefully forward, holding their volley until they were closer to the fort rather than firing and being pinned down while reloading. Finally, the Americans loosed a salvo and then immediately followed it with a bayonet charge. In the ensuing hand-to-hand combat, Mexican troops either died fighting or turned and fled to the safety of the Bishop's Palace, on a low rise 350 yards southeast.

Made of thick squares of gray stone, with flying buttresses and lofty parapets, the castle was a daunting sight. Twice, the Americans attempted to charge the Bishop's Palace, and twice the Americans were repelled. There seemed no way to penetrate the Mexican defenses.

The solution turned out to be simple and yet ingenious. When it became clear that musket fire alone would not drive out the defenders, a twelve-pound howitzer was disassembled at the base of La Independencia and hand-carried up to the American position. The sum of the gun's parts weighed 1,757 pounds, and not a single piece was designed to be manually transported up a steep hillside. But once the howitzer reached the top, those bulky pieces were reassembled into a cannon, and every single bit of firepower implied by that considerable heft was aimed squarely at the Bishop's Palace. "Which piece, with great skill threw shrapnel shells [shells filled with musket balls] right into the palace and the open work in front," wrote Meade.

The besieged Mexicans could see just a few skirmishers — advance scouts — and that gun emplacement. The American force appeared small and easily beatable. Mexican cavalry and infantry soon ventured back out of the castle, eager to drive the Americans off their mountain. The Mexicans had no clue that three full regiments of American infantry rested behind an earthen brow near the twelve-pounder. Their job was to remain hidden so that the Mexicans would underestimate the size of the American force. This tactic, in part, was the brainchild of the West Point instructor Dennis Hart Mahan, America's leading military theorist. Mahan advocated using pickets in front of a main column to draw out the enemy, whereupon the main column would charge and the pickets would fall back and join their ranks. Mahan could not possibly have imagined how that scenario would play out in the fog on the summit of La Independencia: instead of Mexican infantry pickets on foot, lancers on horseback charged out from the castle. The main column of Mexican troops was the infantry regiment right behind them. But while the strategies were somewhat alike, sharp differences soon made themselves clear.

When the lancers had advanced halfway toward the American position, they were suddenly stunned to see twelve hundred U.S. soldiers rise from their hiding place in the rocks and rush toward them. "You never saw such a surprised set of fellows in this world as were those lancers," Dana wrote Sue. "They turned their horse's [sic] tails and struck off like quarter horses for the city, leaving some twenty or thirty of their fellows on the ground."

Now the Americans turned their attention to the Mexican foot soldiers, who had also turned to run for their lives. Most of them raced for the protective walls of the Bishop's Palace, rather than for Monterrey, hoping to get inside before the Americans. The pursuit became a footrace, contested "so hotly that they entered pell-mell with the enemy into the palace before they could close their doors on the position for defense," Dana recalled.

By 3:00 P.M. the battle was won. Four pieces of artillery inside the Bishop's Palace were captured. Like the cannons captured atop La Federación, they were reaimed down onto the Mexican positions inside Monterrey. Few prisoners had been taken: those enemy soldiers who were able had fled—and those who did not run for their lives were dead, clubbed with muskets, shot, or killed by swords.

With the American flag raised over the Bishop's Palace, Taylor's army officially controlled most of the easternmost, and all the westernmost, points in the battlefield. The Mexican army was trapped in between. Now, all Taylor had to do was squeeze the jaws of this vise, and the battle would be won. "I felt confident that with a strong force occupying the road and heights in his rear, and a good position below the city in our possession, the enemy could not possibly maintain the town," Taylor noted optimistically.

To capture Monterrey, Taylor's army would have to reenter the deadly streets and alleys. To the Americans it looked painfully simple, yet this was the showdown General Ampudia had been waiting for all along.

TWENTY-TWO

The Mortar

SEPTEMBER 23, 1846

Just after midnight, Worth's sentries atop La Independencia and La Federación heard commotion on Monterrey's western outskirts. When they looked more closely, however, the streets seemed deserted. Worth ordered Meade to quietly investigate. "The general sent me forward on a reconnaissance, to ascertain what batteries the enemy had in our direction. In doing this, I ascertained the enemy had abandoned all that portion of the town in our direction, and had retired to the central plaza of the town, where they were barricaded, and all the houses occupied by infantry."

Meade had made an amazing discovery: all of Ampudia's perimeter fortifications, with the exception of the Black Fort, had been abandoned in favor of making one final stand at the very heart of the carefully engineered defensive bastion. His troops would focus their activity around the main plaza, a large, square open space that looked very much like a military parade ground. The buildings fronting the plaza were almost all just one story high, with protective shutters that opened from the inside, metal barricades over many windows, and those flat roofs and parapets so perfect for concealing Mexican marksmen. The only multistory building was the cathedral, with its three-story bell tower, which formed a perfect lookout position. Solid masonry walls had been erected across all the streets leading into or out of the plaza, with cannon portals that resembled the openings on the side of an old-fashioned man-of-war. For maximum destructive effect, those guns would fire rounds of grape.

Worth changed his plans accordingly. "Two columns of attack were organized," the general wrote, "to move along the two principal streets in the direction of the great plaza, composed of light troops, slightly extended, with orders to mask the men whenever practicable, avoid those points swept by the enemy's artillery, to press on to the first plaza, get hold of the end of the streets beyond, then enter the buildings, and, by means of picks and bars, break through the longitudinal section of the walls, work from house to house, and ascending to the roofs, to place themselves upon the same, breast-high with the enemy."

The Second Dragoons had been kept out of the fighting, instead acting as couriers, riding their horses back and forth from Taylor's camp at Walnut Springs to Worth's position west of the city. Thus Worth was able to plan his attack knowledgeably, using the information about street fighting that had been gleaned after Garland's debacle. Instead of marching in columns, advancing street by street, the Americans would attempt to advance house to house—from the inside. Most homes shared a common wall, so advancement was as laborious as knocking a hole in the stone and then clearing the next house of enemy occupants. Battering rams, sledgehammers, pickaxes, and even small cannons were assembled for the job.

Couriers weren't the only soldiers making the circuitous loop from Walnut Springs to the Saltillo road. On the morning of the twenty-third, an artillery squad came dragging the ten-inch mortar used during the first day of the battle, giving Worth a gun capable of inflicting enormous damage. Worth planned to station the piece somewhere inside Monterrey and then rain mortar shells down on the main plaza. The location he had in mind was a smaller plaza, known as the Capella, which, by resonant coincidence, housed a cemetery.

Worth had already shifted the bulk of his force to the summit of La Independencia, the summit offering the shortest downhill route into the city. His infantry now began picking their way down through the rocks and grass, even as his twelve-pounder and the captured Mexican cannons opened fire from the Bishop's Palace.

Like it or not, it was time to enter the trap.

AS A LONE dragoon galloped back through the muddy cane fields with the results of Meade's reconnaissance, a small group under Jeff Davis's command probed the Mexican defenses on the other side of town. There, too, the Americans discovered that the enemy had retreated. "On the morning of the 23rd we held undisputed possession of the east end of Monterey," noted Grant, who was then moving back into the outskirts with the Fourth.

Taylor had finally ridden Old Whitey into the city — with elements of the Second Dragoons riding alongside as his personal escort — and set up a command post in La Tenería. American estimates showed that there were seven thousand Mexican regulars in the plaza, with at least another two thousand local conscripts. Ampudia also had forty-two cannons at his disposal, with ample ammunition. "Our artillery," Taylor noted wryly, "consisted of one ten-inch mortar, two 24-pound howitzers, and four light field batteries — the mortar being the only piece suitable to the operations of a siege."

And while it was obvious that the Mexicans had pulled back into the plaza, it soon became clear that their retreat was not total and that they also occupied defensive positions in many streets along the way. The Third and Fourth infantries encountered heavy fire as they moved carefully forward, remaining outdoors in order to travel more quickly. "The streets leading to the plaza," Grant wrote, referring to the Mexican defenses, "were commanded from all directions by artillery...the roofs were manned with infantry, the troops being protected from fire by parapets made of sandbags. All advances into the city were attended with much danger." He added: "A volley of musketry and a discharge of grape shot were invariably encountered."

The constant cannon fire and musket shots were deafening. Oftentimes the American soldiers could not hear their officers' commands and instead relied on visual cues: a line of men abruptly changing direction, signifying a new point of attack; the commander waving his saber, motioning for his men to follow him into battle; a fellow soldier keeling over from the musket shot they never saw coming; or, most horrifically, an entire group of men ripped open and dismembered by a burst of grape.

Death came from all angles at all times. One American soldier estimated that there were "a thousand musketeers on the housetops, and in the barricades at the head of the street up which we advanced, and at every cross street, and you may form some idea of the deluge of balls poured upon us. Onward we went, men and horses falling at every step. Cheers, shrieks, groans, and words of command added to the din.

"I sat down on the ground with my back to the wall of a house. On my left were two men torn nearly to pieces. One of them was lying flat on his back with his legs extending farther in the street than mine. Crash came another shower of grape, which tore one of his wounded legs off. He reared up, shrieked, and fell back a corpse. I never moved, for I was satisfied that one place was as safe as another."

One group of regular soldiers and Texas Rangers managed to

find an extremely safe place in the form of a small market. "We reached a corner house of a block," wrote one of the regulars. "It was a corner grocery full of wine, *aquadenta* and Mescal. On the opposite side of the street we had to cross was another one of those infernal fortified stone walls." Up the street, the Mexicans were bayoneting American wounded, crying out loudly and defiantly as they did so. Sensing that their situation was getting desperate, the soldiers in the market proceeded to get "crazy drunk." Only then did they throw open the door and make a dash for the wall. "Our foes met the rush with so heavy a fire that the air seemed to rain balls. Bullets striking on the stone, pavements and walls, ricocheting and glancing from side to side, as we staggered on. At least a regiment of infantry came up a side street, poured their fire in our flank, and then charged us with bayonet. All fought now on his own hook, and fought more like devils than human beings, with axes, clubbed rifles, sabre, and Bowie knife."

That action took place on the hotly contested eastern side of Monterrey. Davis and the First Mississippi were close by—cold, wet, tired, hungry, and miserable from sleeping in the open and not eating for almost two days and nights. Now they maneuvered street by street, under that same "murderous fire," until the main plaza was in sight. The Rifles were low on ammunition and depleted by casualties, and orders soon arrived for them to retreat from what was clearly a vulnerable position. Obeying that command was not so easy. "The enemy was behind us," Davis noted plainly, with a nod to the artillery battery with a gun aimed squarely down their escape route. He decided to personally test the Mexican response. "If only one gun was fired at me, then another man should follow; and so on, another and another, until a volley should be fired, and then all of them should rush rapidly across before the guns could be reloaded. In this manner the men got across with little loss."

❊   ❊   ❊

GRANT WAS ALSO navigating his way through those streets
with the greatest caution, paying particular attention to the
rooftops. He watched as five of the Third Infantry's twelve
remaining officers went "toes up" in the withering crossfire of
musket and grape, and he could hear the cries of Mexican soldiers exhorting one another in the heat of battle. There were
female voices, too; as the men of Mexico fought for Monterrey,
it was the local women who carried fresh bullets to the rooftops.
"A young woman, Dona María Josefa Zozaya, appeared amid
the soldiers fighting on the roof of the home of Sr. Garza Flores.
She gave them courage and passed them munitions; she showed
them how to face down danger," noted one of the Mexicans.

Many of those female voices were far more anguished. In one
home, two Mexican women, fearful of their young daughters'
being raped, pleaded for the Americans to "spare the senoritas
and use them as we wished," wrote one soldier about entering
a home. In another, the cries were not of a woman but of a young
child, sobbing at the sight of his mother, killed by a random shot.
"In every house," the soldier lamented, "fearful sights told of a
town taken by storm."

Meanwhile, lack of munitions threatened the Third and
Fourth's forward advance. The shortage could hardly have come
at a worse time. They were deep inside Monterrey, just a single
block from the plaza. Colonel Garland needed to get word back
to General Twiggs that reinforcements and ammunition were
urgently required. He asked for a volunteer, someone willing to
travel back out of the city alone and get the message to Twiggs.
It was Grant who stepped forward. The heat of battle and concern for his fellow soldiers had turned the passive observer of
Palo Alto and timid company commander at Resaca de la Palma,
without warning or plan, into a brave-hearted warrior.

Grant's horse that day was named Nelly. He had dismounted once they were inside the city and led her carefully through the fields of fire. But now was not the time to walk. He needed to gallop Nelly back out of town to bring help as quickly as possible.

All of his years on horseback had prepared Grant for this act of daring, and he relied on his skill to devise an unconventional plan. "I adjusted myself on the side of the horse furthest from the enemy, and with only one foot holding to the cantle of the saddle, and an arm over the neck of the horse exposed, I started at a full run." Nelly galloped down the street, Grant clinging to the side of her. "It was only at street crossings that my horse was under fire, but these I crossed at such a flying rate that generally I was past and under cover of the next block before the enemy fired," he recalled. "At one point on my ride, I saw a sentry walking in front of a house, and stopped to inquire what he was doing there. Finding that the house was full of wounded American soldiers, I dismounted and went in."

Soldiers and officers lay about the floor. One of the officers, an engineer named Williams, had been shot in the head. The bowels of a nearby lieutenant spilled from his body. Grant promised the men filling the small home that he would report their location and return with help. Then he ventured carefully back out into the fray.

Dead-running Nelly through the streets of Monterrey, Grant succeeded in reaching Twiggs. But his gallantry was in vain—Garland had once again retreated. His advance position a block from the plaza soon fell back into Mexican hands. As for the wounded soldiers to whom Grant had promised relief, their position was overrun. None of them survived the battle.

ON THE OPPOSITE side of the city, Worth began firing a single mortar round into the main plaza, one every twenty minutes.

The shells, wrote one soldier in position a few blocks away, "rushed over our heads with a strange roaring scream." Each round consisted of a hollow iron cannonball filled with gunpowder. Each explosion killed between six and ten Mexicans. This show of force was meant to simultaneously unnerve Ampudia's men and underscore that they were, in fact, pinned within a relatively small quadrant. American soldiers weren't yet capable of penetrating the plaza, went the message, but the parabolic lob of an exploding mortar shell could reach it quite easily. Ongoing Mexican attempts to silence the mortar with cannon fire from the Black Fort proved futile.

Reaching the Capella, that smaller city plaza where the mortar was positioned, had involved a bloody and vicious fight. Following the lead of a small advance unit, Worth's men had breached the city that morning, spreading wide as they did so; instead of attacking down just one street, American soldiers filled six different avenues. Whenever fire was encountered, they entered private homes and tore down connective walls, slowly making a passage to the heart of the Mexican force. One of the Texas Rangers fighting under Worth later recalled how "the street fighting became appalling—both columns were now closely engaged with the enemy, and steadily advanced, inch by inch. Our artillery was heard rumbling over the paved streets, galloping here and there as the emergency required, and pouring forth a blazing fire of grape and ball—volley after volley of musketry, and the continued peals of artillery became almost deafening. The artillery of both sides raked the streets, the balls striking the houses with a terrible crash, while amid the roars of battle were heard the battering instruments used by the Texans. Doors were forced open, walls were battered down, entrance made through the longitudinal walls, and the enemy driven from room to room, and from house to house, followed by the shrieks of women, and the sharp crack of Texan rifles. Cheer after cheer

225

was heard in proud and exulting defiance, as the Texans or regulars gained the housetops by means of ladders."

By two o'clock, Worth's division was very near the main plaza. "Here we were brought to a stand," wrote Dana. "The tops of the houses were filled with Mexicans and they poured their bullets like hail upon us in the streets. In one place three men of our company were wounded (one of them mortally) in less time than you could count three. We had nothing to do but fight them in their own way. So after constructing ladders we left our artillery and a strong force to keep the streets whilst we took the tops of the houses."

The rooftop fighting that ensued was the day's most intense action. Mexicans and Americans fired at one another from behind parapets and sandbags, raising their heads to shoot and then ducking back down to begin that laborious process of reloading their muskets—the Americans always creeping steadily toward Ampudia's men, who fell back toward the plaza again and again, rather than sally forth and wage an offensive battle. Progress was painfully slow. Protective artillery was nonexistent, the imprecision of cannon and howitzer fire making it impossible to target most Mexican positions without risk of hitting Americans, too.

Still, like clockwork, that mortar dropped a shell into the plaza every twenty minutes. The cathedral and plaza were full to overflowing with Mexican soldiers and citizens. Wounded stretched out on pews. Families slept on the nave's sacred floor. There was no place to run or hide when the mortar rounds fell. The shells did not distinguish between combatant and noncombatant, young and old; and to the plaza's odors of gunpowder, vomit, and overflowing toilets were added the moans of the injured and the anguished weeping of the bereaved.

There was pride among the defenders, for they had proved themselves a lethal fighting force. But the end was clearly in sight, and there was quiet talk of mutiny. In addition to soldiers and civilians, the plaza was home to a huge magazine of ammunition. One lucky mortar round could kill them all. Better to overthrow Ampudia and seek a truce than to get blown to kingdom come.

At 11:00 P.M., Taylor ordered Worth to cease fire until dawn. The mortar's barrel went cold. The starless night turned silent. Worth waited, his troops on alert, not sure what would happen next.

A MESSENGER FROM Ampudia soon galloped through the darkness, flying the white flag of truce. The Mexican general was requesting that his army be allowed to leave the city and to march away unmolested.

The petition wasn't as ludicrous as it first appeared. Ampudia understood Taylor's strengths and weaknesses just as clearly as his own. And despite having the upper hand, Taylor was in trouble. The Mexican army had suffered just 367 killed and wounded. Even with the bulk of his force penned inside the plaza, Ampudia still outnumbered Taylor two to one. Taylor could not launch a full-scale assault on the plaza without losing hundreds more men, and even then the city would not be his. The Black Fort would still have to be assaulted, and thus far it had proved itself impregnable. "Being without siege artillery or entrenching tools, we could only hope to carry this fort by storm, after a heavy loss from our army," Dana observed.

The victory, in those terms, would be Pyrrhic. Taylor's army would be too weakened to fight another day. They were hundreds of miles inside a hostile foreign country, cut off from their supplies. Taylor had only enough rations to feed his troops for ten more days. He needed more bullets, musket balls, shells, and, most of all, men.

By the time Ampudia's messenger came forth, Taylor had

ridden back to Walnut Springs to spend the night. Hours passed as the message was sent by courier to his tent and the general penned a reply. Taylor did not wish to destroy Mexico or the Mexican army; he simply wanted to end the battle—and perhaps the war. He chose his words carefully. "The consideration of humanity was present on my mind," Taylor wrote in his official report, "and outweighed, in my judgment, the doubtful advantages to be gained by a resumption of the attack on the town."

But those thoughts of humanity extended to his own forces, too. Taylor had lost more men than Ampudia, some 120 killed, 368 wounded, and 43 missing in action (a polite term, "missing in action" was the military's way of saying that a cannonball had rendered a soldier's body nonexistent).

Taylor let the Mexican army go—all seven thousand of them.

Meade recorded the terms: "The Mexican Army was to evacuate the place in seven days, and retire beyond the Rinconada, forty miles from here, to which point we were at liberty to advance. The infantry and cavalry to take their arms; the artillery, six pieces of light-artillery; all the rest of the public property and munitions of war to be ours, and the two to be given up to our exclusive possession," he wrote. In addition, the Black Fort, which Taylor had almost completely bypassed while taking the city and which still contained more than two thousand troops, would be evacuated.

Ampudia was given one hour to accept. He required just thirty minutes. A team of commissioners, three from each side, drew up the formal surrender document. Along with General Worth and General J. Pinckney Henderson of the Texas Division, Taylor appointed Jeff Davis to represent the United States—and it was Davis, as junior officer, who acted as secretary, writing out the treaty in longhand.

Taylor and Ampudia met face-to-face during the proceedings,

with the Mexican assuring his American adversary that he had received information that very morning from Mexico City, stating that an American minister (James Buchanan) would soon be received by acting president General José Mariano Salas (since the war's beginning, President Herrera and his equally ineffectual successor, General Mariano Paredes, had been forced from office) to discuss a truce. Taylor came away convinced that the Mexican withdrawal from Monterrey could signify the end of the war. "It was no military necessity that induced General Taylor to grant such liberal terms, but a higher and nobler motive," wrote Meade. "First, to grant an opportunity to the two governments to negotiate for peace, knowing, as he did, that should he destroy the Mexican army, the Government would never listen to overtures of peace under the disgrace. Secondly, to stop the unnecessary effusion of blood, not only of soldiers, but of old and infirm women and children, whom necessity kept in the city, and who were crowded with our troops, from whom every shot told. Thirdly, as a tribute of respect to the gallantry of the Mexicans, who had defended their place as long as it was in their power."

The agreement was signed on the evening of September 24. Two days later, Ampudia began marching his troops out of the city, on their way south to the city of San Luis Potosí. Most of the soldiers were uneducated peasants or local Indians, simple men who had been forced into service. The Americans were unimpressed.

"My pity was aroused by the sight of the Mexican garrison of Monterey marching out of town as prisoners, and no doubt the same feeling was experienced by most of our army who had witnessed it," wrote Grant. "Many of the prisoners were cavalry, armed with lances, and mounted on miserable half-starved horses that did not look as if they could carry their riders out of town.

The men looked in but little better condition. I thought how little interest the men before me had in the results of the war."

Ampudia was downcast and anxious. The route passed directly through the Texas Rangers' encampment, and he was terrified of being shot down from the roadside. But the Texans let him pass, uttering not a sound or oath to their longtime tormentor.

The results, for the Americans, could be counted best in the military lessons learned: well-trained volunteer units made for surprisingly good fighters; an offensive stance was preferable to defensive entrenchment; knocking down walls was a more effective method of street fighting than advancing in column formation; light artillery was effective against cavalry and infantry, but large cannons were necessary for assaulting fortified positions; and, most personally, a vast and terrible grief accompanied the death of longtime friends. "How very lonesome it is here with us now. I have just been walking through camp, and how many faces that were dear to the most of us are missing," Grant wrote to Julia.

Hazlitt was still very much on his mind. The Pennsylvanian was the young officer who had coaxed Julia to marry Grant. Just two weeks earlier, Grant had written to Julia that "Mr. Hazlitt is very well," knowing it would prompt memories of good times at White Haven. Now his twenty-five-year-old former classmate was gone.

Hazlitt's death soon devastated Grant. He would mourn his fallen West Point brethren for months, often bewildered by the power of grief. "I came back to my tent to drive away, what you call the Blues," Grant wrote Julia. But driving away the heartbreak was a challenge. He also struggled to cope with the sadness, looking for solace in his work, his love for Julia, and his optimistic belief that he would return home soon. Grant put enormous faith in Taylor's hope that Monterrey might mark the end of the war. There were rumors in camp that peace negotiations between Mexico and America had already begun. "I hope sincerely that such is the case, for I am very anxious to get out of the country," he confided to Julia.

But General Santa Anna had explicitly stated that he would refer the matter of peace to the Mexican Congress, which did not meet until December. Despite Ampudia's deceptive words to the contrary, no American emissary would be received until then, so the Americans settled in as an occupying force.

Matamoros had marked just the third time in U.S. history that its army had gained control of a foreign territory (the other two being Quebec during the Revolutionary War and various regions of Canada during the War of 1812). Monterrey, however, would be a much greater test of the American's ability to rule another populace. One could only hope that Taylor wouldn't see a repeat of York, in 1813, when Americans had looted and burned the city during a three-day bender. Many Mexican War volunteers had signed up out of impulsive patriotism, but others had been lured by promises of "Roast beef, two dollars a day, plenty of whiskey, golden Jesuses, and pretty Mexican girls." Thus far their experiences had been something far more miserable. Monterrey offered a chance to make amends.

On a more historical note, the predominantly Protestant American force's taking up residence in a strongly Catholic nation had many West Pointers recalling their studies of Napoleon's struggles to subjugate Spain during the Napoleonic Wars. The French disregard for Spain's social practices and Catholic faith had led to a bloody nationalist uprising. Before invading the Iberian Peninsula, Napoleon had estimated that his losses would total some twelve thousand; instead, more than three hundred thousand French troops died at the hands of Spanish partisans. At one point, the frustrated French were shooting priests and burning entire villages in an attempt to maintain order. Taylor, with his puny remaining force, faced a very similar dynamic in Mexico. He began planning the occupation, hoping it would be incident free—perhaps more along the lines of the Duke of Wellington's occupation of Spain, when the British general's forces supplanted Napoleon's. Wellington had been adamant that his troops respect the Spanish citizens' homes and property, and as a result the British occupation was relatively blood free.

Pro-expansionist forces back in Washington had no fears of an uprising. They firmly believed that Mexico's indigenous population would embrace the Americans as a liberating force, bringing democracy to replace tyranny. On the ground, things were more complicated. "This plan of an armed occupation, I, individually, am opposed to, upon the ground of its never having any end," wrote Meade. "For Mexico, though she will hardly undertake to drive us out, will nevertheless be always talking about it and making preparations, which will compel us to be always prepared by having a large army on this frontier."

Monterrey marked the beginning of a very long lull in the fighting. Both sides needed time to lick their wounds and form a new strategy. New leaders and new officers were about to enter the fray, men whose exploits would overshadow anything the war had seen thus far. Less than three months after graduating from West Point, many brand-new young lieutenants from the very noteworthy class of 1846 had already landed in Port Isabel and begun traveling upriver. And anxious as he was to go home, Sam Grant was destined to travel ever deeper into Mexico.

So, finally, was Robert E. Lee.

III

POLITICS AND WAR

The administration had a most embarrassing problem to solve. It was engaged in a war of conquest that must be carried to a successful issue, or the political object would be unattained. Yet all the capable officers of the requisite rank belonged to the opposition, and the man selected for lack of political ambition [Taylor] had himself become a prominent candidate for the Presidency. It was necessary to destroy his chances promptly.

— ULYSSES S. GRANT, *Memoirs*

TWENTY-THREE

Change of Command

OCTOBER 12, 1846

The second front of Taylor's invasion opened on a Monday morning, as engineers supervised the construction of a temporary pontoon bridge across the Rio Grande. Crossing the bridge would be Brigadier General John E. Wool, a former lawyer with a comb-over hairstyle and perpetually downturned mouth, leading a column consisting of nearly two thousand regulars, Illinois volunteer infantry, Arkansas volunteer cavalry, and 118 supply wagons. They were marching from San Antonio toward the Mexican fortress at Chihuahua.

Chihuahua was nestled at the base of the Sierra Madre, 350 miles northwest of Monterrey. Colonel Stephen Watts Kearny, Grant's former commander at the Jefferson Barracks, had marched a large American force from Fort Leavenworth, Kansas, into Santa Fe during the summer and had become its military governor on August 18. Kearny had captured the New Mexico region without incident, but he had left just a small garrison force in Santa Fe as he marched on to California to continue the American conquest of the West. The American troops in Santa Fe were very much at risk from a counterattack by Mexican troops marching due north out of Chihuahua—thus the need to neutralize any forces that might be stationed there.

Wool had been orphaned at a young age, but his stellar organizational skills and battlefield bravery during the War of 1812 had long ago helped him rise above that harsh twist of fate. By the time he led his army toward Mexico, he had risen to prominence as the U.S. Army's third-ranking general, behind Winfield Scott and Zachary Taylor. Even better, at least in President Polk's mind, Wool was a Democrat. From a political and pragmatic point of view, Polk thought Wool the ideal man for the pivotal thrust toward Chihuahua. With any luck, he might win a decisive battlefield victory and deflect some of the American public's growing fascination with Taylor.

The newly arrived general went to work immediately. His greatest task would be turning volunteers into soldiers. At first he faced great opposition, but simple pleasures such as hot coffee, prompt payment of their salaries, and the accoutrement of war proved to be a means of winning them over. "General Wool displayed great activity in organizing his army, and putting the commissariat in the finest possible condition. Sugar and coffee of the best quality have always been a part of his soldier's daily diet," wrote one soldier approvingly. "No army was better provided than this with all the munitions and appliances of war."

Once his men had begun to look and act like an army, there still remained the problem of getting those soldiers to Chihuahua. A quick look at the chart showed Wool that the town definitely existed somewhere out in the foothills of the Sierra Madre, but few maps detailed this region of northern Mexico. The Spanish and then the Mexicans had neglected the area because it was barren and inhabited by hostile Indians—a wasteland dividing the lush farmlands of the south with the rugged lands north of the Rio Grande. "Nobody wanted to go into the vast zone of the north," wrote one Mexican historian, "which, lacking people, was a danger, an invitation to pillage, an open arc."

The few maps that existed were inferior and not to scale, offering vague sketches of the few existent dirt roads. There were no topographical maps at all, nothing to provide specifics about cliffs, mountains, waterfalls, deserts, ravines, or other geographical hazards. As a result, Wool arranged for two teams of engineers to accompany him. The first, a four-man group from the Topographical Corps, would blaze the trail and begin drawing the first serious charts of northern Mexico. The other group was composed of two civil engineers who would supervise the building of roads and assembly of temporary bridges.

Robert E. Lee was a member of the second group, working closely with a fellow West Point graduate named William D. Fraser. As if to emphasize the slothful course of Lee's career thus far, both men were captains, but Fraser was seven years younger — and Lee's superior officer.

Not that Fraser was an ambitious overachiever. He was thirty-three years old, stuck squarely in that no-man's-land between West Point and premature retirement. This was a land that Lee knew all too well. He was just four months shy of his fortieth birthday. A dark brown mustache gave him a rakish air that belied his stolid demeanor, and his muscular shoulders and chest gave him an imposing physical appearance. Lee was a bold man when he had to be, brimming with a quiet confidence about his abilities and intellect. But he could also be deeply conservative, even timid. By his own admission, Lee had stayed in the military out of procrastination, not out of some deep belief that he was thus destined for greatness. "I am waiting, looking, and hoping for some good opportunity to bid an affectionate farewell to my dear Uncle Sam," he had written to a friend more than ten years earlier. Apparently, he was still waiting.

Yet the army was where he belonged, just as it had been for his father. He loved its discipline and emphasis on duty and would have been quite lost without them in his life. When the call to war finally came on August 19, Lee's first priority was the army, not his wife and children: indeed, he had been in such a rush to get to Texas that he didn't bother stopping at home to say good-bye. This despite the fact that Mary had just given birth to a new baby girl, that their Arlington home was just a short jaunt across the Potomac, and that he might be gone in Mexico for several months, at the very least.

Lee had traveled by steamboat to New Orleans and then to the Texas coast. There he eagerly galloped a horse across the brush and chaparral of the coastal plain toward San Antonio, desperate to arrive before Wool marched his army into Mexico. Amazingly, it took him just three weeks to travel some twenty-five hundred miles. Lee had been so speedy that he reached Wool's command with a week to spare. His first assignment upon arriving was typical of an engineer, not a warrior. He was off to make the rounds of the local merchants, purchasing pickaxes, shovels, hammers, and other tools essential to building Wool's vital new infrastructure.

On September 28, at the same time Ampudia was ushering his army from the smoldering remains of Monterrey, Lee rode out of San Antonio with Wool's brigade, off to engage a foreign enemy in battle for the first time in his career.

As in all great military movements, the heady grandeur of setting out was soon replaced by the rigid routine. Each day began with a 3:00 A.M. reveille and inspection of arms. Breakfast followed immediately afterward, with the men gobbling down goat's milk, rice pudding, and gruel. There was no mess tent, nor were there cooks to prepare a hot meal. The men were simply issued their rations, preparing them themselves or pooling them and rotating the cooking chores. They ate in darkness, off tin plates, each man allotted a single tin spoon and tin cup as utensils. Lee and the other officers enjoyed the relative luxury of sleeping in tents. Soldiers from the Quartermaster Corps struck the tents as breakfast was consumed, expertly bundling the canvas, tent poles, and officers' personal belongings for the journey to the next night's campsite.

Those lacking rank slept on the ground, with just a wool blanket between them and the earth, and another wool blanket for warmth. Beginning their daily march was as easy as rolling the two blankets into a bedroll, slinging it over their shoulder, and waiting for the order to move out. This came promptly at 4:00 A.M.—just one hour after rising. Wool's army averaged fifteen miles a day over the rolling hills and chaparral desert between San Antonio and the Rio Grande.

During his time scouring the markets of San Antonio, Lee had local artisans construct four large wooden pontoons. The Quartermaster Corps was responsible for carting these unwieldy behemoths across the Texas wilderness, lashing each to the top of a wagon, praying all the while that the pontoons didn't somehow topple and break. They were precious cargo, designed to build a vast temporary bridge over the Rio Grande in case the river was too deep and fast for Wool's force to march across.

Eleven days and 164 miles after setting out from San Antonio, Lee prodded his horse into the sluggish current, testing the river's depth. His trained eye told him that the distance from the American shore to the Mexican was easily three hundred yards, and the river's depth soon proved too deep for men and material to ford in safety.

The time to build his bridge had arrived. Lee supervised the careful placement of the pontoons out in the current. Strung together with a rope that crossed from one side of the river to the other and then overlaid with wooden planks, they formed what the men called a flying bridge.

It took three days of manual labor and engineering calculation to properly position the pontoons and complete the bridge.

When Lee was satisfied that his new construction was sturdy and ready, men and material were allowed to cross—but not all at once. He watched as two hundred men at a time, marching slowly, balancing themselves carefully on the ever-heaving bridge, invaded Mexico, looking more like circus acrobats than soldiers. Wool was so delighted at the success that he halted his army on October 13 and threw a party for his officers. Port, champagne, and whiskey were proffered. Lee, according to his habit, attended but did not partake. Among the officers was the newly commissioned volunteer colonel John J. Hardin of the First Illinois, the former congressman Lincoln had defeated for the Whig Party nomination.

Before Wool's army could march any farther into Mexico, a steamboat chugged upriver from Camargo and off-loaded Brigadier General James Shields, another political rival of Lincoln's, who was just joining the Illinois regiment. Together, the two men had spent less than six months in uniform, yet both outranked Lee.

THE AMERICANS HOPED that the local populace would see them as liberators and welcome them with open arms. But that hope was based on a naïveté about their neighbors to the south. Mexico was an extremely complicated nation, riven by class division and racial gaps just as wide as those between black and white in the United States. During Spanish rule, the nation had been governed by Spaniards and by those Europeans who had been born in New Spain. The Europeans and criollos, combined, made up just 20 percent of the population, and that minority governed a vast Native American population, who were held in check through terror, random imprisonment, torture, and forced labor.

Nothing changed after Mexico's War of Independence. The Spaniards were gone, but the criollos desperately clung to the vast land holdings they had stolen from the Indians. "The aristocracy of color is quite as great in Mexico as it is in this country," U.S. ambassador to Mexico Waddy Thompson had concluded shortly after Mexico was founded in 1821.

The Indians fought back, staging violent revolts when the Mexican government seized more of their lands. Each time—at Oaxaca in 1827, Veracruz in 1836, Guerrero in 1842, and Alvarez in 1844—the Mexican army ruthlessly crushed the peasants. Once violence had been established as a means of settling disputes, no faction within Mexico was safe. The Mexican army soon got in the habit of staging coups to displace unwanted governmental regimes. With the army's officer corps dominated by criollos and other men of European white heritage, and the enlisted soldiers almost entirely of Native American extraction, the power distribution was no different than in the days before independence. Spain may have left, but the heirs to its colonial legacy still ruled Mexico. Recognizing the hatred for the regime, Polk and his pro-expansion allies in Washington fooled themselves into believing that the Americans would be welcomed into Mexico with open arms—Palo Alto, Resaca de la Palma, and Monterrey notwithstanding.

Despite Taylor's victories, the Mexican army still ruled most of northern Mexico, vastly dampening the chances that the local peasantry would align themselves with Wool's force. Shortly after Wool's crossing, a Mexican officer presented himself and proclaimed that, under the terms of the Monterrey armistice, this new American incursion was illegal. Wool ignored him, preferring to travel farther southward to establish his own armistice boundary rather than let the conquered Mexicans set it for him. While the Mexican army might have been outraged at Wool's perceived arrogance, they were also in the process of escalating the stakes.

On October 8, two weeks after the signing of the armistice, General Santa Anna had arrived in the city of San Luis Potosí with a small army. Pledging his personal fortune as collateral for salaries and munitions, he soon began increasing the size of his force. His goal was twenty-five thousand men. As Ampudia had done at Monterrey, Santa Anna also ordered the construction of new fortifications around San Luis Potosí.

Wool was ignorant of Santa Anna's presence and intentions when he resumed his march on October 16. All his army saw before them was a vast, empty land. The Topographical Corps had verified that the best path was a detour slightly southwest toward the village of Santa Rosa. Other than roving bands of Comanche and Apache Indians and perhaps the stray communal farmer, there didn't appear to be any opposition — or support.

TWENTY-FOUR

The Perils of Occupation

OCTOBER 19, 1846

Jeff Davis was going home. Varina missed him dearly, and Davis had requested a sixty-day furlough to be by her side. A two-month leave was hardly standard procedure among Taylor's officers, but Davis's congressional standing and familial connections allowed him a certain leeway. Davis was confident that he would never see Monterrey again. There was still talk of a U.S. commission that would soon meet with the Mexican leaders in Mexico City to discuss a lasting peace. "They were whipped, and we could afford to be generous," Davis had written his brother Joseph, referring to Monterrey and its aftermath. "The war is probably over."

Three weeks later, with no sign that Mexico planned to quit the war, he took matters into his own hands and left the First Mississippi, if only for a time. It was a Monday as he galloped Tartar out of Monterrey, destined for Camargo and the *Hatchee Eagle,* a 116-ton side-wheel river steamer, for the trip down to the mouth of the Rio Grande, there to catch a sailing ship for New Orleans.

Other than just his chronic restlessness, Davis had several

powerful reasons for leaving. First, the wait for the Mexican Congress to reassemble meant an eight-week armistice, and Davis wasn't the sort to stand idle. Rather than while away his time in the comparative luxury of Monterrey, where many officers were now living in the city's finer homes, he was more than happy to travel a thousand miles back to Davis Bend. Second, racing home ensured that Davis would be the first member of his regiment to return from the war—with all the fanfare and political capital that entailed. But Davis was in for a surprise: he had no way of knowing that on October 17, just two days before saddling Tartar for the trip home, his brother Joseph had submitted Davis's letter of resignation. Davis might be coming home a hero, and definitely a politician, but he was no longer a member of the U.S. House of Representatives.

GRANT, MEANWHILE, REMAINED in Monterrey. The Americans were well into their second month as an occupying force, and the daily urgencies of preparing for battle and waging war had been replaced by boredom, mayhem, and longing—though not always in that order. "I got one of the sweetest letters from you a few days ago that I have had for a long time and the least I can do in return is to write you at least three pages in return; even if I have nothing more to write than that I love you, and how very much," Grant wrote Julia. He and the Fourth were still camped at Walnut Springs. Monterrey had become a bustling American outpost, and his days had settled into a rather comfortable routine. Once again, war seemed very far away. "How happy I should be if I knew that but a few more letters were to pass between my Dearest Julia and myself—as mere lovers—that is to say, how happy I should be if soon Julia was to become mine forever," Grant wrote. "You say in your letter that you wish it was our country that was being invaded instead of

Mexico, that you would ask for quarters, but that you doubted if Mr. Grant would *grant* them. Indeed dearest, I am one of the most humane individuals you are acquainted with, and not only would I give quarters to anyone who implores them; but if Julia says she will surrender herself my prisoner I will take the first opportunity of making an excursion to Mo. But you must not expect your parole like other prisoners of war, for I expect to be the sentinel that guards you myself."

Despite Grant's distance from Julia, Monterrey was proving to be an enjoyable interlude. "Grant was then quartermaster of the Fourth Infantry," remembered the Virginian Dabney Maury, a lieutenant in the Mounted Rifles. "I had been badly wounded hunting near Camargo, so as to disable me from duty while in Monterey. Grant being also, by the duties of his office, free to go when and where he pleased, we were much together and enjoyed the association. Grant was a thoroughly kind and manly young fellow, with no bad habits, and was respected and liked by his fellow officers, especially those of his own regiment."

The tents of each company were laid out in two rows, with a "company street" running between them. At the end of each street, displayed perpendicular to the road, was each company's colors. This "color line" was also where muskets and rifles were stacked and where a company assembled in formation. There was precision and order to this arrangement, for it was the same throughout the army, making Walnut Springs and Camargo and Fort Brown and Corpus Christi and the countless bivouacs in between carbon copies of one another — and in that way, home.

The only regulars inside Monterrey were Worth's Second Division, accompanied by the Texas Mounted Rifles. Having a force simultaneously within the city and outside it kept the Americans from being bottled up in one spot. This was Taylor's way of keeping his army prepared for war, in case of a Mexican counterattack. It was not beyond question: intelligence reports showed that General Santa Anna had a force of eight thousand linking up with Ampudia's tattered thousands far to the south at San Luis Potosí.

But having the army camp outside Monterrey served another purpose, too. Its citizens had been so afraid of the Americans that many had fled to Saltillo and other towns farther inland. They were terrified that they would be captured, sent to the United States, and sold into slavery, although rumors to this effect proved to be false. However, the people of Monterrey still had reason to be scared of the occupying forces. Hoping to prove that the American army would treat them well, Taylor had banned the sale of alcohol in the city, given that violence often accompanied drunkenness (this, however, proved almost impossible to enforce as Americans discovered Mexican spirits such as mescal for the first time).

Gambling and associating with camp followers were also off limits. At a time when he should have been allowed to focus on the war, or at the very least on saving his command, Taylor (who rotated between Saltillo and Monterrey) was forced to spend his time and energy finding ways to keep the bored, vengeful, and sexually frustrated volunteers from causing trouble. Though he had full authority over the regulars, Taylor was forbidden to punish volunteers. His only recourse was to place offenders in chains and send them back to New Orleans for trial, whereupon the guilty volunteer would be released for lack of eyewitnesses. "Reliable information reached Washington, almost daily, that the wild volunteers as soon as beyond the Rio Grande, committed with impunity, all sorts of atrocities on the persons and property of Mexicans," an exasperated General Winfield Scott wrote of Taylor's woes. "There was no legal punishment for any of those offences, for by the strange omission of Congress, American troops take with them beyond the limits of their own country, no law but the Constitution of the United States, and the rules and articles of war. These do not provide any court for the trial or punishment of murder, rape, theft, etc, etc.—no matter by whom or on whom committed."

Mexicans were shot down in the streets. Livestock were stolen. Women were raped. "Many outrages have been committed on respectable females, some of the most hellish, devilish kind, and heart-rending in the extreme. Some volunteers the other night, for instance, entered the house of a very respectable family, and obliged the husband to leave the room. Some held him outside whilst two remained inside. One held a pistol to the lady's head whilst the other fiend incarnate violated her person," Dana wrote Sue.

At one restaurant in town, a group of Tennessee volunteers got drunk and began destroying plates, then took out their guns and began shooting. They killed one of their own in the process. Taylor was forced to banish one group of volunteers, the Louisville Legion, from Monterrey entirely. They were ordered back to Camargo after it was discovered that a large group of them regularly went out on vigilante raids, searching for Mexicans to kill.

Worst of all was the Texas cavalry—the Texas Rangers, as they were known. Thought by many to be an elite unit, they viewed the war as a means of extracting revenge on Mexico and the Mexican people, and Monterrey as a city that was theirs to plunder. Texas Rangers wore buckskin shirts and were fond of tucking their dusty pants into the tops of their riding boots. They disdained bathing and were infested with lice and fleas, wore broad-brimmed hats similar to Mexican sombreros, and were never without a gun belt, knife, or rifle—and sometimes wore all three at once. Few of the Rangers shaved, and their thick beards added to their outlaw appearance, particularly in comparison to the regulars, who were generally clean shaven. When Worth temporarily ceased military patrols, thinking that order had been restored, the thatch-roofed shanties of peasants were burned and at least one hundred Mexicans were murdered. The Texans, under Colonel Hays, were found to be responsible but went unpunished.

The Mexican populace quickly learned to differentiate between the regulars and the volunteers—the good Americans and the bad, to their way of thinking.

And over time the violence died down. Little by little, the citizens of Monterrey returned. Their local economy flourished, thanks to the American soldiers who were willing to pay for goods and services. Thus the waning months of 1846 passed, with Taylor's Monterrey army literally divided into two camps: those in the city and those in the country. Life seemed to be settling back into a normal routine. It was, as Grant wrote, "a quiet camp life."

But not for much longer.

TWENTY-FIVE

Policy and Power

NOVEMBER 7, 1846

Life in Monterrey was good for George Meade—very good. Thanks to the death and illness of several predecessors, he was now the ranking topographical engineer in Taylor's army (four had fallen, and it had become a grim running joke that getting the job of senior topog was akin to being issued a death warrant). He and his housemates, fellow topographical engineers Jeremiah Scarritt and John Pope, had hired a cook, a waiter, and a groom to meet their every need. Their opulently appointed mansion was decorated in mahogany and featured a Monterrey rarity: glass windows. Most important, Meade also enjoyed the confidence of Taylor and Worth, two increasingly powerful generals. Worth thought Meade a man of "intelligent zeal and gallantry" and brought him ever closer into his command circle. The two men had ridden down the Saltillo road together, Worth studying the narrow pass for its strategic importance while Meade made carefully detailed terrain sketches for Taylor—sketches that were later forwarded to Washington and reviewed by Polk and Secretary of War Marcy.

The sketches, however, were not the only missives from Mexico being reviewed by the president and the secretary of war.

Word of Taylor's Monterrey victory and subsequent armistice had reached Washington, D.C., on October 11. This could not have been worse news for Polk. Since late August he had been rethinking the war. With the Texas boundary now all but settled at the Rio Grande, it was becoming unclear why U.S. troops were still in Mexico. Popular support for the war was waning among the American public. Yet for Polk to pull out before achieving a complete Mexican surrender would be an enormous loss of face.

Instead, Polk chose to greatly increase the size of the U.S. force and the scope of the war. He proposed (in a plan borrowed from General Winfield Scott) to abandon military operations in northern Mexico and go straight for that country's jugular. American forces would first take the small eastern port of Tampico for use as a staging area and then travel hundreds of miles south by ship to invade from the sea at the tropical port of Veracruz. It was Mexico's largest and most vital harbor and its conduit to the outside world. From there, they would march inland to Mexico City and seize the Mexican capital.

It was the obvious scheme, for it was becoming clear that the Mexicans had little emotional investment in northern Mexico. Taylor's advances had minimal effect on life in Mexico's lush central valley, where the vast majority of its citizens lived, particularly the white criollos, who controlled the church, the military, and the political hierarchy. To them, the North was a place for establishing military presidios—forts—for national defense, but also a place where hostile Indians held far more sway in the vast open spaces between towns. It had been that way since the time of the Aztecs, who referred to the region contemptuously as the Chichimeca, in reference to the area's nomadic tribes, whose lifestyle they considered barbarian in contrast to their own cultured ways. Mexico's current leaders, while unwilling to cede northern Mexico to the United States without a fight, would never put themselves under America's thumb by surrendering their entire nation over those desert lands. Not until Americans took up residence in the halls of Montezuma—Mexico City, once the epicenter of Aztec rule and still the base of all Mexican power—could the war truly be complete.

On Sunday, September 20, just as hostilities were beginning in Monterrey, Polk convened an emergency cabinet session to discuss this radical change in strategy. He proposed that Taylor be redirected from Monterrey to Tampico and outfitted with seven companies of regulars, a new company of dragoons, and a large body of volunteers. The soldiers would attack the town from the rear, while an American naval fleet commanded by Commodore David Conner would bombard it by sea.

This was a bold tactical shift, a point underscored by Polk's making the unusual move of holding a cabinet meeting on the Sabbath. The president was saying, in essence, that Monterrey no longer mattered. Even after the long summer of moving troops up the Rio Grande, the buildup of men and material, and now the ferocious street fighting that would claim hundreds of Mexican and American lives, Polk had decided it was all for naught.

Thanks to the vast distance between Washington, D.C., and Taylor's army, the courier delivering Polk's new orders had crossed paths with the messenger bringing word of the Monterrey armistice. So even as Taylor—and then Meade—digested the proposed Tampico assault, Polk and his cabinet were just receiving news of Taylor's unilateral act of diplomacy.

The armistice had the potential to be an enormous loss of face for Polk. His own peace efforts, launched in July, had been rebuffed by the Mexicans, who made it clear they would not talk peace until all American forces left their country. Additionally, the British and French were growing more and more hostile toward Polk's war. In an article that the *Times* of London reprinted for British readers, the Parisian *Journal des Débats* succinctly described their view of the war thus far: "A grievance was imagined relative to a strip of land between the Rio Nueces and the Rio Grande, which had belonged to the insurgent Texians, which was manifestly false, and which it was said the Mexicans retained contrary to justice. But once Matamoros was conquered, the Americans were in possession of the disputed territory. Why, then, advance an army, first to Camargo and subsequently to Monterey?...Mr. Polk and his counselors cannot but have perceived this, and they regret having advanced on that side; but to recall General Taylor, at present, would be to cover themselves with confusion in the eyes of their political adversaries and in the eyes of the multitude, whom they have inspired with a fatal passion for military glory."

What some saw as Polk's act of naked aggression was punctuated by the recent congressional proposal for a railway that would travel across the Rocky Mountains and on to the Pacific. With the railway, the sea-to-shining-sea goal of Manifest Destiny would almost be complete.

From the European point of view, Mexico was an impoverished young nation being bullied by a greedy neighbor. It was equally obvious that there was no turning back. "A retreat," concluded the *Journal,* "would be translated into a defeat. The Mexicans would be persuaded that they had beaten the Americans."

Polk's greatest dilemma over Taylor's armistice, however, lay not with the opinions of the British or the French, and certainly not with that of the Mexicans. It was the American people whom he feared most. The problem had its roots in democracy and a politician's need to be elected by the people before being allowed to serve. Americans had historically been an easily malleable, highly illiterate, and ill-informed mass of voters. But that was changing, and quickly. Technological advances in papermaking and the invention of the steam printing press (which printed well over 1,000 pages per hour, as opposed to the 240 of the Gutenberg-style manual press) had made newspapers affordable and more easily mass-produced beginning in the 1830s. Once only for the well-off, papers sprang up all around the country; New York alone had eleven dailies, a quick source of news and opinion available for as little as a penny a day.

This in turn helped catalyze an unexpected rise in literacy among the working class. Most communities had a school of sorts, the most popular being the one-room schoolhouse, where reading was among the educational fundamentals, so the ability to read was already widespread. But the growth of the daily newspaper offered Americans the chance to apply that skill as part of their daily routine and as a means to form their opinion on a broad variety of issues, including politics. That opinion would translate into a yea or nay vote come election time.

In between elections, they voted with their wallets. Competition for readership between newspapers became cutthroat. The paper that published a breaking story first could outsell the others, a fact that became readily visible during the war. The *New York Herald,* in conjunction with the *New Orleans Crescent City,* the *Baltimore Sun,* and the *Philadelphia Public Ledger,* established a network to "express" stories from the battlefield. Traveling via pony express, ship, and steamboat, couriers raced information to the papers. Telegraph service formed the final leg of the network. The system was quicker (by days) than the U.S. Postal Service—so much so that the outraged and embarrassed U.S. postmaster general eventually arrested the *Crescent City'*s owner on charges of moving mail by private means.

So even as military couriers sped Taylor's dispatches to the White House, news of the Monterrey victory was creeping into newspapers across the country well before letters from the front arrived home. "Glorious News from the Army!" read an October 13 headline in the *Richmond (VA) Enquirer.* "Capitulation of Monterey after Three Days of Fighting." The *New York Herald,* that city's most influential and widely read newspaper, seized on the populist idea that the real heroes were the volunteers. "When it is considered that the men who behaved themselves so gallantly on these occasions, were drawn promiscuously from all parts of our extended country—were strangers to each other till the time when they met at the rendezvous to take up arms in defence of their country's honour, and never had heard the roar of cannon or the rattling of firearms except on the 4th of July, we have great reason to be proud of their prowess in time of danger, and the reliance we can place in our countrymen's courage and ability to defend to the death the free institutions that their patriotic sires bequeathed to them, whenever endangered by foreign or domestic enemies."

Taylor was at the center of all that adulation. His seeming battlefield invincibility was rapidly making him a folk hero and thus a political threat. The Whig Party had been revitalized and was in the process of regaining control of the House and the Senate in the elections of 1846. Looking ahead two short years, Polk was fearful that Taylor might run for the presidency—and, with his homespun ways and wartime heroics, might win.

Polk acted quickly. On October 13, he directed Secretary of War William L. Marcy to annul the armistice. Then Polk removed Taylor from command of the Tampico expedition. Leading the American army in his place would be Robert Patterson, an Irish-born Democrat. Patterson was a volunteer who owed his rank to an influential civilian job in banking and his limited service—in the Quartermaster Department—during the War of 1812. Patterson was pompous and soft. At his headquarters in Camargo there was a standing order that "no wagons or horsemen should pass the street facing his palace door" owing to the fine clouds of caliche dust that they soon sent wafting inside. Thanks to Patterson's unlikable personality, it was an edict that some regulars took great pride in ignoring. "Colonel May and Lieutenant Britton, affecting not to understand the order or to forget it, gallop past the palace door a dozen times a day with lightning speed, and raising a devil of a dust, lost in the clouds of their own creation before the sentinel has time to call a halt," wrote one eyewitness.

Patterson's lack of command experience (and his unswerving Democratic allegiance) had prompted Taylor to leave him behind in Camargo with the volunteers rather than allow him to make the march to Monterrey. Patterson and his fellow Democratic volunteers had made their anger known to Washington, and now Polk was letting them know he had heard, loud and clear.

"Well may we be grateful that we are at war with Mexico," wrote a cynical Meade when the news reached Monterrey. "Were it any other power, our gross follies would have been punished severely before now."

An outraged Taylor chose to ignore the follies altogether. After informing the Mexican army by courier that the armistice was no more, he and Worth led a force of a thousand men some fifty-five miles southwest into Saltillo, which he occupied on November 16. The town had once been a major Mexican city, a place where people thronged annually for a great open-air fiesta featuring bullfights and cockfights and gambling on cards. The narrow streets were paved with small stones made smooth by mules' traveling over them, and fountains still lined the plazas, but the city had fallen on hard times. "Saltillo seems to be rather on the decline," wrote one Indiana volunteer. "Many of the buildings look very old and are going to ruin."

General Wool, whose army had camped in nearby Monclova to wait out the armistice, had abandoned their march to Chihuahua after having received word that the Mexican army was no longer there. Wool's men now stood ready to join the rest of the American forces. They would position themselves in Parras, just west of Saltillo, and guard Taylor's right flank. Together they would hold a line that kept the Mexican army bottled up in the southern half of the country. A three-hundred-mile expanse of uncrossable desert lay between the American forces and the combined armies of Santa Anna and Ampudia, in San Luis Potosí. Now the American occupation force was split, with most of the army in Monterrey and the smaller advance contingent in Saltillo. "I presume that General Taylor's idea is to hold this country," wrote Meade, "and keep his troops ready to carry out the orders of the Government."

The orders of the government, however, were for Taylor to remain in Monterrey. Those orders had arrived by courier on November 12. Not only had Taylor ignored them, but he now set in motion a plan to broaden the sweep of his command.

Even before occupying Saltillo on November 16, he had pronounced himself "decidedly opposed to carrying the war beyond Saltillo in this direction," effectively indicating that the quaint old village was the southernmost point his army would occupy. Taylor's ambition was to form a defensive line that stretched eastward from Saltillo to the town of Victoria and then on to Tampico, on the Gulf of Mexico. On December 13, Taylor rode toward Victoria to set that plan in action. With him was a division of regulars commanded by General David E. Twiggs and a brigade under General John A. Quitman. Patterson and the Second Division of Volunteers were to march from Camargo to join up with him in Victoria and then proceed to Tampico, which the U.S. Navy had already taken without a fight.

But soon after the march began, Taylor received a message from General Worth in Saltillo, relaying rumors of a possible Mexican attack on the town. On December 17, he turned and charged back with Twiggs's force, ordering Quitman to continue his march to Victoria. On December 23 he abruptly reversed his course upon hearing that Wool's army had ridden to Worth's aid, to repel what was likely a false alarm. Once again, Taylor rode with Twiggs's division to Victoria.

Back on the Rio Grande, in the disease-ridden outpost of Camargo, a visitor had arrived, searching for the elusive Taylor.

This visitor was none other than General Winfield Scott. He had come not only to rein in Taylor but to steal his beloved army.

IV

SCOTT'S WAR

After the fall of Monterey, [Taylor's] third battle and third complete victory, the Whig papers at home began to speak of him as the candidate of their party for the Presidency. Something had to be done to neutralize his growing popularity. He could not be relieved from duty in the field where all his battles had been victories. The design would have been too transparent. It was finally decided to send General Scott to Mexico in chief command, and to authorize him to carry out his own original plan: that is, capture Veracruz and march on the capital of the country.

— Ulysses S. Grant, Memoirs

TWENTY-SIX

Transfers

JANUARY 16, 1847

O f all days, it was Christmas when General Winfield Scott wrote to General Zachary Taylor, informing him that he needed additional men for his Veracruz invasion. But December 25 was just another day in wartime, and America's top general was not in a giving mood.

Scott had hoped to soften the blow by making the demand in person. He had cruised all the way upriver to Camargo by steamboat before learning that Taylor was no longer in Monterrey, or even Saltillo, but now stubbornly riding toward Victoria.

Someone had to establish order, and Scott was in a hurry to take charge of that task. "My dear general," he wrote Taylor. "I shall be obliged to take from you most of the gallant officers and men (regulars and volunteers) whom you have so long and so nobly commanded. I am afraid that I shall, by imperious necessity—the approach of the yellow fever on the gulf coast—reduce you for a time, to stand on the defensive. This will be infinitely painful to you, and for that reason, distressing to me. But I rely on your patriotism to submit to the temporary sacrifice with cheerfulness."

Taylor, in other words, had fought his last battle.

Divisions of regulars commanded by Worth and Twiggs, and the volunteers under Quitman and Patterson, were immediately transferred to Scott. Taylor was left with just 500 regulars and 4,500 volunteers. Santa Anna had built up a formidable army—estimates now placed Mexican troop strength somewhere between 15,000 and 25,000 men—south across the desert in San Luis Potosí. And though the terrain separating them from the Americans was considered too arid for such a large army to march across, Santa Anna's feints toward Taylor had become so common that U.S. troops had given a name to their frantic deployment into fighting positions: stampedes.

The truth was far less romantic: if Santa Anna actually managed to force-march his conscripts north from San Luis Potosí, Taylor's army would be slaughtered. Scott tried to soften whatever fears his old comrade might have by dangling the prospect of reinforcements sometime very soon.

"You will be aware of the recent call for nine regiments of new volunteers, including one of Texas horse. The president may soon ask for more; and we are not without hope that Congress may add ten or twelve to the regular establishment. These, by the spring, say April, may, by the aid of large bounties, be in the field—should Mexico not earlier propose terms of accommodation; and, long before the spring (March), it is probable you will be again in force to resume offensive operations," Scott concluded.

This was unlikely. Both men knew it. Scott was also ordering him to abandon his defensive line across northern Mexico by leaving Saltillo and falling back into Monterrey. There he would be reduced to fending off desperadoes that had begun to prey on American supply wagons. "No man can better afford to do so. Recent victories place you on that high eminence; and I even flatter myself that any benefit that may result to me, personally, from the unequal division of troops alluded to, will lessen the pain of your consequent inactivity," Scott wrote, concluding his demand as diplomatically as possible.

Word of the coming Veracruz invasion was already making its way into U.S. newspapers. Scott believed that Santa Anna would soon be too consumed with the rumors to bother Taylor much longer. Once Scott's army began thrusting inland toward Mexico City, Santa Anna would be forced on the defensive, without a man or a musket to spare for any other theater of operations.

Taylor would now pass the rest of the war as he had spent so many months of his career: far from his family, occupying a frontier garrison, commanding men, and fending off a foreign enemy as best he could until it was time to go home. His officers in the Monterrey region had been the army's best and brightest. Some had already made their mark, others were just beginning to show their potential, and still more were true longshots to command a fighting force. Yet these officers rubbed shoulders on a daily basis, subconsciously studying Taylor's style of command and getting to know one another's strengths and weaknesses, quirks and talents, emotions and fears—just as they had at West Point: Ulysses S. Grant, Thomas Jackson, George Meade, George McClellan, Napoleon Dana, Braxton Bragg, John Pope, Abner Doubleday, Daniel Harvey Hill, Pete Longstreet, Joseph Mansfield, William Hardee, and many more. Now all of them were gone, transferred to the command of either Patterson or Scott. Meade, whose respect for Old Rough and Ready had blossomed into adulation, was the only topographical engineer to be ripped from Taylor's command. One of the few Monterrey veterans who remained with Taylor was Jeff Davis, freshly back from Davis Bend and Varina, ready and eager to once again take charge of the Mississippi Rifles.

"It is with deep sensibility that the commanding general finds himself separated from his troops," Taylor told them all, using the third person as he addressed the departing ranks. "To those corps, regular and volunteer, who have shared with him the active services of the field, he feels the attachment due to such associations, while to those who are making their first campaign, he must express his regret that he cannot participate with them in its eventful scenes. To all, both officers and men, he extends his heartfelt wishes for their continued success and happiness, confident that their achievements on another theater will redound to the credit of their country and its arms."

General Zachary Taylor had no idea how profoundly those hopes would soon be realized.

TWENTY-SEVEN

The Artillery Officer

JANUARY 7, 1847

Among those singled out by Taylor as "making their first campaign" was the Virginian Thomas Jackson, an artillery officer. Jackson had a lean physique that made his body appear all sharp angles, from the prow of his long nose and sharply sloping forehead to the cant of his elbows. The only feature that appeared soft was his light blue eyes, which seemed perpetually rimmed with fatigue. Lacking a middle name at birth, Jackson had taken it upon himself to adopt the initial J.—some thought it stood for Jonathan, after his father—and took to signing his name T. J.

He had been born in a brick house on the main street of Clarksburg, Virginia, on the night of January 20, 1824. The doctor swore he was born before midnight, but no one was paying close attention to the time, so his actual birth date was never established. Jonathan, a lawyer and Freemason with a history of money problems, died of typhoid fever when young Tom was two. Julia Jackson raised her three children with the help of a dozen slaves and her rather large extended family, before remarrying four years later. When Julia died during childbirth in 1831,

Tom was sent to live with his uncle Cummins, at a place called Jackson's Mill, near Weston.

Julia Jackson had been a devout Presbyterian, but Cummins was cut from a different cloth. Tom grew up in a household without religion, enjoying a backwoods lifestyle centered around outdoor adventure, with minimal restriction. He could drive a wagon and chop wood, among other manual hallmarks of rural living. There were "none to give mandates; none for me to obey but as I chose; surrounded by my playmates and relatives, all eager to promote my happiness." Indeed, when a twelve-year-old Tom asked permission to float a raft eighty miles down the Ohio River, Cummins agreed to let him go.

At seventeen, however, Tom heard a Presbyterian minister deliver a sermon one Sunday morning. Cummins had sent his nephew off to the town of Parkersburg to pick up a part for the mill. While there, Tom happened to hear the minister preaching. His sermon was so powerful that Tom returned for the evening service so that he might hear the passionate words of worship once more. The date was August 1, 1841. A seed of religious fervor had been planted in Jackson that would flourish just a few years later—in Mexico.

Eight months afterward, Jackson received an appointment to West Point. He had a minimal education, thanks to sporadic school attendance and a lack of good schools near Jackson's Mill, but he possessed a solid work ethic and a deep desire to succeed. It helped that the congressman making the appointment, Samuel L. Hays, was the father of Jackson's friend and occasional schoolmate Peregrine. "Jackson," remembered his classmate Dabney Maury of their first day at the military academy, "was awkward and uncultured in manner and appearance, but there was an earnest purpose in his aspect which impressed all who saw him. Birket Fry, A.P. Hill and I were standing together when he entered the South Barracks under charge of a cadet sergeant.

He was clad in gray homespun, and wore a coarse felt hat, such as wagoners or constables — as he had been — usually wore, and bore a pair of weather-stained saddlebags across his shoulders. There was about him so sturdy an expression of purpose that I remarked, 'that fellow looks as if he has come here to stay.'"

Jackson, however, nearly flunked out his plebe year. His lack of education was clearly an impediment to a military career, forcing him to apply himself to his studies with a dedication that bordered on the fanatic. "His barracks room was small and bare and cold. Every night just before taps he would pile his grate high with anthracite coal, so that by the time the lamps were out, a ruddy glow came from his fire, by which, prone on the bare floor, he would 'bone' his lesson for the next day, until it was literally burned into his brain," wrote Maury. "His steady purpose to succeed and to do his duty soon won the respect of all, and his teachers and comrades alike honored his efforts." Jackson began compiling a list of aphorisms to keep himself in line: "You may be whatever you want to be"; "Disregard public opinion when it comes to your duty"; "Sacrifice your life rather than your word"; and "Perform without fail what you resolve," among others. Jackson went on to graduate seventeenth of fifty-nine cadets in the class of 1846. His classmates agreed he would have finished first if there had been one more year.

It was not all a life of the mind along the Hudson. There were rumors, never proved, that Jackson fathered a child out of wedlock while at West Point. Most curiously, after years of hardening his body through work and self-denial, Jackson had become something of a hypochondriac, complaining of phantom illnesses and raising his left arm high in the air to let blood drain back into his body — this because he thought his left arm was larger than his right, throwing his circulation out of balance. Raising it, he argued, was a means of restoring equilibrium. In time, Jackson would also begin to eat standing up whenever possible, with the aim of "straightening the intestinal tract" and enhancing digestion.

Jackson had graduated from West Point on July 1 and gone straight to Brown's Hotel in New York with some classmates to celebrate (getting drunk for one of the few, if not the only, times in his life); by mid-August he was making the journey down the Ohio and the Mississippi and then on to the war via the *James L. Day.* "I belong to a company of light artillery, which is frequently called flying artillery," he wrote to his uncle James while at sea. "In an action, if all the officers of the company should be well, I will have to carry dispatches, unfortunately being too low to have a command."

Jackson, along with twenty-seven men and eighty-four horses, disembarked at Port Isabel on September 25. He was hungry to see action. "I am in hopes of starting up the Rio Grande tomorrow and on reaching General Taylor as soon as possible," Jackson wrote his sister Laura. But Monterrey had fallen by then, and Jackson's unit—Company K, First Artillery—lingered in Port Isabel for two weeks. By Halloween, he had arrived in Camargo by steamer. Jackson openly envied the veterans who had already seen the elephant, but during the long march to Monterrey he developed a growing fascination with the Mexican countryside. "The portion of Northern Mexico which has fallen under my observation is mostly a vast barren waste, cities excepted," he wrote to his sister. "There are but two seasons in Mexico: wet and dry. In consequence there is but little vegetation."

Monterrey, however, was pleasant. Jackson was quartered inside the city with Worth's division, in a home with an orange orchard and a swimming pool in its large backyard. "It is the most beautiful city I have seen in this country," he told Laura. He was awed, in particular, by the ornate churches, the devout religiosity of the local people, and even the fine robes worn during Mass by the Catholic priests.

Jackson had been in Mexico a little over two months when Company K was transferred to Scott's command. Now he and the rest of his unit hitched their horses and mules to the caissons of ammunition and the limbers of the six-pounders to retrace their steps back to Camargo and then the Texas coast. There, he would board yet another ship, on his way, finally, to make his first campaign.

TWENTY-EIGHT

One Step Closer

January 16, 1847

aptain Robert E. Lee was also among the men transferred to Scott's command. The reliable, if heretofore unspectacular, Virginian had shown a dogged brilliance during his time with Wool's army, as if desperate to finally make his mark.

One incident in particular stood out. Wool's six-hundred-mile march south from San Antonio had been incident free, and the subsequent garrison duty in the Saltillo region had been cause for the occasional adventure. But on Christmas morning, just after breakfast, news of enemy troop movements reached Wool's headquarters. Lee volunteered to act as scout, to ascertain the size of the force. He hired a local guide to show the way and rode all day and into the night searching for the Mexican army. He was soon rewarded by the sight of distant campfires. The terrified Mexican guide begged Lee to turn back. When the Virginian refused, the guide fled, forcing Lee to press on alone.

By then, he was forty miles from Wool's army. Yet Lee carefully rode closer to the fires, until he could clearly see a large encampment on a hill. The dingy white tents seemed to be moving. Thinking this odd, Lee edged even closer. The "tents" turned out to be a flock of sheep. The Mexican army was nowhere to be seen.

That could have been the end of the mission, but the indefatigable Lee had been ordered to find the enemy troops, and he would not rest until he had done so. After riding into the shepherds' camp and ascertaining the true location of the Mexican army, Lee galloped back to Wool. "The most delighted man to see me was the old Mexican, the father of my guide, with whom I had last been seen by any of our people, and whom General Wool had arrested and proposed to hang if I was not forthcoming," he later recalled.

Lee promptly teamed up with a group of cavalry and rode back out into the country. By this time he had been in the saddle for more than a day, with just a three-hour break to catch some sleep. Yet he would spend the next day in the saddle as well, finally locating the Mexican forces, precisely calculating their numbers, and charging back to report the news to Wool.

That was the sort of diligent effort Lee had put forth his entire career, but now something finally came of it. Wool promoted him to inspector general of his division. Even better, Scott remembered their long-ago meeting at West Point, when they had administered final exams to the cadets. Lee was not just being transferred to the general's command; he was ordered to join the general staff as they planned the invasion of Veracruz.

The challenges Lee would face were many, and the logistics enormous. Veracruz would be the largest joint amphibious operation in U.S. history. Transport ships needed to be positioned, some ten thousand men needed to be loaded aboard those ships and then fed and housed, and surfboats were needed to row them ashore. Additionally, cannons, munition, and horses needed to be transported, among the myriad objects a self-sustaining force required to invade another nation. It was a great honor for Lee to be chosen. He still had yet to hear a shot fired in anger, but that seemed certain to change come the first week of March, when Veracruz would see the American army crawl out of the sea.

TWENTY-NINE

California

JANUARY 26, 1847

L ieutenant William Tecumseh Sherman was also in a place called Monterey, but nearly three thousand miles from his fellow West Pointers. One hundred and eighty-nine days after sailing from New York, the USS *Lexington* dropped anchor. She was roughly one hundred miles southwest of Yerba Buena, on the coast of California, in the charming mission village that shared a name with its war-torn southern cousin.

"Swords were brought out, guns oiled and made ready, and everything was in a bustle when the old Lexington dropped her anchor," Sherman recalled. "Everything on shore looked bright and beautiful, the hills covered with grass and flowers, the live oaks so serene and homelike, and the low adobe houses, with red tiled roofs and whitened walls, contrasted well with the dark brown pine trees behind, making a decidedly good looking impression on us who had come so far to spy out the land.

"Nothing could be more peaceful in its looks than Monterey in January, 1847."

Therein lay the problem. Sherman had traveled far in search of war — down the coast of North and South America, around

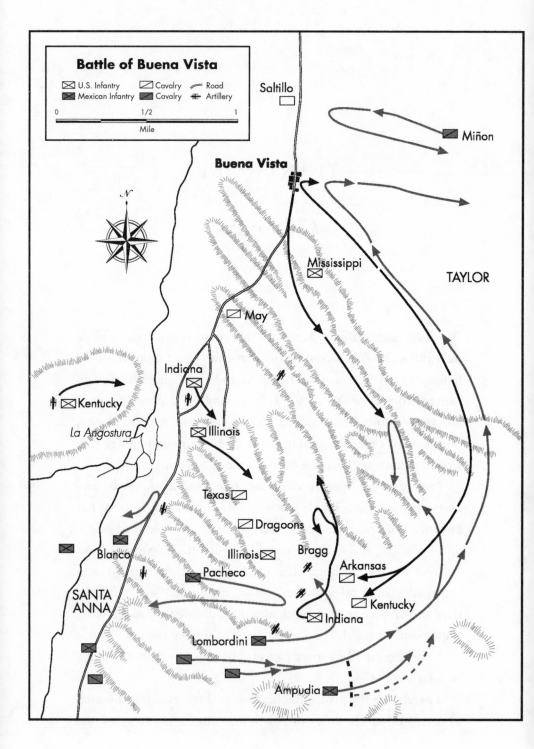

Battle of Buena Vista

U.S. Infantry   Cavalry   Road
Mexican Infantry   Cavalry   Artillery

0   1/2   1
Mile

Saltillo

Miñon

Buena Vista

Mississippi

TAYLOR

May

Indiana

Kentucky

La Angostura

Illinois

Texas

Dragoons

Illinois

Bragg

Arkansas

Blanco

Pacheco

Kentucky

SANTA
ANNA

Indiana

Lombordini

Ampudia

Cape Horn, then back up along the coasts of those same two continents—only to find that the war in California was all but done by the time he got there.

The conquest of California was the fulfillment of Polk's aggressive Manifest Destiny strategy and had initially been led by an eccentric and ambitious adventurer named John C. Frémont. The son-in-law of Senator Thomas Hart Benton, Frémont was a brevet captain in the Topographical Corps who had been sent west to chart the Arkansas and Red rivers. However, he had somehow ended up on the shores of the Pacific, more than a thousand miles west of those rivers' headwaters, and almost single-handedly overthrew the Mexican government at Yerba Buena. On July 4, 1846, at a party in Sonoma to celebrate the victory, he declared California independent of Mexico. The victory was sealed when a naval contingent led by Commodore Robert F. Stockton captured Monterey. Frémont was named military commandant of the region, and Yerba Buena's name was soon changed to San Francisco.

Meanwhile, Colonel Stephen Watts Kearny, who had led a force of dragoons west from Fort Leavenworth in June, successfully captured the Mexican outpost at Santa Fe on August 18. He then left behind an occupying force and marched three hundred dragoons overland on mules toward Southern California, departing on September 25. En route, they encountered the legendary mountain man Kit Carson, who was racing east with news from Frémont that American forces had already conquered California. Kearny immediately transferred the dispatches to one of his officers, pressed Carson into service as a guide, and sent two hundred dragoons back to Santa Fe, thinking that the less volatile conditions in California called for a smaller force.

Over the two months of travel that followed, Kearny's force suffered horribly. Their route took them through the great Mojave and Sonoran deserts of the American Southwest. Their mules died beneath them from lack of water and vegetation. The men became skeletal as their rations were reduced. When Kearny's depleted column finally arrived in the verdant scrublands outside San Diego, a chance encounter with Mexican forces saw eighteen of them slaughtered and another thirteen mutilated by lances and sabers. The Battle of San Pasqual was the first American defeat of the Mexican War. Just as disturbingly, it signaled a shift: the Mexicans had regained control of portions of California.

But Kearny managed to hook up with American naval forces in San Diego on December 12. Working in conjunction with naval commodore Robert F. Stockton, Kearny's soldiers marched north and captured Los Angeles on January 10, 1847. After that, the battle became one of pride, as dueling forces settled the matter of California's American military leadership. Kearny, under orders from Washington, claimed that he was military governor; Stockton backed Frémont.

That was the only semblance of conflict Sherman discovered upon arriving in Monterey. Now he would be fated to spend the rest of the war keeping the peace in a quiet, beautiful, and—with a mere twenty thousand Spanish and American residents—extremely underpopulated territory.

Just as during the Seminole Wars, William Tecumseh Sherman seemed destined to remain on the periphery of yet another conflict, left to hear of the action secondhand, through the accounts of his fellow West Pointers. Slowly, and despite his best efforts to enjoy the beauty of this new land, Sherman settled into a deep and lasting depression.

THIRTY

Taylor Stands Alone

FEBRUARY 22, 1847

It was George Washington's birthday, a most patriotic day to every American soldier. The Mexican request for surrender arrived at 11:00 A.M. An officer on horseback, flying a white flag, galloped toward the American lines. But it was not the Mexicans who were giving up. Rather, Santa Anna's messenger carried a letter requesting that Taylor's forces throw down their weapons and throw up their hands. "You are surrounded by 20,000 men," the demand read in Spanish, forcing Taylor to yell for a translator, "and cannot in any human probability avoid suffering a rout, and being cut to pieces with your troops. But as you deserve consideration and particular esteem, I wish to save you from a catastrophe, and for that purpose give you this notice in order that you may surrender at discretion under the assurance that you will be treated with the consideration belonging to the Mexican character; to which end you will be granted an hour's time to make up your mind, to commence from the moment when my flag of truce arrives at your camp."

Taylor appeared to have little choice. General Santa Anna had done the impossible, marching his 21,533 men and twenty-one pieces of artillery hundreds of miles north from San Luis Potosí across a barren and almost entirely waterless wasteland. He now prepared to slaughter Taylor's depleted force.

Santa Anna had exerted a cruel discipline on the march, shooting anyone attempting to desert. But he had promised his army that they could loot the American corpses after the battle. Now, their long march finally done, the impoverished Mexican soldiers thirsted for their promised riches. Many of these same Mexican troops had marched out of Monterrey in disgrace five months earlier. There was little doubt that the Mexicans had come seeking revenge. Should the Americans surrender, they would be stripped of their belongings and perhaps their lives. Taylor's men chose a name for the grisly fate awaiting them: getting "lanced."

Davis and the First Mississippi anchored the far left—and most vulnerable end—of the American line. Placing the Mississippi regiment at the far left was evidence of Taylor's trust in Davis's leadership. Of all his units, Taylor had personally requested that the First Mississippi remain under his command when other troops were being stripped away. Davis had since become closer than ever with the general, privy to his confidences and anti-Polk opinions.

The Americans were seven miles south of Saltillo, near a sprawling stone hacienda known as Buena Vista. The estate was gorgeously situated on a vast plain, with undulating columns of buttes and ravines arrayed before it. The soldiers were mesmerized by the splendor of their surroundings. "Nature was there in her grandeur and her power," wrote one officer. "And as far as the eye could reach, the peaks of the Sierra Madre were towering in the skies."

THOUGH BEAUTIFUL FROM a distance, the terrain was treacherous and windswept up close, its loose soil lacking in vegetation.

Taylor's scouts had warned him of the Mexican advance just a few days earlier. After the initial shock of realizing that his worst fears were about to come true, Taylor had ordered his army to fall back from their encampment farther south at Agua Nueva. He retreated up the road eleven miles until he found the place where he would make a stand. Taylor, working closely with General Wool, judiciously positioned his small force. The crags and plateaus offered natural defensive positions. A mountain pass known as La Angostura provided a perfect location to place the right side of his line, for the land west of it was far too rugged for an army to traverse. Taylor installed artillery and two regiments in the pass, the Third Indiana and the First Illinois. His remaining regiments, including cavalries from Kentucky and Arkansas, spread out across a mile-long plateau that extended like a long tongue eastward from the Angostura pass. Davis and the First Mississippi were at the far end of the plateau. Thanks to that daunting terrain west of La Angostura, the Mexicans would have no choice but to attack Davis's end of the line.

Despite Santa Anna's boast that his forces already had the Americans surrounded, his army was merely arrayed in a broad arc in front of Taylor's troops. Yet his words weren't too far from the truth: encircling the Americans would be as simple as making a sweep around Davis and marching straight on to Buena Vista. There he would block the road that ran directly through Angostura, into Buena Vista, then on to Saltillo, and into Monterrey. This was the same road Worth's men had battled for on September 20. The Americans had traveled back and forth along the span countless times in the months since. Now the combination of Santa Anna's troops and the terrain would imprison the Americans.

The Mexican messenger was Major Pedro Vanderlinden, a surgeon. As commanding general, it was Taylor who drafted the reply to Santa Anna's demand. The major dutifully galloped back to the Mexican lines and presented it to Santa Anna. The wording had been altered by Major Bliss (Taylor's actual language had been laden with expletives), but the intent remained no less direct: "In reply to your note of this date, summoning me to surrender my forces at your discretion, I beg leave to say that I decline acceding to your request."

Battle was imminent. Wool rode up and down the lines, rousing his division and even the volunteers by invoking the memory of the venerated Washington. The sun was shining brightly, but the air was biting cold. They were upholding a "sacred trust," Wool told the volunteers, by doing battle on the first president's birthday. The American soldiers responded with thunderous cheers, and regimental bands broke into "Hail, Columbia." Wool "nerved the hearts of the soldiers," in the words of one Massachusetts volunteer. Small in numbers, but mightily determined to stand fast, the Americans braced for the Mexican onslaught.

They didn't wait long. As Wool was exhorting the Americans, Catholic priests marched in a long procession before Santa Anna's forces, offering a benediction to the Mexican troops as regimental bands played somber martial music in the background. As soon as the priests finished, the Mexicans attacked. The time was 3:00 P.M. The action began with the firing of a single cannon. That was the signal for squads led by Mexican generals Ampudia and Mejía to begin the predictable move toward Davis and the left side of the American line. Sunlight gleamed off their polished bayonets. The air was filled with the clatter of hooves and the creak of gun carriages being dragged into position. Those two Mexican generals were proud and used to getting their way. They had been humiliated by Taylor three times. Buena Vista marked the beginning of their redemption.

The deep valleys and rocky plateaus made for slow movement. A cold wind whistled up the valley when darkness fell. It began to rain. Muzzle flashes continued until long after sunset. Both sides rested in the field and waited for morning to come again—everyone but Davis and the First Mississippi. Taylor was concerned about his supply depot back in Saltillo. He ordered the First to pull back and march there as a defensive gesture. Finding nothing wrong, the Mississippi Rifles slept a few hours and marched back to Buena Vista at first light.

THIRTY-ONE

The Hacienda

FEBRUARY 23, 1846

The Rifles reached the hacienda at 9:00 A.M.; they had been able to hear artillery for the final two miles of the march. "Excited by the sound, the regiment pressed rapidly forward, manifesting, upon this, as upon other occasions, their more than willingness to meet the enemy," wrote Davis.

Things were going horribly for the Americans. Mexican forces had punched a hole in the American lines, and the Second Indiana had fled in full retreat. "As we approached the scene of action," Davis said, "horsemen, recognized as of our troops, were seen running, dispersed and confusedly from the field; and our first view of the line of battle presented the mortifying spectacle of a regiment of infantry flying disorganized from the enemy." Seven thousand Mexican troops were now driving on Buena Vista, where Wool's terrified soldiers huddled inside the protection of the hacienda. "I rode into the court of the hacienda, and was taken from my horses and carried into a very large room," wrote Lieutenant Samuel French, an artillery specialist who had been shot in the thigh with a musket ball. "The whole floor was covered with wounded. I was placed between two soldiers. One had both legs broken below the knee. The scene almost beggars description. The screams of agony from pain, the moans of the dying, the messages sent home by the despairing, the parting farewells of friends, the incoherent speech, the peculiar movements of the hands and fingers, silence, the spirit's flight—to where? And amidst all this some of the mean passions of humanity were displayed. Near me was a poor soldier hopelessly wounded. He was cold, and yet a wretch came and, against remonstrances, took the blanket off him, claiming it was his."

Zachary Taylor's leadership style was a curiosity to military men. He did not oversee every last detail of a battle, preferring to draw up a broad plan beforehand and then allow his able commanders to execute that plan, utilizing knowledge of their troops and of the battlefield in order to make tactical maneuvers. Now, with chaos descending upon Buena Vista, Taylor's battle plan was disintegrating. He desperately needed at least one commander to step forward and make a bold play that would turn the tide in the Americans' favor—no matter how improbable the odds.

That commander was Jeff Davis. Once considered unworthy of marrying the general's daughter, he would now attempt to save Taylor's entire army.

The Mississippian halted his regiment at Buena Vista and implored the retreating Americans to stop running. "With few honorable exceptions, the appeal was unheeded, as were the offers which, I am informed, were made by our men to give their canteens of water to those who complained of thirst, on condition that they would go back. General Wool was upon the ground making great efforts to rally the men who had given way," Davis remembered.

One common ploy by men not wishing to appear cowardly was to carry a wounded friend back to Buena Vista and then to stay there instead of returning to the battlefield. The hacienda, however, would offer no protection if the Mexicans overran Taylor's position. "No one could have failed to perceive the hazard," Davis later wrote.

While American soldiers fled in the other direction, the First Mississippi marched briskly into the battle. Now numbering just four hundred men, they advanced to within rifle range of a four-thousand-man Mexican force that was "supported by strong reserves, flanked by cavalry and elated by success" and then opened fire.

It worked. "The progress of the enemy was arrested," wrote Davis. After their initial volleys, the Mississippians ran down into a chasm that separated them from the Mexicans, and continued firing as they climbed out on the other side. "The contest was severe—the destruction great on both sides. We steadily advanced, and, as the distance diminished, the ratio of loss increased."

Davis's men were falling and dying. Yet persistently, doggedly, the regiment pressed on. Davis was shot in the heel, and the musket ball drove bits of his brass spurs through his boot and into his foot. He had the wound treated while sitting in the saddle and then resumed the fight. His courage, and that of his men, emboldened their fellow Americans. The Third Indiana joined Davis's men and protected their right flank. Davis sent his sergeant major off in search of artillery to strengthen their attack. Meanwhile, Mexican lancers had caught sight of the First Mississippi and were preparing an attack. "A body of richly caparisoned lancers came forward rapidly, and in beautiful order—the files and ranks so closed as to look like a mass of men and horses. Perfect silence and the greatest steadiness prevailed in both lines of our troops, as they stood at shoulder arms waiting an attack," wrote Davis.

There were fifteen hundred lancers in all, wearing brass helmets plumed in black and scarlet, and blue tunics faced in red. They sang in cadence as they trotted their horses forward, sitting erect in the saddle, the polished tips of their lances pointing straight up at the brilliant blue sky. Davis didn't have time to form his men into a fighting square. Instead, he ordered the Indiana and Mississippi men to make a V to repel the charge, with the tip pointed at the lancers. The formation was born of necessity, not some great stroke of tactical genius. All the while, Davis said, "I repeatedly called to the men not to shoot."

The lancers trotted closer and closer. They did not know what to make of the V, for such a formation had never been used against a cavalry charge in the history of war. Eighty yards away, they came to a complete halt.

A few of Davis's men fired, against orders. That was the provocation the others needed. Davis could only watch as both lines of his impromptu V soon "poured in a volley so destructive that the mass yielded to the blow and the survivors fled."

Against all odds, the battle became a rout.

The surviving Mexican cavalry galloped away. Davis directed his troops to cross a series of ravines to link up with the beleaguered American artillery. Braxton Bragg's flying cannon was anxiously pouring double canister down onto a slowly advancing squad of Mexican infantry. The North Carolinian was such a petulant and dislikable man that two attempts had been made on his life by his own men since the war began. But at Buena Vista he showed the depths of his military prowess, flitting his cannon from one side of the field to the other in almost maniacal fashion, pouring fire into the Mexican lines. Now, the men of Mississippi and Indiana came to Bragg's aid and drove the enemy back before he could be overrun. "Though worn down by fatigue and thirst, the ranks thinned by our heavy losses in the morning, they yet advanced upon the enemy with the alacrity and eagerness of men fresh to the combat," Davis wrote proudly of his troops.

Once again, darkness halted the fighting. Davis, at long last, unable to bear the pain of the musket ball rubbing against bone any longer, galloped from the field to seek medical assistance. He never returned. Davis ended the day among the eight hundred men jammed into the Buena Vista hacienda. His wound was severe enough that he would require crutches to stand upright for the next two years and would undergo intermittent surgeries for the rest of his life.

Davis was placed in a common wagon alongside Lieutenant French and a volunteer lieutenant and carried to Saltillo, where they arrived at 10:00 P.M. The city had become one enormous hospital, particularly the Cathedral of Santiago, which was filled to overflowing with wounded. The First Mississippi had suffered thirty-nine killed and fifty-six wounded, yet Davis was hailed as the great hero of Buena Vista, and his men "conceived him to be superior to any officer in the army—those of them who have no personal fondness for him prefer him as a commander to anyone else."

The next morning, as American troops rose from a night of fitful sleep to continue the fight, they were shocked and greatly relieved to discover that the Mexicans had fled. Santa Anna, who had lost more than four thousand men, was already racing his tattered army back toward Veracruz to head off Scott's invasion. "I passed over the Mexican slain," Captain William P. Rogers of the First Mississippi wrote of the battlefield scene that morning. "There they lay in heaps, the dead and the dying. The wounded have by their sides small sacks of parched meal. They have evidently been poorly fed and clothed, as was indicated by their emaciated forms. Some would eagerly beg for 'Agua and Pan' while others would exclaim 'Ciete me Señor' as I passed. Others also we would see who had passed unhurt through the fight, but who from exhaustion and emaciation were scarcely able to speak."

Mexican critics would swear that Santa Anna had actually

won the battle, despite his retreat. "For lack of provisions and water, General Santa Anna had to retreat, but if General Taylor was left the victor, why did he not attack and conquer the miserable remains of the army which fell back to San Luis?" asked Carlos María de Bustamante, a member of the Mexican Congress who had once been a cavalry officer. "The Battle of Angostura [the Mexican name for Buena Vista] was not in any way won by General Taylor."

Yet the fact remained that Zachary Taylor and his army, against long odds, had held fast. Buena Vista was his last battle and perhaps his greatest victory. His losses were exorbitant: 272 killed and 388 wounded out of the 4,691 Americans who began the fight. He rode from the battlefield and pulled his forces back into garrison duty, there to spend the rest of the war.

THIRTY-TWO

Lobos Island

FEBRUARY 25, 1847

Grant struggled to move his pen across the page, pressing the steel nib down hard on the paper to keep his script from becoming erratic—a nearly impossible task, for he was writing to Julia from inside the USS *North Carolina* as raging swells rocked her from side to side. Once upon a time, the *North Carolina* had been the most powerful vessel in the U.S. Navy, a seventy-four-gun ship of the line that had gun ports for more than a hundred cannons and had twice been the flagship of a commodore. But those days were in the past. Now, even though it still carried ninety enormously powerful cannons (including fifty-six 42-pounders and twenty-six 32-pounders), the outmoded *North Carolina* was less a dreadful weapon than just another vessel filled with seasick American soldiers, bobbing in violent chop off the Mexican coast, two hundred miles north of Veracruz.

Grant lifted pen from page and peered out over the horizon. Thirty other transports bobbed at anchor, riding out the storm as they awaited the arrival of still more troopships. Once the rendezvous was complete, they would sail for Veracruz and the start of the invasion. "There is a report here that General Taylor has had a fight with Santa Anna some place beyond Monterey and repulsed him but it is not generally believed," wrote Grant. "My anxiety to see you my Dearest Julia increases with the space that separates us. Vera Cruz is twenty degrees south of Jefferson Barracks. I have dreamed of you twice since my last letter. All my dreams agree in one particular, that is in our marriage, either that the day is set or the ceremony is being performed."

Grant and the Fourth had been reassigned to General Worth's division, a transfer that he did not enjoy in the least. "I found General Worth a different man than any I had before served directly under. He was nervous, impatient, and restless on the march, or when important or responsible duty confronted him," Grant recalled, having gathered his first impressions while marching from Monterrey back to Port Isabel. "General Worth on one occasion at least, having made the full distance intended for the day, and after the troops were in camp and preparing their food, ordered tents struck and made the march that night which had been intended for the next day. Some commanders can move troops so as to get the maximum distance out of them without fatigue, while others can wear them out in a few days without accomplishing so much. General Worth belonged to the latter class."

The only upside of joining Worth's division was that it reunited Grant with Longstreet, and also with Grant's old West Point acquaintance Thomas Jackson, whose artillery unit had been transferred from Wool's command.

The Mexican War was the first time steamboats were widely used by an army, but the ships that would transport the Americans to Veracruz were nearly all sailing vessels. Grant had boarded the *North Carolina* at the mouth of the Rio Grande. Accommodations were limited, and "the trip was a comfortless one for officers and men." That discomfort increased as the ships sailed farther south into the tropics, where humidity and the cramped conditions conspired. The Quartermaster Department had been unable to procure antiscorbutics or green vegetables, so the daily diet consisted of salt meat and hard bread, and many of the men became ill from the shipboard fare. One vessel had suffered an outbreak of smallpox, and one hundred men had perished, their bodies buried at sea. "The character of the recruits that have recently joined is of such a nature that disease and death must be expected among them," noted one army surgeon. "Many of them are boys too young to undergo the hardship of a soldier's life, while others are old and worn out men who should never have been enlisted."

Young and old, sick and well, officer and enlisted, regular and volunteer, they were all part of an ongoing logistical marvel. Since Polk had approved the Veracruz landing three months earlier, the U.S. Army's Quartermaster Department had labored long and hard to assemble the supplies and transportation necessary to put Scott's hoped-for twenty-five thousand American soldiers on the beach. This was not just a matter of locating brigs, barks, and schooners for naval transport (163 vessels were eventually gathered from Port Isabel, Tampico, and New Orleans, then pressed into service as transports); men had to be off-loaded from their sailing ships and rowed ashore. The Quartermaster Department had hastily ordered the construction of special "surfboats," which could carry fifty men without foundering in the shore break. The boats were built in three lengths—40 feet, 37 feet 9 inches, and 35 feet 9 inches—that nested inside one another on the deck of the transport ship during the month-long journey to Mexico. They were flimsy and designed to be used just once, but of the 141 that were contracted, only 65 were built in time for the landing, meaning that the eight crewmen aboard each surfboat (seven seamen and a petty officer) would off-load men and then row back out to the transport to take on another load. Once the troops were ashore, the operation would be repeated, but with munitions, animals, and other miscellaneous supplies. Each soldier would carry enough provisions to last him three days—just long enough for the ships to be off-loaded, if all went well. Artillery and horses would go last.

Veracruz was a significant target. It was no provincial backwater, nor even a small regional hub like Monterrey or Saltillo. It was a bustling city and a strategic port, with that mix of the purely nautical and the basely commercial that defined ports around the world. Veracruz was just as vital to Mexico's economy as Boston or Charleston was to the United States'. Landing at an established harbor gave Scott a more formidable jumping-off point—and a far more daunting defensive position than a simple beachhead. Almost all oceangoing European and American trade into Mexico had been conducted at Veracruz since the first Spaniards arrived in 1518. Veracruz could rightfully claim that it was the first European city on the American mainland. Even better, it was one of the oldest existent cities in all of the Americas. The highly sophisticated Huastec Indians had settled the area three thousand years earlier, giving way to the Totonacs, who were linguistically related to the Mayas but under Aztec rule.

When the first Spaniards arrived, they witnessed four Totonac priests giving offerings to the Aztec god Tezcatlipoca on the small island where the San Juan de Ulúa fortress would one day be constructed. The Spaniards made Veracruz pivotal to their empire in the Americas, and all silver and gold from Mexican mines that was bound for Europe was loaded aboard ships in its harbor. As a result, Veracruz became a favorite target of pirates seeking plunder.

Among those to attack the port was a young Sir Francis Drake, whose unsuccessful 1568 assault made him a national hero in England. The Spaniards recognized that Drake's would not be the last attempted invasion, and they worked hard to make the city impregnable. Everything about its posture was defensive: the fifteen-foot-high city walls that protected Veracruz from invasion by land; the two forts and nine redoubts studding the wall; and the city's crown jewel, the fortress of San Juan de Ulúa, considered by many military experts to be the strongest fortification in North America — and equal to the renowned fortress at Gibraltar. San Juan de Ulúa was not one bastion, but three, a sprawling gray eminence seven hundred acres in size, built on an island a thousand yards offshore, its various sections divided by canals and drawbridges. It was all but invasion-proof, with fifteen-foot-thick stone walls (and a similarly thick stone roof in key areas) designed to absorb cannonball blasts with ease. There were 250 gun ports, and many of the cannons were enormous sixty-eight- and eighty-four-pounders. The fort featured a moat, battlements, parapets, an internal system of bridges, cisterns filled with a two-year supply of water — and deep dungeons where prisoners were chained to the walls, even when high tide brought in waist-high ocean water. Appropriately, San Juan de Ulúa being of Spanish design, a broad open-air plaza lay at the center, lined by tall houses. In preparation for the American invasion, shells and shot had been heaped in the center of the plaza.

The most intriguing of all the fort's European characteristics were the cannons. Many were Spanish and made of brass, dating back a century to the reign of Philip V. Others were French. There was no precise count, but the fort was filled with more than two hundred such guns. The Spanish king Charles V had spent forty million pieces of gold to begin construction of San Juan de Ulúa in the sixteenth century, but it would not be completed for more than a hundred years after his death in 1558. For more than eighteen months after Veracruz fell during the War of Independence, Spanish Royalists had remained in the fort, safe from any and all attack. But although they had enough munitions to last for years, they were ultimately reduced to starvation. The fortress was the last place in Mexico to fly the Bourbon flag of Ferdinand VII. With its lowering, all of Mexico finally belonged to the Mexicans. Thus Veracruz and the fort were more than just a city and its castle; they were symbols of a nation's greatness. The military academy at Veracruz had trained many a Mexican officer, including Santa Anna. To capture this jewel of a city was to strike a solid blow against Mexican national morale.

"In my next," Grant wrote, referring to the letter he would write after the invasion, "no doubt I will have some news of a great battle to relate."

That battle would be for Veracruz.

THIRTY-THREE

Invasion

MARCH 6, 1847

R obert E. Lee finally heard a shot fired in anger—and it was coming right at him.

He was at sea, of all places, when the adrenaline-inducing blast was launched. General Winfield Scott had taken his staff and engineering corps for an offshore reconnaissance of Veracruz. Lee and George Meade were among those onboard the small steamship *Petrita* as it traveled up and down the coast, observing landing locations and the Mexican defenses. When the *Petrita* came within a mile and a half of San Juan de Ulúa, cannon fire from the castle began arcing shells in their direction.

For a moment it appeared that Scott had made a stupid tactical error, for onboard were his entire general staff as well as his top engineers. They would all be lost if a cannonball struck the boat. But each of the eleven shots missed. Scott and his staff went unscathed. The invasion would proceed.

If ever there was a general whom Lee could emulate, it was Scott. A heavyset man whose military correctness had led the Texas Rangers to call him Old Fuss and Feathers, he outranked Zachary Taylor and often behaved in the manner of an older and far more stodgy individual, yet he was actually younger than Taylor by almost two years. Scott was a Virginian, like Lee, born on his family's farm outside Petersburg on June 13, 1786. He was educated as a lawyer at the College of William and Mary but abandoned that career for the army life. Enlisting as a corporal in the Virginia militia, he rose to the rank of brigadier general during the War of 1812. Scott was taken captive after the Battle of Queenston Heights, an American debacle on the Canadian shore of the Niagara River, wherein a small British force routed the invading army. After having been returned in a prisoner swap, Scott went on to victories as a commander at the Battle of Chippewa (a second attempt to establish an American toehold on the Canadian side of the Niagara River) and then at Fort Erie in the summer of 1814, only to be wounded at the Battle of Lundy's Lane on July 25, 1814, and forced to sit out the remainder of the war. Scott could be vainglorious and argumentative, but in the decades that followed he became a passionate student of military history (translating Napoleon from the original French in order to better understand his meaning) and wrote several army manuals. Among these were two books on infantry tactics, one written in 1830 and the other in 1840, that became standard throughout the U.S. Army. By putting that knowledge to use in the Black Hawk and Seminole wars, and by carefully cultivating power and political connections, he rose swiftly through the military. Luckily, his heroics during the War of 1812 had left him with a general's rank at war's end, preventing Scott from falling into that midcareer malaise so typical of the army's officer corps between 1814 and 1846.

As the Mexican War began, Scott had been a general for three decades. No one in the U.S. Army, not even Zachary Taylor, possessed such standing. Scott had all but forgotten what it felt like to hold a lesser rank.

In the months leading up to Veracruz, Lee watched the

venerable figure prepare his battle plans. Unlike George McClellan, who was just twenty when he was assigned to Scott, Lee did not ape Scott's mannerisms (the diminutive McClellan, for instance, took to posing for portraits with a Napoleonic hand in his tunic, as did his superior). Rather, he reveled in spit and polish, taking great pride in his personal uniform, just as his commander did.

And he saw that Scott was substance as well as style. The general was a fiend for preparation. He had a propensity for setting up spy networks and sending his soldiers off on daring missions to gather as much information about his enemies as possible. This instilled in Lee a profound belief in reconnaissance.

Nevertheless, Scott's invasion plan was not guaranteed. The road between Veracruz and Mexico City was the same path Cortés's conquistadores had followed three centuries earlier (indeed, Cortés had also landed in Veracruz), a winding track from sea level up through a series of mountain passes. The lack of alternate roads and the narrow stricture of each pass ensured that the Mexicans knew exactly which direction Scott was headed, and gave them ample time to select the optimal location to stop him in his tracks. There was also the great distance between Veracruz and Mexico City, which would make it difficult for Scott's quartermasters to ferry bullets and food up to the front lines via wooden wagons and mules. Like Taylor in Monterrey, Scott would have to curry favor with the local population in order to keep his supply lines from being decimated by Mexican insurgents. He issued a general order that made rape, robbery, assault, and other crimes committed by American forces against the Mexican people illegal, hoping to prevent the sort of mayhem the volunteers were so infamously perpetrating in Monterrey. Scott further prepared himself by rereading Sir William Francis Patrick Napier's three-volume *History of the War in the Peninsula* so he could learn from Napoleon's failings as the commander of an occupying army in Spain.

*　　*　　*

THE INVASION WAS scheduled to proceed on the eighth, but a blustery "norther" made for choppy seas and thundering surf. Not wanting to lose a single life during the amphibious assault (the cautionary precedent was the French invasion of Algeria in 1830, when Charles X's army lost men to drowning while putting ashore), Scott pushed it back a day.

At 2:00 P.M. on March 9 (coincidentally, it was Good Friday, the exact same holiday on which Cortés had landed), soldiers began lowering themselves carefully over the side of the transports, down into waiting surfboats. "The tall ships of war sailed leisurely along under their topsails, their decks thronged in every part with dense masses of troops, whose bright muskets and bayonets were flashing in the sunbeams; the jingling of spurs and sabers; the bands of music playing; the hum of the multitude rising up like the murmur of a distant ocean; the small steamers plying about, their decks crowded with anxious spectators; the long lines of surf boats towing astern of the ships, ready to disembark the troops," one sailor aboard the sloop of war *Albany* wrote, describing the scene.

It had been a year to the day since Taylor's army had marched out of Corpus Christi looking for a fight. This time the Americans weren't just hoping to find a battle—they were itching to start one.

The weather was perfect, a cloudless sky and flat surf. Three miles south of Veracruz, the landing boats would be rowed directly inland to a chosen landing zone on Collado Beach, a broad stretch of shorefront lined with rolling dunes and chaparral. In the far western distance, Mount Orizaba's snowcapped peak reminded the men that if they made it ashore safely, the path to the high altitudes of Mexico City led ever upward. For Scott, the mountain served a dual purpose, for when the setting sun dropped low enough to rest atop the mountain, the invasion would begin.

Scott's hoped-for twenty-five thousand troops had been reduced to a much smaller force of thirteen thousand, but it had still taken four hours to assemble the boats. When the sun and Mount Orizaba met, Scott ordered a single cannon blast fired from the *Massachusetts:* the attack was on.

"The landing was made in whale-boats rowed by sailors of the fleet," wrote Lieutenant Dabney Maury. "In each boat were from fifty to sixty soldiers, and it was a glorious sight to see the first division, under General Worth. The fifty great barges kept in line, until near the shore, when General Worth himself led the way to make the landing first of all, and being in a fine gig he accomplished this, and was the first man of the army to plant the American flag upon that shore of Mexico."

Sailors cheered from the ship's decks. Bands played "The Star-Spangled Banner." The Mexicans knew they were coming—with so many American vessels anchored just beyond cannon range, the invasion was hardly a surprise. The residents of Veracruz crowded atop the city walls and on rooftops to watch the gringos come ashore. Mexican lancers could be seen in places along the beach, surely a harbinger of a greater hidden force. American naval guns soon drove them back.

The soldiers were tense as they approached shore, peering into the chaparral for signs of hidden guns and men. They affixed bayonets and nervously prepared to launch themselves over the gunwales before sprinting up the beach to engage the enemy. Not a man among them had experienced an ocean landing before, so no one knew what to expect. They prayed they might race far enough forward on the sand to find some sort of protective cover. A hailstorm of Mexican musket balls would surely be aimed their way—and they knew it. With each dip of an oar blade, the soldiers could see the invasion beach looming closer and closer.

Then it was time.

"Without waiting for the boats to strike [the beach] the men jumped in up to their middles in the water and the battalions formed on their colors in an instant," wrote Second Lieutenant George McClellan, who had entered West Point at the age of fifteen and recently graduated second in the class of 1846. Like Jackson, he had made his way to Mexico almost immediately afterward. "Our company and the Third Artillery ascended the sand hills and saw—nothing."

There was no gunfire, no cannon blasts. Utter silence and a perfectly empty shoreline greeted the Americans. It soon became obvious that the Mexican army had no plans to contest the landing. Their commander, Brigadier General Juan Morales, had withdrawn his force from the beaches and city and was now safely protected behind the impregnable walls of the castle of San Juan de Ulúa and within the city's defenses. Morales's retreat was deeply unexpected. Small bands of Mexican cavalry and infantry soon sallied forth to probe the American position, resulting in minor casualties on both sides, but otherwise the American encirclement went unmolested.

Scott's army soon prepared to move on to the next step of the invasion plan. Theoretically, it was possible to bypass Veracruz and begin marching straight to Mexico City. Yet as long as the castle was in Mexican hands, American ships would never be safe from its many guns, and Scott would always have the Mexican army at his rear, capable of harassing his men throughout the long march inland. Just as pragmatically, Scott required the great port as a means of off-loading supplies and reinforcements. The city needed to be taken.

But he would do so through siege. The siege was a timeless military tactic, wherein a force surrounds a city or fortress that refuses to surrender, and then cuts off all movement of supplies in or out. As an offensive gambit, the siege dated back to antiquity and the building of walls around cities, but its use was coming to an end as artillery became more powerful and mobile in the Napoleonic era. Yet the tactic had worked against Veracruz before. Scott hoped it would work again.

The plan, if all went well, would proceed in four phases: invasion, encirclement, investment, and surrender. The invasion had already gone off flawlessly, and Scott's landing would go down in the annals of warfare as one of the most successful of its kind. Encirclement would mean just that: spreading a line of troops around the city by land, and ships by sea, to completely surround Veracruz. No Mexican citizens or soldiers would be allowed to go in or out. *Investment* was the formal military term for commencement of siege hostilities, the relentless firing of cannons, slowly destroying the city's walls and the will of its defenders and noncombatant citizens. Surrender, theoretically, was just a matter of time.

On March 10, as Scott came ashore from the wooden steamship *Massachusetts,* his army made the transition from invasion to encirclement. American troops proceeded north from their landing beach to take up positions a mile west of the city walls and also block the main road from Veracruz to Mexico City. Their siege lines were seven miles long, stretching from the Collado Beach landing zone all the way north to the village of Vergana. Twiggs's division anchored that end of the line, while Worth's anchored the southern end, near where Scott set up his headquarters. In the center was the division led by Patterson, the unproven general and political appointee. Should his leadership, or lack thereof, allow his section to be breached, the Whig generals on either side of him would rush in to cover his ass.

The lines were vital to a successful siege. The less porous they were, the better. Scott's initial goal was to prevent any of the 15,000 residents or 3,360 Mexican soldiers from exiting the city, and to prevent Mexican irregulars from riding to their rescue.

Once the line was sealed, the next step to a successful siege was to cut off necessities vital to daily living. The city's water supply came from a series of ponds and marshes that fed into a stream at the southwest corner of the city, which in turn filled the cisterns of Veracruz. Scott ordered the stream blocked. When the cisterns ran dry, the good people of Veracruz would begin the agonizing process of death by dehydration. The tropical climate would only hasten their anguish.

Scott's plan then called for cannons to be positioned south of the city and to lob shells into the Mexican defenses. It was imperative that these cannons begin firing as soon as possible. Scott was fearful that the seasonal yellow fever—*el vómito,* in local slang—would soon spread along the Mexican coast. Initially contracted by a mosquito's bite, yellow fever was viral and easily passed between humans who remained in close proximity to one another—such as soldiers. The symptoms were horrendous, ranging from severe flu to severe hepatitis, profuse fevers, internal bleeding, and then a black, gut-wrenching vomit. An epidemic of yellow fever presented as great a threat to Scott's army as the Mexican guns.

The general knew firsthand the insidious effects disease could have on an army: cholera had swept through his troops as they traveled toward the front lines of the Black Hawk War, cutting a force of one thousand down to two hundred in a matter of weeks. For this reason, Scott had not seen action in that conflict.

Now, fearful that a similar devastation might strike his much larger army, he was eager to be off the beach and climbing into the mountains, where yellow fever did not exist.

But another fierce norther blew through Veracruz before the heavy ordnance could be rowed to shore. All the Americans could do was sit and wait for the ocean to calm—or for the unlikely possibility that the Mexicans would surrender without a fight. Boredom, that by-product of any siege, set in as the days adopted a sameness: there was intense heat from sunrise until 10:00 A.M., when the sea breeze shifted direction and began blowing onshore to cool the men. The men often passed the time reading, with many of the troops favoring patriotic books about the great George Washington (Washington books had come into vogue during the war) or an elocution primer called the *United States Speaker,* which contained patriotic speeches that fired their hearts with the glory of their cause. At night came thick clouds of mosquitoes and sand fleas. It was the fleas that bothered the troops most of all. "I have never seen anything like those Vera Cruz fleas. If one were to stand ten minutes in the sand, the fleas would open up on him in the hundreds. How they live in that dry sand no one knows," marveled one officer, who then noted the bizarre extremes some men went to in battling the fleas. "The engineer officers, G.W. Smith and McClellan, slept in canvas bags drawn tight about their necks, having previously greased themselves in salt pork."

Like Scott, America's officers and men were clearly eager to be away into the mountains.

On March 17, after five days of stormy weather, the skies cleared. Scott's force finally received heavy artillery. The ten mortars, four 24-pounders, and smattering of howitzers were set in the sand and aimed toward the castle. Scott had also succeeded in borrowing six large guns from the navy, thinking that he could use the additional firepower. He gave Lee personal command over their emplacement: too far from the castle and they would pose no legitimate threat, but too near and they were within range of the enemy guns.

On the surface it was an unusual gesture. Lee was not an artillery specialist, and his position among Scott's four-officer "little cabinet" of close advisers (Lee, Colonel Ethan Allen Hitchcock, Colonel Joseph Totten, and the general's son-in-law and chief of staff, Henry Lee Scott) would seem to make him ill suited for frontline work. But the job was actually a test, with Scott giving Lee the opportunity to shine or fail. Lee's many thankless years of building fortifications and otherwise laboring in engineering anonymity had prepared him well for the challenge. He chose a risky location, high and exposed, but with a clear view down into the city that would effect maximum damage. Lee was boldly willing to risk his reputation on the site and eagerly awaited the arrival of the big guns.

Additional foul weather delayed the arrival of the navy's thirty-two-pounders. Soldiers instead focused their attention on positioning the army's cannons a half mile south of the city. There would be four batteries in all. It was rough and sweaty work, muddy at times, conducted amid clouds of mosquitoes and flies, scorpions, biting ants, fleas, and the raging humidity that followed every break in the weather.

At 4:15 P.M. on March 22, shortly after the Mexicans rejected Scott's demand for a surrender, American mortars dropped the first exploding rounds into the city. The mortars were stamped with the initials GR, for Georgius Rex (King George): they had been seized from the British general Burgoyne at the Battle of Saratoga, during America's Revolutionary War, and were still more than effective seven decades later.

U.S. Navy ships opened fire, focusing their guns on the castle and receiving heavy fire in return. Neutral British and French vessels bobbed offshore, watching the action but never joining in. The pounding continued all evening but ceased as night fell.

The six navy guns finally arrived onshore on the twenty-second. Lee, who had almost been killed three nights earlier when an American sentry mistakenly fired at him and singed the sleeve of his jacket with the bullet, got to work immediately. His job was to oversee their emplacement and then turn them over to the naval gun crews for the bombardment. The cannons consisted of three 32-pounders weighing more than three tons and three French-made 8-pounders known as Paixhans. The 32-pounders, which would be the largest guns ever used in a siege, fired a solid chunk of shot capable of knocking down thick walls and crashing through to underground ammunition bunkers. The Paixhans were smaller but perhaps far more deadly. The invention of the French general Henri-Joseph Paixhans twenty years earlier, they were known for their extreme horizontal accuracy and for the lethal 68-pound exploding shells launched from their barrels. During a naval battle, these shells would spray shrapnel across an opposing ship's decks, maiming and killing sailors, while simultaneously slashing holes in sails and shredding rigging and masts. In close naval combat, they could be aimed directly at an enemy's gun ports, with the intention not only of killing the gun crews but of ripping open a hole in the side and sinking the ship. Paixhans were so adept at lacerating a battleship's wooden hull that they would change the course of naval warfare. Gone would be vulnerable wooden vessels; in their place would be warships constructed from iron.

Lee knew full well that if he did his job, collateral damage in the form of dead civilians was likely to ensue. But he had never been in combat or seen the aftermath of a siege. The destructive power of military weaponry was still an abstract concept, to be gleaned from textbooks. He approached the gun emplacement as just another engineering task, albeit with higher stakes.

Lee's guns were officially known as Battery Number Five. He positioned them seven hundred yards south of the Mexican position. They were carefully concealed within a network of sand dunes just to the left of the army batteries. Working in a driving wind that sandblasted his exposed skin, he supervised several hundred soldiers as they dragged the mighty guns from the beach and then over the dunes. The work was slow and frustrating. At one point a set of railroad tracks that went nowhere blocked their path. As they drew closer to the chosen position, a particularly vile form of mesquite, with thorns so large that they were actually longer than the branches on which they grew, drew blood as it ripped at their clothes and flesh.

Meanwhile, Lee had ordered the construction, atop a low hill and nestled among the mesquite, of deep gun pits that were seven feet wide and covered with a thick protective roof. "The large cannon stand on a high platform, with their muzzles sticking out of the embrasures towards the city," was how one American soldier described the typical gun pit. He went on to describe a "deep hole in the trench, slanting double roof of plank and timber, upon which are three tiers of bags, filled with earth or sand, to protect it from the bombs of the enemy."

The naval gun crews were unused to digging. They chafed at building the fortifications, arguing they were so far from the city that there was no need. Lee was sure of himself. He coolly ordered the sailors to take up shovels and pickaxes alongside their army brethren and to lean hard into their labors.

The task was completed within twenty-four hours. On the morning of the twenty-fourth, Lee transferred control of Battery Number Five to the navy's Captain John Aulick—and not a moment too soon: as the naval artillery crews were sponging the last bit of sand from the guns' barrels, Mexican scouts spotted the emplacement.

All hell broke loose. Mexican cannons focused their shells on the naval battery, which was more exposed owing to its position atop the dunes. "I wish you could hear one of these huge projectiles in the air as they are coming, and see the scattering they make. The roar they make may be compared to that of a tornado, and every man within a quarter-mile of the spot where they strike thinks that they are about to fall on his individual head. The consequence is, that there is a general scampering to and fro," wrote one American, "and so deceptive is the sound that one is just as apt to run directly towards as from them."

Battery Number Five responded in kind, firing alongside their four army counterparts, aiming heavy solid shot and exploding shells into the heart of the city. Blasts landed in the main plaza, and huge chunks of the city's wall were torn away. The primary purpose of the American barrage was to destroy the Mexican forts within Veracruz, and their powder magazines in particular. But the precise location of those forts was hard for the gunners to pinpoint. It was inevitable that the shells would take the lives of civilians. Most were residents, but the city was also home to visiting diplomats from Britain and France who had foolishly refused to leave, forgetting that there was no diplomatic immunity from a cannonball. These noncombatants huddled in their homes, terrified of stepping outside. Mexican soldiers placed protective sandbags around the damaged walls of their forts and were unable to break away from the fighting to offer relief or protection.

Wrote Napoleon Dana, "Our immense shells would fall through the tops of houses, go through both stories, and then, bursting, would shatter the whole house, throw down walls, and blow two or three rooms into one. Doors and windows are blown to pieces all over the city. Some houses had as many as a dozen ten-inch shells burst in them. One of their splendid churches is completely ruined inside. Several ten-inch shells fell in among the altars, and a number of 42-pounder shot went through it. These splendid altars, costly and old oil paintings, cut-glass chandeliers and large vases and shades, gilt and silver work, ornamental flowers and drapery, priests' robes and church linen, books, bricks, mortar shot, and pieces of shells formed one confused mass of fragments, the most costly work of a costly Catholic tabernacle, totally destroyed."

The dying were often left unattended, and the dead littered the streets. Two women breastfeeding their babies on the steps of a church were killed by the first shells of the siege, and all four bodies would go untouched for days. One family of seven took refuge together in their house and were all killed at once by the same exploding shell. Priests would not step into the crossfire to administer last rites, and there was no hospital to speak of. Artillery fire from the army and constant broadsides by the naval vessels at sea made for an endless barrage, slowly reducing the city to rubble. Civilian casualties rose quickly to a hundred and kept on climbing. Veracruz was being laid to waste.

On the night of March 23, American cannons scored a direct hit on a Mexican storehouse, setting fire to the city. Flames shot up into the night, whipped by a harsh norther. Just as the wind abated and the fire had been put out, the American cannons resumed firing. The lethal Paixhans were scoring direct hits on the walls and houses of the city, landing with such force that the effects were clearly visible from a mile away. The only thing slowing the American guns was the Quartermaster Department's inability to ferry ammunition to the batteries. Mules pulling the wagons were exposed to Mexican cannons and often stubbornly refused to go forward when a shell landed too near. On the night of the twenty-fourth, that problem was solved by a massive resupply effort under cover of darkness, so that on the morning of the twenty-fifth, every American gun was once again clobbering Veracruz. "Nothing but a continuous roar of artillery can be heard," wrote one American. "Above the roar of the cannon a dense smoke is rising, plainly pointing out the scene of this conflict. For close work—for hand-to-hand combat—Monterey was far ahead of this. But for grandeur and sublimity this far exceeds any attempt that has ever yet been made by the American arms."

On March 25, the Mexicans sent forth an emissary proposing that women and children be allowed to leave the city. Scott refused. A sharp wind raked Veracruz that night, a gale so terrifying that one veteran U.S. naval commander called it one of the worst he'd ever seen. The city's homeless residents struggled to

find shelter, and the American soldiers camped in the field struggled in vain to stay dry as they lay down upon the sand. Some
divisions had tents; others camped in the open. Officers and soldiers alike were filthy and tired and, except for the very busy gun
crews, growing grumpy and bored as the siege wore on. "We are
out here in the sand beyond the reach of the city and the castle,
and we can see all that is going on from our little hillocks without
being exposed at all. It is true that we are in a very uncomfortable
fix still, having no tents and no baggage," Dana wrote home that
day. "I am now so accustomed to sleeping with my clothes on that
I do not know how it feels to go to bed regularly. I have not had
off my pants to go to bed for a month, and I pulled off my coat
and boots night before last for the first time in a fortnight."

And still the siege continued. In just four days, the Americans had leveled Veracruz. They did so dispassionately. Between
them, the four army batteries fired sixty-seven hundred mortar
and cannon rounds—almost a half-million pounds of munitions. Artillery Lieutenant Thomas Jackson was in command of
a gun crew, as were fellow West Point graduates A. P. Hill, Abner
Doubleday, J. B. Magruder, and Joseph Hooker. Sam Grant was
fond of venturing forth to watch the gunners in action and was
nearly killed when a Mexican shell struck an adobe building in
which he and P. G. T. Beauregard had taken cover. Both men
were shaken up, but neither was seriously hurt.

Captain John R. Vinton, of the West Point class of 1817, was
one of the few American gunners killed. He stepped from a
gun pit and was struck on the side of his body. The cannonball
glanced off him and didn't so much as break the skin, but the
men around Vinton could hear the wind being knocked out of
him, and then watched as he keeled over.

Four members of the naval battery died far more violently:
they were standing out in the open to observe the siege when a
single cannonball tore off all their heads.

That lone naval battery had fired a staggering eighteen hundred cannonballs and exploding shells in just two days—this despite running out of munitions at 3:00 P.M. on the twenty-fourth and having to wait until morning before being resupplied by sea.

At sunrise on March 26, the terrifying norther continued to rake Veracruz. The wind was so severe that some twenty sailing ships were ripped from their anchors and run up onto the beach. By sunset, however, that harsh gale was stiffening a white surrender flag: the Mexicans had finally quit. Scott's terms were just as generous as Taylor's had been at Monterrey: no prisoners of war; all Mexican troops were free to leave their weapons and march out of the city unmolested. By March 29, the Stars and Stripes was flying over Fort San Juan de Ulúa. Scott had lost just thirteen men, with fifty-five wounded. Mexican fatalities were never tallied but numbered just below a thousand soldiers and civilians. Scott's invasion of Veracruz was the largest-ever landing of American troops on foreign soil and would not be surpassed until June 6, 1944—D-day.

Despite that remarkable achievement, the Mexican people were unbowed—and unimpressed. "The Americans should not even speak of the bombardment of Veracruz. The walls of Veracruz are in no way strong or impregnable," one Mexican journalist wrote. "More than 500 innocent children, women, and old people perished under the enemy cannonade, and the valiant garrison under General Morales had to submit to a capitulation, because the entire city would have been ruined and all the innocents sacrificed to no avail."

The writer concluded with a disgusted nod to the changing face of warfare: "A military action which relied solely on the superiority of the missiles should not even be mentioned."

Scott soon assembled a list of men to be commended for their "noble services" during the battle. Lee was on it. Colonel Totten, his direct superior, was soon dispatched to Washington to deliver news of the victory. When Major John L. Smith, the senior man, then became ill, Lee was instantly elevated to a position as Scott's senior engineer.

MEADE, ON THE other hand, was all but forgotten. As the navy spent its days off-loading munitions and supplies, and the army steeled itself for the dramatic march to Mexico City, the topographer had been ordered home. "I found myself at Veracruz a perfect cipher; the major, three captains, and one lieutenant I had over my head depriving me of any opportunity I might otherwise have of distinction," he groused in a letter to Margaretta. Meade was known to be deeply fond of Zachary Taylor and was something of a rogue among the topogs in Veracruz, owing to the fact the orders had not yet been cut reassigning him to Scott's command. He had fallen into a military limbo, still technically under Taylor's authority while physically in Scott's theater of war. Meade had complained about his inactivity to General Worth, who in turn demanded an explanation from Major William Turnbull, the ranking topographer. Turnbull shrugged, saying that he had more than enough topographers to do the limited jobs to which his unit had been assigned.

Before Scott sent him back to Washington, Colonel Totten had seen to it that the prime assignments fell to men under his command and not to the Topographical Corps. Now, the duties of mapping and forward reconnaissance that Meade had done so well since Matamoros were being turned over to men like Lee. Meade groused that Totten "wishes to make as much capital for his own corps, and give us as little as possible."

In the midst of a monumental invasion, with a rugged and potentially bloody stretch of road between the American army and Mexico City, and at a time when experienced cartographers would be vital to analyzing the lay of the land, Meade was being told that there was nothing for him to do.

He was ordered home. Meade was not happy about the transfer. There was the slightest whiff of failure to his homecoming, for so few other officers were leaving the front. "What will you say to my return?" he wrote his wife. "And what will your dear father say? I will frankly acknowledge that I had a most anxious time in making up my mind what to do. I, however, reasoned, that it was my intention, from the first moment I left you, to perform my duty and remain so long as duty required me, but to retire whenever I could do so honorably, and could not retire in a more honorable manner than I have done."

Meade's departure was swift, even if his journey home was not. He boarded the steamship *Alabama* on March 31, stopped two days in Tampico and a third on Brazos Island, and then endured another twenty-four hours stuck on a sandbar at the mouth of the Mississippi. His ten-day trip to New Orleans should have ended six days earlier, but the duration gave Meade plenty of time to reflect. Although there was little chance that he would see combat again, this did not sadden him. Meade knew that there would be no more significant warfare in northern Mexico (insurgents and bandits had taken to harassing American supply columns and lone American soldiers) and was afraid that his commanding officer would reassign him to Monterrey, where the work would be administrative. And he was also afraid of being posted somewhere out on the Great Plains, surveying wagon trails in the middle of nowhere. The postwar promotions would go to the warriors, and the personal connections that arose from being part of a large army on the move would benefit those soldiers even more.

Meade knew that, and he struggled to find a silver lining to the cloud that had just thrown a shadow over his career. It was not a cloud of shame, for he had performed his job admirably and with courage. Rather, it was a cloud of bad fortune, sending him back to the safety of Washington at a time when the men of West Point were finally getting the chance to be soldiers.

Meade set those thoughts aside and allowed himself to dream of being home. And when he did, Meade was eager to be with his wife and children after more than a year's absence. "Rest assured," he wrote Margaretta from New Orleans, "I shall leave no exertion unspared to hasten the moment when I shall hold you and my ever dear children in my arms."

THIRTY-FOUR

National Road

APRIL 8, 1847

The weather was blazing hot, tempered ever so slightly by a
fresh sea breeze. Just a little more than a week after the fall
of Veracruz, Scott had ordered General David Twiggs to march
his division on to Mexico City. Their first stop would be Jalapa,
seventy-four miles inland, at an altitude of 4,680 feet. From a
military standpoint, the march presented major obstacles in the
form of a river crossing (the Río Antigua) and mountain passes
at Plan del Río, Cerro Gordo, and Corral Falso. Each of these
presented a potential bottleneck of American troops and offered
the Mexicans prime opportunities to thwart the invasion.

Thomas Jackson was among the twenty-six hundred men and
two batteries of flying artillery setting out from Veracruz. An
advance screen of dragoons rode before them to suss out the terrain. They were an army in a hurry, and each man was stripped
down to the essentials of uniform, canteen, bedroll, and weapons. Extra baggage was forbidden, and each company was limited to three tents, to be used only for the sick or the wounded
and for the protection of weapons in case of rain.

Though ravaged by the bombardment, in some ways occupied

Veracruz had been lovely, and after their bland shipboard diet the men had exulted in delicacies like oysters, fresh tomatoes, eggs, and lemonade. But the soldiers were glad to be away. Yellow fever had a gestation period of just three to five days, and already many men were getting sick, thanks to their weeks of exposure to the elements—and to the mosquitoes in particular. They drank little alcohol for fear of weakening their immune systems and falling prey to *el vómito* or to the diarrhea they had come to know all too well back on the Rio Grande. Each soldier, even the hard-headed volunteers, had begun to treat disease with the same cautious fear as they would the enemy. But for some it was too late, and American corpses began to pile up. (Some 1,721 Americans would have been killed in combat and 4,102 wounded when the war in Mexico finally came to an end, but an astonishing 11,562 would have succumbed to disease or accidents.)

Contrarily, Jackson, the quiet hypochondriac, was feeling not only well but better than he had in a very long time. "I probably look better than I have in years," he wrote to his sister.

Jackson had been busy during the siege. There had been no time for advanced artillery training after his West Point graduation, but he had been more than adequately educated on the sands of Veracruz. Jackson's battery was on the front lines, his commanding officer John Bankhead Magruder. "Prince John," who had built the theater at Corpus Christi and fought at Resaca de la Palma before being reassigned to the recruiting service for several months, had been promoted to captain in June. His gregarious personality, imposing physical size, pronounced lisp, and determination to be in the thick of every battle made Magruder a flamboyant and deeply charismatic leader. He was also a strict disciplinarian, which made him an ideal commander for Jackson, whose zeal for rules and restraint bordered on the fanatical.

For Jackson there had been great satisfaction in the destruction of Veracruz, which he saw as a necessary step toward defeating

Mexico. He had not been shaken in the least when an enemy cannonball missed him by just a few feet, and he was more than content to deflect glory onto the artillery commanders who had already plied their craft with steady brilliance under Taylor's command. "That portion of praise which may be due to me must of course go to those above me or be included in the praise given to the army," he wrote Laura.

The aftermath brought out yet another side of Jackson's very complicated personality. He was known by many for the twang of his backwoods Virginia accent, and by his West Point brethren for his determination to succeed at all costs. But there was also an outspoken side to Thomas Jackson, one that few soldiers ever saw, for he preserved his sharpest comments for his letters home. "This capitulation has thrown into our hands the strong hold of this republic and being a regular [siege] in connection with other circumstances must in my opinion excel any military operations known in the history of our country," he wrote Laura. Jackson could not and would not understand the logic of releasing enemy prisoners. "I approve of all except allowing the enemy to retire that I can not approve of in as much as we had them secure and could have taken them prisoners of war unconditionally."

What might have been seen as a cold heart was, in fact, canniness. Rumors were flying that General Santa Anna was racing back from Buena Vista with the remainder of his army to confront Scott. The Mexican soldiers from Veracruz were sure to flee westward toward their military brethren, where they would be rearmed and sent straight back into battle. Jackson realized that in the long run, keeping prisoners now would save lives later.

The rumors were true: Santa Anna had marched straight from Buena Vista to Mexico City, seized control of the Mexican government in order to quell the growing dissent at his performance in the field, and then on April 2 hurried his troops east toward Jalapa, which was not only the American's intermediate destination, but also the location of Santa Anna's personal hacienda.

Santa Anna arrived in Jalapa on April 5, and after a two-day reconnaissance, he chose the mountain pass at Cerro Gordo, as the site where his army would position themselves and throw the Americans back into the sea.

Now, a day later, Jackson marched toward this showdown. He had been with Worth's division during the siege, stationed on the southern end of the American line. But Worth would linger a few days more to serve as temporary military governor of Veracruz. Elements of his division were being divided between other generals. Now Jackson was commanded by Twiggs, the towering and somewhat dim-witted Georgian with the prebattle bowel superstitions.

Jackson's performance at Veracruz had resulted in a promotion to full second lieutenant. He was eager to continue his upward advance by making a name for himself in another battle. But the National Road was a twisting route, and if battle came, it was hard to imagine that artillery would be as effective as infantry, for its mobility would be minimal when the passage turned mountainous. Many of the men were making the situation more precarious by falling behind during the march, thanks to the heat and an overall lack of fitness, making them a perfect target.

Jackson and his gun crews were not among the stragglers. They slogged slowly away from the beach. The trail was lined with palm trees and resplendent with exotic flowers and vegetation, but it was also thick with sand until the army finally linked up with the National Road. The Spaniards under Cortés had leveled the road and covered it in pavers three centuries earlier, making it the ideal path for yet another invading army. With his left arm raised high to enhance his circulation, Jackson slowly rode forward into the mountains.

THIRTY-FIVE

Twiggs's Dilemma

APRIL 15, 1847

J ust outside the village of Cerro Gordo, the National Road
passed through a long valley. Steep cliffs and sudden drop-
offs defined the wooded terrain. Mexican gun batteries had
been placed atop hills on either side of the road, and troops were
stationed at the mouth of the ravine. Should Twiggs have made
it past the Mexican cannons, his outnumbered army would be
penned inside the valley as Mexican forces swarmed over them.
Santa Anna had selected an invincible position.

Twiggs was a confrontational sort. A head-on attack suited
his personality. Tactically, it wasn't the prettiest way to get at
Santa Anna, but on a practical level, there was no other way to
get an army from one side of the pass to the other. Twiggs knew
it. Santa Anna knew it. As bloody as it would be, Twiggs's suicidal charge made perfect logistical sense.

On April 12, Twiggs probed the pass with an advance unit
led by William Hardee, which immediately came under fire
and withdrew. Determined to test the Mexican defenses again,
this time under cover of darkness, Twiggs decided to invade the
pass at 4:00 A.M. on the thirteenth. The plan fell through when

units led by Generals Gideon Pillow and James Shields, a pair
of young volunteer Democrats (forty and thirty-six, respec-
tively) appointed to their ranks by President Polk, arrived shortly
before the attack was to begin. The volunteers were too tired to
be effective, claimed the generals. Twiggs was reluctantly forced
to postpone his charge for twenty-four hours.

The mood in the camp turned somber as the hours counted
down, and the soldiers dreaded the coming morning. They knew
that few of them would survive the attack. Wrote one soldier,
"On the night before the expected engagement the camp wore an
air of stillness unusual at other times, the men generally appear-
ing more thoughtful, and conversing less, and in more subdued
tones than usual. On the evening of the 13th, General Twiggs,
who, during the sickness of General Patterson, commanded the
forces at Plan del Río, after having spent two days in reconnoiter-

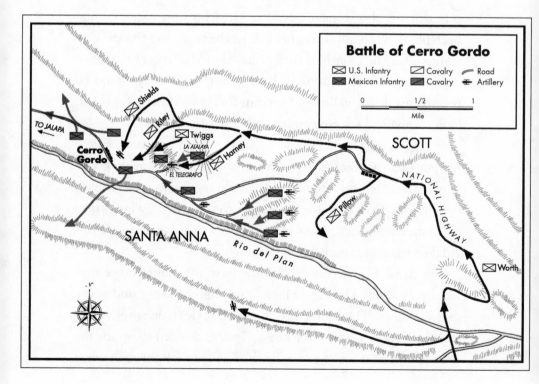

ing, gave the order for an attack on the enemy's batteries, which we were to take at the point of the bayonet by assault, early next morning. The bugle having sounded for the troops to assemble a little before sunset, the captains of companies addressed their men, informing them of the General's intention, and explaining as much of the plan of the meditated attack as would tend to facilitate its execution. They concluded with a hope that all would do their duty gallantly, and required us to give three cheers, an invitation which was very faintly responded to. The want of enthusiasm displayed by the men, arose, I am persuaded, from a want of confidence in the judgment of General Twiggs, and not from any deficiency of the necessary pluck required for the occasion. But that General, though always admitted to be a brave old cavalry officer, was considered, from his peculiar temperament, and previous school of education and discipline, to be totally incapable of successfully directing an operation of such magnitude as the present, which any person might easily see required both military talent and skill."

Of all people, it was General Patterson who saved the day. The political appointee, who outranked Twiggs, rose from his sickbed and took command, calling off the attack. The American army would hold its present position and wait for Scott to tell them how best to move forward up the valley. This rare example of a volunteer general's making a sound decision saved countless American lives.

Dana, still on the road to Cerro Gordo, could hear the distant sounds of artillery as Mexican guns took aim on the American positions. Dana had recently been promoted to first lieutenant and was in command of a company, marching inland with the Fourth Infantry. All he knew of the action were rumors that Santa Anna's twelve-thousand-man army had been located at Cerro Gordo, and that Twiggs had nearly attempted a premature head-on assault of the position. Those rumors sent shivers through the American army, who knew all too well that their inferior numbers would likely spell doom in waging such a battle against a fortified position. "General Twiggs intended to attack," Dana wrote. "But I rather think that General Scott got up in time to stop him until he gets ready. He will probably wait for us to come up, and then he will put Santa Anna in a mighty bad fix." Dana hadn't played an active part in a battle since Monterrey and was eager to get back into action.

"It may be that the fight will be over before we reach there," he wrote to Sue. "I have no doubt that there are a good many in Santa Anna's army who surrendered and were paroled at Veracruz. If so, and we can get hold of any of them and detect them, they will be shot to a certainty."

Dana's bold predictions had been correct throughout the war, but Cerro Gordo would be a different story. Dana's luck in battle would finally run out.

THIRTY-SIX

Reconnaissance

L ee walked out of Scott's command tent, mentally girding himself for the arduous physical challenge before him. Once again, the general had given him a task crucial to the army's success. This would be no mere placement of siege guns, with hundreds of men doing his beckoning. Joseph Johnston of the Topographical Corps, a close friend of Lee's, had taken musket balls in the thigh and arm while performing the early reconnaissance at Cerro Gordo, but his injuries were not in vain. Johnston's scouting had shown that there might be a secondary path that would allow the American forces to maneuver around the Mexican defenses and avoid Santa Anna's National Road snare. Now Lee was setting out to confirm if such a path existed. If he failed, Scott would be forced to follow the same risky plan Twiggs had nearly attempted, with all the carnage that was sure to ensue.

The particular tactic Scott had in mind—provided Lee could find an alternate route—was something known as a turning movement. This maneuver entailed seizing objectives behind the enemy line and forcing the Mexicans to turn to face this new threat. A successful turning movement would allow Scott to have more say in how the battle would be fought and to use his strengths (speed, better-trained and better-equipped troops, superior battlefield leadership) rather than let Santa Anna's fortifications dictate the action.

Scott's army was camped at Plan del Río, three miles east of Cerro Gordo. The bivouac was on a small, verdant plain hemmed by a swift river on one side and mountain crags on the other. It was here that the National Road began its winding path up through the mountains. Lee appraised the situation: "The right of the Mexican line rested on the river at a perpendicular rock, unscalable by man or beast, and their left on impassable ravines; the main road was defended by field works containing thirty-five cannon; in their rear was the mountain of Cerro Gordo, surrounded by entrenchments in which were cannon and crowned by a tower overlooking all—it was around this army that it was intended to lead our troops."

The river—the Río del Plan—was swift but shallow and was lined with cliffs that would prevent a turning movement on the American left. Outlandish as it seemed, Lee would have to find a route through the "impassable ravines" on the American left for Scott to turn Santa Anna. It was the only chance to avoid a head-on attack.

Lee trekked out of camp on foot, knowing that the ground he'd be traveling over would be too steep for a horse. The morning air was heavy after a night of rain. He hiked carefully uphill and then continued farther north up a ravine. The ground was rugged, with scrub oaks, vines, thorns, and dry, rocky streambeds making for slow going. It was no place for an army to move quickly or quietly, but it was certainly not impassable. Lee pressed on into a valley between two large hills. On his right rose Atalaya and to his left El Telégrafo. Santa Anna had placed gun batteries atop both of them.

Lee came upon a clear spring and stopped to drink. He had been hiking for hours. His tunic was ringed with sweat and dust. As he paused for that much-needed mouthful of water, Lee noticed a small, well-worn trail, the first he'd seen in a while. Suddenly, Lee heard Spanish-speaking voices. He dropped down behind a log next to the spring. The log was large enough to hide behind, and the vegetation so thick that his blue uniform did not stand out. He pressed his body into the mud and lay motionless as a squad of Mexican soldiers settled in for their own water break.

One soldier sat down on the log. His body was inches from Lee. Bugs began biting Lee's hands and face and working their way inside his uniform. He had no choice but to lie motionless and pray that he wouldn't be noticed.

The soldiers stood to leave, but other soldiers soon replaced them. From the limited knowledge of Spanish he had picked up over the past eight months, Lee knew they were talking about the Americans and wondering about the attack to come. Many of the Mexicans thought Scott's army was unbeatable. Bronchial and digestive illnesses had become rampant among the Mexicans, and those who had served with Santa Anna at Buena Vista were exhausted from the month-long, thousand-mile march from there to Cerro Gordo. All in all, they were a sympathetic bunch, destined to fight a war that would gain them little in terms of money or social standing if they won. Yet Lee knew that if his presence became known, they would kill him on the spot.

Morning turned into afternoon, which became evening. Finally, the Mexicans wandered slowly back to their camp. In the darkness of the night, Lee did the same, picking his way through the rocks, thorns, and scrub oaks in the darkness.

He had succeeded. By locating the Mexican army, even inadvertently, Lee had found Scott's trail to the Mexican rear.

Lee announced the news to a jubilant Scott, who ordered Lee to march out again immediately with a fatigue detail. This time he would not just search for a path but would widen the existing trail into something more suitable for an entire army, including cannons and horses. What Scott wanted, in just a single night, was nothing less than a road.

Once again, Lee delivered.

Grant would later marvel at the accomplishment. "Roadways had been opened over chasms to the right, where the walls were so steep that men could barely climb them. Animals could not. These had been opened under cover of night, without attracting the notice of the enemy."

Once again deeply pleased with Lee's actions, Scott sent him off on a third great mission. This time, instead of scouting or supervising construction, Lee would show the way for a division of soldiers. He would be leading men into battle, so to speak, for the very first time in his life.

AT 4:30 ON the morning of April 17, with Lee as their guide, Twiggs's division began a broad flanking movement to the left of the Mexican lines, following Lee's impromptu mountain road. Their goal was to occupy the hill at Atalaya as inconspicuously as possible. There they would take up positions, rest for the night, and then swoop down on the town of Cerro Gordo on the morning of the eighteenth. Their ultimate goal was to block the National Road to prevent Santa Anna's army from escaping.

After a somber predawn breakfast of coffee, biscuits, and salted beef ("the last meal for many a poor fellow," one soldier sagely noted), they lined up in battle order. Each man placed his rucksack in a supply wagon, to be retrieved farther up the road after the battle—if all went well. The mood was heavy, and even those men who normally talked in the ranks were quiet.

Few expected to do much more than skirmish with the enemy while driving them off Atalaya, with the big battle expected to take place the following day. But they had been camped at Plan del Río long enough to know the scale of the enemy's fortifications. Anything could happen.

Walking quietly, Twiggs's army set out. "It was no great wonder either that the men were rather more reflective than usual, considering that very few of our number had ever been close in front of an enemy before, and we were approaching fortifications which we should have to carry by assault, at whatever sacrifice of life," wrote one soldier in the First Artillery. "On coming to the head of the ravine, we were ordered to form in file, trail arms, and keep perfect silence, the staff and field officers dismounting and leading their horses."

Moving at a slow, deliberate pace, Twiggs's men somehow remained undetected. By early afternoon, they were in position. Heeding Twiggs's order that the American soldiers "charge them to hell," they routed a small Mexican force, driving them clear off the hill. From the summit, the Americans could clearly see Santa Anna across the valley on the slopes of El Telégrafo, wearing civilian clothes and riding a gray charger as he maneuvered his troops into position for a counterattack. "Several of my men fired at him, but such a long range forbade accurate shooting," wrote Lieutenant Dabney Maury, who was just moments away from having his left arm destroyed by a musket ball.

But Santa Anna's counterattack was too modest and slow in coming. Before he could close, the Americans had time enough to hand-carry a lightweight cannon known as a mountain howitzer into accurate range. The howitzer was leveled at the Mexican troops as they marched toward the American lines at the base of Atalaya, its barrel loaded with rounds of grape. The American soldiers would long remember the howitzer's opening salvo, cutting down more men with a single shot than most soldiers

323

could ever remember having seen before. The Mexicans seemed utterly surprised. As Santa Anna watched from the safety of El Telégrafo's summit, a Mexican band marched into battle with the counterattack. They kept playing their instruments right up until the instant that rounds of grape tore their bodies apart.

With the hill secured, Lee turned his attention to armament. Lieutenant Thomas Jackson was one of the artillery specialists who helped haul a 24-pounder, a 12-pounder, and a 24-pound howitzer over the cliffs and rugged terrain in order to position the weapons. The grueling labor was designed to put men and arms in place for the crucial action of the next day, when Scott would send the soldiers atop Atalaya charging through the valley below and up the slopes of El Telégrafo, desperately hoping they would turn Santa Anna's army.

THE BATTLE FOR Cerro Gordo got under way at 7:00 A.M. on April 18. Lee was galloping a horse named Creole westward. He led a brigade of soldiers, once again showing the way. In all his reconnaissance missions, Lee had never actually seen the place where the National Road linked up with his trail. The time had come to find it.

While Lee went searching for the road, several interconnected maneuvers took place at once: Colonel William Harney led the assault of El Telégrafo, with its fortress and batteries on top; General Gideon Pillow formed a diversionary attack to the left, hoping to mislead Santa Anna into thinking his was the main assault; General James Shields followed a path roughly similar to Lee's, seeking to capture the main body of troops at Cerro Gordo; and the rear elements of Scott's army continued their movement up the Mexicans' left flank, following the road Lee had engineered. General Scott, meanwhile, rode as far up the National Road as safety allowed in order to watch his grand plan be set into motion. The dragoons and most of the field artillery lingered nearby to provide reinforcement and to protect the general, just in case.

"The attack was made as ordered," Grant recalled, "and perhaps there was not a battle of the Mexican War, or of any other, where orders issued before an engagement were nearer being a correct report of what afterwards took place."

He was right: Scott's plan unfolded brilliantly. The main body of Twiggs's division had crept up the left flank entirely undetected, with Santa Anna believing that the previous day's skirmish had revealed the extent of the American force on his left. As a result, even though Pillow's forces moved forward along the wrong route, the Mexicans had no inkling that a large force was in their rear. Lee and elements of Shields's and General Bennet Riley's brigades completely cut off the National Road out of Cerro Gordo. (During the movement, Shields was felled by a rocket that tore through his lung but did not kill him. Edward D. Baker, until just a few months earlier an Illinois congressman, assumed command of the brigade.) Scores of Mexicans fled toward Jalapa before the road could be closed, but once the American noose was cinched, others risked their lives to escape by scrambling down the cliffs above the cold waters of the Río del Plan and wading to the other side. Then they fled back up the road, soon to fight another day.

As he charged into battle atop Creole, Lee thought of his son, Custis, wondering how he might protect the child if he were there alongside him. As if to echo those thoughts, he came across a Mexican drummer boy whose arm was crushed and whose body was pinned beneath a fallen soldier. A girl stood over the child, distressed. Lee dismounted to help. "Her large black eyes were streaming with tears," he would write to Custis a week later. "I had the dying man lifted off the boy, and both carried to the hospital."

The battle of Cerro Gordo was over by 10:00 A.M. More than three thousand Mexicans were taken prisoner. Hundreds of Mexican soldiers died. Santa Anna had been forced to escape by clambering hastily out of his stagecoach, cutting a saddle mule away from the rest of the team, and then galloping off through the chaparral. The Mexican general was in such a rush that he left behind his personal papers, a chest full of money, and even his wooden leg.

Scott was not without his own losses. Two hundred and sixty-three Americans died. "The rough and rocky road, cut through the rugged defiles and dense chaparral by our troops, is now lined with our wounded," wrote one American. Corpses lay in thick piles about the vast battlefield, drawing their first flies, even as the Americans cheered Scott when he rode into their midst. He delivered an impromptu speech to his men after the battle, telling of his pride in their gallant action. He was so overcome by the unlikely triumph that he let a tear roll down his cheek as he spoke. Many of the soldiers cried right along with him, thrilled at their victory but far more happy just to be alive.

Back at the battlefield, a cold rain fell all day. Burial parties picked through the bloated corpses, finding Mexican and American bodies side by side on the steep and rocky slopes of what the Americans called Telegraph Hill. The air smelled of rotting flesh and decay. Thick clouds of flies buzzed around the corpses, which were already turning black. Many of the bodies lacked limbs, and some had already been shorn of their boots, wallets, and wedding rings by scavenging volunteers who had crept out onto the battlefield to steal from their fellow soldiers.

One member of the burial detail thought something was unusual about one of the dead. For starters, he wasn't bloated and didn't smell of death. There was just a small round hole in the right side of his uniform, where the musket ball had passed through his intestine. On closer examination, he appeared to be breathing. The man was an officer, and his body was quickly placed atop a stretcher and taken to the surgeon of the regiment, Dr. Adam McLaren. The wound was cleaned and patched, and the patient placed under close supervision. Further investigation revealed that he had been in reserve with the rest of Worth's division but was so eager to do battle that he'd found his way into the fight.

"Among the wounded on our side," Grant wrote to Julia in his description of Cerro Gordo, "was Lt. Dana, very dangerously."

Dana would live, but his war was over.

Lee's first taste of combat had left him a changed man. He had seen for the first time the effects of cannon fire on the human body and the emotional cost of injury to noncombatants. He would never view war the same way again. "You have no idea what a horrible sight a field of battle is," he wrote his son.

But Cerro Gordo had altered him professionally, too. Lee was now on the fast track to greatness. Twiggs took pains to praise Lee in his official after-battle report. "Although whatever I may say may add little to the good reputation of Captain Lee, of the engineer corps, yet I may indulge in the pleasure of speaking of the invaluable services which he rendered me from the time I left the main road, until he conducted Colonel Riley's brigade to its position in the rear of the enemy's strong work on the Jalapa road. I consulted him with confidence, and adopted his suggestions with entire assurance. His gallantry and good conduct on both days deserve the highest praise."

Scott was no less sparing. "I am impelled to make special mention of the services of Captain R. E. Lee, engineers. This officer, greatly distinguished at the siege of Vera Cruz, was again indefatigable, during these operations, in reconnaissance as daring as laborious, and of the utmost value."

THIRTY-SEVEN

Pressing the Advantage

APRIL 19, 1846

W hile it was a most serious and inspiring sight, it was a painful one to me," Grant wrote of Cerro Gordo. "I stood there watching the brigade slowly climbing those ragged heights, each minute nearer and nearer the works of the enemy with our missiles flying over their heads, while white puffs of smoke spitefully flashed out in rapid succession along the enemy's line and I knew that every discharge sent death into our ranks. As our men finally swept over and into the works, my heart was sad at the fate that held me from sharing in that brave and brilliant assault."

Grant and most of Worth's division had been held in reserve and did not see any action. Their absence from the fighting was difficult, for it was clear to all that Cerro Gordo was a battle that would live on in history. Many would later compare it to the Battle at Thermopylae, in 480 B.C., where two armies of vastly different sizes waged war on precarious terrain. To have watched from afar was a bitter sort of pill.

Still, by the following morning reality had set in: the war was not over. Scott's army recognized the prize for what it was: a very vital piece of real estate that had been captured on the way to Mexico City. Now it was time to move on.

The elated soldiers marched to Jalapa, a lovely town set on a mountain slope, facing down toward the ocean. There, among the fragrance of flowers and fruit orchards, they would halt and await further orders, content in the knowledge that yellow fever would not pose a threat at such a high altitude.

General Worth's division dashed even farther inland, chasing Santa Anna's army. The fleeing Mexicans were before them the whole time. Worth expected them to turn and fight at any moment. Yet even though the Mexicans once again outnumbered the Americans, there was no battle. The Mexicans raced toward Puebla, pushing through Jalapa (even though Santa Anna's favorite daughter lived there and it was the site of Perote, a fortified castle the American soldiers had heard about for weeks). That meant that Puebla now represented the last true obstacle between the American army and Mexico City.

"My dear Julia," Grant wrote, "the pursuit was so close that the Mexicans could not establish themselves in another strong pass which they had already fortified, and when they got to the castle at Perote they passed on, leaving it too with all of its artillery to fall into our hands." By early May, the American army left Perote and advanced to Puebla, taking it without a battle. Now only Mexico City remained. For the time being, however, Puebla would be home. There, Scott would halt the army for three long months as the volunteers returned to the United States, their one-year period of enlistment having come to an end at a most ill-timed moment. Only when he received reinforcements, later in the summer, would Scott push on to Mexico City.

AMONG THOSE TO depart the Mexican War were Jeff Davis and the First Mississippi—they had served out the war in

Monterrey. As Zachary Taylor looked on, wearing full dress uniform for one of the few times that anyone could remember, Davis assembled the Rifles rank and file. "We had never seen the old hero in uniform, but on this occasion he came out in our front in the regulation blue 'from tip to toe.'" Taylor gave a short speech, tugging self-consciously on his uncomfortable vest. He wished the First Mississippi well, saying he hoped that they arrived home safely and that their private lives would be just as memorable as their "bright and glorious" military careers.

Davis then ordered the ranks to move into the same place that they had stood the night before the battle of Monterrey. The 1,000-man force now reduced to just 376, there were huge gaps between the men where the lost soldiers had once stood. "In dress parade on the same ground in the same place they did the even before the battle of Monterey," wrote a North Carolina volunteer looking on. "Each standing in the tracks he then stood in near as he could be. It was a solemn sight. There were great gaps and not a man to fill it up—here were three—then farther along two. The Regiment looked like an old comb with most of the teeth broken out."

Then the time came to close ranks and march home.

"My daughter, sir," Taylor said to Davis, finally admitting that he had been at fault by opposing his marriage to Knox, "was a better judge of men than I was."

And then they were off. Great crowds greeted the First Mississippi in New Orleans three weeks later. They were feted at banquet after banquet. Their rifles were their calling card, and the people of New Orleans were insistent that the First carry their guns to every social occasion.

On June 14, Davis and four companies of the First Mississippi disembarked from the steamboats *Natchez* and *Saint Mary* in Vicksburg, home at last. But Davis and the First did not step off those steamships in the garish red and white uniforms that once made them so easily visible. The State of Mississippi had sent a new outfit to the unit that was more in keeping with the national spirit. The new uniforms had reached them at the mouth of the Rio Grande. When the First Mississippi walked down the gang-plank and back onto Mississippi soil, they now wore blue uniforms, just like their regular army brethren. And so, on that day, after a lively barbecue that included thirteen rounds of toasting, the military career of Jefferson Davis came to an end—in blue.

V

THE AZTEC CLUB

The route followed by the army from Puebla to the City of Mexico was over Río Frío Mountain, the road leading over which, at the highest point, is about eleven thousand feet above tide water. The pass through this mountain might have been easily defended, but it was not; and the advanced division reached the summit in three days after leaving Puebla. The City of Mexico lies west of Río Frío Mountain, on a plain backed by another mountain six miles farther west, with others still nearer on the north and south. Between the western base of Río Frío and the City of Mexico there are three lakes: Chalco and Xochimilco on the left and Texcoco on the right, extending to the east end of the City of Mexico. Chalco and Texcoco are divided by a narrow strip of land over which the direct road to the city runs. Xochimilco is also to the left of the road, but at a considerable distance south of it, and is connected to Lake Chalco by a narrow channel. There is a high rocky mound, called El Peñon, on the right of the road, springing up from the low rocky flat ground dividing the lakes. This mound was strengthened by entrenchments at its base and summit, and rendered a direct attack impracticable.

— ULYSSES S. GRANT, *Memoirs*

THIRTY-EIGHT

"Nothing Can Stop This Army"

AUGUST 18, 1847

Grant, much to his disgust, was still a quartermaster. When he had attempted to resign the post, Colonel Garland pointedly reminded him that quartermaster was "an assigned duty, and not an office that can be resigned." As "this duty was imposed by a military order from a superior officer," Garland told him, "the duty cannot be revoked except by a like order relieving Lieutenant Grant from the duty."

Grant was not unaware that his job had been an important one. To consolidate his forces and ensure that no American food or ammunition fell into the hands of Mexican soldiers who might hijack them along the National Road, Scott had cut the 175-mile supply line with Veracruz and forced his army to live off the land. Grant's job during the three-month delay in Puebla was to ride out with empty wagons and purchase produce and goods from local farmers. As a result, he often returned looking dirty and unkempt, his uniform unbuttoned for comfort. The date has been lost to history, but sometime during this period, Lee paid a visit to Garland's command and remonstrated Grant for his lack of spit and polish. It was the first time the two men

335

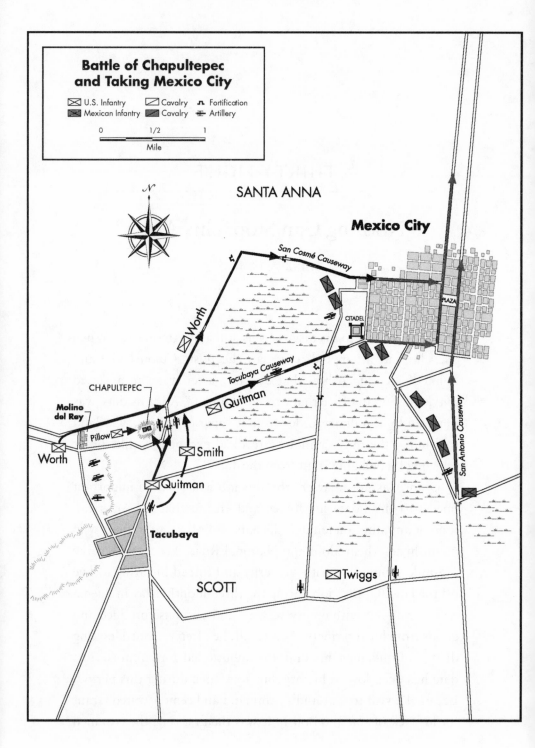

ever met, and the wording was harsh enough that Grant would remember it for the rest of his life—and would remind Lee of it again when next they met on a Palm Sunday far in the future.

Meanwhile, Scott's ambitious plan had left many observers predicting his doom. Britain's Duke of Wellington, the vaunted hero of Waterloo, had even proclaimed that "Scott is lost." But while Scott's army was cut off in Mexico, they were certainly not lost, thanks to the efforts of diligent quartermasters like Grant. The very fate of the army had depended upon his initiative, and Grant had come through. But now, as Scott's army gazed upon Mexico City after those months of boredom and rest in Puebla, he longed to fight. Ever since the day he had left Saint Louis and made his way through the war, Grant had been certain that his homecoming was right around the corner. And finally it was. If the Americans succeeded in capturing the Mexican capital, there would be no more war. Santa Anna's army would be defeated once and for all, and the long-delayed moment when Grant took Julia into his arms once again would be imminent.

The movement from Puebla to Mexico City had begun on August 7, with Twiggs in the lead. Divisions under the command of Worth, Quitman, and Pillow followed at one-day intervals. New volunteers had been trickling in all summer, replacing the seven regiments that had departed for Veracruz and home on June 6 and 7. Scott's army had dwindled to 7,113 men at that point, but the ranks had now swelled to 10,738 officers and men. By August 11, Twiggs was within fifteen miles of the capital, in the village of Ayotla. Scott joined him later that day and ordered the other divisions to spread out and occupy the neighboring towns of Chimalpa and Chalco. It had been almost a year to the day since Santa Anna returned from exile in Cuba, on August 14, 1846. Numerous attempts had been made to broker a peace. Santa Anna had rebuffed them all. Now he waited inside Mexico City with a force of 30,000, aching for one last desperate chance to crush the Americans. He had forbidden any information about the city's defenses to be published in any way, had conducted rigorous rifle training for his new troops and prepared for a state of siege by grinding every last bit of local wheat and storing it inside the city, and had evicted all American citizens. He had circulated an order forbidding civilian horses and carriages to be in the streets when the Americans attacked, and another making it illegal for anyone other than old men, women, and children to leave Mexico City without a special pass. Most ominously, Santa Anna had ordered that a Mexican version of the Paixhans gun be cast and poured for the city's defense. If Mexico City would be the battle that would end the war, Santa Anna wanted that finale to be on his terms.

Grant, meanwhile, had been in the war since the very beginning, back when it was just a rumor. Barring calamity, fighting or not, he would be there at the finish, too.

MEXICO CITY PRESENTED a puzzle. The capital was nestled high in the mountains, in a low valley forty-six miles wide. Three large lakes—Chalco, Texcoco, and Xochimilco—lay just east of the city. The road from Puebla wound around them. The terrain was marshy in some areas and a volcanic moonscape in others. A reconnaissance of the approaches was in order. For that, Scott once again called upon Lee.

The Virginian had been promoted for his work at Cerro Gordo, and now it was Major Robert E. Lee who rode forth on August 12 and 13 to observe the Mexican defenses. As suspected, the main road into Mexico City was heavily defended. Santa Anna had anticipated Scott's strategy and placed a massive force atop a hill known as El Peñon. The final seven miles into Mexico City was a narrow causeway built over marshy ground, hardly ideal for rapid troop or artillery movement. In an attempt to save the city from bombardment, the Mexican commander was positioning his forces around El Peñon's perimeter to stop the Americans long before they could enter.

"The hill of El Peñon is about 300 feet high," Lee observed, "having different plateaus of different elevations. It stands in the waters of Lake Texcoco. Its base is surrounded by a dry trench, and its sides arranged with breastworks from its base to its crest. It was armed with thirty pieces of cannon, and defended by 7,000 men under Santa Anna in person."

That was just the beginning. Batteries lined the causeway, and a secondary road that circumvented El Peñon was also fortified with cannons. That path came to a swampy end in the village of Mexicaltzingo, which meant that the American troops could either fight on the wide-open road, exposing them to fire and providing nowhere to run, or they could attempt the impossible by trying to wage war in a swamp, which would make them easy targets for Mexican artillery. Santa Anna's decision to fall back into Mexico City, they now realized, had been an act of brilliance. Everything favored him and his men.

Scott wrestled for a solution to this complex military problem. He had long ago decided against invading from the north, even though his scouts suggested that the city was weakly fortified from that approach. He briefly considered storming El Peñon, but he knew that the cost in lives would be too great. And the secondary road into Mexicaltzingo was just as fraught with peril.

There was one final option. It was a huge loop down around Lake Chalco and Lake Xochimilco that would bring Scott's troops up under the belly of Mexico City. They would enter from a point due south, near the village of San Augustin, far to the left of the marshes and fortified causeways that were sure to spell doom.

But this southern route was further proof that there was no easy way into the capital. For while the road around the two lakes was well worn (though covered in water at times), a vast lava barrier would stop the army cold at San Augustin. Known as the Pedregal, the volcanic terrain was so daunting that the Mexican army believed it was impossible for a bird to make it from one side to the other. "This Pedregal is a vast surface of volcanic rocks and scoria broken into every possible form, presenting sharp ridges and deep fissures, exceedingly difficult even in the daytime for passage of infantry, and utterly impassable by artillery, cavalry, or single horsemen," wrote Lieutenant Henry Hunt, an 1839 West Point graduate. "Indeed, it appears like a sea of such lava suddenly congealed, with here and there a clump of hardy bushes or dwarf trees which have managed to force an existence from the apparently sterile rocks."

On the opposite side was a plateau, guarded by six thousand entrenched Mexican troops with a complement of twenty-nine guns. But beyond that was Mexico City. If Scott could somehow send his army through the Pedregal, he would hit Santa Anna at his weakest spot.

On August 18, Lee was ordered to find a path through the lava.

The Pedregal was five miles wide and three miles from south to north. On August 18, Lee and Lieutenant P. G. T. Beauregard, a Louisiana Creole who had graduated from West Point in 1838, ventured out into the wasteland. Carefully and cautiously, they picked their way through the craggy terrain. On its western side they came across what looked to be a game trail or a smuggler's path. They followed the trail for three miles, until they surprised a group of Mexican pickets who had ventured in from the Pedregral's northern rim. As the Mexicans ran off, Lee scurried up a ridge. From the top he was able to look down and see the 6,000 Mexican forces on the opposite side of the Pedregal: he had found the way across.

Lee and Beauregard reported their findings to Scott. After some deliberation, it was decided that Lee would return the next morning with a company of engineers to help him build a road through the Pedregal, a task that would make the boulevard he had constructed overnight at Cerro Gordo look like child's play. It was to be large enough to handle men and artillery. A fatigue detail of five hundred men from General Gideon Pillow's division would provide the labor. The rest of Pillow's division, along with all of Twiggs's and two batteries of flying artillery, would protect them.

They set out early the next morning. Among Lee's engineers was young George McClellan. Thomas Jackson and John Magruder manned two of the mobile gun batteries. The going was arduous but surprisingly quick. The Pedregal was "precipitous and generally compelling a rapid gait in order to spring from point to point of rock, on which two feet could not rest, and which cut through our shoes," American soldiers complained. "A fall upon this sharp material would have seriously cut and injured one, whilst the effort to climb some of it cut the hands."

By early afternoon the Mexicans had caught sight of the Americans—and reacted violently. Lee ordered that the mobile guns be dragged up to the edge of a steep ravine, angling for the best possible field of fire. Lieutenant McClellan assisted, and while taking rounds from the enemy, the men soon positioned the guns to return those rounds with well-aimed shots of their own. It was hardly an equal battle. The Mexicans had twenty-nine cannons, including a number of the terrifying eighteen-pounders. On the American side, guns were limited to the six-pounders of John Magruder's batteries and the twelve-pound howitzers of Captain Franklin D. Callender. The ravine walls were perpendicular in places, and the Mexicans were just thirty yards away on the opposite side. The distance was the artillery equivalent of point-blank range—a fact that soon made itself all too well known when Lieutenant Preston Johnston, the young nephew of Lee's good friend Joseph Johnston and commander of a gun battery, promptly had his leg torn off by a solid Mexican cannonball.

Johnston's six-pounder was one of Magruder's four guns. As the firing continued, the captain scanned the escarpment in search of the other three. One of them—that of Thomas Jackson—appeared to be missing, and Magruder assumed that his determined young lieutenant was dead. In fact, Jackson had found a better spot from which to fire. "Lieutenant Jackson," Magruder wrote later, "kept up the fire with briskness and effect. His conduct was equally conspicuous throughout the whole day, and I cannot too highly recommend him."

As the artillery battle raged, Lee could look down from the ravine onto the Mexican position. He could clearly see the road to San Ángel behind them, and columns of infantry in the far distance, marching closer to serve as reinforcements. Persifor Smith, one of Twiggs's generals, took command, moving right to seek another way out of the Pedregal. As Lee held back, a force of thirty-three hundred American soldiers soon followed Smith. The American force successfully found a new path out of the Pedregal and up onto the road a mile north of the Mexican lines.

Lee and the American engineers had not completed their impromptu highway, but the time for road building was past. The focus now was on moving forward, ever forward, into Mexico City. Whatever surprise they may have hoped for by attacking through the Pedegral was lost. Santa Anna, still determined to keep the fight outside Mexico City, rushed fresh armies to the front. The American force took up positions in the cornfields and orchards near the road. They were caught between this oncoming force of twelve thousand men and the soldiers under Major General Gabriel Valencia, who had already been holding the land along the Pedregal.

But night soon fell, and with it came an utter darkness and driving rain that prevented any more hostilities. To get his troops out of the cruel downpour, Santa Anna pulled them back inside San Ángel, on the northwest side of the Pedregal, where they took refuge in houses, barns, and simple sheds. General Valencia and his troops held their positions in an encampment just outside the village of Contreras.

The American brigades trapped between those two great armies found shelter as best they could. Shortly after 9:00 P.M., in a small Catholic church in the village of San Gerónimo, the American commanders held a council of war. There was no way to communicate with Scott, so Generals Persifor Smith, George Cadwalader, and Bennet Riley were being forced to plot their own course of action. (Lee was there as Scott's representative, and as such, his presence had a heft that belied his rank—but he was still no general.) In a dire position, the men decided to take an extreme risk. Despite the darkness and weather, they abandoned their positions at 3:00 A.M. and then began preparing for their attack by swinging silently into position behind the lines of General Valencia. Riley had been a soldier for more than thirty years and had led the first military escort along the Santa Fe Trail in 1829; Cadwalader was a forty-one-year-old member of the Pennsylvania state militia who had once suppressed riots in Philadelphia. But it was Smith, the gallant Louisiana native who had fought in the Seminole Wars and distinguished himself at Monterrey, who would command the battle. If all went well, the brigades would be in position by dawn and would launch their attack at sunrise.

As the generals made their decision, Lee stunned them all by announcing that he was headed back to Scott's headquarters to convey the news. "During the council and for hours after, the rain fell in torrents, whilst the darkness was so intense that one could move only by groping," Lieutenant Hunt later wrote, marveling at Lee's journey. "It has always seemed incredible to me when I recollect the distance amid darkness and storm, and the dangers of the Pedregal which he must have traversed, and that, too, I believe entirely unaccompanied. Scarcely a step could have been taken without danger or death; but that to him, a true soldier, was the willing risk of duty in a good cause. I would not believe it could have been made, that passage of the Pedregal, if he had not said he had made it."

Unbeknownst to Lee, Scott had sent out seven separate officers from his headquarters since sundown, hoping that at least one could make it through the Pedregal and get word to the stranded American brigades. Each messenger had returned in failure.

Lee made it through. Dripping wet and chilled to the bone, his normally immaculate uniform filthy and torn, he reached Scott's headquarters back at San Augustin just before midnight and relayed a message from General Smith, requesting a diversionary predawn attack to keep Valencia off balance. This force would attack Valencia from the front, adding the element of surprise when Smith and the other two brigades swooped down from behind.

As Lee was explaining himself, division commanders Twiggs and Pillow came in out of the rain. They, too, had turned back after an unsuccessful nighttime attempt to march across the Pedregal to the American positions. Scott decided to send Twiggs back out, with orders to command the requested diversionary force. To do that, Twiggs had to be united with his men. Lee was the only man who knew the way, and so he was obliged to go out into the cold, wet night, this time to guide the barrel-chested Twiggs through the Pedregal. Halfway across, they found an American brigade hunkered down for the night. This would be Twiggs's diversionary force. At 1:00 A.M. they began the slow march toward the front of Valencia's position.

The diversionary attack was launched shortly after dawn. Twiggs had been exhausted after the late night march. It was Lee who guided the American troops into position. The place he chose was the exact same ridge where Jackson and Magruder's cannons had been positioned the day before. As the sun rose, Mexican pickets caught sight of the Americans' blue uniforms and opened fire. Soon, American troops could be seen racing down the hillside behind the Mexican lines, as Smith, Cadwalader, and Riley charged their men onto the enemy. It was a scenario that could not have unspooled more perfectly, nor could it have succeeded without the bravery of Robert E. Lee. Later, when Scott was asked to describe Lee's actions that night, he was unsparing in his praise. It was, Scott said, "the greatest feat of physical and moral courage performed by any individual, in my knowledge, pending the campaign."

Valencia's stunned forces broke and ran after just seventeen minutes of fighting. Lee crossed to the far side of the Pedregal and found his good friend Joe Johnston "shrunk and shivered with agony" about his nephew's death. Lee moved to offer his condolences, extending his hand to Johnston. But the fatigue, the cold, and the battle, and now this empathy toward a man he had known since their days at West Point, finally broke him. Lee burst out in tears, and together he and Johnston mourned the loss of a good young officer.

LEE COULD NOT linger long in his grief.

Even as the first American elements slipped into the Mexican position, Scott's army back in San Augustin was on the move, racing up the eastern edge of the Pedregal via the San Antonio road. Lee saddled a horse and charged east down the San Ángel road toward the village of Churubusco. They soon routed a Mexican force ensconced in the Convent of San Mateo.

The Mexican army hastily retreated inside the gates of Mexico City. They jammed the causeways, a sea of men and horses racing to flee the American invaders. "The soldiers, in general, are Indians, forcibly made to serve," noted one Mexican government minister. "These Indians have little or no concept of nationality, and no interest whatever in maintaining an order of things in which they figure only as beasts of burden. Nevertheless, it must be truthfully said that as soldiers they are really quite good, because—aside from not being cowards—they have great endurance in the campaign. They have shown that they can cross hundreds of leagues over bad roads, barefoot, badly clothed and worse fed, and this without complaining or committing any notable act of insubordination. Without doubt, if these same Indians were led by officers with good quality training and some sensibility, they would be as good as the soldiers of any other country. The trouble therefore, with the Mexican army is not with the soldiers but with the officers, who, with a few and honorable exceptions, are assuredly the most ignorant and demoralized on earth."

That fact was very clear as the terrified Mexicans jammed the causeway. Scott did not pursue them, preferring to seek a Mexican surrender. Just like that, hostilities ceased. Nicholas P. Trist, a commissioner representing Polk and the U.S. government, was traveling with Scott's army to broker an armistice. On August 23, he succeeded. The deal allowed for the release of all Mexican prisoners and the delivery of supplies into the city (where, strangely, American quartermasters such as Grant would be allowed to venture to purchase provisions), with an agreement by both sides that reinforcement and strengthening of their positions were forbidden.

On September 2, Trist dictated additional terms, as stipulated by Polk: Mexico would abandon any claims on Texas and accept the Rio Grande as its northern boundary; New Mexico and California would be ceded to the United States in exchange for a cash payment; and Americans would have transit rights across the Isthmus of Tehuantepec, allowing goods to be shipped from one side of the United States to the other without enduring the treacherous journey around Cape Horn.

Santa Anna said no. On September 3, his hubris restored

after the break in hostilities, he once again adopted a wartime posture. Sales of provisions to American quartermasters were suspended, every Mexican soldier within a hundred miles was recalled to the city, and Mexico City's fortifications were once again manned.

Carlos María de Bustamante, a Mexican congressman from Oaxaca, summed up the mood of the nation's leaders. "It would be better that a conquest be completed, that the cities be reduced to ashes, than to enter into conditions which would reduce the Mexican nation to a status worse than when it had been a colony of Spain," he wrote. "Mexico is alone, but that does not matter, nor do the reverses it has suffered as long as it maintains its constancy. That is what made the United States triumph in its war of independence, and that is what will make us triumph."

Yet the Americans kept coming. On September 7, after Scott confirmed Mexican troop movements on the southern side of Mexico City, he ordered that Worth's division attack the foundry at the King's Mill, or Molino del Rey. It was rumored that church bells were being melted down to make new cannons at the heavily defended complex, which lay just one thousand yards from the hilltop castle at Chapultepec, whose formidable guns stood ready to rain fire on any American advance. "Chapultepec is a mound springing up from the plain to a height of probably three hundred feet, and almost in a direct line between Molino del Rey and the western part of the city," Grant observed in his usual detached manner.

Molino del Rey was not one single structure, but a series of one-story stone buildings sprawling over a three-hundred-yard radius directly west of Chapultepec. The defenses ringing the complex were astonishingly powerful: Two brigades of Mexican soldiers occupied the foundry itself. The flat roof provided cover for Mexican gunners and brought back eerie memories of Monterrey for those Americans who had fought there. Sandbags lined the rooftops and the low walls forming Molino del Rey's perimeter.

The Casa Mata, another fortified structure just five hundred yards away, was surrounded by earthworks that garrisoned fifteen hundred men. Scott rightly believed that the building was a key enemy gunpowder storage unit. Seven Mexican cannons hidden within a wall of cactus defended the gap between the two buildings. And finally, four thousand Mexican cavalry were stationed at a hacienda just a mile away, ready to ride forth at a moment's notice.

Yet somehow, Scott assumed that the structure was lightly defended. He ordered Worth's division of 3,250 men to capture the foundry. "I have just learned that the plan of attack is arranged," Captain Kirby Smith wrote to his wife on the eve of battle. "A forlorn hope of five hundred men commanded by Major G. Wright is to carry the foundry and blow it up. At the same time, an attack from our artillery, the rest of the first division, and Cadwalader's Brigade is to be made upon their line and Chapultepec, with our battalion forming the reserve. This operation is to commence at three in the morning. Tomorrow will be a day of slaughter."

At 3:00 A.M. on September 8, Worth's men quietly jogged into position. Grant, with Garland's brigade, was on the far right end of the American lines. A shortage of officers accounted for his being pressed into combat. When the Mexicans didn't return fire during the initial artillery salvo, and there was no sign of Mexican soldiers anywhere, Worth ordered the fire halted. Clearly the foundry had been abandoned. Worth ordered Wright's advance party to charge.

Smith's gut prediction soon proved all too true: it was a day of slaughter. The Mexicans had not retreated but were merely hiding. General Simeón Ramírez had concealed his soldiers and artillery so well that when Wright's men raced toward the foundry, they were torn apart in the same violent manner in which American cannons had so often torn apart the Mexicans. Not only were the Americans forced to retreat after thirty brief minutes of firing, but the casualties were horrendous. Mexican troops brazenly took aim at the American wounded during the lull in the battle, shooting helpless men where they lay, even as lancers galloped forth to spear the bodies and slash the throats of others.

The Americans attacked repeatedly over the next ninety minutes, searching for some way inside the foundry's heavy locked iron gates. Over to the far left of Worth's lines, First Lieutenant Thomas Jackson galloped forward with a complement of flying artillery. His timing was impeccable: their deadly fire stopped a Mexican cavalry attack.

It was Garland's men on the right flank that finally broke through a gate and breached the foundry, working as a series of small units fighting independently of one another. Grant was among the first in the door. He was in the thick of the fighting, leading men from building to building, flushing out Mexican resistance. He was later commended for his "gallant and meritorious conduct."

Scott, meanwhile, rushed reinforcements into the field as soon as he discovered his tactical error. The Americans finally took Molino del Rey after the two-hour battle (Casa Mata was attacked late in the action and exploded when a magazine caught fire), but at great cost: 116 dead, 671 wounded, and 22 missing. Brevet Colonel James McIntosh lost 44 men and 104 horses in one span of ten seconds.

For their part, the Mexicans suffered the loss of roughly 2,000 soldiers, with another 685 taken prisoner. Among the American fatalities was Captain Kirby Smith, who had so prophetically predicted the battle's exorbitant body count. He was shot in the face while climbing over a wall into an enemy gun position.

But even Captain Smith—who had shown the depth of his prebattle fears by closing his final letter to his wife with the words, "I am thankful you do not know the peril we are in"—had understated the outcome: American losses amounted to a staggering one-fourth of Worth's division. And the men had been slain for little gain, for the Americans found a few paltry cannons inside Molino del Rey. Instead of masses of destructive weapons, they found great mounds of grain, so vital to feeding the vast Mexican army.

Worth's division retreated to their former positions. It was clearly an American victory, but the retreat left Grant furious. He had by now seen enough war to know good tactics from bad and was more than comfortable venting his frustrations at the way good men had died unnecessarily. Of the twenty-one officers that had begun the war with the Fourth Infantry, just Grant and a handful of others remained. His evolution from timid young lieutenant to future general was complete. He could see the entire battlefield in his head, and he struggled to analyze his mixed emotions about Scott's tactics. No longer were generals revered elder men in Grant's estimation; they were very fallible human beings making choices that affected the lives of thousands. His journeys as quartermaster, seeking to feed the army, had allowed him to see the topography on a daily basis and had led him to form his own views on the optimal way to attack Mexico City. He wrote in a letter:

> You can see the difficult and brilliant work our army has been doing. If Santa Anna does not surrender the city, or peace be negotiated, much more hard fighting may be expected, as I foresee before the city is captured. My observations convince me that we have other strong works to reduce before we can enter the city. Our position is such that we cannot avoid these. From my map and all

the information I acquired while the army was halted at Puebla, I was then, and am now more than ever, convinced that the army could have approached the city by passing around the north of it, and reached the northwest side, and avoided all the fortified positions, until we reached the gates of the city at their weakest and most indefensible, as well as most approachable points. The roads and defenses I had carefully noted on my map, and I had communicated the knowledge I had acquired from Mexican scouts in our camp, and others I met at Puebla who were familiar with the ground, to such of my superiors as it seemed proper, but I know not whether General Scott was in possession of the information. It is to be presumed, however, that the commanding General had possessed himself of all the facts.

It seems to me the northwest side of the city could have been approached without attacking a single fort or redoubt, we would have been on solid ground instead of floundering through morass and ditches, and fighting our way over elevated roads, flanked by water where it is generally impossible to deploy forces.

What I say is entirely confidential, and I am willing to believe that the opinion of a lieutenant, where it differs from that of his commanding general, must be founded on ignorance of the situation, and you will consider my criticisms accordingly.

The letter's addressee was never discovered, as if Grant was writing it to himself. But whatever his conflicted emotions, he was much more confident when writing to Julia: "There is no force in Mexico that can resist this army," Grant boasted. "To fight is to conquer."

THIRTY-NINE

Old Glory

SEPTEMBER 13, 1847

The walls of Mexico City were now tantalizingly close to the Americans, just over a mile as the crow flew. "To the northeast, apparently at but a little greater distance, lies amid its lakes and marshes the boasted city of the Aztecs, its spires and domes, its walls and aqueducts, all plainly visible," wrote one officer.

That short distance between the American position and the Mexican capital was bewitching—and deceptive. For in that brief divide lay still more of the soupy swamps and mud that, by necessity, defined a city that had originally existed on an islet in the southwest portion of a saltwater lake. Tribes had been settling on the shores of Lake Texcoco (an S-shaped geographic oddity known as an endorheic body of water, lacking any type of outflow such as a river or an underground aquifer) since 1700 B.C., but it was the Nahua Aztec tribe—the original Mexicas—who realized the defensive potential of this massive body. In 1325, they ventured out onto a small islet and built a great new city, which they called Tenochtitlán. Over time, as the Aztecs prospered and their expanding population outgrew that original outcropping, artificial islands were constructed. To

352

prevent flooding, and to capture (as a source of drinking water) the fresh water that flowed into the lake from nearby rivers, the Aztecs constructed a series of dams. The aquatic barrier proved such a wondrous natural defense that Cortés required a seventy-nine-day siege to take the city in 1519.

But Cortés soon destroyed those all-important dams, and the Spanish drained those portions of Lake Texcoco on which the city had been built. Flooding became a way of life in what had come to be known as Mexico City, recurring often enough that the great salt marshes that now surrounded the city never lacked for moisture and once again formed a vast defensive barrier.

A series of narrow causeways bisected the soup between the American forces and the walls of Mexico City. The roads would make the Americans easy fodder for Mexican cannons whenever the moment for that final advance came. But before Scott's armies could even begin to advance on those causeways, one other very formidable obstacle stood in their path. "To the north," wrote one American officer, peering up at the fortified structure atop the tallest hill for miles around, "lies Chapultepec."

Chapultepec was the name both of the highest point for miles around and of the castle perched atop its summit. Aztec royalty had once retreated to the verdant slopes of Chapultepec—"Grasshopper Hill"—during the summer months, enjoying the commanding view and the cool shade of its many cypress trees. The castle was built during the Spanish occupation, by a man, ironically enough, who had been instrumental in helping America win the Revolutionary War.

Count Bernardo de Gálvez y Madrid had been ordered by the Spanish government to aid the American colonists, knowing that Spain could only benefit from Britain's misfortunes. As governor of Louisiana, he was instrumental in defeating the British at Baton Rouge in 1779 and then pushing them out of the lower Mississippi River valley with subsequent triumphs at Mobile and

Pensacola. He later helped draft the 1783 Treaty of Paris, which ended the war, and was then reassigned to serve as viceroy of New Spain in Mexico City. In 1785 he ordered workers to begin construction on a new summer house atop Chapultepec. What began as a simple baroque getaway soon took on the appearance of a fortress, with the great walls, parapets, and generally defensive appearance of a castle. There were rumors among higher-ups in New Spain's government (soon communicated to his superiors in Spain) that the popular Gálvez was quietly conspiring to hole up in this mountaintop refuge and rally the local people to seek independence from their European master. That talk came to an end with Gálvez's untimely death on November 30, 1786. Some said he was poisoned.

Chapultepec fell into disrepair. The castle on the hill was entirely abandoned during the Mexican War of Independence. By the Mexican War, it had been refurbished to house the country's military academy, and it now claimed an area a quarter mile wide and three-fourths of a mile long. The main gate was on the east side, facing the city. Molino del Rey anchored its western end, and seven-foot-high walls of stone ringed the remainder of the facility. A gap in the south wall had been filled in with piles of sandbags, and a low, swampy ditch along the western wall had been mined. Within the complex, those cypress trees where Montezuma had once rested on hot summer days now formed a grove that led up to a second set of high white walls, which encompassed the actual castle. Inside that castle were 852 Mexican infantry, along with a handful of engineers and military cadets. They had ten cannons.

The American troops thought Chapultepec was impregnable and dreaded the moment of vulnerability when they would have to scale those white walls that led to the summit. Yet the castle was far from a military stronghold: the parapets were unfinished, the roof was too thin to deflect artillery shells, and those stone walls could easily be breached by troops carrying scaling ladders.

Scott could not afford another blunder like Molino del Rey. His army numbered just a little more than seven thousand men; Santa Anna had three times that. Scouts reported that a second Mexican force comprising two divisions and as many as eight thousand men might be approaching from Scott's rear, potentially pinning the Americans between two vastly superior Mexican forces. If, for instance, Scott threw his army at Chapultepec, and Santa Anna was able to rush his army from the city in time to reinforce the defenders, Scott could easily be overwhelmed. Despite failure after failure, Santa Anna still had the upper hand. The American general's next move in this tactical game of cat and mouse was of vital importance, and no one was more aware of that than he.

Scott's solution was, as always, Robert E. Lee. The general sent his most trusted source of reconnaissance out to probe the Mexican defenses, hoping he would yet again find some brilliant alternate path toward their military objective. But when Lee, along with Lieutenants P. G. T. Beauregard and Zealous B. Tower, studied the southern approach, which would have allowed the Americans to bypass Chapultepec and head straight into Mexico City, it became obvious that Santa Anna was expecting the attack from that direction. A series of three parallel causeways a thousand yards apart ran into that side of the city. The Mexican general had connected them all with a perpendicular trench, which he soon fortified with breastworks and then filled with troops and cannons.

When Lee reported this news to Scott, the general personally rode out from his command post in Tacubaya to see the position. On the morning of September 11, Scott called a council of war in the tiny village of Piedad. Present were his engineers and his generals, the two groups of men most imperative to any victorious attack. The topic of debate was finding the best possible route into the Mexican capital. Lee argued in favor of isolating the garrison at Chapultepec and invading Mexico City from the south by hitting those entrenched positions hard and then advancing en masse up the causeways. There were obvious strategic liabilities: marshy ground; the need to follow causeways into the city, making flanking movements impossible; and carefully planned Mexican fortifications alongside the causeways, designed to pin American troops with a withering crossfire. Yet Lee saw the southern approach as the Americans' best hope and boldly made his case.

Beauregard, on the other hand, favored an attack from the west. He presented a long and masterly dissection of the southern route, which ended with his making a strong case for the Chapultepec assault. Nobody, with the exception of Scott, agreed with him at first, but Beauregard's argument was persuasive enough that General Franklin Pierce crossed over and took his side. "Gentlemen," Scott finally announced, as he had been planning to do all along, "we will attack by the western gates."

Yet Scott respected the opinions of both Lee and Beauregard enough that he combined their arguments into a single ingenious attack. On the morning of September 12, units of U.S. soldiers would march over to the southern side of Mexico City, showing themselves to Santa Anna's army, in the hopes that he would continue to reinforce that approach. But at night the Americans would march silently over to the west and take up positions around Chapultepec.

Lee spent the night of the eleventh supervising the construction of gun batteries for Chapultepec's bombardment. Four positions had been selected, and a host of eight-pound howitzers, along with a ten-inch mortar, were soon aimed at the fortress. The emplacement with the greatest fire was near Molino del Rey, where a twenty-four-pounder stood ready to belch forth its wrath.

Scott described their locations in his official report to Polk: "No. 1, on our right, under the command of Captain Drum, 4th artillery," he wrote, "and No. 2, commanded by Lieutenant Hagner, Ordnance—both supported by Quitman's division. Nos. 3 and 4 on the opposite side, supported by Pillow's division, were commanded, the former by Captain Brooks and Lieutenant S. S. Anderson, 2d artillery, alternately, and the latter by Lieutenant Stone, Ordnance. The batteries were traced by Captain Huger and Captain Lee, Engineer, and constructed by them with the able assistance of the young officers of those corps and artillery."

The mortars opened fire first. Starting on the morning of the twelfth and continuing into the evening, Chapultepec came under heavy fire. First the mortars and then American cannons lobbed exploding shells and solid balls at the fortress. According to plan, those volunteer divisions commanded by Generals John Quitman and Gideon Pillow drew the heated Mexican fire as they feinted toward the southern approach to the city.

It was Scott's desire that the Mexicans abandon the castle without a fight or that the barrage destroy it altogether. This was not to be. Even when cannon fire punctured the castle's roof and otherwise damaged the parapets, forest, and stone walls at the base of the complex, Chapultepec was very much intact—and very much occupied. The Mexicans were cowed, exhausted, and low on food, but they stood fast. For the Mexican soldiers up in the castle, the night of the twelfth was spent vigilantly, for they were unsure whether the cessation of American bombardment portended a stealthy nighttime infantry attack.

But the Americans were waiting (and resting) until dawn. Scott summoned Lee to his command post two miles to the rear, fearful that the Mexicans would spend the night repairing

Chapultepec's damage. The general was angry with Lee, who had been so consumed with observing the artillery fire that he had not seen fit to check in with his commander. This left Scott without his most trusted battlefield eyes and ears.

Lee, for his part, was exhausted. He had been so busy positioning guns and preparing for the assault that he had not slept in thirty hours. The Virginian informed Scott that the Mexicans would most likely refortify their position during the night. The general immediately prepared to order an American attack under cover of darkness.

Lee stopped him. Arguing that there was only so much the Mexicans could do to fix the damage, he reminded Scott that if the Americans succeeded in taking Chapultepec quickly, it would be easier to press the advantage and race into Mexico City during daylight.

Scott agreed. The order was rescinded. The attack would take place at dawn, as planned.

Up and down the American lines, the atrocities of Molino del Rey still fresh in their memories, U.S. soldiers girded themselves for the battle ahead with a sense of vengeance. "General Pillow addressed his men, telling them that they were to assault the castle early next morning, when he said he had no doubt they would easily carry it at the point of the bayonet in less than half an hour; which intimation the soldiers received with three cheers," one soldier later wrote.

The barrage resumed promptly at 5:30 A.M. Santa Anna still remained convinced that Chapultepec was a diversion and that Quitman and Pillow would soon be followed by the main body of American troops. He shifted elements of his army eastward, to defend the gate at San Lázaro, clear on the opposite side of the city from Chapultepec, not knowing that Quitman and Pillow's divisions had already moved over to the base of Grasshopper Hill.

At 8:00 A.M. the American cannons went silent. As the defenders of Chapultepec watched from the castle parapets, U.S. infantry stood ready to advance. The attack would not come from a single direction but from the four points of the compass. Lee, who was now forty-eight hours without sleep, was with General Pillow's division, tasked by Scott to show them the way on the eastern approach from Molino del Rey. They would charge up to the castle through the hanging moss of the cypress grove. Lieutenant Thomas Jackson and his flying artillery would skirt the northern flank of the castle, in support of the Eleventh and Fourteenth infantries. Lieutenant Sam Grant was in reserve with Worth's command, preparing to dash up the San Cosmé causeway into Mexico City once Chapultepec fell. Pete Longstreet was nearby, also with Worth's division.

A quiet thrill coursed through the American ranks. If all went well, they would be in Mexico City by nightfall. The war might be over in a matter of hours.

The charge began just moments later. American artillery fired rounds of canister and grape overhead, up onto the highest reaches of Chapultepec. Lee guided Pillow's men forward to the first set of castle walls. Pillow was shot in the heel by a musket ball and went down. Lee stayed with the general as the rest of the army raced forward, now supplemented by Quitman's volunteers and 160 U.S. Marines, who had joined up with Scott's army in Puebla during the summer.

On the other side of the hill, Jackson was so eager to see combat again that he took the concept of flying artillery to its most extreme definition. His complement of horses, men, and six-pounders left the infantry far behind as they raced forward to assault the Mexican positions. Far from merely supporting the foot soldiers, he was preparing to blast a hole through the enemy defenses so the infantry could march right through.

Mexican muskets along Chapultepec's walls and a Mexican gun battery defending the road now focused their fire on Jackson's audacious charge. A ditch soon blocked his path, forcing Jackson to order his men to dismount and then push and pull the two 6-pounders to the other side by hand. They were fully exposed to Mexican fire. One gun was successfully dragged across, but Jackson's men then lost their nerve and raced for cover. "The horses were killed or disabled, and the men became so demoralized that they deserted the guns and sought shelter behind a wall or embankment," one American officer later wrote. "Lieutenant Jackson remained at the guns, walking back and forth, and kept saying, 'See, there is no danger. I am not hit.'"

Jackson stopped for a moment and planted his feet. As he did so, a cannonball passed between his legs.

One man, a sergeant, gamely stepped to Jackson's side. With just one gun at their disposal, the two men strained to spin it around toward the enemy position. Turning the six-pounder, with a weight of 880 pounds, was no easy task, but Jackson would not be deterred. He and the sergeant successfully took aim at the Mexican lines, manning the gun by themselves when the rest of his troops still refused to stand up and fight. The turning point was Captain John Magruder's coming to Jackson's aid—though on foot, after his horse had been shot out from under him. Jackson's men finally rose and dragged the remaining cannon out of the ditch and destroyed the Mexican cannons that were blocking the road. Soon the Eleventh and Fourteenth infantries moved forward, as planned. "Imagine...my situation at Chapultepec, within full range, and in a road which was swept with grape and canister, and at the same time thousands upon thousands of muskets from the castle itself above pouring down like hail upon you," Jackson later marveled in a letter to his sister. "Nothing but the strong and powerful hand of Almighty God could have brought me through unhurt."

Jackson would be highly praised for his service. Magruder wrote that "if devotion, industry, talent, and gallantry are the highest qualities of a soldier, then he is entitled to the distinction which their possession confers."

WORTH'S DIVISIONS, WAITING in reserve, were now ordered into battle. The lead elements of the American column had already reached the castle walls and were waiting for scaling ladders so they could scramble up and over. Soon the ladders arrived, so many that fifty men at a time could clamber up the white walls side by side. Once they entered the fortress, the fighting was hand-to-hand, a bloody and gruesome scene of bayonets, musket butts, sabers, knives, and even bare-knuckle fighting. The Americans were seeking their revenge for Molino del Rey — and they got it, slaughtering the Mexicans almost to a man. One of the Mexican cadets martyred himself by cloaking his body in the national tricolor and leaping from a parapet rather than die at the hands of the Americans.

The battle was still far from decided as Longstreet came over the wall, clutching the Stars and Stripes. Iowa had recently been added to the Union, and the flag now showed twenty-nine stars. But the tall and athletic Virginian, who had fought in every major battle of the war except Buena Vista without suffering so much as a scratch, was hit in the thigh by a musket ball. Right next to him was Lieutenant George Pickett, the fun-loving goat of West Point's 1846 class who had secured his appointment to the academy through the help of Abraham Lincoln's law partner. Longstreet handed him the colors before they could touch the ground, and it was Pickett who carried the American flag into Chapultepec Castle. Racing for the flagpole under heavy enemy fire, Pickett lowered the Mexican tricolor and, in one of the war's seminal moments, raised the Stars and Stripes so that everyone for miles around immediately knew the outcome of the battle.

At that very instant, on a nearby hillock, a group of Irish American deserters were far from thrilled to see Old Glory snapping in the breeze. The San Patricios had gone over to the Mexican side early in the war and had become heroes among their new comrades for their ferocious conduct under fire. But the Patricios had been captured at the Battle of Churubusco and sentenced to death by Scott. Rather than kill them immediately, the general had decreed that the thirty men be positioned so that they faced Chapultepec as the battle raged. Each prisoner stood atop the bed of a mule cart (one man was legless and sat atop a mule), hands tied behind his back, ankles bound together, and a noose cinched tightly about his neck. The other end of that rope was affixed to a hastily constructed gallows. The raising of the American flag was the signal for the executioner to whip the mules forward, sweeping the carts out from under the Irishmen's feet and hanging them.

Meanwhile, from the National Palace in Mexico City, a sullen Santa Anna could clearly see that very same flag. "If we were to plant our batteries in hell, the damned Yankees would take them from us," he vented to General Ampudia as they looked out into the distance. They could see Mexican soldiers fleeing Chapultepec. It was a scene of panic and disarray, the causeways jammed with emotionally broken men running for their lives toward Mexico City.

"God," Ampudia replied, "is a Yankee."

FORTY

Conquest

SEPTEMBER 13, 1847

The Mexico City that now stood before the American army was a far cry from the island fortress the Aztecs had created so long before. Three centuries of Spanish rule had transformed it into a New World version of a fine European city, with plazas, grand citadels, towering cathedrals, boulevards broad enough for a fine military parade, and a population numbering nearly two hundred thousand. It was as if a majestic slice of Spain had been built directly on top of the former Aztec sanctuary.

The embattled nature of Mexico City's inhabitants was one variable that had not changed. In the days leading up to Chapultepec, they had heard repeated admonitions from the Catholic clergy to take up arms against the American heretics. Horror stories about American atrocities at Buena Vista, Monterrey, and Veracruz were enough to make old men sharpen their knives and hatchets, and even send women and little children to the rooftops, lugging heavy stone pavers to be thrown down onto the invaders. A portrait of the Virgin of Guadalupe, Mexico's patron saint, had been paraded through the streets as part of a religious procession. And Santa Anna, who had been reviled by Mexico City's people after his failure at Cerro Gordo, was now cheered wherever he went.

Fortified customs houses, known as *garitas*, stood at each of the many gates situated around the city walls. These were the Mexicans' last line of defense—choke points that would force the Americans to funnel through narrow passages where they might easily be thwarted. But Santa Anna had depleted the *garitas* blocking the western and southwestern approaches to the city when he shifted the bulk of his army to the city's southeast quadrant. The Americans had great hopes of overwhelming the city's western approaches by thrusting immediately from Chapultepec into the city.

Quitman's division now raced up the Belén causeway, which had been precisely engineered to form a straight line from the main gate of Chapultepec to the Belén *garita*, on Mexico City's southwest corner. Church bells pealed the signal for citizens to prepare for battle. As Quitman, the Mississippi volunteer general, and his troops charged pell-mell up the crowded causeway, residents of Mexico City clambered onto their rooftops to witness the titans' approach. The Americans wore threadbare uniforms, and Quitman had somehow lost a boot during the action. So what the Mexican people saw was not a spit-and-polish corps of conquerors, but a band of filthy, unshaven men led by a shoeless officer on horseback.

Meanwhile, Worth's division was delayed at Chapultepec for several hours. Many of the men ransacked the castle in search of plunder and liquor. It was late in the afternoon as they proceeded, as best they could, up the San Cosmé causeway to Quitman's far left. San Cosmé traveled due north before turning sharply to the right to enter the city.

Jackson was one of the few soldiers who had not stopped fighting when the castle fell. As he had dashed up the San Cosmé causeway, Mexican soldiers fleeing back into the city had clogged the road, slowing his advance. Jackson solved the problem by firing his six-pounders into the mob to clear a path. "Every shot told on the huddled and demoralized thousands of Mexicans," wrote one officer. "But their fire back upon the thirsty, pursuing Americans was harmless."

Jackson later told his sister that he felt no guilt or sadness about shooting men in the back and perhaps killing those innocent civilians who had gotten caught in the crossfire. His actions would not go unnoticed, and even Scott would soon publicly confront Jackson about how he had "slaughtered" those Mexicans. Yet Jackson did not care. "What business had I with results?" Jackson wrote defiantly to his sister. "My duty was to obey orders."

Finally, Jackson's advance was halted when a complement of two thousand Mexican cavalry under General Ampudia rode out from the city to challenge the invaders. Jackson, now joined by Magruder, quickly unlimbered their guns. "A rapid fire was opened on the Mexicans, who retreated without attacking the artillery," noted one officer.

Only then did Jackson stop to wait for Worth. "It was not," wrote one American, "judged prudent to proceed further."

GRANT, TOO, WAS impatient to be inside Mexico City. He was now moving up the San Cosmé road toward Jackson's position. Rather than travel on the causeway, he and the rest of Garland's detachment followed a parallel route beneath the arches of a city aqueduct. They encountered pockets of Mexican resistance but pressed forward. "When opposition was encountered our troops sheltered themselves by keeping under the arches supporting the aqueduct, advancing an arch at a time," Grant remembered. But at the point where the causeway turned sharply to the right, "our progress was stopped for a time by the single piece of artillery and the infantry occupying the housetops back from it."

Grant remained calm. As Jackson directed his flying six-pounders at that lone Mexican gun, Grant set out by himself to find a way around it, soon coming upon another Mexican position.

"West of the road from where we were, stood a house occupying the southwest angle made by the San Cosmé road and the road we were moving upon. A stone wall ran from the house along each of these roads for a considerable distance," wrote Grant. "I watched my opportunity and skipped across the road and behind the south wall. Proceeding cautiously to the west corner of the enclosure, I peeped around and, seeing nobody, continued, still cautiously, until the road running east and west was reached. I then returned to the troops and called for volunteers. All that were close to me, or that heard me, about a dozen, volunteered."

Grant safely led these men up the road, ordering them not to fire, lest they give themselves away. In this way, they stealthily crept up on the Mexican positions. Jackson's cannons had succeeded in their chores, and Grant was equally successful in his impromptu flanking movement. The Mexicans, catching sight of the approaching U.S. soldiers and having no more artillery support, fled back into the city.

At the San Cosmé *garita*, however, the Mexicans made a stand. If Worth had simply raced from Chapultepec right after it fell, he would have found the *garita* undefended. But he had lingered to take on more ammunition and had then had to fight off a last-ditch charge by fifteen hundred Mexican lancers who had ventured forth from the city. So it was 4:00 P.M. when his men finally got under way. As Chapultepec had fallen at 9:30 in the morning, Santa Anna had finally realized his great tactical error and guessed—correctly this time—that the bulk of the American forces would be entering the city at San Cosmé. Men and weapons had been rushed to the *garita*, and by the time Worth's men approached, three cannons (including a twenty-four-pounder) and three fresh battalions now manned the roofs and hid inside the arches of the aqueduct. The Americans' path was completely blocked.

It was Grant who noticed that a local church overlooked the enemy positions. It "looked to me as if the belfry would command the ground back of the garita San Cosmé," he wrote. Seizing command of the situation, Grant persuaded an artillery unit to dismantle one of their lightweight mountain howitzers. Taking the long route to the church, they were forced to carry the cannon through a series of chest-deep swamps. When he finally arrived at the church, Grant politely knocked on the door. A priest answered. "With the little Spanish then at my command, I explained to him that he might save property by opening the door, and he would certainly save himself from becoming a prisoner, for a time at least: and besides, I intended to go in whether he consented or not. He began to see his duty in the same light that I did, and opened the door, although it did not look as if it gave him special pleasure to do so," Grant later wrote.

The gun was hauled up the belfry's narrow wooden steps, piece by piece, then reassembled in the steeple. Grant then gave the order to open fire. The results were immediate. "Shots from our little gun dropped in upon the enemy and created great confusion. Why they did not send out a small party and capture us, I do not know."

Grant and the artillery specialists kept right on firing. Worth's forces soon saw the value in outflanking the Mexican positions. The twenty-four-pounder was knocked out of commission shortly before 5:00 P.M., and a group of U.S. Marines successfully climbed to the roof of a three-story house behind the enemy position and decimated the Mexican infantry and baggage mules with a display of precision musketry.

Worth ordered his men to halt and to settle into their new positions for the night. Over at the Belén *garita,* Quitman's men were doing the same. He sent one of his staff officers, Lieutenant John Pemberton, to bring Grant to him. "He expressed his gratification," Grant wrote simply of his meeting with Quitman.

LEE ENTERED THE city long after Grant and Jackson, via the very same route. He had spent the day riding back and forth from the various battlefields to Scott's headquarters, not wishing to anger the general again by failing to provide a steady stream of reports. There had still not been any time to sleep. By the time he and Scott began riding down the San Cosmé causeway, he was struggling to stay awake in the saddle. Just as he and Scott reached Worth's position, Lee fainted.

And that was how, after months of bravery and daring, Robert E. Lee's Mexican War came to an end. At 1:00 A.M. the next morning, Santa Anna opened Mexico City's jails and freed every prisoner. At the request of the city fathers, who did not wish to see the horrors and destruction of Veracruz inflicted upon their city, he then evacuated with his army and fled to the village of Guadalupe Hidalgo.

By 4:00 A.M., Mexico City's authorities had sent a delegation to Scott, requesting terms of surrender. As the sun rose over the capital the following morning, the American flag was raised over Mexico's National Palace. Scott slept there that night, guarded by a squad of U.S. Marines, in what was also known as the Halls of Montezuma.

Sam Grant could finally rest easy and make plans for his eventual return home — because, after so many battles and so much uncertainty about his future, that day would now soon come. He reflected with pride on his service and that of his army brethren: "I had gone into the battle of Palo Alto in May, 1846, a second lieutenant, and I entered the city of Mexico sixteen months later with the same rank, after having been in all the engagements possible for any one man and in a regiment that lost more officers in the war than it ever had present at any one engagement," wrote Grant. "I would not have the anniversaries of our victories celebrated, nor those of our defeats made fast days spent in humiliation and prayer. But I would like to see truthful history written. Such history will do full credit to the courage, endurance, and soldierly ability of the American citizen, no matter what section of the country he hailed from, or in what ranks he fought. The justice of the cause which in the end prevailed, will, I doubt not, come to be acknowledged by every citizen of the land, in time."

FORTY-ONE

Fourth of July

July 4, 1848

It was a Sunday. Rain had fallen during the night, tamping down the midsummer dust that so often drifted over Washington's undeveloped riverfront. As the crowd of thousands flocked to the Mall in front of the Capitol, there was a "delicious freshness to the air," in the words of one local paper.

They had come to witness the laying of the Washington Monument's cornerstone. Local ferries and other transportation services had lowered their rates just for this special ceremony, which had begun early that morning with a grand parade and the pealing of church bells. The people came from near and far—local dignitaries, representatives of various Indian tribes, members of Congress and the judiciary, and names now synonymous with America's earlier generations: Mrs. Elizabeth Schuyler Hamilton, the wife of Alexander Hamilton; Mrs. Dolley Payne Madison; Martin Van Buren; Sam Houston; John Quincy Adams; and Millard Fillmore. A forty-year-old bald eagle that had been in attendance when the legendary Lafayette visited nearby Alexandria in 1825 now perched atop a temporary archway. It was during his 1824–25 return to the United States (during which he had paid a poignant visit to the widow of Light-Horse Harry Lee and met a teenage Robert E. Lee) that the French general had presided over the dedication of the Bunker Hill Monument in Massachusetts. The eagle represented not just America and Lafayette's visit but also the spiritual continuum between America's early years of independence and the bold new future that now lay ahead. As if to remind one and all of the bird's importance, it had ridden into the city on a stone wagon, as part of the grand procession, perched atop the 24,500-pound block of Baltimore marble that would soon become the cornerstone.

"In a hollow spread with boards and surrounded with seats the crowd gathered. Around two sides of this space were high and solidly constructed seats, hired out to spectators, covered with awnings, and affording a favorable position for seeing and hearing," wrote one newspaper account. "From 15,000 to 20,000 persons are estimated to have been present, stretched over a large area of ground from the southern hill, gradually sloping to the plain below."

Unbeknownst to most in attendance, the U.S. Senate had ratified the Treaty of Guadalupe Hidalgo that morning, formally bringing an end to the Mexican War. Worth's division, with Grant still among its members, had finally marched away from Mexico City on June 12, marking the end of the capital's American occupation. Now, with the treaty's ratification, the war was truly done.

Almost all of Polk's demands had been met: Texas and all the lands west to the Pacific were now part of the United States, in exchange for fifteen million dollars, with the Rio Grande now specified as Texas's southern boundary. The lone exception was that the United States had failed to secure control of transit rights across the Isthmus of Tehuantepec, which the British had magically finagled for themselves through deft diplomatic maneuvering. Nonetheless, America's Manifest Destiny was complete.

For that reason, and for the powerful emotion accompanying the commencement of construction on the long-delayed Washington Monument, the Fourth of July, 1848, as one Washington newspaper noted, was truly "one of the most splendid and agreeable Washington has ever witnessed."

THE WRITER DIDN'T even know the half of it. The Treaty of Guadalupe Hidalgo's biggest prize was California, with its deepwater ports and abundant natural resources. Now, as Lieutenant William Tecumseh Sherman prepared to celebrate the Fourth of July clear across the continent from Washington, those riches were about to take on a brand-new meaning. Sherman was working for the military governor of California, Colonel R. B. Mason, a stern yet fair individual who had been appointed when Kearny was ordered to take over as military governor of Veracruz. "I remember, one day in the spring of 1848, that two men, Americans, came into the office and inquired for the Governor. I asked them their business, and one answered that they had just come down from Captain Sutter on special business, and they wanted to see Governor Mason in person," wrote Sherman, who ushered them into Mason's office and then returned to his duties.

But Mason came to the door a moment later and summoned Sherman back into his office. A pair of dull yellow rocks lay atop a pile of papers on Mason's desk. "What is that?" Mason asked him.

Sherman hefted one of the rocks. "Is it gold?" he asked.

It was. And soon Mason and Sherman struck out from Monterey, on their way up to an outpost known as Sutter's Fort, in Sacramento. When they stopped at San Francisco, the soldiers were shocked to see the city almost empty of men. As they moved inland up the long, broad river delta that would take them to Sutter's Fort, they saw that mills and shops in towns along the way were deserted and that farmers were allowing cattle and horses to wander about aimlessly in mature fields of wheat and corn, trampling and ruining the crops. Clearly, news of gold at Sutter's Mill had already spread throughout northern California.

They had arrived on July 2. "Sutter's Fort," Sherman wrote, "stands about three miles back from the river, and about a mile from the American Fork, which is also a respectable stream. The fort encloses a space of about two hundred yards by eighty; the walls are built of adobe, or sun-dried brick. All the houses are of one story, save one, which stands in the middle, which is two stories."

There they had met Sutter, a balding German immigrant in his midforties who had made a small fortune selling supplies to the local Indians, Californians (as the local Mexican population was known), and those Americans coming west to make a new life in California.

Sherman and Mason celebrated the Fourth of July at Sutter's Fort in lavish fashion. "Sutter presided at the head of the table, Governor Mason on his right and I on his left. About fifty sat down to the table, mostly Americans, some foreigners, and one or two Californians. The usual toasts, songs, speeches, etc. passed off, and a liberal quantity of liquor was disposed of: champagne, Madeira, sherry, etc.; on the whole, a dinner that would have done credit in any frontier town."

But that Fourth of July was just a prelude to the momentous events that would follow. Mason and Sherman set out two days later, riding twenty-five miles up the American River, to the place where miners were scrambling over the sand and pebbles of the water's shallows, panning for gold. A bemused Sherman rode back to Monterey with Mason shortly afterward. Under the governor's orders, Sherman drafted the letter back to Washington that would spark a worldwide rush to the California gold fields. "I have no hesitation now in saying that there is more gold in the country drained by the Sacramento and San Joaquin Rivers than will pay the cost of the present war with Mexico a hundred times over. No capital is required to obtain this gold, as the laboring man wants nothing but his pick, shovel, and tin pan," wrote Sherman. "Many frequently pick gold out of the crevices of rock with their butcher knives in pieces from one to six ounces."

Sherman's letter was handed to a courier, who sailed south, crossed the Panamanian isthmus on a mule, and then sailed to New Orleans via Jamaica and finally on to Washington. On December 5, 1848, in his final State of the Union address, President Polk announced the discovery of gold: "The accounts of abundance of gold are of such an extraordinary character as would scarcely command belief were they not corroborated by the authentic reports of officers in the public service," he said, crediting Sherman.

Within days, thousands upon thousands of Americans were flooding toward California, along with immigrants from Australia and South America. This "gold rush," in turn, would see the settlement of those lands between California and the Mississippi River, thanks to the countless pioneers who trailed along in the miners' wake, seeking farmland instead of gold.

Manifest Destiny had been realized. Lieutenant William Tecumseh Sherman never actually saw combat in the Mexican War, but in most unique fashion, his role in America's sea-to-shining-sea expansion was as pivotal as any contribution by his West Point band of brothers.

EPILOGUE

On October 13, 1847, the American regular and volunteer officers stationed in Mexico City gathered to form a social group. They were a very special breed of men, and Scott had singled out the West Point graduates in particular when describing the outcome of the Mexican War: "I give it as my fixed opinion, that but for our graduated cadets, the war between the United States and Mexico might, and probably would have lasted some four or five years, with, in its first half, more defeats than victories falling to our share; whereas, in less than two campaigns, we conquered a great country and a peace without the loss of a single battle or skirmish."

At first their aims were merely to establish a place to enjoy one another's company while on duty in Mexico, but the Aztec Club, as they called themselves, would meet on a regular basis, long after they returned home from the occupation. The meetings would cease during the Civil War but would resume after the conflict and be conducted with a great deal of joviality and nostalgia.

Sam Grant arrived back in Saint Louis on July 28, 1848. He had been among the first men to march into Mexico at the start of the war and marched out of Mexico City with Worth's division as the very last American troops to leave. He was belatedly promoted to first lieutenant for his heroism at Molino del Rey, and then to captain for his courage at the San Cosmé *garita*. However, at war's end, he was still a quartermaster. Julia had waited more than four years for his return, and they married just a little over three weeks after his arrival. **Pete Longstreet** served as Grant's best man. Fellow officers Cadmus Wilcox and Bernard Pratte were also in the wedding party, both of whom would fight for the Confederacy. "My wedding cake was a marvel of beauty.... We had music, and I think two of my bridesmaids took a turn around the room," wrote Julia. The Grants honeymooned with a riverboat ride to Cincinnati. Julia described the craft as "almost human in its breathing, panting, and obedience to man's will." They were often alone on deck, and she would sing something "low and sweet" to him.

Life for the Grants soon turned turbulent. Sam Grant was eager to stay in the military, but his pay would not cover the expense of having his family live with him at frontier outposts. Homesick for Julia and their growing family, he abruptly resigned his commission in 1854 and returned home. Rumors that drunkenness was the cause have been greatly exaggerated, as Grant was known for his inability to drink more than a few sips of alcohol owing to his light weight and diminutive size. He struggled to find a new profession and soon failed at a number of business ventures that included farming, tanning, and bill collecting. When the Civil War began, Grant was commissioned as a colonel in the Illinois militia. Within three years he had risen to become general-in-chief of all U.S. armies. Following the war, he returned to civilian life. Grant successfully ran for president in 1868 and served two terms. He died on July 23, 1885, shortly after completing his memoirs, which were edited by Mark Twain. Julia and he were loyal to each other throughout their nearly four decades of marriage. She survived him by seventeen years and is buried next to him in New York.

Robert E. Lee became commandant of cadets at West Point shortly after the Mexican War. Following that, he was posted to Texas to serve in the ongoing battles against the Comanches and the Apaches, and he put down the insurrection at Harpers Ferry just before the Civil War. General Winfield Scott asked Lee to command the Union forces during that conflict, but he could not turn his back on his beloved Virginia. Lee's brilliant tactics very nearly won the war for the South, but his defeat at Gettysburg proved his undoing. His family estate in Arlington had been used as a cemetery by Union forces, seeking to ensure that the house would never again be inhabited by Lee. They were correct. After the war, he served as president of Washington College (later Washington and Lee University) from 1865 until his death from complications of pneumonia in 1870. He is buried in Lee Chapel on that campus.

Thomas "Stonewall" Jackson returned from Mexico as a battle-tested veteran and a brevet, thanks to battlefield promotions for bravery at Cerro Gordo, Churubusco, and Chapultepec. But he had also found himself deeply impressed by the Mexicans' religious faith. He would later become a deacon in the Presbyterian Church. Jackson left the military soon after the war, and in 1851 he became an instructor at the Virginia Military Institute. He married in 1853, but his wife died in childbirth. Jackson married again in 1857, and his second wife bore him two daughters, only one of whom lived. When the Civil War broke out, Jackson became Lee's top general. He was mistakenly shot three times by a sentry during a nighttime lull in the Battle of Chancellorsville. His left arm was amputated as a result, but he died of pneumonia on May 10, 1863.

William Tecumseh Sherman married in 1850. He and his wife, Ellen, had eight children. He resigned his commission in 1853 and served as president of a bank until it failed in 1857. He moved to Kansas to practice law, failed at that, and then moved on to Louisiana, where he taught at a military academy. He would become legendary for his relentless Civil War march through Georgia. Sherman died on Valentine's Day, 1891. One of his pallbearers was Confederate general **Joe Johnston,** who was eighty-four at the time. The day of Sherman's funeral was rather cold; Johnston refused to wear a hat, soon took sick, and died of pneumonia one month later.

Zachary Taylor was elected president in 1848, succeeding James K. Polk. Taylor died in office on July 9, 1850, after a Fourth of July celebration dedicating the newly completed Washington Monument.

James K. Polk served just one term as president. He died on June 15, 1849, at the age of fifty-three, just five months after leaving office.

On December 6, 1847, **Abraham Lincoln** formally took his seat in the House of Representatives as the Thirtieth Congress came to order. Over in the Senate, **Jefferson Davis** had been appointed to fill a vacancy from the Mississippi delegation, and the popular "hero of Buena Vista" made his triumphal return to Washington. After several passionate antiwar speeches from the House floor (known as the Spot Resolutions), Lincoln gained political renown all his own. However, he was not reelected in 1848 and struggled politically and personally for much of the next decade. He was elected president in 1859 and was assassinated on April 15, 1865, six days after the Civil War ended, by a single .44-caliber shot through the head. His guests that evening at Ford's Theatre were to have been Ulysses and Julia Grant.

Jefferson Davis served as secretary of war from 1853 to 1857, then ran successfully to regain his Senate seat. However, when the Civil War broke out, he abandoned the Senate and was named a major general in the Mississippi militia, reclaiming his former Mexican War command. He soon accepted the position of president of the Confederate States of America, which he held throughout the war. Davis was briefly imprisoned afterward and then made his living selling insurance. He died at the age of eighty-one in New Orleans. His body was marched nonstop back to Richmond, Virginia, and was attended throughout by a throng of mourners.

ACKNOWLEDGMENTS

It was my agent, the incomparable Eric Simonoff, who called one day with the idea that later became this book. On the surface, it was a very simple concept, a sort of *Young Guns* take on the great generals of the Civil War. But as I researched and began writing, it became much more than that, as books like this always do. So as I grappled with structure and the sometimes-daunting task of weaving together the various biographies and battle scenes that fill these pages, Eric availed himself as a sounding board. I am deeply indebted to him for the time and thought he has put into this project. If not for him, *The Training Ground* would simply not exist.

Likewise, my editor, Geoff Shandler. It was Geoff who coaxed me into writing a longer and more sprawling book than I had originally envisioned. This gave me and the characters room to breathe as I told their stories, allowing me to know them and their exploits on a much more intimate level. Geoff likes to deflect credit back onto the writer rather than bask in the limelight himself. But his skill with a red pencil is second to none, and this book is stronger for his suggestions, comments, queries, and even deletions.

Special thanks to Michael Pietsch at Little, Brown.

Thanks also to Junie Dahn and Amanda Erickson.

My friend Jim Yount, a former Marine Corps officer, was a fount of military knowledge, and I am deeply indebted to him for his insights. Thanks also to Marc Spizzirri, Jeff Davis, Chris and Wendy Teske, Tom Silber, and Gary Shutler, and to all the members of the JSerra High School Running Lions cross-country and track teams, whom I have had the privilege of coaching these past few years.

Thanks to John Trowbridge.

Dr. Dave Vogel was very helpful in my education on yellow fever and the other maladies incurred by American troops in Mexico, as was Dr. Matthew Dugard.

Rachel Careau and Peggy Freudenthal did the heavy lifting on copyediting. Thanks for catching my mistakes and inconsistencies.

Finally, if you happened to be sitting at my family dinner table over the past two years, you would have overheard an inordinate amount of talk on my part about Mexican War trivia. Thanks to my wife, Calene, and our three sons for putting up with my endless stream of "fun facts" as I returned from my daily mental journeys down into Mexico.

APPENDIX A

THE BROTHERHOOD

West Point graduated 1,365 officers between the years of 1802 and 1847. Approximately one-third of these men soon left the military for civilian life, and 268 died in the Mexican War. A great number of those still serving after the Treaty of Guadalupe Hidalgo left the military during the 1850s, when the army once again settled into a life of routine and garrison duty during America's westward expansion. It's interesting to note that many military establishments along America's seaboard were named for Revolutionary War figures, while the forts and cities of the American West were named for men like Bliss, Worth, and Ord, the next generation of men who fostered America's growth—the heroes of the Mexican War. When the Civil War began, many of those who had left the military quickly made themselves available for service on both sides of the great divide. The Mexican War, which had been until then the greatest military conflict of their lives, suddenly paled by comparison. Here is a short list of those officers, compiled as part of Meade's memoirs.

GEORGE G. MEADE'S LIST OF U.S. OFFICERS WHO SERVED IN MEXICO AND LATER ACHIEVED DISTINCTION IN THE CIVIL WAR

REGULAR ARMY

George A. McCall, assistant adjutant-general, afterward commanded the Pennsylvania Reserves in the Federal Army of the Potomac.

Joseph Hooker, assistant adjutant-general, afterward commanded the Army of the Potomac at the Battle of Chancellorsville, May 1863.

Irvin W. McDowell, assistant adjutant-general, afterward commanded the Federal forces at the First Battle of Bull Run, July 1861.

Robert E. Lee, captain Engineer Corps, afterward commander-in-chief Confederate States Army, and commanded the Confederate Army of Northern Virginia at the Battle of Gettysburg, July 1863.

P. G. T. Beauregard, first lieutenant Engineer Corps, afterward commanded the Confederate forces at the Battle of Shiloh, 1863.

George B. McClellan, second lieutenant Engineer Corps, afterward organizer and commander of the Army of the Potomac.

Joseph E. Johnston, captain Topographical Engineer, afterward commanded the Confederate forces at the First Battle of Bull Run, July 1861; also commanded the Confederate forces opposing General Sherman's march to Atlanta, 1865.

George G. Meade, second lieutenant Topographical Engineers, afterward commanded the Army of the Potomac at the Battle of Gettysburg, 1863.

John Pope, second lieutenant Topographical Engineers, afterward commanded the Army of the Potomac at the Battle of Cedar Mountain, August 1862.

Richard S. Ewell, first lieutenant First Regiment of Dragoons, afterward commanded the Third Corps, Army of Northern Virginia, at the Battle of Gettysburg.

George Stoneman, second lieutenant First Regiment of Dragoons, afterward commanded the cavalry of the Army of the Potomac in the campaign known as "Stoneman's cavalry raid," May 1863.

Alfred Pleasanton, second lieutenant Second Regiment of Dragoons, afterward chief of cavalry Army of the Potomac, at the Battle of Gettysburg.

Abner Doubleday, first lieutenant First Regiment of Artillery; afterward, on the death of General Reynolds, commanded the First Corps, Army of the Potomac, at the Battle of Gettysburg.

William H. French, first lieutenant First Regiment of Artillery, afterward commanded the Federal forces at Harpers Ferry during the Gettysburg campaign.

Seth Williams, first lieutenant First Regiment of Artillery, afterward assistant adjutant-general of the Army of the Potomac at the Battle of Gettysburg.

Ambrose P. Hill, second lieutenant First Regiment of Artillery, afterward commanded Third Corps, Army of Northern Virginia, at the Battle of Gettysburg and was killed at the Battle of Petersburg, April 1865.

Henry J. Hunt, first lieutenant Second Regiment Artillery, afterward chief of artillery, Army of the Potomac at the Battle of Gettysburg.

John Sedgwich, first lieutenant Second Regiment of Artillery, afterward commanded the Sixth Corps, Army of the Potomac, at the Battle of Gettysburg, and was killed at the Battle of Spotsylvania C.H., May 1864.

Richard Rush, second lieutenant Second Regiment of Artillery, afterward colonel Sixth Pennsylvania Volunteer Cavalry (Rush's Lancers), Army of the Potomac.

Braxton Bragg, captain Third Regiment of Artillery, afterward commanded Confederate forces in the Civil War.

Edward O. C. Ord, first lieutenant Third Regiment of Artillery, afterward commanded the Federal forces at the Battle of Dranesville, December 1861.

John F. Reynolds, first lieutenant Third Regiment of Artillery, afterward commanded the left wing of the Army of the Potomac at the Battle of Gettysburg, and was killed July 1, 1863.

George H. Thomas, first lieutenant Third Regiment of Artillery, afterward commanded the Federal Army of the Cumberland.

Ambrose E. Burnside, second lieutenant Third Regiment of Artillery, afterward commanded the Army of the Potomac at the Battle of Fredericksburg, December 1862.

John Gibbon, second lieutenant Fourth Regiment of Artillery, afterward commanded the Second Corps, Army of the Potomac, at the Battle of Gettysburg.

George Sykes, first lieutenant Third Regiment of Infantry, afterward commanded the Fifth Corps, Army of the Potomac, at the Battle of Gettysburg.

Ulysses S. Grant, second lieutenant Fourth Regiment of Infantry, afterward commander-in-chief United States Army and President of the United States.

Lewis Armistead, first lieutenant Sixth Regiment of Infantry, afterward commanded a brigade in "Pickett's Charge" at the Battle of Gettysburg and was wounded and died within Union lines.

Edward Johnson, first lieutenant Sixth Regiment of Infantry, afterward commanded a division in the Army of Northern Virginia at the Battle of Gettysburg.

Winfield S. Hancock, second lieutenant Sixth Regiment of Infantry, afterward commanded the center of the Army of the Potomac at the Battle of Gettysburg.

Lafayette McLaws, first lieutenant Seventh Regiment of Infantry, afterward commanded a division in the Army of Northern Virginia at the Battle of Gettysburg.

James Longstreet, first lieutenant Eighth Regiment of Infantry, afterward commanded the First Corps, Army of Northern Virginia at the Battle of Gettysburg.

George E. Pickett, second lieutenant Eighth Regiment of Infantry, afterward commanded a division in the Army of Northern Virginia and led the assault known as "Pickett's Charge" at the Battle of Gettysburg.

VOLUNTEERS

Jefferson Davis, colonel First Regiment Mississippi Rifles, afterward President of Confederacy.

John W. Geary, colonel Second Regiment Pennsylvania Volunteers, afterward commanded a division of the Twelfth Corps, Army of the Potomac, at the Battle of Gettysburg.

Jubal Early, major Virginia Volunteers, afterward commanded a division in the Army of Northern Virginia at the Battle of Gettysburg.

APPENDIX B

THE SPOT RESOLUTIONS

Abraham Lincoln's "Spot Resolutions," Presented in Congress on December 22, 1847. In Which Lincoln Refuted Polk's Waging of the War, and Challenged Him to Show the Specific "Spot" on U.S. Soil Where Blood Had Been Shed to Begin Hostilities

Whereas the President of the United States, in his message of May 11th, 1846, has declared that "The Mexican Government not only refused to receive him" (the envoy of the U.S.) "or listen to his propositions, but, after a long continued series of menaces, have at last invaded *our teritory* [sic], and shed the blood of our fellow *citizens* on *our own soil*"

And again, in his message of December 8, 1846, that "We had ample cause of war against Mexico, long before the breaking out of hostilities, but even then we forbore to take redress into our own hands, until Mexico herself became the aggressor by invading *our soil* in hostile array, and shedding the blood of our *citizens*

And yet again, in his message of December 7, 1847, that "The Mexican Government refused even to hear the terms of adjustment which he" (our minister of peace) "was authorized to propose; and finally, under wholly unjustifiable pretexts, involved the two countries in war, by invading the teritory of the State of Texas, striking the first blow, and shedding the blood of our *citizens* on *our own soil*"

And whereas this House desires to obtain a full knowledge of all the facts which go to establish whether the particular spot of soil on which the blood of our *citizens* was so shed, was, or was not *our own soil,* at that time; therefore

Resolved by the House of Representatives, that the President of the United States be respectfully requested to inform this House —

First: Whether the spot of soil on which the blood of our *citizens* was shed, as in his messages declared, was, or was not, within the teritories of Spain, at least from the treaty of 1819 until the Mexican revolution

Second: Whether that spot is, or is not, within the teritory which was wrested from Spain, by the Mexican revolution.

Third: Whether that spot is, or is not, within a settlement of people, which settlement had existed ever since long before the Texas revolution, until its inhabitants fled from the approach of the U. S. Army.

Fourth: Whether that settlement is, or is not, isolated from any and all other settlements, by the Gulf of Mexico, and the Rio Grande, on the South and West, and by wide uninhabited regions on the North and East.

Fifth: Whether the *People* of that settlement, or a *majority* of them, or *any* of them, had ever, previous to the bloodshed, mentioned in his messages, submitted themselves to the government or laws of Texas, or of the United States, by *consent,* or by *compulsion,* either by accepting office, or voting at elections, or paying taxes, or serving on juries, or having process served upon them, or in *any other way.*

Sixth: Whether the People of that settlement, did, or did not, flee from the approach of the United States Army, leaving unprotected their homes and their growing crops, *before* the blood was shed, as in his messages stated and whether the first blood so shed, was, or was not shed, within the *inclosure* of the People, or some of them, who had thus fled from it.

Seventh: Whether our *citizens,* whose blood was shed, as in his message declared, were, or were not, at that time *armed* officers, and *soldiers,* sent into that settlement, by the military order of the President through the Secretary of War—and

Eighth: Whether the military force of the United States, including those *citizens,* was, or was not, so sent into that settlement, after Genl. Taylor had, more than once, intimated to the War Department that, in his opinion, no such movement was necessary to the defence or protection of Texas.

APPENDIX C

AMERICAN ARMY ORDER OF BATTLE

Palo Alto/Resaca de la Palma

Brigade	Commander	Composition
1st Brigade (Left Wing)	Lt. Col. William G. Belknap	8th Infantry: Capt. Montgomery[a] Light Artillery: Capt. James Duncan Childs's Artillery: Lt. Col. Thomas Childs
2nd Brigade (Right Wing)	Col. David E. Twiggs	5th Infantry: Lt. Col. James S. McIntosh 3rd Infantry: Maj. L. M. Morris Ringgold's Artillery: Maj. Samuel Ringgold Garland's Artillery: Lt. Col. John Garland[b] 2nd Dragoons: Capt. Charles May 2nd Dragoons: Capt. Kerr

[a]Longstreet
[b]Grant

Monterrey

Division	Commander	Composition

1st Division of Regulars	Brig. Gen. David E. Twiggs	3rd Brigade: Lt. Col. John Garland
		  3rd Infantry: Maj. W. W. Lear
		  4th Infantry: Maj. George W. Allen
		  Mississippi & Texas Volunteers: Capt. Shivor
		  Company E, 3rd Artillery: Capt. Braxton Bragg
		4th Brigade:[a] Lt. Col. Henry Wilson
		  1st Infantry: Maj. John J. Abercrombie
		  Baltimore & District of Columbia Battalion: Col. William H. Watson
		  Company C, 3rd Horse Artillery: Capt. Ridgely

2nd Division of Regulars	Brig. Gen. William J. Worth	1st Brigade: Lt. Col. Thomas Staniford
		  8th Infantry: Capt. George Wright
		  Childs's Artillery Battalion: Lt. Col. Thomas Childs
		  Company A, 2nd Artillery: Capt. James Duncan
		2nd Brigade:[a] Col. Persifor F. Smith
		  5th Infantry: Lt. Col. James S. McIntosh
		  7th Infantry: Maj. Dixon S. Miles
		  "Phoenix Company": Capt. Albert C. Blanchard
		  Company K, 1st Artillery: Capt. William W. Mackall

1st Division of Volunteers	Maj. Gen. William O. Butler	1st Brigade: Brig. Gen. Thomas L. Hamer
		  1st Ohio: Col. Alexander Mitchell
		  1st Kentucky: Lt. Col. Stephen Ormsby

[a]Forces stationed at Camargo

Monterrey *(continued)*

Division	Commander	Composition
		2nd Brigade:[a] Brig. Gen. John A. Quitman 1st Tennessee: Col. William B. Campbell Mississippi Rifles: Col. Jefferson Davis
Texas Division	Maj. Gen. J. Pinckney Henderson	1st Texas Mounted Rifles (Texas Rangers): Col. John C. Hays 2nd Texas Mounted Rifles: Col. George T. Wood
Unattached		2nd Dragoons: Lt. Col. Charles May Company C, 1st U.S. Heavy Artillery: Capt. Webster
2nd Division of Volunteers	Maj. Gen. Robert Patterson	1st Brigade: Brig. Gen. Thomas Marshall 2nd Brigade: Brig. Gen. Gideon Pillow

[a]Forces stationed at Camargo

Buena Vista

Commander	Composition
Brig. Gen. Zachary Taylor Second-in-Command: Brig. Gen. John E. Wool	**Indiana Brigade** Brig. Gen. Joseph Lane 2nd Indiana: Col. William A. Bowles 3rd Indiana: Col. James H. Lane **Infantry** Mississippi Rifles: Col. Jefferson Davis 1st Illinois: Col. John J. Hardin 2nd Illinois: Col. William H. Bissell 2nd Kentucky: Col. William R. McKee

Buena Vista *(continued)*

Commander	Composition
	Cavalry Arkansas Mounted Regiment: Col. Archibald Yell Kentucky Mounted Regiment: Col. Humphrey Marshall 1st Dragoons: Capt. Enoch Steene 2nd Dragoons: Lt. Col. Charles May **Artillery** 1st Artillery: Capt. Thomas W. Sherman 2nd Artillery: Capt. Braxton Bragg 4th Artillery: Capt. John M. Washington

SELECTED NOTES AND BIOGRAPHIES

The bulk of this text came from the personal journals, letters, and memoirs of the officers who fought in the Mexican War and from various biographies about these men. Of that second category, I leaned most heavily on Jean Edward Smith's *Grant*, Douglas Southall Freeman's *Lee*, and William J. Cooper Jr.'s *Jefferson Davis, American*. Grant's *Personal Memoirs of U. S. Grant*, in addition to being extremely well-written (it helped to have Twain as his editor), is a detailed and analytical look back at his life. Grant's personal papers, particularly his correspondence with Julia (and her correspondence, too), gave me an even more intimate look at the budding soldier. All quotes by Grant in this volume were taken either from the *Memoirs* or from *The Papers of Ulysses S. Grant*. Julia's comments are all taken from *The Personal Memoirs of Julia Dent Grant*.

Also, George Gordon Meade's letters and memoirs were exceptionally detailed, as befits a topographical engineer. Meade's direct quotes and comments are all from that work. Another standout memoir was that of William Tecumseh Sherman, who is candid and almost poetic in his descriptions of the natural beauty he encountered during the Mexican War. Again, I relied on this volume for all of Sherman's quotes and descriptions.

A third category of memoir that proved especially helpful was memoirs written by less famous men. The letters of Napoleon Dana, William French, and other officers from West Point and the volunteer corps are remarkable in their descriptiveness and honesty. Enlisted soldiers such as Joshua Chamberlain, George Ballentine, and Samuel Chester Reid were, if anything, even more forthright. In describing battle scenes, I found that the best accounts came from these men, who, lacking the burden of celebrity and the incumbent need for diplomacy, often wrote about warfare with vividness, passion, and a blunt sort of honesty that detailed their fear and horror without diminishing their own heroism or that of their fellow soldiers. I interjected their descriptions wherever possible, and it is with some sadness that I couldn't use even more. Thanks to the current phenomenon of digitizing books, many of these works (some written within months of returning from Mexico), which were long forgotten and unavailable owing to their age and lack of circulation, are now easily obtained through online download. I would encourage the inquisitive reader to take advantage of this opportunity.

Finally, officials at West Point have been very helpful in my research, in particular Major Michael Bonura. The U.S. Army's Center of Military History's publications on the Mexican War, the actual after-action reports filed by Taylor and Scott, newspaper reports from battlefield correspondents, Robert W. Johannsen's *To the Halls of Montezumas,* and K. Jack Bauer's *The Mexican War* all proved to be indispensable road maps, providing me with detailed overviews of the war and specific statistics on troop size, regimental position, and casualties, the international reaction, and the mood of the American public.

APPOMATTOX

Many histories have been written about the Confederate surrender, but the best descriptions come from those who were in the room. Colonel Charles Marshall observed the proceedings as one of the few officers of Lee's who were present, and three decades later he published the most elaborate and thoughtful narrative of the goings-on at McLean's home. Grant's own memoirs tell the story with grace and dignity, not seeking to offend or grandstand in any way. In fact, Grant insisted that his memoirs be entirely accurate when he wrote, uncluttered by historical bias. Twain, as his editor, marveled that Grant painstakingly researched each point in that book, checking his version of events against the historical record.

PROLOGUE

Lee: On September 22, 1779, Congress voted to award Light-Horse Harry Lee a medal for his gallant bravery at the Battle of Paulus Hook. The medal would be struck in Paris and was to be made of gold. However, through an oversight, Lee's medal was never ordered. Ten years later, Secretary of State Thomas Jefferson attempted to correct that error by having the Philadelphia Mint strike a replacement, but the die broke before the medal was cast. Lee eventually received a silver medal with the words TO HENRY LEE FOR VALOUR AND PATRIO-TISM on the front and WASHINGTON AND INDEPENDENCE 1775–1783 on the back. It was confiscated to meet his debts in 1810 and disappeared until 1935, when it was sold at auction for one hundred dollars. Today it is housed in the library at Princeton University, Lee's alma mater.

Charles Mason, who bested Lee as the top graduate in the class of 1829, served just two years in the army. Both those years were spent teaching engineering at West Point. He left to study law, later served as the editor of the *Saturday Evening Post,* and eventually moved to Iowa. Whatever potential he might have had as a soldier was never fulfilled.

Grant: Sherman's comments about Grant were from an interview in the *New York Herald* that ran on July 24, 1885, the day after his old friend died. Grant's comments about his early antipathy toward West Point were taken from his *Memoirs.* Dabney Herndon Maury's memoirs tell of Grant's prowess on horseback, and D. M. Frost's quote about Grant's discomfort with the fair sex is taken from Jean Edward Smith's *Grant.* Longstreet's warm words about their friendship comes from his own memoir. Julia Dent's personal letters recount her version of the courtship with Grant, while Grant's *Memoirs* tell his.

An interesting footnote to West Point's role in the use of class rings came in 1879, when that year's class chose cuff links instead.

Richard "Dick" Ewell was promoted to captain for bravery at Contreras and Churubusco. He remained in the army after the war and saw duty in the West, where he was wounded during a battle with the Apache Indians in 1859. Though pro-Union, he opted to join the Confederate cause because of his allegiance to Virginia, his home state. Ewell was injured again, early in the war, at the Battle of Fairfax Court House, but quickly recovered. He went on to fight at Bull Run and served under Thomas Jackson during the lengthy Valley Campaign. Ewell fought at the Second Battle of Bull Run but was injured yet again at Groveton. This injury was quite severe and resulted in the amputation of his left leg, just below the knee. Ewell returned to service and, upon Jackson's death, took over Jackson's command. His stellar reputation took a beating, however, when he failed to attack the pivotal Cemetery Hill at the Battle of Gettysburg. Many later felt that this inability to capture the high ground early on cost the Confederates the battle. Lee later relieved him of command. Placed in charge of the garrison at Richmond, Ewell was captured by Union forces at Sayler's Creek, just days before Lee's surrender. However, Ewell would be held as a prisoner of war until July 1865, confined to Fort Warren in Boston Harbor. He became a farmer after the war and died of pneumonia in 1872, at the age of fifty-four.

John L. O'Sullivan, who coined the term "Manifest Destiny," unsuccessfully urged President Polk to include Cuba in that mandate. He later backed the Confederacy during the Civil War, exiled himself to Europe when the war ended, and became a great believer in spiritualism and contacting the dead through mediums upon his return. O'Sullivan died from the flu in a New York residential hotel at the age of eighty-one.

CHAPTER ONE

Captain George McCall was promoted to brevet major shortly after the Battle of Resaca de la Palma. He served throughout the war with Mexico and remained in the army until 1853, when he resigned his commission and became a farmer. McCall was named a brigadier general in the Pennsylvania Volunteers when the Civil War broke out, then promoted to major general soon after. He commanded forces at the battles of Dranesville, Mechanicsville, Gaines's Mill, and New Market Cross Roads, where he was captured by the Confederate army. McCall was held as a prisoner of war at Libby Prison in Richmond, Virginia, then released owing to illness. He died on February 25, 1868.

CHAPTER TWO

The descriptive comment about wildflowers was that of Captain Kirby Smith, writing to his wife. He was a passionate man, with a strong chin and long muttonchop sideburns that stretched to the corners of his mouth, and had once been dismissed from the army for two years for "inflicting corporal punishment on mutinous soldiers." Smith's letters in *To Mexico with Scott* are notable for their emotion, their detail, and the disheartening fact that he died just days before the war ended.

During the long march from Corpus Christi to the Rio Grande, all that soot coating soldiers' uniforms led the mounted dragoons to refer to the men on foot as *adobes*, in reference to the dun-colored Mexican building material. Legend has it that *adobes* was later shortened to *dobies* and then to *doughboys*—the tag that would become synonymous with American troops during World War I.

CHAPTER THREE

The comments of Longstreet and Smith are from their memoirs. Ewell's comment about Missouri women was taken from Sanger and Hay's *James Longstreet*.

Captain Charles Ferguson Smith, commander of the red-legged infantry, served as judge advocate in the impromptu military court that heard the Whistler case. Though **Colonel William Whistler** was convicted of all charges of drunkenness and sentenced to be cashiered from the army, President Polk granted him a pardon. Thus protected, Whistler did not retire from military service until October 9, 1861. He died on December 4, 1863, at the age of eighty-three. Whistler's nephew James McNeill Whistler would go on to become one of America's best-known artists.

Smith served with distinction throughout the Mexican War and was promoted several times for bravery. By war's end, he was a lieutenant colonel. Smith served in the American West during the 1850s and was on active duty when the Civil War began. He would go on to serve under Grant, who had once been his student at West Point. At Savannah, Tennessee, Smith inadvertently suffered a wound while leaping into a rowboat. He died of the subsequent infection and a bout of chronic dysentery on May 25, 1862.

CHAPTER FOUR

William Hardee's comments are taken from his official report. Taylor's words denoting the start of the war come from his official message to Washington.

When **Captain Seth Thornton** was charged with cowardice for his role in the battle at Carricitos, soon after having been returned to the American side in a prisoner swap, Hardee, fearful that his good name as an officer would be tainted, requested a court of inquiry to clear him. Both men were cleared of all charges.

Hardee went on to serve with distinction in the Mexican War and rose to the rank of lieutenant colonel by its conclusion. In 1855 he wrote a seminal book on tactical warfare titled *Rifle and Light Infantry Tactics for the Exercise and Manoeuvres of Troops When Acting as Light Infantry or Riflemen* (often shortened to *Hardee's Tactics*).

From 1856 to 1860, Hardee served as commandant of cadets at West Point. He resigned his commission on January 31, 1861, when Georgia left the Union, and accepted a new commission in the Confederate army. Lieutenant General Hardee led troops at the battles of Shiloh, Chattanooga, Perryville, Stones River, and Murfreesboro and during the fall of Atlanta. Hardee commanded his men with such distinction that he was nicknamed Old Reliable. Somewhat ironically, *Hardee's Tactics* was the standard tactical manual for both the Union and the Confederacy.

Hardee's last engagement was in March 1865, at the Battle of Bentonville, in which his only son was killed in a cavalry charge. One month later, Hardee surrendered his depleted forces to Union general William Tecumseh Sherman. He died in Wytheville, Virginia, on November 6, 1873.

As for Thornton, the man who inadvertently started the Mexican War with his tactical blunder, he was shot in the chest at the village of San Augustin, just outside Mexico City. He died instantly.

CHAPTER SIX

Napoleon Jackson Tecumseh Dana's poignant, hilarious, and often extremely bawdy letters home are easily some of the most entertaining wartime correspondence ever written. All comments attributed to him come from those letters, now published. Dana recovered from his wartime injuries and remained in the army until 1855, then moved to Minnesota with Sue and began a successful banking career. He was appointed a brigadier general when the Civil War broke out, and he served with distinction at Antietam and Second Bull Run. He was wounded once again at Antietam during the thick of the fighting. Dana recovered from those wounds, too, and resigned his commission once again in May 1865. He went on to another successful business venture, this one in the railroad industry. He died in 1905.

The account of Major Jacob Brown's surgery is from the official battle report, written by Captain Hawkins, and from Dana's own eyewitness accounts. Brownsville, the town that grew up around Fort Brown, still bears the major's name.

Captain Edgar S. Hawkins was promoted to brevet major for his heroism. Later in the war, he was placed on indefinite sick leave for injuries and illness suffered in the line of duty. Though technically still an active-duty major when the Civil War began, he was declared unfit for service and retired. He died shortly after that war ended, at the age of sixty-four.

CHAPTER SEVEN

Longstreet's quotes are taken from his memoirs. Curiously, though Longstreet fought in the Mexican War until the fall of Chapultepec, his personal story ends rather abruptly after Resaca de la Palma. Either he got tired of trying to remember those years of his life (his memoirs were published in 1895), or he was being modest about his wartime accomplishments.

The discussion of Jomini and tactics is elaborated quite well in Grady McWhiney and Perry D. Jamieson's *Attack and Die*. My knowledge of artillery and armament was greatly enhanced by Naisawald's *Grape and Canister* and Manucy's *Artillery through the Ages*. For further information on the battles of Palo Alto and Resaca de la Palma, the official reports filed by Taylor make for a fine overview.

Artillery specialist **"Prince" John Magruder** fought for the South during the Civil War but fell out of favor with Robert E. Lee and was reassigned to Texas. He was victorious at the Battle of Galveston in January 1863 but spent the rest of the war away from the larger action. Afterward he served as a mercenary in the Mexican army, but when Emperor Maximilian was toppled, Magruder fled back to Texas, where he lived out his days. He died in 1871, at the age of sixty-three.

CHAPTER EIGHT

Meade's comments can all be found in his letters and memoirs. Freeman Cleaves's excellent *Meade of Gettysburg* offers great history and insights into this man. All quotes attributed to and referring to Meade in this section come from those two sources. Adrian George Traas's *From the Golden Gate to Mexico City,* published by the U.S. Army's Center of Military History, not only tells the story of the Topographical Corps during the Mexican War but also describes the job requirements of a topo in great detail.

SELECTED NOTES AND BIOGRAPHIES

CHAPTER NINE

The differing battlefield accounts of Longstreet, Grant, and Meade make for a nice study of each individual. Grant shows himself to be pensive and prone to study before acting; Meade is heroic, though uncharacteristically vainglorious; and Longstreet is humble and reflective. General Díaz de la Vega's comment is taken from K. Jack Bauer's *The Mexican War* and was originally overheard by Captain McCall.

CHAPTER TEN

Of all the characters in this story, none was quite so enigmatic and difficult to understand as Jefferson Davis. He is undoubtedly one of the most accomplished Americans of his, or any, time. I leaned heavily on various biographies of him, as his own letters and personal papers were not often revealing. The quote from the *North American* was taken from Johannsen, and notes on the nation's mood were influenced both by Johannsen and by Justin W. Smith's compelling *The War with Mexico*.

CHAPTER ELEVEN

Grant's comments about his beard can be found in his letters, as can Dana's reference to Brown's death. Grant wrote of Taylor's "no pillaging" policy in his memoirs, which were also the source of his comments on the volunteers. Meade was extremely outraged about the influx of volunteer regiments, particularly when his worst fears about their character and bravery were proved all too true in Matamoros. It is interesting, by the way, to read the different descriptions of that riverfront city by the wide variety of soldiers who served there and wrote down their impressions. Some soldiers were pleasantly surprised at the city's quaint character, while others found it filthy and oppressive.

CHAPTER TWELVE

The "bake one's brains" comments came from Dana, with his typical tendency toward the dramatic, as did the descriptions of fandangos. *Monterrey Is Ours!* a collection of Dana's letters, shows a man conflicted by his love and concern for his wife, and the more carnal desires arising from such a lengthy separation. His words describe that

405

timeless conflict fighting men struggle with to this day, and he is alternately lusty, flirtatious, jealous, and quietly accusing in letters to his wife, Sue. The fandango descriptions were just the tip of the iceberg.

The insights into the Quartermaster Department can be found in Dr. Alvin P. Stauffer's article in the May–June 1950 edition of the *Quartermaster Review*. He displays a deep zeal for logistics in the piece, and it is a treat to read.

Walt Whitman's comments and the description of religion and the American psyche lean heavily on Johannsen.

CHAPTER THIRTEEN

The Mexican-American War and the Media (http://www.history. vt.edu/MxAmWar) Web site, compiled by the University of Vermont, was an astounding source of newspaper knowledge, with complete articles from newspapers around the nation and around the world detailing the war as it unfolded. Such a resource saved countless hours in newspaper libraries, staring at microfilm in the hope of finding that one sentence or paragraph to fit a particular passage. Most newspaper articles mentioned in this book can be found there, including this chapter's quote from the *Times*.

As always, the simple overview came courtesy of Bauer's *The Mexican War*. Davis's quotes came from William J. Cooper's and Felicity Allen's works on Davis.

CHAPTER FOURTEEN

Sherman's trip aboard the *Lexington* was quite well documented in his memoirs. All quotes are taken from there. It's interesting to note that Charles Darwin visited Puerto Soledad, the site of the *Lexington*'s participation in the 1831 Falklands crisis, aboard the HMS *Beagle* in 1833. He made a point to note that the small port and former penal colony was populated by "runaway rebels and murderers."

CHAPTER FIFTEEN

The story of the Mississippi Rifles is told in splendid detail in Joseph Chance's *Jefferson Davis's Mexican War Regiment*. Anyone seeking to know more about that regiment would do well to give it a read. Both that book and the various Davis biographies offer a compelling discussion of the superior ballistic capabilities of the rifle over the standard-issue musket.

CHAPTER SIXTEEN

There is no lack of research on Abraham Lincoln, but I relied mostly on Carl Sandburg's *Abraham Lincoln: The Prairie Years* as the definitive source on his life and political ambitions. *Illinois in the Mexican War,* by Samuel Bigger McCartney, offered details about the men from that state and the economic reasons they were eager to volunteer for duty. Among those men was Lincoln's friend **Edward Dickenson Baker,** who went on to live a long and prolific life. During the Mexican War, he served as a colonel with the Fourth Regiment of the Illinois Volunteers, seeing action at Veracruz and Cerro Gordo. After the war, he served another term in Congress as a representative from Illinois and then moved to San Francisco to practice law. In 1860 he moved to Oregon, where he was promptly elected to the U.S. Senate. When the Civil War broke out, he was authorized to form a volunteer infantry regiment and was killed in action during the Battle of Ball's Bluff on October 26, 1861. The Senate mourned him for thirty days, wearing black crepe armbands in Baker's memory. A city and a county in Oregon are named in his honor, as are several military forts. A life-size marble statue of Baker stands in the Capitol.

Edward Baker Lincoln, his namesake, died of tuberculosis in Springfield, Illinois, in 1850. The boy was just three years old.

Another political acquaintance of Lincoln's who went off to fight was **General James Shields.** He was seriously wounded at Cerro Gordo, recovered, and then was wounded again in the fighting around Mexico City. Shields returned to civilian life after the war. He represented Illinois in the U.S. Senate from 1849 to 1855 and Minnesota in the same capacity from 1858 to 1859. He resumed his military service during the Civil War and was notably defeated by Thomas "Stonewall" Jackson during the Valley Campaign of May and June 1862. He died on June 1, 1879, in Ottumwa, Iowa.

CHAPTER SEVENTEEN

The tortuous journey upriver to Camargo was something Grant and Dana wrote home about in great detail. Their comments are taken from those letters, as are Dana's descriptions of Camargo. A fascinating reference source was *The March to Monterrey: The Diary of Lieutenant Rankin Dilworth,* though for an unusual reason. Although his journal was insightful, the book's editors saw fit to add great amounts of historical minutiae to round out Dilworth's words. Among those facts were the specifics on the *Aid.*

CHAPTER EIGHTEEN

The man responsible for making sure Grant remained a quartermaster was Taylor's chief of staff, **Major William W. S. "Perfect" Bliss.** This young officer was an extraordinary individual. He graduated from West Point in 1833 at the age of seventeen, finishing ninth in a class of forty-three. It was there that he earned his nickname, thanks to his classmates' belief that he was a genius. Indeed, Bliss could read thirteen languages and speak six fluently. He had an encyclopedic knowledge of philosophy, military tactics, and even poetry. After a year fighting the Cherokees as an infantry officer, Bliss returned to the academy and taught math for seven years. He fought against the Seminoles in 1840–41 and then began a decade of service to Zachary Taylor. Bliss served as Taylor's chief of staff until the end of the Mexican War, married the general's daughter in 1848, and served as personal secretary to Taylor during his presidency. He returned to military life in 1850 and died three years later in Pascagoula, Mississippi, from yellow fever. Both the Fort Bliss Military Reservation and the Fort Bliss National Cemetery bear his name.

Second Lieutenant Alexander Hays, the son of a congressman, graduated from West Point a year behind Sam Grant, finishing twentieth in a class of twenty-five. The two became close friends during the Mexican War. Hays resigned his commission in 1848 and headed out for the gold fields of California. Failing utterly as a miner, he returned home to Pittsburgh and worked as an engineer.

During the Civil War he enlisted as a private, but he distinguished himself on the field of battle, was promoted steadily, and soon became an officer again. Hays was injured at the Seven Days' Battles near Richmond, Virginia, in June 1862 and then had his leg shattered by a bullet during the Second Battle of Bull Run. Shortly after his convalescence from that wound ended, he was promoted to brigadier general. Hays's most famous moment came while commanding the Third Division of the Second Corps during the Battle of Gettysburg. Hays played a pivotal part in repelling Pickett's Charge, riding up and down the lines on horseback and ordering his troops to "stand fast and fight like men." He had two horses shot out from under him that day, but his actions broke Pickett's attack and preserved the Union victory. When the battle was won, Hays promptly kissed his aide and then rode up and down his lines dragging a captured Confederate flag in the dirt. Hays was later killed at the Battle of the Wilderness in April 1864, shot through the head by a rebel bullet.

Hays's quotes in this text come from Smith's *Grant*.

Texas Ranger **Samuel Walker** was lanced in the back by Mexican guerrillas while escorting a supply convoy from Veracruz to Mexico City in October 1847. He was originally buried in Mexico, but in 1856 his remains were exhumed and moved to the Odd Fellows Cemetery in San Antonio.

Abner Doubleday's comments are taken from the footnotes to Dilworth's journal. Doubleday, who was a major at the start of the Civil War, was present at Fort Sumter when the first shots were fired, and over the course of the war he was promoted all the way up to colonel, with a secondary rank as a major general of volunteers. He led men at the battles of Second Bull Run, Antietam, and Gettysburg. He was relieved of his command on the second day at Gettysburg, however, when Major General George Meade questioned his combat effectiveness. Returning to the field in a lesser capacity, Doubleday was soon wounded in the neck. He served in Washington for the remainder of the war. He died on January 26, 1893, at the age of seventy-three. Despite prevailing myths to the contrary, he did not invent baseball.

CHAPTER NINETEEN

Taylor's comments can be found in *The Mexican War and Its Heroes.* Dana was the officer who made reference to Monterrey's being a veritable Gibraltar. The comments about military life for regular soldiers come from Ballentine.

Brigadier General William Worth became a major national hero after the Mexican War. He was a boastful man, and proud of saying that he was the first man to go ashore during the invasion of Veracruz and the last man to leave Mexico City at the end of the American occupation. He died of cholera shortly after returning, however, at the age of fifty-five. Worth's remains were buried in Worth Square in New York City. A massive obelisk at the juncture of Broadway and Fifth Avenue marks the site. Fort Worth, Texas, bears his name.

CHAPTER TWENTY

As one of the Mexican War's seminal and most viciously fought battles, Monterrey was a favorite memoir topic. Even though Meade, Grant, and Dana all wrote capably about the action, my favorite is John R. Kenly's *Memoirs of a Maryland Volunteer.* His descriptions of the battlefield have a powerful narrative quality that transports the reader into the action. Also worth noting is Samuel Chamberlain's *My Confession: Recollections of a Rogue.*

Major Joseph Mansfield, designer of Fort Brown, ended the Mexican War as a colonel. He remained in the army for the rest of his life and was promoted to brigadier general at the start of the Civil War. Mansfield, whose beard and hair were snowy white by then, was known for being vigorous and more than a little fussy. He was, however, a very capable leader and in September 1862 assumed command of the Army of the Potomac's XII Corps. Shortly thereafter, he was shot in the stomach at the Battle of Antietam and died of his wounds — one of six generals killed in that engagement. A monument marks the spot where he fell.

The comments of Meade and Grant are taken from their letters and memoirs. Worth's comments come from *The Mexican War and Its Heroes*. The description of Twiggs is from Maury. Davis's quotes come from Chance's *Jefferson Davis's Mexican War Regiment* and Cooper's *Jefferson Davis, American*. Kenly's *Maryland Volunteer*, Reid's *Scouting Expeditions of the Texas Rangers*, and Chamberlain's *Recollections* paint a vivid picture of the hellish fighting inside Monterrey. Meade attempts to tell the same story in his letters and does so well enough, but as he was on the other side of the city, all of his observations are secondhand. Nevertheless, I chose to include his comment about "ten of our gallant officers" being slaughtered.

In John Russell Bartlett's 1848 *Dictionary of Americanisms*, he noted that *seeing the elephant* was primarily a southern term but was later adopted by soldiers throughout the Mexican War. In time it came to mean more than just the first taste of battle and soon included the entire weary experience of military life in Mexico. "Men who have volunteered for the Mexican war, expecting to reap lots of glory and enjoyment, but instead have found sickness, fatigue, privations, and suffering, are currently said to have 'seen the elephant,'" wrote Bartlett.

Colonel John Garland was breveted to brigadier general after the Battle of Churubusco. He was shot in the chest by a Mexican sniper after Chapultepec, while marching his army into Mexico City. He recovered and returned to active duty as a full colonel once the war ended. He would remain in the army for the rest of his life. During the Civil War he chose to side with the Union, although he hailed from Virginia. Both his son-in-law, James Longstreet (who had married Garland's daughter in 1848), and his nephew Samuel Garland Jr. became generals in the Confederacy. Garland died suddenly while in New York City, just months after the Civil War began.

The tactic of advancing house by house instead of street by street, which was pioneered at Monterrey, would be used once again by American forces in World War II, during the advance through Germany and Italy.

CHAPTER TWENTY-TWO

Grant had Monterrey in mind when drafting the terms of surrender at Appomattox. They are, in many ways, alike. George C. Furber's *The Twelve Months Volunteer* contains the full text of the surrender terms, along with the correspondence between Taylor and Ampudia leading up to the cessation of hostilities. This is a fine resource and all the more remarkable for the fact that the author was not even present in Monterrey. *Twelve Months* is one of those rare Mexican War memoirs where the author attempts to show the war from a broader perspective than just his own personal frame of reference. At 677 pages, it is rather weighty, but the level of detail is extraordinary.

Meade makes it sound as if he ventured down into the city all alone that morning, though few other accounts have written it that way. I chose to let Meade's interpretation stand, as individual units and men were prone to operate independently of one another, and, in its own way, Worth's story of his entry into western Monterrey may be correct. It is interesting to read Meade's comments on the city's surrender. His letters read like a personal debate, with Meade trying to convince himself that Taylor had done the right thing.

The account of Mexican women passing bullets to their soldiers can be found in Libura and Morales's *Echoes of the Mexican American War.*

The lengthy quote about the street fighting is from Reid, and the passage about soldiers' getting drunk during the battle is Chamberlain's. Despite his habit of referring to himself as a rogue, the young volunteer Chamberlain was skilled at painting watercolors. His renditions of Monterrey and Buena Vista bring the battle to life.

CHAPTER TWENTY-THREE

Brigadier General John E. Wool was seventy-six when the Civil War began, but he immediately offered his services to the Union. He led the expedition that secured Norfolk, Virginia, in 1862, which saw him promoted to major general. However, his advanced age made Wool unfit for the rigors of battlefield living, and he retired from the military halfway through the war. Wool died after suffering a fall in 1869, in Troy, New York. His lengthy *New York Times* obituary referred to Wool as "the last of the old heroes who connect us with the early military history of the Republic" and noted that Wool was born on February 29, meaning that he had only seen twenty-one birthdays—one of which came just after Mexican War hostilities ceased in 1848.

Colonel Stephen Watts Kearny, the Father of the Modern Cavalry, so named for forming the first division of dragoons, served as military governor of California through August 1847. He returned to Fort Leavenworth and was then ordered to Veracruz to serve as military governor during the American occupation. However, he contracted a tropical disease and returned to his home in Saint Louis, where he died on October 31, 1848, at the age of fifty-four. Several military installations, streets, and cities were later named for this gallant and widely respected gentleman. The U.S. Naval Air Station at Miramar, near San Diego, which served as the home of the famous "Top Gun" air combat school, was known as Camp Kearney (his name was misspelled) until 1946, owing to the site's being near the Mexican War battlefield of San Pasqual. Kearny, whose exhausted dragoons had just barely survived an epic journey across the deserts of the American Southwest, lost that battle, the lone American defeat of the Mexican War.

The criollos discussion is clearly elaborated in the U.S. Army Training and Doctrine Command's report of May 2003.

CHAPTER TWENTY-FIVE

John Pope was promoted to brevet captain by the end of the Mexican War. He spent the 1850s surveying Minnesota and seeking a route for a railway to the Pacific. When the Civil War broke out, he was promoted to brigadier general, and he won several major victories against the Confederate forces before being crushed by Robert E. Lee, Stonewall Jackson, and Pete Longstreet at the Second Battle of Bull Run. He was relieved of command shortly afterward and spent the rest of the war in Minnesota's Department of the Northwest. After the Civil War, he was a Reconstruction commissioner in Atlanta, until President Andrew

Johnson replaced him with his former Monterrey roommate, George Meade. Pope later fought in the Apache Wars and was promoted to major general in 1882. He died ten years later at the old soldier's home in Sandusky, Ohio.

Captain Jeremiah Scarritt, an 1838 graduate of West Point and the son of a Revolutionary War soldier, was posted to Mobile, Alabama, after the Battle of Monterrey, where he surveyed the Flint and Chattahoochee rivers. Scarritt died in Key West, Florida, in 1854, at the age of thirty-seven.

Prisoner exchanges were not conducted on a one-for-one basis. The value of every rank was measured in privates. Thirty privates, for instance, were equal to one brigadier general. Kenly's *Maryland Volunteer* includes the specific transcript of the correspondence between Scott and Taylor concerning the removal of Old Rough and Ready's troops to a second front.

The comments of the "Indiana volunteer" come from Oran Perry's *Indiana in the Mexican War.*

Grant's letters show how much he was enjoying the interlude in Monterrey, and it was nice to come upon Maury's quote in *Virginia General* about his spending time with his old West Point acquaintance. **Dabney Maury,** for his part, recovered well enough from his wounds at Cerro Gordo that he was later posted to America's western frontier during the 1850s, returned to serve as an instructor at West Point for five years, and then served as a major general in the Confederate army during the Civil War. Maury lived until the turn of the twentieth century and is buried in Fredericksburg, Virginia.

The comments of Dana and Scott come from their letters and the footnotes to Dilworth.

CHAPTER TWENTY-SEVEN

Jackson's life is thoroughly documented, and though his letters were few and far between, they are archived at the Virginia Military Institute. I found the most interesting comments about Jackson to come from Dabney Maury, for he was immediately overwhelmed by his fellow cadet's presence when they first met. Maury writes about Jackson and Grant from the perspective of a man who did not achieve their measure of fame but was content to stand back in admiration for them and their accomplishments. His insights were valuable in showing Jackson's determined character. Another invaluable source was the *Life and Letters of General Thomas J. Jackson,* by his widow, Mary Anna Jackson.

CHAPTER TWENTY-EIGHT

Lee's escalating ingenuity is well documented, but I chose to rely on Freeman.

CHAPTER TWENTY-NINE

Once again, Sherman's memoirs provide vivid descriptions of his life in California. The various biographies document his depression about missing out on the fighting (and often with a certain relish, as if foreshadowing his March to the Sea through this time of career impotence). The travails of Kearny at San Pasqual are told well by Bauer and in great detail by Sides.

CHAPTER THIRTY

Of all the descriptions of Buena Vista, I am most deeply indebted to Johannsen, not so much for an account of the battle as for describing the mood of this group of men about to do battle on George Washington's birthday. Jackson's role is well known, as is the initially ineffective role played by Taylor. Samuel French describes what it was like to be there, alternately telling of the U.S. soldiers' awe at the natural beauty and their great fear of being overrun by Santa Anna. Another great source is Benjamin Franklin Scribner's *Camp Life of a Volunteer.*

CHAPTER THIRTY-ONE

An entire book could be written about the events at Buena Vista, which stands as one of the great and almost entirely overlooked battles in American history. Bragg's and Davis's gallant behavior are well documented, and I found Chance's *Mexican War Regiment* greatly helpful because it told the story of the First Mississippi through eyes other than Jefferson's. *The View from Chapultepec* offers a snapshot of the battle from a Mexican point of view, while Bauer's *Mexican War* and Justin Smith's two-volume *War with Mexico* provide their usual highly detailed overview. Perry's *Indiana in the Mexican War* discusses the rush to rebut charges of cowardice by Indiana troops after the battle. Furber's *Twelve Months Volunteer* offers specifics about the battle, eyewitness accounts, and transcripts of Santa Anna's surrender demand and even includes a copy of Taylor's official after-action report. Meade's letters, written from Scott's far-off command, show the great relief among American soldiers that their brethren were not slaughtered at Buena Vista.

CHAPTER THIRTY-TWO

Grant's writings come from his letters home. Mooney's *Dictionary of American Naval Fighting Ships* offers significant details and histories of various vessels and reads like a tangential history of the United States by showing where the navy sent its ships (and, by proxy, where its interests resided at various moments in history). Mosely and Clark's article in the *Joint Forces Quarterly* comparing Veracruz and D-day is apt and very detailed. Harry Kelsey's *Sir Francis Drake,* Francisco López de Gómara's *Cortés,* and Hugh Thomas's *Rivers of Gold* offer specifics about the history of Veracruz and its previous invasion by the Spanish—and attempted invasion by the English. Meade also writes of the buildup to the invasion and the increasingly violent Gulf of Mexico weather. It is worth noting that the U.S. Naval Academy in Annapolis was founded in 1845, just months before the Mexican War began.

CHAPTER THIRTY-THREE

Again, Mosely and Clark are masterly in describing the buildup to this historic amphibious landing. Johannsen offers fine detail, as do Smith and Bauer. The writings of so many men involved in the landing, from Grant to Dana to Lee to Kirby Smith, add drama and a gut-tightening insight that can only come from a first-person perspective. Dana, in particular, was horrified by the carnage inside the city once it fell, and was eloquent in describing the unsettling sight. Kenly's *Maryland Volunteer* offers specific figures for the number of cannons inside the castle and marvels at the size of the fortress but expresses disappointment that American guns didn't destroy more of the city.

Lieutenant George McClellan became the protégé of Secretary of War Jefferson Davis in the years following the Mexican War. The young officer was sent on a secret mission to Santo Domingo, scrutinized the American railroad to assess the possibility of building a transcontinental rail system, and was an official American observer of the Crimean War. Upon his return, he wrote a tactics manual and designed a new cavalry saddle based on one used by the Prussian hussars. The McClellan Saddle would become standard issue for the remaining years of the U.S. Army's cavalry.

McClellan resigned his commission in 1858 to run the Illinois Central Railroad. When the Civil War broke out, however, he immediately went back into uniform. On July 26, 1861, at the age of thirty-four, McClellan was given command of the Military Division of the Potomac by President Abraham Lincoln. This was the main military force responsible for the defense of Washington, D.C., and the new commander quickly sought to expand its size and rename it the Army of the Potomac.

Yet McClellan, who had been such an ambitious overachiever throughout his entire life, soon proved to be a cautious and timid commander. He clashed with the aging general-in-chief of the army, Winfield Scott, who soon retired rather than lose face when Lincoln sided with McClellan in the debate over tactics. After a series of bruising defeats by a heavily outnumbered Robert E. Lee, and then a stalemate at the bloody Battle of Antietam, McClellan was relieved of command on November 5, 1863. One year later, he ran against Lincoln for the presidency and was soundly defeated. McClellan later served as governor of New Jersey and died of a heart attack at the age of fifty-eight.

CHAPTER THIRTY-FOUR

Jackson's comments come from letters to his sister Laura. Dana writes of the rumors about Santa Anna's movement south from Buena Vista.

CHAPTER THIRTY-FIVE

Once again, Dana provides a commentary on the move inland. It is Ballentine who wrote of the dread experienced by the American soldiers at the prospect of Twiggs's suicide charge on the pass, and Bauer and Freeman who expertly describe the lay of the land and Patterson's unlikely maneuver to halt Twiggs.

CHAPTER THIRTY-SIX

Cerro Gordo was perhaps Lee's finest moment in the Mexican War, particularly that day spent behind the log hiding from the Mexican army while in search of an alternate route. All Lee biographies describe this moment, but few with the detail and fervor of Freeman, who dedicated several years to documenting Lee's life. His unabridged text of *Lee* contains specifics of Lee's comments, Scott's praise, and the topographical layout of the battlefield. Maury describes the action with fine detail, and it was particularly memorable in his case because it marked the end of the war for him. Ballentine writes eloquently about the mood of the men before combat.

CHAPTER THIRTY-SEVEN

Grant's comments about missing out on the Cerro Gordo action come from his letters to Julia. The description of Jackson's departure from Monterrey comes from Cooper and from Chance's *Mexican War Regiment*. Interestingly, the many memoirs published by volunteers almost all end at this point in the war, as their time in uniform terminates. Though it was a patriotic time in America, many of the volunteers felt that they had paid their dues during their year at war and were no longer constrained by the emotions of patriotism to stay in the military any longer.

Santa Anna had lost his leg during the 1838 Pastry War with the French. His prosthetic leg was made of wood and cork. The Fourth

Illinois claimed the artificial limb as a spoil of war and brought it back with them when they returned home. Santa Anna's amputation had been poorly performed, and two inches of bone protruded through the skin, which made wearing the leg all the more painful.

CHAPTER THIRTY-EIGHT

The movements of Scott's army toward Mexico are well described in Bauer, Smith, and Freeman. The topography of Mexico City is meticulously described by Grant in his memoirs. It's worth noting that Grant's time as a quartermaster during the Mexican War served him well during the Civil War. Not only was he proficient at logistics and the complex needs of a supply line, but he was not above mimicking Scott and allowing his army to get cut off and live off the land, as U.S. forces did during the summer in Puebla.

The movement into the Pedregal, the fight at Churubusco, and the Battle of Molino del Rey are all thoroughly laid out in Scott's after-action reports; the writings of Bauer, Smith, Freeman, and Johannsen; the memoirs of Grant, Smith, and Hunt; and the various biographies of several key players. I have to admit that Smith's death was a sudden blow to me. Having read his memoir from the beginning, as the army marched from Corpus Christi, I was unprepared to turn the page and read that he had been killed in action. Despite his misgivings on the eve of Molino del Rey, I assumed that he would make it through the battle without injury, just as Grant and the others whom I had come to know so well did. Writing that scene was a reminder of life's brevity.

Henry Jackson Hunt was promoted to captain for his bravery at Churubusco and then to major for gallantry at Chapultepec. He remained in the army during the years between the Mexican and Civil wars. As a Union officer, he fought at Bull Run, Fredericksburg, Chancellorsville, and, most notably, Gettysburg. His artillery was pivotal to repulsing Pickett's Charge, and his concealed gun emplacements atop Little Round Top were particularly effective against Confederate artillery. He ended the war as a brigadier general and managed the siege of Petersburg. He died in 1889.

CHAPTER THIRTY-NINE

Writing about Chapultepec—figuring out the complex defenses surrounding the fortress and the tactical requirements necessary to enter the battle—was as much a logistical challenge as anything else. Bauer was a fine source, but Smith's descriptions and detail were outstanding. For the best description of Jackson's heroics at Chapultepec and manic behavior on the San Cosmé causeway, see his wife's *Life and Letters of General Thomas J. Jackson.*

CHAPTER FORTY

Smith and Bauer were invaluable for understanding the position of various roads and fortifications leading into Mexico City. Grant's descriptions of his brave action entering Mexico City are taken from his memoirs. Bauer and Smith were very helpful in establishing a time line for troop movements during the course of the battle and the position of various individuals. It was interesting to discover that Jackson, Grant, and Lee were all on the same San Cosmé route into the Mexican capital.

CHAPTER FORTY-ONE

Johannsen begins his *To the Halls of the Montezumas* with a description of the July 4, 1848, festivities in Washington, D.C., and their cultural significance. However, I also found Bauer's writing and Frederick L. Harvey's *History of the Washington National Monument* invaluable. For the section on Sherman, I once again relied on his memoirs and supplemented his time line with that of H. W. Brands's *The Age of Gold.*

SELECTED BIBLIOGRAPHY

BOOKS

Addey, Markinfield. *The Life and Military Career of Thomas Jonathan Jackson*. New York: Charles T. Evans, 1863.

Alfriend, Frank H. *The Life of Jefferson Davis*. Cincinnati: Caxton Publishing House, 1868.

Allen, Felicity. *Jefferson Davis: Unconquerable Heart*. Columbia: University of Missouri Press, 1999.

Anderson, Robert, and Eba Anderson Lawton. *An Artillery Officer in the Mexican War: The Letters of Robert Anderson, Captain Third Artillery, USA*. New York: G. P. Putnam's Sons, 1911.

Bache, Richard M. *Life of George Gordon Meade*. Philadelphia: Herry T. Coates and Co., 1897.

Baker, Jean H. *Mary Todd Lincoln*. New York: W. W. Norton, 1987.

Ballard, Michael B. *Pemberton*. Jackson: University Press of Mississippi, 1991.

Ballentine, George. *Autobiography of an English Soldier in the United States Army*. Ann Arbor: University of Michigan Library, 2005.

Barry, John M. *Rising Tide: The Great Mississippi Flood of 1927 and How It Changed America*. New York: Touchstone, 1997.

Bartlett, David W. *The Life of General Franklin Pierce, of New*

Hampshire: The Democratic Candidate for President of the United States. New York: G. H. Derby, 1852.

Bauer, K. Jack. *The Mexican War, 1846–1848*. Lincoln: University of Nebraska Press, 1974.

———. *Zachary Taylor: Soldier, Planter, Statesman of the Old Southwest*. Baton Rouge: LSU Press, 1985.

Bergeron, Paul H. *The Presidency of James K. Polk*. Lawrence: University Press of Kansas, 1987.

Bill, Alfred Hoyt. *Rehearsal for Conflict*. New York: Knopf, 1947.

Bowers, John. *Stonewall Jackson: Portrait of a Soldier*. New York: William Morrow, 1989.

Boyd, James P. *Military and Civil Life of General Ulysses S. Grant*. Dallas: Texas Book and Bible, 1885.

Brands, H. W. *The Age of Gold: The California Gold Rush and the New American Dream*. New York: Doubleday, 2002.

Brooks, Eldredge Streeter. *The Story of the American Soldier in War and Peace*. Boston: D. Lothrop, 1889.

Brooks, Nathan Convington. *A Complete History of the Mexican War: Its Causes, Conducts and Consequences*. Chicago: Rio Grande Press, 1849.

Brown, Charles H. *Agents of Manifest Destiny: The Lives and Times of the Filibusters*. Chapel Hill: University of North Carolina Press, 1980.

Caruso, A. Brooke. *The Mexican Spy Company: United States Covert Operations in Mexico, 1845–1848*. Jefferson, NC: McFarland, 1991.

Chamberlain, Samuel. *My Confession: Recollections of a Rogue*. Austin: University of Texas Press, 1965.

Chance, Joseph E. *Jefferson Davis's Mexican War Regiment*. Jackson: University Press of Mississippi, 1991.

Chance, Joseph E., ed. *The Mexican War Journal of Captain Franklin Smith*. Jackson: University Press of Mississippi, 1991.

Chartrand, Renae. *Santa Anna's Mexican Army, 1821–48*. New York: Osprey, 2004.

Claiborne, J. F. H. *Life and Correspondence of John A. Quitman*. New York: Harper and Brothers, 1860.

Cleaves, Freeman. *Meade of Gettysburg.* Dayton: Morningside Bookshop Press, 1980.

Cooke, John Esten. *A Life of General Robert E. Lee.* New York: D. Appleton, 1871.

Cooper, William J., Jr. *Jefferson Davis, American.* New York: Vintage, 2001.

Cozzens, Peter. *General John Pope: A Life for the Nation.* Chicago: University of Illinois Press, 2000.

Crawford, Mark. *Encyclopedia of the Mexican-American War.* Santa Barbara: ABC-CLIO, 1999.

Curtis, Nathaniel Cortlandt. *New Orleans: Its Old Shops and Public Buildings.* London: J. B. Lippincott, 1933.

Dabney, Robert L. *Life and Campaigns of Lieutenant General Thomas J. Jackson (Stonewall Jackson).* New York: Blelock, 1866.

Davis, Varina Howell. *Jefferson Davis: Ex-President of the Confederate United States.* Vol. 1. New York: Belford, 1890.

Davis, William C. *Jefferson Davis: The Man and His Hour.* New York: HarperCollins, 1991.

Dilworth, Rankin. *The March to Monterrey: The Diary of Lieutenant Rankin Dilworth, U.S. Army.* El Paso: Texas Western Press, 1996.

Dodd, William Edward. *Jefferson Davis.* Philadelphia: George W. Jacobs, 1907.

Dyer, Brainerd. *Zachary Taylor.* New York: Barnes and Noble, 1946.

Eicher, John H., and David J. Eicher. *Civil War High Commands.* Palo Alto: Stanford University Press, 2001.

Eisenhower, John D. *So Far from God.* New York: Random House, 1989.

Ellis, Joseph J. *American Sphinx: The Character of Thomas Jefferson.* New York: Alfred A. Knopf, 1997.

Farwell, Byron. *Stonewall: A Biography of General Thomas H. Jackson.* New York: W. W. Norton, 1992.

Fehrenbach, T. R. *Lone Star: A History of Texas and the Texans.* Cambridge: Da Capo Press, 2000.

Ferrell, Robert H., ed. *Monterrey Is Ours! The Mexican War Letters of Lieutenant Dana, 1845–1847.* Lexington: University of Kentucky Press, 1990.

Field, Ron. *Forts of the American Frontier, 1820–91. Central and Northern Plains.* New York: Osprey, 2005.

Foley, J. P. *The Jeffersonian Cyclopedia.* Vol. 1. New York: Russell and Russell, 1967.

Freeman, Douglas Southall. *R. E. Lee.* New York: Charles Scribner's Sons, 1934.

———. *Lee's Lieutenants.* 2 vols. New York: Charles Scribner's Sons, 1942.

French, Benjamin Brown. *Witness to the Young Republic: A Yankee's Journal, 1828–1870.* Hanover: University Press of New England, 1989.

French, Samuel G. *Two Wars: An Autobiography of General Samuel G. French.* Nashville: Confederate Veteran, 1901.

Frost, J. *The Mexican War and Its Warriors.* New Haven: H. Mansfield, 1848.

Furber, George C. *The Twelve Months Volunteer.* Cincinnati: U. P. James, 1857.

George, Isaac. *Heroes and Incidents of the Mexican War.* Hollywood: Sun Dance Press, 1971.

Gilman, Bradley. *Robert E. Lee.* New York: MacMillan, 1915.

Gómara, Francisco López de. *Cortés: The Life of the Conqueror by His Secretary.* Berkeley: University of California Press, 1964.

———. *Cortés: The Life of the Conquistador.* Berkeley: University of California Press, 1964.

Graham, Wm. A. *Life of General Winfield Scott, Commander of the United States Army.* New York: A. S. Barnes, 1852.

Grant, Julia Dent. *The Personal Memoirs of Julia Dent Grant.* Carbondale: Southern Illinois University Press, 1975.

Grant, U. S. *Personal Memoirs of U. S. Grant.* Cambridge: Da Capo Press, 2001.

Grant, Ulysses S. *The Papers of Ulysses S. Grant.* Vol. 1, *1837–1861.* Carbondale: Southern Illinois University Press, 1967.

Hackenburg, Randy W. *The War with Mexico: The Volunteer Regiments.* Shippensburg: White Man, 1992.

Hamilton, Holman. *Zachary Taylor: Soldier in the White House.* New York: Bobbs-Merrill, 1951.

Harvey, Frederick L. *History of the Washington National Monument and of the Washington National Monument Society.* Washington, D.C.: Norman T. Elliott Printing, 1902.

Hay, Thomas Robson. *James Longstreet.* Vol. 1, *Soldier.* Baton Rouge: Louisiana State University Press, 1952.

Herr, John Knowles. *The Story of the U.S. Cavalry, 1775–1942.* Boston: Little, Brown, 1953.

Hetzel, Susan Rivere. *The Building of a Monument.* Lancaster: Press of Wickensham, 1903.

Horgan, Paul. *Great River: The Rio Grande in North American History.* New York: Holt, Rinehart and Winston, 1954.

Jackson, Mary Anna. *Life and Letters of General Thomas J. Jackson.* New York: Harper Brothers, 1892.

———. *Memoirs of Stonewall Jackson.* Louisville: Courier-Journal Job Printing, 1895.

Johannsen, Robert W. *To the Halls of the Montezumas: The Mexican War in the American Imagination.* New York: Oxford University Press, 1985.

Johnson, Andrew. *The Papers of Andrew Johnson.* Vol. 1, *1822–1851.* Knoxville: University of Tennessee Press, 1967.

Jones, Wilmer L. *Generals in Blue and Gray.* Westport: Praeger, 2004.

Kearney, Milo, ed. *More Studies in Brownsville History.* Brownsville: Pan American University, 1989.

Kelsey, Harry. *Sir Francis Drake: The Queen's Pirate.* New Haven: Yale University Press, 1998.

Kendall, George Wilkins. *Dispatches from the Mexican War.* Norman: University of Oklahoma Press, 1999.

Kenly, John R. *Memoirs of a Maryland Volunteer.* Philadelphia: J. B. Lippincott, 1873.

Kennett, Lee. *Sherman: A Soldier's Life*. New York: HarperCollins, 2001.

Knotel, Herbert, and Herbert Sieg. *Uniforms of the World, 1700–1937*. New York: Charles Scribner's Sons, 1937.

Lecke, Robert. *From Sea to Shining Sea*. New York: HarperCollins, 1993.

Lee, Robert E. *The Recollections and Letters of Robert E. Lee*. New York: Konecky and Konecky, 1992.

Lewis, Lloyd. *Captain Sam Grant*. Boston: Little, Brown, 1950.

Libura, Krystyna, Luis Morales, and Jesus Marquez. *Echoes of the Mexican American War*. Berkeley: Groundwood Books, 2004.

Long, A. L. *Memoirs of Robert E. Lee: His Military and Personal History*. New York: J. M. Stoddart, 1886.

Longstreet, James. *From Manassas to Appomattox: Memoirs of the Civil War in America*. New York: J. B. Lippincott, 1895.

Mansfield, Edward D. *Life and Services of General Winfield Scott: Including the Siege of Vera Cruz*. New York: A. S. Barnes, 1852.

———. *The Mexican War: A History of Its Origin*. New York: A. S. Barnes, 1851.

Manucy, Albert. *Artillery Through the Ages: A Short Illustrated History of the Cannon, Emphasizing Types Used in America*. University Press of the Pacific, 2001.

Marshall, Charles. *Appomattox: An Address Delivered before the Society of the Army and Navy of the Confederate States*. Baltimore: Society of the Army and Navy of the Confederate States, 1894.

Marti, Werner H. *Messenger of Destiny: The California Adventures, 1846–1847, of Archibald Gillespie, USMC*. San Francisco: John Howell, 1961.

Martinez, Orlando. *The Great Land Grab: The Mexican War, 1846–1848*. London: Quartet Books, 1975.

Maury, Dabney Herndon. *Recollections of a Virginian in the Mexican, Indian and Civil Wars*. New York: Charles Scribner's Sons, 1894.

McCall, George Archibald. *Letters from the Frontier*. Gainesville: University Presses of Florida, 1974.

McCartney, Samuel Bigger. *Illinois in the Mexican War*. Chicago: Northwestern University, 1939.

McFeely, William S. *Grant*. New York: W. W. Norton, 1981.

McIntosh, James T., ed. *The Papers of Jefferson Davis*. Vol. 2, *1841–1846*. Baton Rouge: Louisiana State University Press, 1981.

———. *The Papers of Jefferson Davis*. Vol. 3, *1846–1848*. Baton Rouge: Louisiana State University Press, 1981.

McSherry, Richard. *El Puchero; or, A Mixed Dish from Mexico, Embracing Scott's Campaign*. Philadelphia: C. Sherman, 1850.

McWhiney, Grady, and Perry D. Jamieson. *Attack and Die: Civil War Military Tactics and the Southern Heritage*. Tuscaloosa: University of Alabama Press, 1984.

Meade, George. *The Life and Letters of George Gordon Meade*. Vol. 1. New York: Charles Scribner's Sons, 1913.

The Mexican War and Its Heroes. Philadelphia: Grigg, Elliot, 1849.

Miller, Robert Ryal. *Shamrock and Sword: The Saint Patrick's Battalion in the U.S.-Mexican War*. Norman: University of Oklahoma Press, 1989.

Miller, Robert Ryal, ed. *The Mexican War Journals and Letter of Ralph W. Kirkham*. College Station: Texas A&M University Press, 1991.

Monroe, Dan. *The Republican Vision of John Tyler*. College Station: Texas A&M University Press, 2003.

Mooney, James. *Dictionary of American Naval Fighting Ships*. Washington, D.C.: U.S. Naval Historical Center, 1981.

Moore, Joseph West. *Picturesque Washington: Pen and Pencil Sketches*. Providence: J. A. and R. A. Reid, 1884.

Myers, William Starr. *The Mexican War Diary of General George P. McClellan*. New York: Da Capo Press, 1972.

Naisawald, Louis VanLoan. *Grape and Canister: The Story of the Field Artillery of the Army of the Potomac*. New York: Oxford University Press, 1960.

Nelson, Anna Kasten. *Secret Agents: Polk and the Search for Peace with Mexico*. New York: Garland, 1988.

Nies, Judith. *Native American History*. New York: Ballantine Books, 1996.

Oswandel, J. Jacob. *Notes of the Mexican War, 1846–48: Comprising incidents, adventures and everyday proceedings and letters while with the United States Army in the Mexican . . . of Mexico; also influence of the church.* Philadelphia, 1885.

Patterson, Gerard A. *Rebels from West Point.* New York: Doubleday, 1987.

Perry, Oran. *Indiana in the Mexican War.* Indianapolis: Wm. B. Burford, 1908.

Pollard, Edward Alfred. *The Early Life, Campaigns and Public Services of Robert E. Lee.* New York: E. B. Treat, 1871.

Ramsey, Albert C. *The Other Side; or, Notes for the History of the War between Mexico and the United States Written in Mexico.* New York: J. Wiley, 1850.

Reid, Samuel Chester. *Scouting Expeditions of the Texas Rangers.* Philadelphia: G. B. Zieber, 1848.

Remlap, L. T., ed. *The Life of General U. S. Grant.* Chicago: Fairbanks, Palmer, 1885.

Roberts, Wm. Hugh. *Mexican War Veterans: A Complete Roster of the Regular and Volunteer Troops in the War between the United States and Mexico, from 1846 to 1848.* Washington, D.C.: Brentano's, 1887.

Sandburg, Carl. *Abraham Lincoln: The Prairie Years and the War Years.* Norwalk: Easton Press, 1954.

Sanger, Donald Bridgman, and Thomas Robson Hay. *James Longstreet, I: Soldier. II: Politician, Officeholder, and Writer.* Baton Rouge: Louisiana State University Press, 1952.

Scott, Winfield. *Infantry Tactics; or, Rules for the Exercise and Manoeuvre of United States Infantry.* 3 vols. New York: Harper and Bros., 1846.

———. *Memoirs of Lieutenant-General Scott.* Freeport: Books for Libraries Press, 1970.

———. *The Memoirs of Lieutenant General Winfield Scott.* 2 vols. New York: Sheldon, 1864.

Scribner, Benjamin Franklin. *Camp Life of a Volunteer: A Campaign in Mexico; or, A Glimpse at Life in Camp by One Who Has Seen the Elephant.* Philadelphia: Grigg, Elliot, 1847.

Seitz, Don C. *The James Gordon Bennetts*. Indianapolis: Bobbs-Merrill, 1928.

Sides, Hampton. *Blood and Thunder: The Epic Story of Kit Carson and the Conquest of the American West*. New York: Doubleday, 2006.

Simpson, Brooks D. *Ulysses S. Grant: Triumph over Adversity, 1822–1865*. Boston: Houghton Mifflin, 2000.

Singletary, Otis A. *The Mexican War*. Chicago: University of Chicago Press, 1960.

Smith, George Winston, and Charles Judah. *Chronicles of the Gringos: The U.S. Army in the Mexican War, 1846–1848*. Albuquerque: University of Mexico Press, 1968.

Smith, Gustavus Woodson. *Company "A" Corps of Engineers, U.S.A., 1846–1848, in the Mexican War*. Kent: Kent State University Press, 2001.

Smith, Jean Edward. *Grant*. New York: Simon and Schuster, 2001.

Smith, Justin H. *The War with Mexico*. 2 vols. New York: Macmillan, 1919.

Smith, Kirby. *To Mexico with Scott: Letters of Captain E. Kirby Smith to His Wife*. Cambridge: Harvard University Press, 1917.

Snow, William P. *Lee and His Generals*. New York: Richardson, 1867.

Tarr, David R., and Ann O'Connor. *Congress A to Z*. 3rd ed. Washington, D.C.: Congressional Quarterly, 1999.

Taylor, Fitch W. *The Broad Pennant; or, A Cruise in the United States Flag Ship of the Gulf Squadron during the Mexican Difficulties*. New York: Leavitt, Trow, 1848.

Taylor, Zachary. *Letters from the Battlefields of the Mexican War*. New York: Kraus Reprint, 1970.

Thomas, Emory. *Robert E. Lee*. New York: W. W. Norton, 1995.

Thomas, Hugh. *Rivers of Gold: The Rise of the Spanish Empire, from Columbus to Magellan*. New York: Random House, 2003.

Traas, Adrian George. *From the Golden Gate to Mexico City: The U.S. Army Topographical Engineers in the Mexican War, 1846–1848*. Washington, D.C.: U.S. Army, 1993.

Windrow, Martin, and Gerry Embleton. *Military Dress of North America, 1665–1970*. New York: Charles Scribner's Sons, 1973.

Wright, Robert K., and Morris J. MacGregor. *Soldier-Statesmen in the Constitution*. Washington, D.C.: U.S. Government Printing Office, 1987.

GOVERNMENT DOCUMENTS

O'Bright, Alan W., and Kristen R. Marloff. *Farm on the Gravois: Historic Structures Report. Ulysses S. Grant National Historic Site*. Saint Louis, 1999.

U.S. Army Training and Doctrine Command, Fort Monroe, Virginia, and Combat Studies Institute. *Armed Diplomacy: Two Centuries of American Campaigning*. Fort Leavenworth, Kansas, 2003.

JOURNAL ARTICLES

Clark, Paul C., and Edward Mosely. "D-Day, Veracruz 1847, A Grand Design." *Joint Forces Quarterly*, Winter 1995–96, 104–115.

Klafter, Craig Evan. "United States Involvement in the Falkland Islands Crisis of 1831–1833." *Journal of the Early Republic* 4, no. 4 (Winter 1984): 395–420.

O'Sullivan, John L. "The Great Nation of Futurity." *United States Democratic Review* 6, no. 23 (November 1839): 426–430.

Stauffer, Alvin P. "The Quartermaster's Department and the Mexican War." *Quartermaster Review*, May–June 1950.

Wilson, Herbert M. "Topography of Mexico." *Journal of the American Geographical Society of New York* 29, no. 3 (1897): 249–60.

WEB SITES

http://www.archives.gov
http://www.army.mil/cmh
http://www.history.navy.mil/index.html
http://www.inaugural.senate.gov/history/chronology/jkpolk1845.htm
http://www.whitehouse.gov

ARCHIVES

Virginia Military Institute Archives

INDEX

Abercrombie, John J., 394
Abraham Lincoln: The Prairie Years
    (Sandburg), 407
Adams, John, 43
Adams, John Quincy, 20, 21, 97, 112,
    113, 370
Age of Gold, The (Brands), 420
Alamo, the, 61, 74, 178, 180, 187
    casualties at, 21
    Mexican revenge for, 22–23
Alexander the Great, 106
Algeria, French invasion of (1830), 295
Allen, Felicity, 406
Allen, George W., 394
American flag. *See* Stars and Stripes
Ampudia, Pedro de, 63–64, 65, 71, 99
    at Buena Vista, 278
    in defense of Mexico City, 362, 365
    in defense of Monterrey, 178, 188–89,
        196, 199, 217, 220, 226, 242; abandons
        perimeter, 218; casualties, 212;
        surrenders, 227–31, 238, 412
    and Mier, 179–80, 187
    Santa Anna's forces combined with, 246,
        255
Anderson, S. S., 357
Anglo-American alliance urged, 21.
    See also Britain
Anglo-American Convention (1818), 32
Angostura. *See* Buena Vista
Antietam. *See* Battles, Civil War
Apache Indians, 242, 377, 400
    Apache Wars, 414
Appomattox, Lee's surrender at, xi–xiii,
    337, 398–99, 400, 412
Argentina
    as independent republic, 19–20
    and Falklands crisis (1831), 143

Arista, Mariano
    as commander of Army of the North, 65
    at Fort Texas, 81
    at Palo Alto and Resaca de la Palma,
        87–88, 92, 101, 104–8; replaced as
        commander, 187
    prisoners of, 72
    retreats from Matamoros, 121, 124;
        moves inland, 129; Taylor's pursuit
        of, 122
Armistead, Lewis, 386
Army, Mexican
    at the Alamo, 21; revenge for, 22–23
    Army of the North, 60, 65, 106, 187
    artillery, *see* artillery, Mexican
    cavalry, *see* cavalry, Mexican
    coups staged by, 241
    described by London *Times*, 55
    engineering corps (Zapadore), 96
    Grant's view of, 37
    illness among, 321
    Indians forced to serve in, 345–46
    revenge sought by, 22–23, 60, 276
    ruse by, 58
    size and organization, 54–55, 64, 65;
        numerical superiority, 42, 48,
        100–101, 104–6, 227, 260, 275,
        (against Grant and the Fourth) 83, 92,
        (against Scott) 355
    uniforms of, 83, 106, 282
Army, U.S.
    artillery, *see* artillery, U.S.
    casualties, 82, 180, 312, 330, 349 (*see
        also* Mexican War)
    cavalry, *see* cavalry, U.S.
    Center of Military History, 398, 404
    clothing and gear, 152
    desertion from, 63, 190, 362

Army, U.S. *(cont.)*
  discomfort and illness: in camps, 41,
    62, 98, 129, 131–32, 151–53; lack
    of supplies and, 177; on the march,
    47–48, 84, 196, 199, 300, 301, 306;
    on shipboard, 166–69, 287–88
  food, 47–48, 153, 238, 312, 322
  infantry units: First, 166, 200, 204, 394;
    First Illinois, 277; First Kentucky,
    First Ohio, 191, 394; First Tennessee
    "Bloody First," 191, 205, 208, 212;
    First Texas Division, 181, 194; First
    and Second Illinois, 395; Second
    Division, 170, 194, 196, 245; Second
    Indiana, 280, 395; Second Kentucky,
    395; Third, 24, 91, 393, (at Monterrey)
    191, 194, 200, 205, 208, 221, 223, 394;
    Third Indiana, 277, 282, 283, 395;
    Fourth, 91–92, 174, 177, 350, (first
    weeks in Texas) 24–27, 39, 42–43,
    48, 64, (march on Mexico City) 317,
    (at Monterrey) 197–98, 204–7, 211,
    220–21, 223, 244–45, (reassigned) 287;
    Fourth Illinois, 418–19; Fifth, 91, 200,
    201, 393, 394; Seventh "Cotton Balers,"
    166, 387, (at Fort Texas) 74, 76, 79, 110,
    (at Monterrey), 200–201, 204, 394;
    Eighth, 53–54, 89, 200–201, 387, 393,
    394; Eleventh and Fourteenth, 359, 360
  logistics, 59, 113, 165, 269, 288, 406, 419;
    three units, 173–74
  officers, 40, 67, 95, 106; election or
    appointment of, 122–23; Jefferson
    Davis, 113, 115
  official flag, 134. *See also* Stars and
    Stripes
  overland marches in Southwest, 235,
    273–74
  payment of soldiers, 39–40, 41, 137, 152,
    231, 236
  as prisoners, *see* prisoners of war, U.S.
  prisoners of, *see* prisoners of war,
    Mexican
  Quartermaster Department, 41, 129,
    172–75, 239, 254, 288–89, 294, 305,
    406; negotiations by, 166
  size of, 20, 42, 106; outnumbered, 48,
    100, 106, 227, 315, 318, 355
    (*see also* Army, Mexican [numerical
    superiority])
  structure of (battalion, regiment,
    brigade, division, company), 171
  Texas Rangers, 204, 221, 225–26, 230;
    atrocities committed by, 247–49
  troops under Taylor's command, *see*
    Taylor, Zachary "Old Rough and
    Ready"
  uniforms of, 39, 331, 364; volunteer
    regiments design their own, 150, 191
  volunteers, 133, 174, 235, 326, 418;
    animosity between regulars and,
    189–91; at Camargo, 169–70, 247,
    254–55; enlistment period ends, new
    contingents arrive, 329, 337; Fourth
    Regiment, 160, 407; from Illinois,
    162–63, 407; lack of discipline among,
    123, 124, 125, 191; Maryland and
    District of Columbia, 204–5, 206,
    207–8; Mississippi and Texas, 394;
    at Monterrey, 205, 208, (atrocities)
    247, 294; from Northeast, 148;
    numbers of, 42, 106; Pennsylvania,
    387, 401; Polk calls for, 148; promises
    made to, 231; punishment of, 190,
    246–47; Second Division, 256; seen
    as heroes, 254; Virginia, 387. *See also*
    Mississippi Rifles (First Mississippi
    Regiment)
Army Corps of Engineers, 4, 95, 148, 384
Army Corps of Topographical Engineers,
    237, 242, 273, 319, 384, 404
  Meade in, 95–96, 98–99, 124, 201, 249,
    308
"army of conquest," 127
Army of Invasion, 135
Army of Northern Virginia (Civil War), xi,
    385, 387
Army of Observation, 34, 41, 42
Army of Occupation, 41–42, 59. *See also*
    Taylor, Zachary "Old Rough and
    Ready" (troops of)
Army of the Potomac (Civil War), 384–87,
    410, 417
Arnold, Benedict, 3
artillery, Mexican, 64, 77, 81–82
  camouflaged or concealed, 84, 86, 102,
    188, 200, 209
  in defense of Mexico City, 315, 320,
    338–42, 347–50, 353
  marksmanship, 78–79, 201; tactical
    mistakes, 87–88, 93, 199
  at Monterrey, 193, 195, 200, 201,
    206–12, 216, 220–27, 276
  outdated: "Brown Bess" muskets,
    103–4; cannons, 106, 186, 290; lances,
    55 (*see also* cavalry, Mexican)
  spiked or hidden, 122
  U.S. captures, 109, 212, 216, 220
artillery, U.S., 48–49, 57–58
  First, 89, 323, 385; Company K, 266,
    267, 394
  First Heavy, 198, 200
  Second, 357, 385, 394
  Third, 141–42, 146, 297, 386, 394
  Fourth, 357, 385
  Sixth, 386
  for dragoons (standard issue), 70
  failure of supply, 151–52, 157, 223, 305

French Paixhans (cannon) used by,
    301–2, 305, 338
horse-drawn ("flying"), 42, 194–96,
    197–98, 201–2, 210, 267, 283; Jackson
    and, 266, 311, 349, 359–60, 366
in march to Mexico City, 323–24, 339,
    341–42
at Monterrey, 193–96, 197–202, 207–10,
    215, 219–20, 222–27
muskets: in hand-to-hand combat, 107;
    ineffectiveness of, 90, 154; vs. rifles,
    153–56, 407, (rifles delivered) 165
Navy, 286, 300–303
at Palo Alto, 85–93, 198–200
"redlegs," 57, 204, 401
in siege of Fort Texas, 74, 75–76, 77–79, 99
transport of, 59, 86, 102
at Veracruz, 299, 300, 301–7
Artillery through the Ages (Manucy), 404
Attack and Die (McWhiney and
    Jamieson), 404
Aulick, John, 303
Austin, Moses, 18
Austin, Stephen, 18
Austria (in Holy Alliance), 20, 21
Aztec Club, 375
Aztec Indians, 18, 250–51, 289, 352, 363
    dams built by, 353

Babcock, Orville, xii
Baker, Edward Dickenson, 159, 163, 325, 407
Ballentine, George, 398, 410, 418
Baltimore Sun, 253
Barragan, José, 55–56, 57
Bartlett, John Russell, 411
Battles
    of Hastings, 55
    of San Jacinto (Alamo), 22
    of Thermopylae, 328
Battles, Civil War, 401, 402–4, 407, 409,
    410, 419
    of Bull Run, *see* Bull Run, Battle of
    of Cedar Mountain, 384
    of Chancellorsville, 377, 384
    of Dranesville, 386
    of Fairfax County Courthouse, 400
    of Fredericksburg, 386
    of Gettysburg, *see* Gettysburg, Battle of
    of Petersburg, 385, 419
    of Shiloh, 384, 402
    of Spotsylvania Courthouse, 385
Battles, Mexican War
    of Buena Vista, *see* Buena Vista
    of Cerro Gordo, *see* Cerro Gordo
    of Chapultepec, *see* Chapultepec
    of Churubusco, 362, 377, 400, 419
    of Mier, 178–81, 187
    of Molino del Rey, *see* Molino del Rey
    of Monterrey, *see* Monterrey, Battle of

of Palo Alto, *see* Palo Alto, Battle of
of Resaca de la Palma, *see* Resaca de la
    Palma, Battle of
of San Pasqual, Americans defeated in,
    274, 413, 415
Battles, Revolutionary War
    of Bunker Hill, 12
    of Paulus Hook, 7, 399
    of Saratoga, 301
    of Yorktown, 7, 12
Battles, War of 1812
    of Crysler's Farm, 5
    of Lundy's Lane, 195, 293
    of New Orleans, 74, 150
    of Queenston Heights, 293
Bauer, K. Jack, 398, 405, 406, 415, 419
Beagle, HMS, 406
Beauregard, P. G. T., 306, 340, 355–56, 384
Belknap, William G., 393
Benton, Thomas Hart, 113, 273
Bernard, Simon, 148
Bissell, William H., 395
Black Bean Episode, 180–81, 187
Black Hawk War (1832), 115, 159–60,
    161–62, 293, 299
Blake, Jacob, 99–100, 124
Blanchard, Albert C., 394
Bliss, William W. S. "Perfect," 278, 383, 408
Bolivia as independent republic, 19
Bonura, Michael, 398
Bowles, William A., 395
Bradford, Alexander, 151
Bragg, Braxton, 74–76, 77, 81, 147, 261, 386
    at Buena Vista, 283, 396, 415
    at Monterrey, 197–99, 210, 394
Brands, H. W., 420
Brazos Island, 152–53, 165, 168–69, 191, 309
Britain
    Anglo-American alliance urged, 21
    artillery of, 154; "horse artillery," 194;
        outdated guns sold to Mexico, 103–4,
        106; seized from Burgoyne, 301
    diplomatic efforts to free Texan Alamo
        prisoners, 181
    fears U.S. expansion, 31–32, 33
    holds Oregon, 4, 21, 29, 41, 112, 113;
        Anglo-American Convention and
        (1818), 32; signs Treaty of Oregon
        (1846), 136–37
    Mexican War as viewed by, 251–52
    recognizes Texas as independent
        territory, 22
    secures transit rights across Isthmus of
        Tehuantepec, 371
    during siege of Veracruz, 301, 304
    U.S. distrust of, 28
    in wars with America: Revolutionary
        War, 3–4, 7, 12, 40, 301, 353; War of
        1812, 4–5, 8, 19–20, 28, 40, 43

Britton, Lieutenant (cavalry officer), 254
Brooklyn Daily Eagle, 134
Brooks, Captain (Second Artillery), 357
Brown, Jacob, 74, 76
  wartime surgery on, 79–81, 120–21,
    403, 405
"Brown Bess" (musket), 103–4
Buchanan, James, 229
Buena Vista, 276
  battle of, 277–79, 280–85, 287, 321,
    415–16, 418; atrocities following,
    363; map of, 272; order of, 395–96;
    watercolor paintings of, 412
  Santa Anna at, 313
Bull Run, Battle of, 384, 400, 419
  Second, 403, 409, 413
Bunker Hill, Battle of, 12
Bunker Hill Monument, 371
Burgoyne, John, 301
Burnside, Ambrose E., 386
Bustamente, Carlos María de, 285, 347
Butler, William O., 394

Caddo tribe, 17
Cadwalader, George, 343, 345
Caesar, Julius, 106
Calhoun, John C., 9, 28, 113, 146, 156
California Territory, 17, 21, 29, 136, 149
  gold rush, 372–74
  troops on way to, 141–43, 235, 271;
    conquest of, 273–74; U.S. acquires,
    346, 372
Callender, Franklin D., 341, 348
Camargo, 129–33, 174–75, 182, 245, 259, 267
  steamboat journey and march to, 153,
    165–68, 172, 178, 191, 408
  volunteer force at, 169–70, 247, 254–55
Campbell, William B., 395
Camp Life of a Volunteer (Scribner), 415
Canada and Canadian border, 4, 31, 106,
    231, 293
Canning, George, 21
Carricitos, Thornton's blunder at, 67, 402,
    403
Carson, Kit, 273
Cartwright, Peter, 162
casualties
  at the Alamo, 21
  in Mexican War, *see* Mexican War
Catholic Church, 145, 266, 278, 304
  as Mexican national religion, 19, 134, 363
  missions built by, 17, 18
  Protestant bias against, 63, 125, 231
cavalry, Mexican, 63, 90–91, 107, 215
  as elite corps, 55
  lancers, 50, 58, 91, 216, 296; at Buena
    Vista, 282–83; Jalisco and Guanajuato,
    202; losses at Monterrey, 202–3; U.S.
    fears of getting "lanced," 276

cavalry, U.S.
  First Dragoons, 7, 115, 384–85, 413
  Second Dragoons, 34–35, 42, 66–67,
    219–20, (trapped by Torrejón,
    surrender) 68–71
  First and Second Texas Mounted Rifles,
    194, 245
  Third, 394
  advances ahead of horse-drawn "flying"
    artillery, 311
  Kentucky and Arkansas, 277
  overland march by, 136–37
  Rush's Lancers, 385
  weapons and gear issued to, 70;
    McClellan Saddle, 417
  See also Pickett's Charge; Texas Rangers
Central American isthmus, 17
Cerro Gordo, 311, 314, 315–18, 319–21,
    341
  Battle of, 322–27, 328, 338, 364, 377,
    418; map of, 316
Chamberlain, Joshua, 398
Chamberlain, Samuel, 410, 411, 412
Chance, Joseph, 406, 411, 416, 418
Chapultepec, 353–56
  Battle of, 347–51, 357–62, 363–64, 366,
    416, 419–20; map of, 336; Stars and
    Stripes raised at, 361–62
Charles V, king of Spain, 290
Charles X, king of France, 295
Cherokee Indians, 408
Chihuahua, march toward, 235–36
  abandoned, 255
Childs, Thomas, 393, 394
Chippewa Indians, 53
Churubusco, 345
  Battle of, 362, 377, 400, 419
Civil War, U.S., 375, 383, 400–414 *passim,*
    417
  Confederacy, 376; Davis as president,
    379; Lee as commander in chief, 377,
    384
  Grant as general, 376, 419; Lee
    surrenders to, xi–xiii, 337, 398–99,
    400, 412
  Meade's list of officers who achieved
    distinction in, 384–88
  Pickett's Charge, 6, 361, 386, 387, 409,
    419
  Sherman in, 403; march through
    Georgia, 378, 384, 415
  Valley Campaign, 400, 407
  See also Battles, Civil War
Clay, Henry, 30, 94, 97, 146
Cleaves, Freeman, 404
Comanche Indians, 15, 178, 242
Confederate States of America, 376, 379,
    384, 386–87, 400, 402. *See also* Civil
    War, U.S.

Congress, U.S., 8, 246, 370, 407
  considers abolishing West Point, 14, 192
  Davis in House of Representatives,
    112–14, 118, 138, 155–56; letter of
    resignation, 139, 244
  declaration of war reaches, 113; funding
    for war, 113, 118, 154–55, 260; takes
    formal vote on war, 119, 122
  decrees design of flag, 134
  and expansionism, 28–29, 31
  Lincoln elected to Thirtieth, 158–59,
    161–62
  Monroe Doctrine announced to, 20
  Senate demands Richard Meade's
    return, 97
  Senate ratifies Treaty of Guadalupe
    Hidalgo, 371
  and tariff bill, 156
  Whig Party in, 254; Whig-Democrat
    divide, 164, 192
Conner, David, 251
Constantinople, siege of, 85
Constitution, U.S., 7, 162, 246
  Twentieth Amendment, 31
Cook, James, 4
Cooper, William J. Jr., 397, 406, 411, 418
Coronado, Francisco, 18
Corps of Discovery (Lewis and Clark), 4
Corpus Christi, 39–46, 54, 147, 173, 245,
  295, 312
Cortés, Hernando, 294, 295, 314, 353
Cortés (Gómara), 416
"Cotton Balers" (Seventh Infantry).
  See Army, U.S.
Crimean War, 417
criollos, 240–41, 250, 413
Cross, Trueman, 62–63, 65, 99
Cuba, 19, 400
  Santa Anna exiled to, returns, 187, 337
Custis, Mary Anne Randolph. See Lee,
  Mrs. Robert Edward

Dana, Napoleon Jackson Tecumseh,
  130–31, 172, 261, 403
  at Fort Texas, 77–78, 81, 121
  in march to Mexico City, 317–18, 416,
    418; wounded, 327
  at Monterrey, 201, 405–6; describes
    conditions, 196, 204, 210–11, 216,
    226, 227, 410, (after battle) 247
  and trek to Camargo, 166–68, 408
  at Veracruz, 304, 306
Dana, Mrs. Napoleon (Sue), 403
  husband's letters to, 77, 167–68,
    196, 204, 216, 247, 318, 398; on
    "fandango," 131, 405–6
Darwin, Charles, 406
Davis, Jefferson, 405
  ambitions of, 112–19, 138–40

biographies of, 379, 397, 406
  in Black Hawk War, 115, 160
  in Civil War, as president of the
    Confederacy, 379
  in House of Representatives, 112–14,
    118, 138, 155–56; letter of resignation,
    139, 244
  resigns commission in U.S. Army, 113,
    117; court-martial overturned, 114, 116;
    reapplies for and accepts, 118, 119, 138
  as Secretary of War (1853), 417
  Taylor's trust in, 276
  as West Point graduate, 6, 10, 112, 114,
    115–16, 118
  AND MEXICAN WAR, 158, 186
  eagerness to serve, 112, 115, 118–19;
    embarks for, 137–40
  First Mississippi Regiment of,
    see Mississippi Rifles
  Grant rides into battle with, 205
  probes Mexican defenses, 220
  represents U.S. in Ampudia's surrender,
    228
  returns home, 243–44, 329–31;
    triumphal return, 378
  with troops at Buena Vista, 276–79,
    280–84, 395, 415
Davis, Mrs. Jefferson (Sarah Knox Taylor
  "Knox," first wife), 113, 115–17, 139,
  193, 330
Davis, Mrs. Jefferson (Varina Howell,
  second wife), 112–19 passim, 137–39,
  156, 208, 243, 261
Davis, Joseph, 114, 117, 118, 243–44
Davis, Lucinda, 138
Dawson Massacre (1842), 179
Declaration of Independence, signers of,
  6, 144
Democratic Party, 236, 254–55, 316
  Davis in, 118, 191
  and expansionism, 29, 30
  and Mexican War, 113, 162, 164
  vs. Whigs, 164, 192–93
Democratic-Republican Party, 3
Dent, John, 27
Dent, Julia Boggs. See Grant, Mrs. Ulysses S.
Dent, Mary Ann. See Longstreet, Mrs. James
de Soto, Hernando, 18
Díaz de la Vega, Rómulo, 108
Dictionary of Americanisms (Bartlett), 411
Dictionary of American Naval Fighting
  Ships (Mooney), 416
Dilworth, Rankin, 408, 409
disease
  casualties from, 132, 169, 288
  yellow fever and cholera, 35, 137, 299,
    312, 329, 410
  See also Army, U.S. (discomfort and
    illness)

Donelson, Andrew Jackson, 31
Doubleday, Abner, 183, 261, 306, 385, 409
"doughboys," origin of term, 401
dragoons. *See* cavalry, U.S.
Drake, Sir Francis, 289
Drum, Captain (Fourth Artillery), 357
Duncan, James, 92, 393, 394

Early, Jubal, 387
Echoes of the Mexican American War (Libura et al.), 412
elections, presidential and congressional, 29–30, 32, 94, 158–59, 161, 254. *See also* Congress, U.S.
elephant. *See* "seeing the elephant"
Ewell, Richard S. "Dick," 26, 52–53, 384–85, 400, 401
Ewing, Thomas and Maria, 145–46
expansionism, U.S., 16, 19
    advocates of, 29–30, 232; Jackson, 21, 22, 30, 97, 115; Polk, 30–36, 113, 136, 273, 371, 400, (increases aggression toward Mexico) 250, 252
    and Black Hawk War, 159–60
    colonists in Mexico, 18–19, 32
    conquest of California, 273–74
    European fears of, 31–32, 33
    opponents of, 30, 113
    in Pacific Northwest, 4, 21, 30, 32, 112, 136; territories purchased: California, 346, 372; Florida, 97; Louisiana, 4, 137; New Mexico, 346
    See also Manifest Destiny

Falkland Islands crisis (1831), 132, 406
Ferdinand VII, king of Spain, 96, 291
Fillmore, Millard, 370
First Mississippi. *See* Mississippi Rifles
Fitzhugh, William H., 9
Florida, 66
    U.S. disputes with Spain over, 20; buys from Spain, 97
    See also Seminole Wars
Fort Brown. *See* Fort Texas
Fort Sumter
    construction of begins (1829), 148
    first shots fired at (Civil War, 1861), 409
Fort Texas (or Fort Taylor, later Fort Brown), 129, 166, 245
    building of, 61–62, 64, 73, 193, 410
    renamed Fort Brown, 121, 124, 403
    siege of, 74, 75–76, 77, 83–93, 99, 110–11, 199; casualties, 78–82, 120–21; temporarily suspended, 101
    Stars and Stripes raised at, 60, 110–11
    volunteers stationed at, 124

France
    aids in construction of U.S. forts, 148
    artillery of, 154; Paixhans cannons, 301–2, 305
    battle tactics of, 87
    fears U.S. expansion, 31–32, 33; in Holy Alliance, 20, 21
    invades Algeria (1830), 295
    Louisiana Territory purchased from, 4
    Mexican War as viewed by, 251–52
    Santa Anna's war with (1838), 418
    during siege of Veracruz, 301, 304
    in Texas, 18; recognizes independence of, 22
    See also Napoleonic Wars
Franklin, Benjamin, 3
Fraser, William D., 237
Freeman, Douglas Southall, 397, 415, 418, 419
Frémont, John C., 273, 274
French, Samuel, 176, 280, 284
French, William H., 385, 398
French and Indian War, 12
From the Golden Gate to Mexico City (Traas), 404
Frost, D. M., 14, 399
Furber, George C., 412, 416
Fry, Birket, 264

Gaines, Edmund P., 127
Gálvez de Madrid, Bernardo, 353
Garland, Bessie, 53
Garland, John, 52–53
    in Mexican War, xii, 393, 394, 411; as Grant's commander, 173, 335, 348–49, 365; at Monterrey, 204–5, 208, 223, (retreats) 209–10, 219, 224
Garland, Louise. *See* Longstreet, Mrs. James "Pete"
Garland, Samuel Jr., 411
Geary, John W., 387
Genghis Khan, 140
Gettysburg, Battle of, 377, 384–87, 400
Gibbon, John, 386
Gibraltar
    Monterrey compared to, 189, 410
    San Juan de Ulúa at Veracruz compared to, 290
Goliad, prisoners shot at, 22, 187
gold rush, California, 372–74
Gómara, Francisco López de, 416
Grant, Jesse, 12–13
Grant, Matthew, 12
Grant, Noah, 12
Grant, Mrs. Noah (Hanna Simpson), 12
Grant, Ulysses S. (Hiram Ulysses) "Sam," 378, 386
    biographies of, 375–77, 399

courtship and marriage, 23–28, 53, 176, 230, 287, 376–77, 400; letters to Julia, see Grant, Mrs. Ulysses S.
as general in Civil War, 376, 419; Lee surrenders to, xi–xiii, 337, 398–99, 400, 412
grows beard, 120, 405
horsemanship and horses of, 12, 14, 23, 26–27, 34, 43–46, 172, 224, 399
memoirs, 397, 399–400, 405; quoted, xiii, 37, 127, 233, 257, 333
as U.S. president, 376, 386
as West Point graduate, 12, 13–15, 23, 52, 57, 402; name changed, 13, 191
AND MEXICAN WAR, 338
and artillery and transport, 59, 89, 90
Davis rides into battle with, 205
early postings, 34–36, 47, 54, 181, 235; false alarm, 58
with Fourth Infantry, 48, 245, 350 (see also Army, U.S. [infantry units])
future plans, 123, 232
and Lee: meets, is rebuked by, xii, 335, 337; quoted on, 322
and march to Matamoros, 60–61, 64
in march on Mexico City, 346, 348–51, 359, 365–69, 371, 416, 420; quoted on, 325, 327, 328, 329, 347, 350–51
at Monterrey, 205, 207, 211–13, 214, 244–45; bravery of, 223–24; quoted on, 182–83, 186, 200, 206, 220–21, 229–30, 248
opinion of Taylor, 49–50, 213, 257, 261, 405
as quartermaster, 181, 197, 245, 346, 376, 408; dislikes job, 172–73, 176, (attempts to resign) 173, 335; success of, 174–75, 177, 337; value of experience, 350, 419
and slavery as issue, xiii
and Veracruz, 286–87, 291, 306
war begins, 73–74, 76, 83–84, 86; "army of invasion," 135; discusses provocation of / eagerness for, 35–36, 40–41, 42; first sees action, 89–93, 94, 154; hopes for negotiation, 64–65, 132, 230–31, 337; takes command, 104–5, 108–9, 171–72; waits for further action, 133, 166–67
Grant, Mrs. Ulysses S. (Julia Boggs Dent), 23–28, 206, 337, 400
marriage, 376–77, 378
Personal Memoirs of, 397
Sam's letters to: courtship, 53, 76, 120, 123, 132–33, 177, 244–45; on war, 40–41, 42, 60–61, 109, 167, 286–87, 327, 329, 351, 418, (on possibility of negotiation) 64, 230–31
Grant (Smith), 397, 399, 409

Grape and Canister (Naisawald), 404
Green, Jim, 140, 207

Hagner, Lieutenant (Ordnance), 357
Hamer, Thomas L., 191, 394
Hamilton, Alexander, 370
Hamilton, Mrs. Alexander (Elizabeth Schuyler), 370
Hancock, Winfield S., 386–87
Hannibal, 106
Harbors and Rivers Bill, 156–57, 158
Hardee, William Joseph, 66–70, 73, 261, 315, 402–3
surrenders to Torrejón, 71–72
Hardin, John J., 159, 163, 240, 395
Harney, William, 324
Harpers Ferry insurrection (1859), 377, 385
Harvey, Frederick L., 420
Hawkins, Edgar S., 81, 403–4
Hay, Thomas, 401
Hays, Alexander, 177, 248, 408–9
Hays, John C., 395
Hays, Peregrine, 264
Hays, Samuel L., 264
Hazlitt, Robert, 25–26, 34, 212, 230
Henderson, J. Pinckney, 228, 395
Herndon, William H., 162
Herrera, José Joaquin de, 32–33, 35, 229
Hill, Ambrose P., 264, 306, 385
Hill, Daniel Harvey, 261
History of the War in the Peninsula (Napier), 294
History of the Washington National Monument (Harvey), 420
Hitchcock, Ethan Allen, 300
Holy Alliance (Russia, Austria, Prussia, France), 21
Hooker, Joseph, 306, 384
horses and horsemanship. See cavalry, Mexican; cavalry, U.S.; Grant, Ulysses S.
horse-drawn ("flying") artillery. See artillery, U.S.
Hoskins, Charles, 206–7
Houston, Sam, 22, 370
Huastec Indians, 289
Huger, Captain (Second Artillery), 357
Hunt, Henry J., 340, 343, 385, 419

Illinois, volunteers from state of, 162–63
Illinois in the Mexican War (McCartney), 407
Illinois Territory, 116
Indiana divisions. See Army, U.S. (infantry units)
Indiana in the Mexican War (Perry), 414, 416
Indians
Apache, 242, 377, 400, 414
Aztec, 18, 250–51, 289, 352–53, 363

Indians *(cont.)*
 Caddo, 17
 Cherokee, 408
 Chippewa, 53
 Comanche, 15, 178, 242
 Huastec, 289
 Shawnee, 144–45
 forced to serve in Mexican Army, 345–46
 represented at laying of Washington
   Monument cornerstone, 370
 subjugated by Spanish explorers, 18
 See also Black Hawk War
infantry, U.S. *See* Army, U.S.
investment, as military term, 298
Iowa Territory, 116
 joins Union, 361
Irish Americans, 44, 63, 78, 125, 362.
 See also Catholic Church
isolationism, 19–20
Isthmus of Tehauntepec, transit rights
   across, 346
 U.S. fails to acquire, Britain obtains, 371

Jackson, Andrew, 31, 98, 146, 192
 expansionism of, 21, 30, 97, 115; meets
   Santa Anna, 22
 in War of 1812, 150
Jackson, James, 266
Jackson, Jonathan and Julia, 263–64
Jackson, Laura, brother Thomas's letters
   to, 266, 313, 365, 418
Jackson, Thomas J. "Stonewall," 6, 261,
   263–67, 287, 297, 414–15
 biography and *Life and Letters* of, 377,
   415, 420
 in Civil War, 377, 400, 407, 413
 first Mexican campaign, 267
 and march on Mexico City, 311–13,
   314, 324, 341–42, 344, 361, 368, 420;
   "flying artillery" of, 266, 311, 349,
   359–60, 366; Scott reprimands for
   "slaughter" by, 364–65
 at Veracruz, 306
Jackson, Mrs. Thomas J. (Mary Anna), 415
Jalapa, 311, 314, 325, 327, 329
James Longstreet (Sanger and Hay), 401
Jamieson, Perry D., 404
Jefferson, Thomas, 3–4, 115, 118, 399
Jefferson Davis, American (Cooper), 397
Jefferson Davis's Mexican War Regiment
   (Chance), 406, 411, 416, 418
jingoism, 133
Joaquin del Arenal, Ignacio, 211
Johannsen, Robert W., 398, 405, 406, 415,
   416, 419, 420
Johnson, Andrew, 413–14
Johnston, Joseph E., 10, 319, 341, 345, 378,
   384
Johnston, Preston, 341–42, 345

Joint Forces Quarterly, 416
Jomini, Antoine-Henri, 87, 404
Jones, Anson, 31, 32–33, 35
Journal des Débats (Paris), 252

Kearny, Stephen Watts, 235, 273–74, 372,
   413, 415
Kelsey, Harry, 416
Kenly, John R., 410, 411, 414, 417
Kerr, Captain (Second Dragoons), 393

Lafayette, Marquis de, 9
lancers. *See* cavalry, Mexican
Lane, James H., 395
Lane, Joseph, 395
Lear, W. W., 394
Lee, Custis, father Robert's letters to, 325,
   327
Lee, Henry "Light-Horse Harry," 6–9,
   148, 371
 medal for, 399
Lee, Mrs. Henry (Matilda, first wife;
   Ann Hill Carter, second wife), 7–9, 10
Lee, Robert Edward
 biography of, 397
 birth and childhood, 7, 8–9, 371; siblings
   of (Carter, Ann, Smith, Mildred), 9
 in Civil War, 377, 384, 404, 413, 417;
   surrenders to Grant, xi–xiii, 337,
   398–99, 400, 412
 as West Point graduate, 6, 9–11, 269;
   commandant of cadets, 6, 377
   AND MEXICAN WAR, 232, 237–38,
   292
 builds bridge, 239–40
 in march on Mexico City, 325–27,
   342–45, 355–59, 368, 420; searches
   for, constructs alternate route,
   319–22, 324, 340–41, 418
 promoted, 338
 rebukes Grant, xii, 335, 337
 as scout for Scott, 11, 268–70, 319–22,
   338–40, 343–45
 and Veracruz, 269, 293–94, 301–3,
   307–8, 416
Lee, Mrs. Robert Edward (Mary Custis),
   10–11, 238
Lee's Legions, 7
Lewis, Meriwether, 4
Lexington, USS, 141, 143–44, 148, 271, 406
Libura, Krystyna, 412
*Life and Letters of General Thomas J.
   Jackson* (M. Jackson), 415, 420
Lincoln, Abraham, 158–64, 361, 407
 early life and education, 160–61
 and McClellan, 417
 political life, 161–64, 240; assassinated, 378
 serves in army, 160, 161
 "Spot Resolutions" of, 389–91

Lincoln, Mrs. Abraham (Mary Todd), 161
Lincoln, Edward Baker, 161, 407
Lincoln, Robert, 161
literacy, rise in, 253
London *Times*, 32–33, 55, 136, 137, 251–52
Longstreet, James, 51–52, 71
Longstreet, Mrs. James (Mary Ann Dent), 51, 52
Longstreet, James "Pete," 23, 50–52, 261
  in Civil War, 387, 411, 413
  and Grant, 15, 53–54, 287, 376, 399
  memoirs of, 399, 400, 401, 404, 405
  in Mexican War, 87; at camp, 34, 53–55, 181; false alarm, 58; first battles, 89, 109; march on Mexico City, 359, 361; at Monterrey, 200, 214; at Palo Alto, 84
Longstreet, Mrs. James "Pete" (Louise Garland), 52–53, 109, 411
Longstreet, William, 50–51
Los Angeles, Kearny takes, 274
Louisiana Purchase, 4, 137
Louisville Legion (volunteers), 247
Lowd, Allen, 77, 81

McCall, George Archibald, 44–45, 47, 100, 106, 384, 401, 405
  temporarily retreats, Grant takes over command, 101, 104
McCartney, Samuel Bigger, 407
McClellan, George, 261, 294, 297, 300, 341, 384
  and McClellan Saddle, 417
McDowell, Irvin, 384
McIntosh, James S., 349, 393, 394
Mackall, William W., 394
McKee, William R., 395
McLaren, Adam, 327
McLean, Wilmer, home of as Civil War surrender site, xi–xii, 399
McLung, Alexander K., 151, 208–9
McWhiney, Grady, 404
Madison, James, 33
Madison, Mrs. James (Dorothy "Dolley"), 370
Magnus, Heinrich, 153–54
Magruder, "Prince" John Bankhead, 306, 312, 360–61, 404
  with First Artillery, 89; guns of, 341–42, 344, 365
Mahan, Dennis Hart, 216
Manifest Destiny, 135, 162, 252, 273, 371, 374
  term coined, 29, 400
  See also expansionism, U.S.
Mansfield, Joseph K. F., 61–62, 81, 261, 410–11
  at Monterrey, 193, 199, 201–2, 205, 209–10

Manucy, Albert, 404
March to Monterrey, The: The Diary of Lieutenant Rankin Dilworth (Dilworth), 408, 409
Marcy, William L., 113, 127, 249, 254
Marines, U.S., 359, 367–68
Marion, Francis "the Swamp Fox," 7
Marshall, Charles, xii, 398–99
Marshall, Humphrey, 396
Marshall, John, 8, 51
Marshall, Thomas, 395
Mason, Charles, 399
Mason, George T., 71
Mason, R. B., 372–73
Massachusetts, USS, 296, 298
Matamoros, 55, 59–60, 107, 180, 405
  Mexican forces in, 63–64, 65, 100, 105; retreat from, 121–22, 124, 129; U.S. prisoners held by, 71–72
  U.S. occupation of, 121–25, 133, 181, 231; camp just outside, 61, 124, (church service held in) 135; European view of, 252; "fandangos" in, 131; as frontier depot, 129–30; march to Camargo from, 166–67, 172, 178
Maury, Dabney Herndon, 245, 296, 323, 399, 411, 418
  quoted on Stonewall Jackson, 264–65, 414–15
Maximilian, emperor of Mexico, 404
May, Charles A., 90, 254, 393, 395, 396
Meade, George Gordon, 96, 404–5, 409
  in Civil War, 384
  letters and memoirs, 397, 416
  list of officers compiled by, 384–87
  as Taylor's aide, 89–90, 94–95, 98–100, 102, 261; in Matamoros, 121, 123–25; at Monterrey, 200–203, 215, 218–19, 411, (after battle) 228, 229, 251, 255–56, 412; at Palo Alto, 89, 94, 100; at Resaca de la Palma, 109–10; at Veracruz, 292, 308, (ordered home) 309–10
  quoted on occupation of Mexico, 232
  in Topographical Corps, 95–96, 98–99, 124, 201, 249, 308
  as West Point graduate, 6, 89, 98, 125
Meade, Mrs. George Gordon (Margaretta Sergeant), 94–95, 98–100, 124, 200, 308–9, 310
Meade, Richard, 96–97
Meade, Sra. Margarita Coates Butler de (Margaret), 96–97, 98
Meade of Gettysburg (Cleaves), 404
Mejía, Francisco, 55, 60, 187, 207, 278
Memoirs of a Maryland Volunteer (Kenly), 410, 411, 414, 417
mestizo as term, 18

Mexican War
  break in diplomatic relations with U.S., 31
  casualties, Mexican, 93, 110, 202–3, 212,
    227; at Buena Vista, 284; civilian, 305;
    by drowning in Rio Grande, 110; at
    Mier, 180; at Molino del Rey, 349; at
    Monterrey, 223; at Veracruz, 304–5, 307
  casualties, U.S., 62–63, 65, 99, 110, 330;
    at Buena Vista, 284, 285; first official,
    78, 120; from disease, 132, 169, 288,
    312; at Fort Texas, 78–82, 120–21; in
    march on Mexico City, 326, 349–50;
    at Mier, 180; at Molino del Rey,
    349–50; at Monterrey, 206, 208–13,
    221, 223–24, 228, 330; at Palo Alto,
    92–93; at Veracruz, 306, 307; West
    Point graduates, 306, 383
  compared to Crusades, 135
  European view of, 251–52
  first and only American defeat in, 274,
    413
  forced by U.S., xiii, 35–36, 56, 57; U.S.
    goal in, 136, 178
  hostilities increase, 11, 23, 24, 32–36,
    72; Mexican proclamation, 55–56,
    57; U.S. builds fort, see Fort Texas;
    U.S. officially invades, 177–78; U.S.
    officers killed, 62–63, 65, 99; war
    begins, 73–74, 403; war officially
    declared, (secretly, by Mexico) 65, (by
    U.S.) 113
  "and the Media" (Web site), 406
  Mexican map falls into Taylor's hands,
    108, 124
  naval blockade and bombardment, 137,
    165, 251
  officers who achieved distinction in,
    384–87; West Point and, 375
  as political war, 127, 233
  Polk stipulates armistice terms, Santa
    Anna rejects, 346–47
  prisoners of, see prisoners of war,
    Mexican; prisoners of war, U.S.
  Santa Anna requests U.S. surrender,
    Taylor refuses, 275–78, 416
  steamboats first used in, 287, 298
    (see also steamboats)
  surgery in, 79–81, 403, 419
  U.S. sentiment against, 113–14, 131,
    133–34; and politics, 162, (Whigs) 163
  U.S. sentiment favoring, 113, 119,
    134–35, 162–64; support wanes, 250
  U.S. volunteers in, see Army, U.S.
  war ends, 368, 371–72
  women and children in, 223, 305, 307,
    325–26, 363, 412
  See also Battles, Mexican War
Mexican War, The (Bauer), 398, 405, 406,
  416

Mexican War and Its Heroes, The, 410, 411
Mexico
  armed forces of, 21, 23; governing power
    of, 241–42; Texians surrender to, 22
    (see also Army, Mexican)
  citizens' rebellions in, 63
  Congress of, 231, 244, 285
  Constitution of, xiii
  Emperor Maximilian of, 404
  as independent republic, 241; U.S.
    colonization of, xiii, 18–19
  northern, 236, 250–51, 266, 309;
    topographical charts of, 237; U.S.
    defensive line across, 260
  racial problems in, 240–41
  territory belonging to, 21
  Texas as buffer between U.S. and, 16, 31
  Texas (as nation) at war with, xiii, 15,
    21–23, 179–81; declares independence
    from, 21–22
  U.S. offers to buy Texas from, 21; later
    demands as condition of armistice,
    346
  U.S. war with, see Mexican War
  War of Independence, 56, 184, 241,
    290–91, 354
Mexico City
  history of, 363–64
  Spanish viceroy in, 17
Mexico City, march on, 311–14, 334, 335,
  352–61, 420
  alternate route sought, 319–22, 324,
    340–41, 418
  assault planned and executed, 170,
    250–51, 261, 297–98; preparations
    for, 308; tactics of, 315–18, 323–27,
    328–30, 337–51
  Battle of Cerro Gordo, 324–27, 328, 364;
    map of, 316
  Battle of Chapultepec, 347–51, 357–62,
    363–64, 366; map of, 336
  Stars and Stripes raised, 361–62, 368;
    occupation ends, 371
Mier, Battle of, 178–81, 187
Miles, Dixon S., 394
Military Peace Establishment Act, 3
Minnesota Territory, 116
Mississippi Rifles (First Mississippi
    Regiment), 406–7
  at Buena Vista, 276–77, 279, 280–84,
    395, 416
  Davis commands, 137, 139, 150–57, 170,
    184, 261, 276; returns home, 243,
    329–31
  journey to Camargo, 165–69, 171
  at Monterrey, 193–94, 205, 212, 222,
    243, 395; hostility between regulars
    and, 189–91; "seeing the elephant,"
    207–9

Mississippi River, travel on, 137–38
Mitchell, Alexander, 394
Molino del Rey, 354, 357
    Battle of, 347–50, 355, 359, 376, 419;
        slaughter at, 349; U. S. revenge for,
        358, 361
Monroe, James, 8, 20–21, 148
Monroe Doctrine, 20, 113
Monterey, California, 141, 271, 274, 372, 373
    U.S. captures, 273
Monterrey
    attack planned, 124, 125, 129, 133;
        Arista plans resistance, 121; Taylor's
        march to, 169–70, 175, 178, 181–83,
        184–87, 191, 266, 294; viewed as
        "perfect Gibraltar," 189, 410
    as U.S. outpost, 309; Taylor and,
        244–47, 249; atrocities at, 246–48,
        294, 363; divided into two camps, 248
    Monterrey, Battle of, 201–213, 214–17,
        218–27, 277, 343, 347
    battle plans, 193–96, 197–200; tactics
        used, 411
    casualties, 206, 208–10, 211–13, 221–23,
        227–28, 330; cannonball narrowly
        misses Taylor, 201
    First Mississippi at, see Mississippi
        Rifles
    Garland retreats, 209–10, 219, 224
    map of, 185
    order of, 394–95
    Santa Anna at, 187–88
    Taylor quoted on, 217, 220, 228
    truce and Mexican surrender, armistice,
        227–32, 241–42, 249–52, 256, 266,
        412; armistice annulled, 254–55;
        citizens return, 248; Grant quoted
        on political effect of, 257; Mexican
        revenge for, 276; newspaper accounts
        of, 253–54; Stars and Stripes raised
        at, 217
    watercolor paintings of, 412
    women in, 223, 412
Monterrey Is Ours! (Dana), 405
Montezuma, 354
Montgomery, Captain (Eighth Infantry),
    393
Mooney, James, 416
Morales, Juan, 297, 307
Morales, Luis, 412
Morris, L. M., 393
mules as transport, 172, 174–76, 206,
    273–74, 305
My Confession: Recollections of a Rogue
    (Chamberlain), 410, 411, 412

Naisawald, L. VanLoan, 404
Nájera, Juan, 202
Napier, Sir William Francis Patrick, 294

Napoleon Bonaparte, 4, 51, 231–32, 294
    Scott translates works of, 293
Napoleonic Wars, 19, 96, 106–7, 148, 231,
    298
National Road, 314, 315, 319–20, 322,
    324–25, 335. See also Mexico City,
    march on
Navy, U.S., 20, 308, 416
    aids Kearny in taking Los Angeles, 274
    blockades and bombardments by, 137,
        165, 251
    sailing vessels still in use, 286–88 (see
        also steamboats)
    takes Monterey, California, 273
    takes Tampico, 256
    at Veracruz, 296; artillery, 286, 300–303
New Mexico
    as Mexican state, xiii, 17, 29; missions
        built in, 18
    U.S. forces capture, 235, 273; U.S.
        purchases, 346
New Orleans, 246, 310
    steamboat traffic to, 139–40, 238, 309
    supplies gathered from, 288
New Orleans Crescent City (newspaper),
    253
New Spain, 17–18, 31, 240, 354.
        See also Spain
newspapers, 399, 413
    antiwar, 133
    battlefield reports in, 398
    rise and influence of, 253–54, 261
    Web site information, 406
        See also London Times
Newton, Isaac, 153
New York Herald, 253–54, 399
New York Times, 413
New York Tribune, 133
North American (journal), 119, 405
North Carolina, USS, 286, 287
Northwest Territory, 163. See also Pacific
    Northwest

Oñate, Juan de, 17
Ord, Edward O. C., 143–44, 383, 386
Oregon, 17, 113
    annexation of, 29, 30, 32, 112
    occupation of, 21, 40–41
    Treaty of, signed by U.S. and Britain,
        136–37
Ormsby, Stephen, 394
O'Sullivan, John L., 29, 400

Pacific Northwest, 4, 21. See also Oregon
Padre Island, 18
Page, John, 90
Paixhans, Henri-Joseph, 302
Paixhans guns, 301–2, 305
    Mexican version, 338

Palo Alto, Battle of, 83–93, 94, 99–100, 130, 142, 181
  Arista loses, 187
  army formation at, 193, 194
  artillery at, 85–93, 198–200
  casualties at, 92–93; Mexican, 121
  Grant's observations at, 83–84, 90, 154, 223, 369
  map of, 84
  order of, 393
  as turning point, 105, 120, 176
Papers of Ulysses S. Grant, The, 397
Paraguay as independent republic, 19
Paredes y Arrillaga, Mariano, 35, 229
patriotism, 114, 125, 133–35, 151, 231, 418
Patterson, Robert, 256, 260, 261, 316, 395
  disobedience of orders of, 254–55
  as political appointee, 254, 298; makes crucial decision, 317, 418
Pedregal, the, 340–41, 342–45, 419
Pemberton, James, 139
Pemberton, John, 368
Pendleton, W. N., 10
Perry, Oran, 414, 416
Personal Memoirs of Julia Dent Grant, The, 397
Personal Memoirs of U. S. Grant, 397
Philadelphia Public Ledger, 253
Philip V, king of Spain, 290
Pickett, George, 6
Pickett's Charge (Civil War), 6, 361, 386, 387, 409, 419
Pierce, Franklin, 356
Pillow, Gideon, 316, 324–25, 337, 341, 344, 357–59, 395
Pleasanton, Alfred, 385
Poinsett, Joel Roberts, 66
Polk, James K. "Young Hickory," 378, 402
  announces discovery of gold in California, 374
  as Democrat, 236; vs. Whigs, 191–92
  distrusts army, 191–92
  expansionism of, 113, 241, 250, 252, 273, 400; annexation of Texas, 30–33, 34–36, 136, 250, 371
  frees Santa Anna, 187
  opposition to, 276
  AND MEXICAN WAR, 236, 316
  as commander in chief, 106, 123, 249
  eagerness for war, 30, 72, 73, 113, 127; Lincoln challenges, 389–91; Lincoln quoted on, 163–64
  and Monterrey armistice, 250–53, 255; annuls, 254–55
  promises rifles in exchange for votes on tariff bill, vetoes Harbors and Rivers Bill, 156–57, 158
  requests more troops, 113; calls for volunteers, 148
  stipulates final armistice terms, 346
  and Veracruz landing, 288
Pope, John, 249, 261, 384, 413–14
Porter, Theodore H., 40, 63, 65
Port Isabel, 76, 152, 166, 178, 232
  supply center at, 61, 62, 64, 86, 129, 174, 288; caravans to, 130; road to, 101, (blocked) 81; troops stationed at, 73, 84, 266, 287, (volunteers) 123
Pratte, Bernard, 376
Princeton University, 7, 399
prisoners of war, Mexican, 229–30, 362
  at Cerro Gordo, 326
  deal for release of, 347
  Jackson's view of, 313
  paroled at Veracruz, 318
  prisoner exchange, 414
  at Resaca de la Palma, 108–10
  Taylor's treatment of, 121
prisoners of war, U.S.
  Civil War, 401
  prisoner exchange, 414
  shot, 22; Black Bean Episode, 180–81, 187
  treatment of, (cordial) 71–72, (rumors about) 64–65
Prussia (in Holy Alliance), 21

Quartermaster Department. *See* Army, U.S.
Quartermaster Review, 406
Quitman, John Anthony, 260
  in march to Mexico City, 337, 357–59, 364, 368
  at Monterrey, 208, 256, 395

Ramírez, Simeón, 348
Reid, Samuel Chester, 398, 411
R. E. Lee (Freeman), 397, 415, 418
religion, 134–35, 231, 264, 406. *See also* Catholic Church
Resaca de la Palma, Battle of, 101–2, 121, 130, 142
  Arista loses, 187
  artillery in (U.S. and Mexican), 102, 103–8; U.S. captures, 109
  map of, 95; topographical map captured during, 108, 124
  order of, 393
  prisoners taken, 108–10
  as turning point, 120, 176
  veterans of, 181, 312, 401; Grant, 223
Revolutionary War, 3–4, 28, 103, 383
  Spanish aid in, 353–54
  U.S. occupation of Quebec during, 231
  veterans and descendants of veterans of, 6–9, 12, 40, 43, 67, 204, 414
  See also Battles, Revolutionary War
Reyes, Mariano, 188
Reynolds, John F., 385, 386
Richmond (VA) Enquirer, 253

Ridgely, Randolph, 197–98, 199, 212, 394
Rifle and Light Infantry Tactics (Hardee), 402, 403
Riley, Bennet, 325, 327, 343, 345
Ringgold, Samuel, 198, 393
Rio Colorado, crossing of, 48–50, 57–59, 204
Rio Grande
  conditions of life on, 169
  Mexican soldiers drown in, 110
  Taylor's army reaches, 59–60; builds fort, 61–62, 74; crosses by boat, 121; follows the course of, 178
  temporary bridge across (Lee builds), 235, 239–40
  as Texas-Mexico boundary, 17, 136, 250, 346, 371
Rivers of Gold (Thomas), 416
Robles, Luis, 188
Rogers, William P., 284
Rush, Richard, and Rush's Lancers, 385
Russia (in Holy Alliance), 20, 21

Salas, José Mariano, 229
Saltillo, 186, 189
  Mexican forces retreat to, 202; citizens flee to, 246
  Saltillo road, 193, 195–96, 200, 202; U.S. controls, 203, 219, 249
  Santa Anna moves toward, 188, 277; defense of, 279
  U.S. march to, 195–96
  U.S. occupation of, 255–56, 259, 260, 268, 276
  wounded taken to, 284
Sandburg, Carl, 407
San Francisco, 273, 372
Sanger, Donald, 401
San Juan de Ulúa (fortress at Veracruz), 290–91, 292, 297; U.S. takes, 307
San Luis Potosí, Mexican Army in, 246, 255, 260, 276
San Pasqual, Americans defeated in battle of, 274
San Patricios, 362
Santa Anna, Antonio López de
  at the Alamo, 21–22
  artificial leg, 326, 418–19
  captured, xiii; returns from exile, 187, 337
  cruelty of, 21–22, 180
  defends Mexico City: at Cerro Gordo, 314, 315, 322–25, 363; flees, 326, 329; inside city, 320, 337–40, 342, 355, 358, 362, 366–67; prisoners freed by, 368; viewed as hero, 364
  forces raised by, 187–88, 242, 246, 255, 260; size of, 317, 355
  and peace with U.S., 231; refuses truce, 346–47

requests American surrender, Taylor refuses, 275–78, 416; battle of Buena Vista follows, 284–85, 287, 313, 321, 415, 418
seizes control of government, 313–14
and Veracruz, 261, 291, 318
Santa Fe, U.S. occupies, 235, 273. *See also* New Mexico
Santa Fe Trail, 343
Satterlee, R. S., 169
Saturday Evening Post, 399
Scarritt, Jeremiah, 249, 414
Scott, Henry Lee, 300
Scott, Winfield "Old Fuss and Feathers," 236, 292
  in Civil War, 377, 417
  AND MEXICAN WAR
  after-action reports filed by, 398
  drafts plans for, 136, 250; passed over for command, 127; takes command from Taylor, 256, 257, 259–62
  in march on Mexico City, 311, 313, 317–18, 328–29, 337–40, 345–51, 419; Battle of Cerro Gordo, 324–27; Battle of Chapultepec, 353, 355–59, 362; Jackson reprimanded by, 365; Lee as scout for, xii, 11, 268–70, 319–22, 338–40, 343–45, 418; Mexicans surrender to, 368
  quoted: on volunteers, 246; on West Point graduates, 375
  at Veracruz, 257, 269, 284, 288, 292–301, 307–8; terms of surrender, 305, 307
Scouting Expeditions of the Texas Rangers (Reid), 411
Scribner, Benjamin Franklin, 415
Sedgwick, John, 385
"seeing the elephant," 207, 266, 411
Seminole Wars, 50
  veterans of, 36, 54, 66, 69, 100, 293, 343, 408; Sherman, 142, 146–47, 274; Taylor, 34
Sergeant, John, 94
Shakespeare, William, 6
Shawnee Indians, 144–45
Shea (Irish soldier), 78
Sherman, Charles and Mary, 144–45
Sherman, Charles and James, 145
Sherman, Roger, 144
Sherman, Thomas W., 396
Sherman, William Tecumseh "Cump," 144–45
  biography and memoirs of, 378, 397, 406, 415, 420
  in Civil War, 403; march through Georgia, 378, 384, 415
  in Seminole Wars, 142, 146–47, 274
  sent to California, 141–44, 148–49, 271, 274; and gold rush, 372–74
  as West Point graduate, 6, 13, 142, 146

Shields, James, 159, 240, 316, 324–325, 407
Shivoc, Captain (Mississippi and Texas Volunteers), 394
Sides, Hampton, 415
Simpson, Hanna, 12
Sir Francis Drake (Kelsey), 416
slavery
  antislavery vs., 118, 133, 157
  forbidden in Mexico, xiii, 19
  as political issue, xiii, 113, 157, 162
  in Texas, xiii, 28, 31
  volunteers and, 124
Smith, Charles Ferguson, 57–58, 100–101, 204, 211, 401–2
Smith, G. W., 300
Smith, Jean Edward, 397, 399, 409
Smith, John L., 308
Smith, Justin W., 405, 416, 419, 420
Smith, Kirby, 58, 348, 349–50, 401, 416, 419
Smith, Persifor F., 342, 343, 344–45, 394
Smithson, James, 115
Spain
  in Napoleonic Wars, 231–32, 294
  in New Spain (Texas and Mexico), 17–18, 240–41, 314, 353; first arrival, 289–90; founds Monterrey, 184; loses colonies, 19, 291; in Mexico City, 363; in northern Mexico, 236; shipwrecked sailors massacred, 18
  in Revolutionary War, aids colonies, 353–54
  U.S. disputes with, 20, 97; Richard Meade imprisoned, 96–97
  Washington portrait presented to, 96
Staniford, Thomas, 394
Stars and Stripes
  as official army flag, 134
  raised at Bishop's Palace, Monterrey, 217
  raised at Chapultepec, 361–62
  raised at National Palace, Mexico City, 368
  raised at Rio Grande (Fort Texas), 60, 110–11
  raised at Veracruz, 296, 307
Star-Spangled Banner (riverboat), 138, 139
Stauffer, Alvin P., 406
steamboats
  first use of, 287, 298
  passengers transported by, 137, 139, 238, 309
  prototype invented, 50–51
  troops and supplies shipped by, 35, 129–30, 153, 165–68, 174, 240, 330
  See also Navy, U.S.
Steene, Enoch, 396
Stewart, R. A., 135
Stockton, Robert F., 273, 274
Stone, Lieutenant (Ordnance), 357
Stoneman, George, 385

Stuart, Gilbert, 96
Summary of the Art of War (Jomini), 87
Sumter, Thomas "the Gamecock," 7, 148
"surfboats," 288–89, 295. *See also* Navy, U.S.
surgery, wartime, 79–81, 403, 419
Sutter, John, and Sutter's Mill, 372
Swift, Joseph, 3, 5
Sykes, George, 386

Tabasco uprising (1844), 63
Tampico, 309
  assault planned on, 250, 251
  Navy takes, 256; vessels at, 288
  Taylor removed from command, 254
Tartars, the, 140
Taylor, Sarah Knox. *See* Davis, Mrs. Jefferson (first wife)
Taylor, Zachary "Old Rough and Ready," 33–34, 40, 236, 292–93
  Bliss marries daughter of, 408
  Davis marries daughter of, 115–17, 281, 330
  Davis serves under, 137, 152, 330
  Grant as viewed by, 173, 174
  Grant's opinion of, 49–50, 213, 257, 261, 405
  as presidential candidate, 233, 254, 257; as president, 378, 408
  in Seminole Wars, 147
  as Whig, 163, 191
  AND MEXICAN WAR, 391
  after-action reports, 398, 404
  horse of ("Old Whitey"), 44, 88, 173, 220
  hostilities begin, command falls to, 72, 127
  Mexican map falls into hands of, 108
  Meade as aide to, *see* Meade, George Gordon
  and Monterrey (march on and battle for), *see* Monterrey; Monterrey, Battle of
  public support for, 113, 163
  refuses to surrender, 275–78; battle of Buena Vista, 277–79, 281–82, 285, 287, 395, 415
  removed from command, 252, 254; ignores order, 255, 256; Scott takes over from, 256, 257, 259–62
  shortage of supplies and transport, 130, 165–66, 170, 175, 227
  troops of (Army of Occupation), 41–43, 54, 56, 65, 67, 111; artillery of, 48–49, 86, 102; compassionate policy, 121, 181; number of, 63, 106, 260; as occupation forces, 121–25, 168–69, 235; officers of, 313; Taylor maneuvers, 34–36, 100–102, 104–8, (crosses Rio Colorado, builds fort), 57–62, 73, (at Palo Alto) 85–89, 92–93, (returns to front) 76, 81, 82;

Taylor's knowledge of, 172; victories of, 113, 134; volunteers in, 119, 122–25, 131–32, 191, 260, (atrocities of, in Monterrey) 247, 294

Tecumseh (Shawnee chief), 144–45, 148

Texas
American colonists settle in, xiii, 18–19, 21
annexation of, xiii, 23, 28–33, 40, 346, 371; accepts statehood offer, 35; admitted to Union, 134
as independent nation, 15–17, 22–23, 28, 32; Mexico offers to recognize, offer withdrawn, 31, 33; wars with Mexico, xiii, 15, 21–23, 179–81
as New Spain, 17–18 (see also New Spain)
U.S. offers to buy, offer refused, 21; secessionist rebellion and the Alamo, 21–22

Texas Rangers, 204, 221, 225–26, 230, 292, 409
atrocities committed by, 247–49

Thermopylae, Battle of, 328

Thirtieth Congress, 161–62. See also Congress, U.S.

Thomas, George H., 386

Thomas, Hugh, 416

Thompson, Waddy, 241

Thornton, Seth, 67–72, 402, 403

To Mexico with Scott (Smith), 401

Topographical Corps. See Army Corps of Topographical Engineers

Torrejón, Anastasio, 64, 70–71, 73, 90–91

To the Halls of the Montezumas (Johannsen), 398, 420

Totten, Joseph, 300, 307–8

Tower, Zealous B., 355

Traas, Adrian George, 404

Treaties
of Guadalupe Hidalgo (1848), 371–72, 383
of Oregon (1846), 136–37
of Paris (1783), 354
of Velasco (1836), 22

Trist, Nicholas P., 346

Turnbull, William, 308

Twain, Mark, 376, 397, 399

Twelve Month Volunteer, The (Furber), 412, 416

Twiggs, David E., 42, 204, 298, 393, 411
in march on Mexico City, 311, 314, 322–23, 325, 337, 341–44; praises Lee, 327; suicide charge, 315–18, 319, 418
at Monterrey, 256, 260, 394; Grant delivers message to, 223–24

Tyler, John, 23, 28–29, 31

United States
elections in, see elections, presidential and congressional
expansion by, see expansionism, U.S.

isolationism of, 19–20; Monroe Doctrine vs., 20–21, 113

Military Academy, see West Point

northern border formally defined, 137

Postal Service, 253

recognizes Texas as independent territory, 22

two-front war threatened, 113; Treaty of Oregon ends threat, 136–37

war with Mexico, see Mexican War

See also Congress, U.S.; Constitution, U.S.

United States Democratic Review, 29

United States Speaker (elocution primer), 300

Valencia, Gabriel, 342–45

Van Buren, Martin, 29–30, 146, 370

Vanderlinden, Pedro, 277–78

Vega, Díaz de la, 405

Venezuela as independent republic, 19–20

Veracruz, 313
Cortés lands at, 294, 295
history and symbolism of, 286–91, 416
invasion planned, 250, 257, 259, 261, 269–70, 292–95; carried out, 296–308, 327, 335, 410; casualties at, 304–7; compared to D-day, 416; horrors of, 363, 368; Mexican prisoners, 318; Santa Anna vs., 284; Stars and Stripes raised at, 296, 307; surrender, 311, 312
military governors of: Kearny, 372, 413; Worth, 314

Victoria, 256, 259

Vinton, John R., 306

Virginia Military Institute, 377, 414

volunteers. See Army, U.S.

Vose, Josiah H., 34

Walker, Robert J., and Walker Tariff bill, 156–57

Walker, Samuel, 181, 409

Walnut Springs campground, 189–96 passim, 197–99, 205–7, 213, 219, 228, 244–45

War Department, U.S., 137, 391

War of 1812, 4–5, 8, 19, 20, 28, 34, 57
mind-sets of, in Mexican War, 165
U.S. forces in Canada during, 231
veterans and descendants of veterans of, 40, 43, 62, 67, 74, 144, 236, 254
See also Battles, War of 1812

War with Mexico, The (Smith), 405, 416

Washington, George, 3, 7, 10, 51
Gilbert Stuart portrait of, 96
honored, 8, 115, 275, 278
popularity of books about, 300

Washington, John M., 396

INDEX

Washington and Lee University, 377
Washington, D.C., 115
  burned by British (1814), 5
Washington Monument, 115
  cornerstone laid, 370–71, 372, 420
  monument completed, 378
Watson, William H., 394
Webster, Amos, xii, 395
Webster, Daniel, 146
Weigart, Sergeant (first casualty), 78, 120, 130
Wellington, Arthur Wellesley, duke of, 232, 337
West Point
  academy established, 3, 4
  cadets at, 5–6, 13, 52, 269; literary and secret societies, 14; rules governing, 5–6
  class rings, 14, 24–25, 27–28, 400
  commandants of: Hardee, 402; Lee, 6, 377; Smith, 57; Worth, 195
  Congress considers abolishing, 14, 192
  graduates of, 9–15, 31, 74–75, 143, 399; Davis, 112, 114, 115–16, 118; Grant, 12, 13–15, 23, 52, 57; Lee, 6, 9–11, 269, (as commandant of cadets) 377; Longstreet, 51–52; Meade, 6, 89, 98, 125; Sherman, 6, 13, 142, 146; Stonewall Jackson, 6, 264–66
  graduates in Mexican War, 58, 81, 176, 183, 206, 232, 297, 340; killed, 306, 383; Scott's view of, 375; as veterans of previous wars, 36, 40, 66, 69
  public view of, 125
  tactics taught at, 59, 100
Whig Party, 146
  antiwar, 114, 162–63; "Conscience Whigs," 162
  army officers in, 127, 191, 298
  and expansionism, 28–30
  Lincoln and, 158–59, 164, 240
  Whig-Democrat divide, 164, 192
  revitalized, 254
  and Taylor as presidential candidate, 257

Whistler, James McNeill, 402
Whistler, William, 43, 64, 402
Whitman, Walt, 134, 406
Wilcox, Cadmus, 376
Williams, Jonathan, 3, 4
Williams, Seth, 385
William the Conqueror, 51, 55
Wilson, Henry, 394
Wisconsin Territory, 115, 116
women and children
  Indian or *mestizo*, 18
  in war, 223, 305, 307, 325–26, 363, 412
Wood, George T., 395
Woods, Thomas, 99
Wool, John E., 136, 235–42, 255–56, 268–69, 287
  at Buena Vista, 277–78, 280–81, 395
  in Civil War, 412–13
World War I, 401
World War II, 411
Worth, William, 147, 170, 383
  Grant's opinion of, 287
  in march on Mexico City, 327, 328–29, 337, 347–50, 359, 361, 364–68; occupation ends, 371, 376
  at Monterrey, 175, 193–96, 228, 249, 394; artillery and tactics of, 197, 202–4, 211, 214, 218–20; breaches defenses, enters city, 224–27, 245, 247, 266, 412
  and Saltillo, 255, 256, 277
  at Veracruz, 260, 296, 308, 410; as military governor, 314
  at West Point, as commandant of cadets, 195
Wright, G., 348

Yell, Archibald, 396
yellow fever, 35, 137, 299, 312, 329, 408
Yerba Buena (later San Francisco), 271, 273
Yucatán, citizens' rebellion in (crushed), 63

Zozaya, María Josefa, 223

ABOUT THE AUTHOR

Martin Dugard is the *New York Times* bestselling author of such nonfiction titles as *The Last Voyage of Columbus*, *Farther Than Any Man*, *Knockdown*, *Chasing Lance*, and *Into Africa*. He has written for *Esquire*, *Outside*, *Sports Illustrated*, and *GQ*. Dugard lives in Orange County, California, with his wife and three sons.

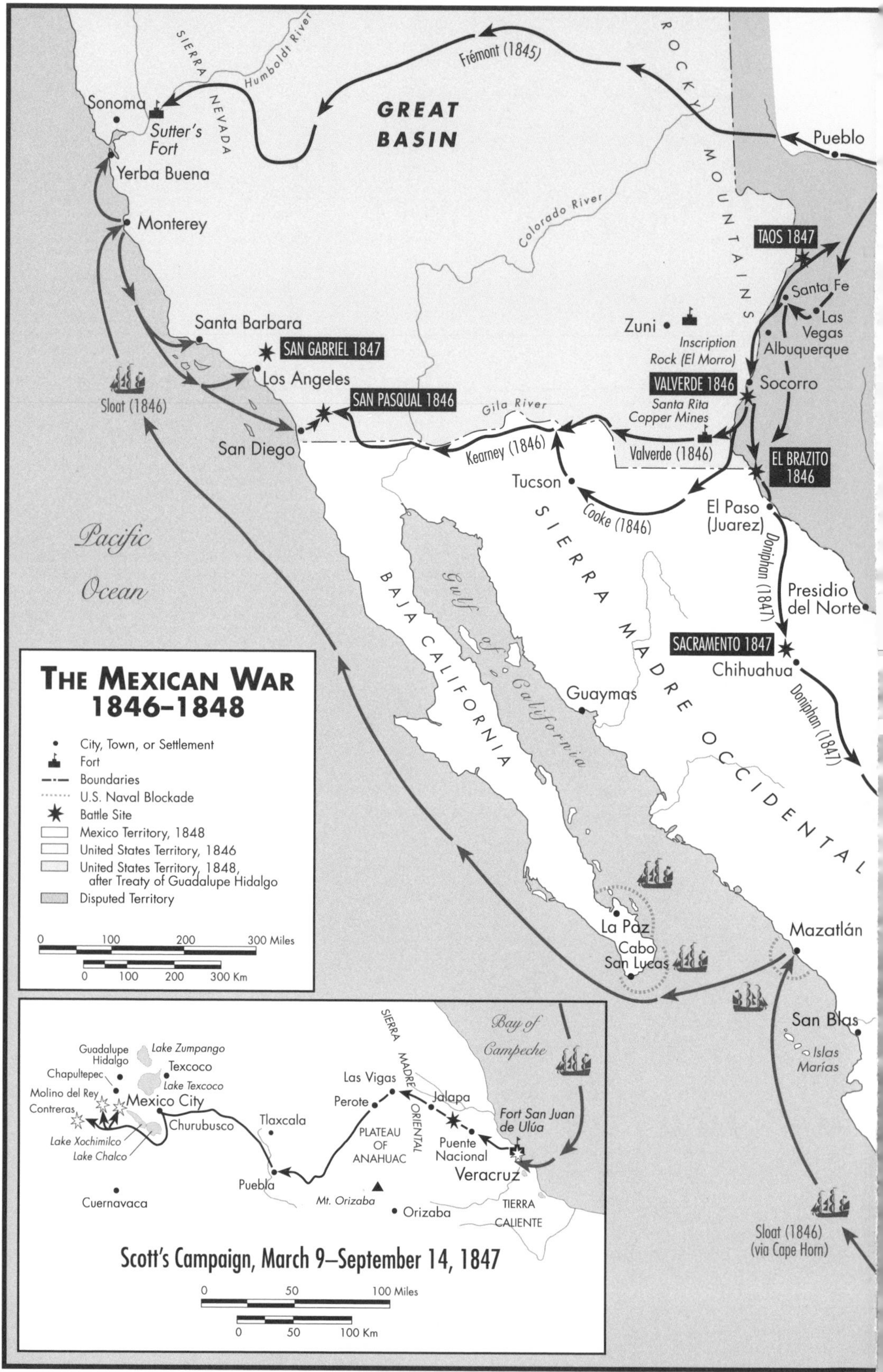

THE MEXICAN WAR
1846–1848
City, Town, or Settlement
Fort
Boundaries
U.S. Naval Blockade
Battle Site
Mexico Territory, 1848
United States Territory, 1846
United States Territory, 1848, after Treaty of Guadalupe Hidalgo
Disputed Territory
0 100 200 300 Miles
0 100 200 300 Km
SIERRA NEVADA
Humboldt River
Frémont (1845)
ROCKY MOUNTAINS
GREAT BASIN
Sonoma
Sutter's Fort
Yerba Buena
Monterey
Pueblo
Colorado River
TAOS 1847
Santa Fe
Las Vegas
Albuquerque
Zuni
Inscription Rock (El Morro)
Santa Barbara
SAN GABRIEL 1847
Los Angeles
Sloat (1846)
SAN PASQUAL 1846
Gila River
VALVERDE 1846
Socorro
Santa Rita Copper Mines
San Diego
Kearney (1846)
Valverde (1846)
EL BRAZITO 1846
Tucson
Cooke (1846)
El Paso (Juarez)
Doniphan (1847)
Pacific Ocean
SIERRA MADRE OCCIDENTAL
Presidio del Norte
Gulf of California
BAJA CALIFORNIA
SACRAMENTO 1847
Chihuahua
Guaymas
La Paz
Cabo San Lucas
Mazatlán
San Blas
Islas Marías
Sloat (1846) (via Cape Horn)
Bay of Campeche
SIERRA MADRE ORIENTAL
Guadalupe Hidalgo
Lake Zumpango
Texcoco
Lake Texcoco
Chapultepec
Molino del Rey
Mexico City
Contreras
Churubusco
Lake Xochimilco
Lake Chalco
Tlaxcala
Las Vigas
Perote
Jalapa
Fort San Juan de Ulúa
PLATEAU OF ANAHUAC
Puente Nacional
Veracruz
Puebla
Mt. Orizaba
Orizaba
TIERRA CALIENTE
Cuernavaca
Scott's Campaign, March 9–September 14, 1847
0 50 100 Miles
0 50 100 Km